TA

VICTORIAN ORIGINS of the

BRITISH WELFARE STATE

by David Roberts

Archon Books   1969

©Copyright 1960 by Yale University Press
Reprinted 1969 with permission
in an unaltered and unabridged edition

[Yale Historical Publications Miscellany: 73]

SBN: 208 00692 3
Library of Congress Catalog Card Number: 69-11553
Printed in the United States of America

TO MY MOTHER AND FATHER

PREFACE

BRITAIN TODAY IS NOTED for both its Parliamentary government and its welfare state. Histories of the first are long and distinguished; by comparison, studies of the origins of the latter are meager indeed.

Its history is, of course, more recent. As the term is used by most people, the welfare state was suddenly born around 1911 and reached maturity after 1945. The more romantic chroniclers of Elizabethan and Stuart England, to be sure, note faltering beginnings in the Old Poor Law, but students of the eighteenth century can certainly discover little evidence in the Whiggish government of Sir Robert Walpole or the Tory government of William Pitt that the central government, or even the justices of the peace, did much for the lower classes besides dispense poor relief.

It is not until after 1832 that the central government seriously assumes responsibility, and the concern it then developed was not at first fully realized by historians, who saw the period, rather, as the high-water mark of laissez-faire capitalism. But since Karl Polanyi's *The Great Transformation* (1944) and J. Bartlett Brebner's "Laissez Faire and State Intervention in Nineteenth Century Britain" (*Journal of Economic History*, Supplement 8, 1948), there can no longer be doubt that the origins of British collectivism run back to the Victorian era, alive with social reforms and bureaucratic growth.

It is the aim of the following work to describe this growth, to analyze its powers and organization, to discuss the men who became its civil servants, and to show in some detail how well it worked.

Many able historians have written on the first of these four aspects. Sydney and Beatrice Webb in their monumental administrative studies describe the establishment of the Prison Inspectorate and the Poor Law Commission; Cecil Driver vividly narrates, in *Richard Oastler, Tory Radical* (1946) the story of the formation of the Factory Inspectorate; and John and Barbara Hammond's *Lord Shaftesbury* (1923) discusses the creation of the Lunacy Commission and the Mining Inspectorates. R. A. Lewis in *Edwin Chadwick and the Public Health Movement* (1952) and Samuel Finer in *Edwin Chadwick and His Times* (1952) give detailed accounts of the passage of the Factory Act of 1833, the Poor Law Amendment Act of 1834, and the Public Health Act of 1848. Roger Prouty's *The Transformation of the Board of Trade* (1957) has a sound account of the beginnings of the Merchant Marine Department. Much then of the first aspect of the following study has been told elsewhere in greater detail and with greater insight. But to view the emergence of a centralized administration in its entirety it is necessary to tread old ground as well as new. A comparative study of the establishment of all these new departments allows one to judge more judicially the broad social forces and intellectual attitudes that led to the sudden bureaucratic growth.

Few historians have yet dealt with the second of the above aspects, the powers and organization of the early Victorian administrative state. Lewis and Finer, to be sure, have trenchant remarks on the essential nature of the new bureaucracy, but it was not their task to give a complete picture of all the departments. It is my intention to do so.

No historian has dealt with the third of the aspects mentioned above—the men who became its inspectors, secretaries, and commissioners. Emmeline Cohen's *Growth of the British Civil Service* (1941) and J. Donald Kingsley's *Representative Bureaucracy* (1944) are devoted to civil service reform and the changing character of the men who, increasingly by examination, joined the lower ranks of the government. But they do not discuss the civil servants themselves, as individuals with particular ideas and prejudices. The background, capabilities, and convictions of the bureaucrat is too often overlooked in administrative histories. A centralized administrative state, whatever its organization or powers, can govern no better than the capacity and zeal of its officials will allow. For that reason I have described in considerable detail the backgrounds, education, character, and ideals of the men who became Her Majesty's civil servants. Their abilities and ideas define to no little extent the direction and the achievements of the early Victorian administrative state.

The fourth aspect of this study deals with the day-to-day work of England's new bureaucracy, analyzing the inspectors' investigations and reports, the complex process of the formation of policy, and the execution of this policy through the cooperation of central inspectors and local officials. The formation and execution of policy involved, between 1833 and 1854, lively and violent clashes. Administrative history, from its very nature, can be dull. Perfunctory reports and routine decisions mark much of the daily history of many bureaucracies. But fortunately the administrative efforts of England's central government after 1833 involved fundamental changes, new policies, and in the minds of Tories and local officials some impudent and radical innovations. The angry responses to the Poor Law Commission and the strong opposition to the General Board of Health are events of dramatic intensity— and have been so depicted by Finer and by Lewis. But still untold were the tribulations of the poor-law assistant commissioners confronted with obdurate Welsh guardians or the frustrations of mining inspectors before evasive mine owners. The opening up, in 1952, of the voluminous correspondence of the poor-law guardians and poor-law assistant commissioners with the Poor Law Commission has given the historian a remarkable opportunity to observe administrative conflicts in detail.

The method adopted has been comparative and analytical and not, except in Chapters 2 and 3, narrative. I have attempted not to tell the full story of each department but to sketch in the broader lines of the nature and work of the administrative state

Preface

and of the men who worked in it. I hope that thereby a more coherent picture is given to its growth, its characteristics, its civil servants, and its achievements and failures.

This study grew out of a dissertation submitted to Yale University in 1952 on the establishment of the central inspectorates in England, 1833–54. Since then I have gone through more materials and have broadened the scope. During these years I have received valuable help and advice from many persons. The idea for the project arose from a conversation in 1949 with John Gaus of Harvard and was furthered by the lively suggestions of Lewis P. Curtis of Yale. In its dissertation stage Ralph Turner, of Yale, offered many ideas and Cecil Driver, also of Yale, was most generous with his wise counsels. J. Bartlett Brebner, of Columbia University, read the dissertation and made excellent suggestions. My brother, Clayton Roberts of Ohio State University, has been an exacting critic of all inconsistencies of thought and awkwardnesses in style. And in its final stages John Gazley, Ted Hill, and James Winter of Dartmouth College have labored conscientiously to catch any error of fact or style. All these people have given generously of their time and wisdom and deserve the warmest acknowledgment and thanks, which I extend also to the Yale Fund for Young Scholars, a grant from which has greatly assisted with publication.

D.R.

Hanover, N.H.
June 1959

CONTENTS

Preface   vii

Abbreviations   xiii

1. The Problems of Government in 1833   1
    Social and Economic   2
    Local Government   7
    The Central Government   12
    Opinions and Theories   22

2. Social Reform and Administrative Growth   35
    Factory and Poor-Law Reforms   36
    Prison, Tithe, and Church Reforms   45
    The Education Controversy, 1839   51
    Conservative Reforms and Tory Paternalism   59

3. The Issue of Centralization   67
    The Public Health Act   70
    Further Administrative Growth, 1849–1854   85
    Political Attitudes toward Centralization   95

4. Powers and Organization   105
    The Powers   106
    The Organization   118

Contents

5. Her Majesty's Public Servants   137
   Ministers and Commissioners   138
   Inspectors   152

6. The Inspectors' Outlook and Character   168
   The School Inspectors   185

7. Inquiry and Report   203
   The Inspectors' Reports   206
   Public Criticisms and Uses of the Reports   219

8. Formulation of Policy   232
   The First Step: Inspectors, Secretaries, and Commissioners   232
   Basic Decisions: The Cabinet   244
   Parliament Has Its Say   252
   Public Opinion   260

9. Execution of Policy   272
   The Resistance of Local Government   273
   The Art of Persuasion   287
   By Order of the Court   293
   A Working Cooperation   300

10. The Central Government and Social Progress in 1854   310

Appendix   327

Bibliographical Essays   334

Index   355

ABBREVIATIONS

In the notes the following papers from the Public Record Office in London are abbreviated:
1. HO, Home Office papers.
2. MH, Ministry of Health papers. These include both poor-law and Board of Health papers.

The Sessional Papers of Parliament are abbreviated *PP* (*Parliamentary Papers*), followed by the volume number and year. The number in the parenthesis after the page number for the volume is the page number of the report. Often more than one report is bound in a volume so that there is both a volume pagination and a report pagination. There are two editions of the Sessional Papers, those of the House of Lords and those of the House of Commons. When the House of Lords edition is used, the *PP* has an accompanying asterick.

T. C. Hansard, ed., *The Parliamentary Debates of Great Britain* (Ser. 3, London, 1830–90), is abbreviated Hansard, followed by volume number (year), and column number.

Chadwick Papers. The manuscripts of Edwin Chadwick, University College, London.

The references to the *Quarterly, Edinburgh,* and *Westminster* Reviews are to the American editions, as is the one reference to *Household Words.*

1.

THE PROBLEMS OF GOVERNMENT IN 1833

BRITAIN'S FIRST REFORMED House of Commons met in the crowded hall of St. Stephen's Chapel on January 29, 1833. For over two years, and to the exclusion of nearly all else, the English had fought bitterly over the constitution of this House. Now, reformed and more representative, invaded by William Cobbett and the Philosophical Radicals and full of the spirit of improvement, the House turned to reform England's other institutions. The same rapid industrial and commercial advances that had brought representation to Birmingham manufacturers and Liverpool traders raised pressing social and economic problems on a national scale, while the same traditionalism and conservatism that had kept the Commons so long unreformed continued to weigh heavy on England's local and central government. Ineffective local authorities and an antiquated and jealously restricted central administration could not cope with the many acute problems of a changing society. The great transformations of the previous half century, having made much of England prosperous and strong, had also brought overcrowded towns, depressed trades, rural pauperism, and other social grievances. The results of an increasingly industrial and urban society, these developments defined in 1833 the basic problems of English government, the problems which now confronted the newly reformed Commons.

1

The Government in 1833

The changing society of the 1830's presented a varied and complex picture. While England's farms produced the most fertile crops in Europe, millions still lived off parish relief. Her ingenious manufacturers had made her one of the wealthiest nations in the world, yet they ruthlessly exploited the cheap labor of children. In no country in the world did a larger proportion of the people live in towns, with their promise of good schools, comfortable living, and cultural opportunities, yet in the midst of an advancing prosperity large areas in these towns were congested centers of crime, ignorance, and disease. Statisticians who recorded that the value of cotton exports exceeded nineteen million pounds had also to report that the poor rates totaled over seven million. Alongside the new factories were slums; next to the enclosed farm was the pauper's hovel.

The cause of this contrast was the impact on England of three unexpected economic changes: a rapid increase in population, the enclosure movement, and the industrial revolution. The introduction of a scientific agriculture, demanding the enclosure of farms, meant more and cheaper food but not sufficiently more to keep pace with the increase in population caused by a rising birth rate and improved medical care. Between 1801 and 1831 the population of England grew from 8,900,000 to 13,900,000. As Thomas Malthus had gloomily predicted, agricultural production could not keep pace. If it had not been for the expansion of manufacturing and commerce, especially in textiles, England would not have escaped the fate of Ireland, where population growth pressed the people down to a subsistence level. Fortunately this expansion, with some help from emigration, absorbed much of the growing population. The surplus of laborers of the North became the cotton operatives of Lancashire and Yorkshire. The redundant labor of the South flowed into Bristol, Plymouth, and London, there to build houses, enter a trade, or join the merchant marine. Some found their way into the iron works of Birmingham or the potteries of the Midlands. All earned higher wages. An industrious family could earn

15 or 20 shillings a week in a cotton mill, although they lost the amenities of rural life: the small village community, the lax winter season, the clean air and open field.

The sudden transformation from rural living to urban was to pose a serious challenge to English society. But in 1833, with more Englishmen still living in the country than in towns, the most widespread social problem was rural pauperism—the most ancient of all problems, and since the French wars the most acute. In 1795 the Berkshire magistrates meeting at Speenhanland made an ill-fated attempt to meet the problem. They ordered the overseers of the poor to supplement wages with outdoor relief whenever the price of the "gallon loaf" exceeded one shilling. This benevolent but fateful order meant the subsidizing of agricultural wages out of the poor rates. It was an attractive, easy, and apparently humane policy. By 1833, under the name of the allowance system, it had become general throughout southern England. But in matters of poor relief there was no uniformity. Some parishes forced the farmers to hire the parish poor at a fixed wage; others simply provided easy outdoor relief. A few clung to the workhouse. Most of these policies encouraged pauperism: the allowance system because it kept wages low and thus forced the independent worker to accept poor relief, the hiring out of paupers to farmers because it reduced the demand for independent laborers, easy relief (often as high as six shillings for a family) because it placed a bounty on idleness. With farm wages often a barely adequate eight shillings a week, any barely adequate poor relief not given in a workhouse appeared attractive.

There was no easy solution to the problem of rural pauperism. It had its roots in persistent overpopulation and was increased by periods of distress: there were too many hands, too few jobs, and too many bad harvests. Cobbett describes the misery of the agricultural laborer, his meager diet, his rags, and his hovels of mud and straw. Bulwer Lytton in 1833 wrote that "they are born, they are wretched, and they die." [1] In 1833 their plight constituted Eng-

1. William Cobbett, *Rural Rides* (London, 1930), 2, 664. Sir Edward Bulwer Lytton, *England and the English* (London, 1833), p. 64.

land's greatest social problem. Speenhanland had provided no answer: it had led only to the expenditure of seven million pounds in poor rates and the creation of widespread pauperism.

The town laborer, though he had more money than the farm hand, suffered more dramatic evils. The distress of the rural poor could be ignored by the wealthy, or at least accepted as customary; but the mills and tenements of the new manufacturing towns brought into the open the employment of child labor, the erection of unsanitary dwellings, and the pervasiveness of ignorance, crime, and drunkenness. Richard Oastler, the evangelical Tory Yorkshire bailiff, delivered his philippic, *A Letter on Yorkshire Slavery*, against the barbarism of employing children of six for twelve hours in crowded, ill-ventilated, dangerous factories.[2] The Scottish physician James Kay, in his study of the working class of Manchester, painted a melancholy picture of the Manchester slums, of streets unpaved, undrained, and full of refuse, of tenements overcrowded, badly ventilated, and without privies, of workers dulled by incessant toil and dissipated by drink, of an "atmosphere loaded with the smoke and exhalations of a larger manufacturing city." P. Gaskell echoed Kay's indignation at the immorality of the working classes and the sordidness of their life. He found that one person out of 840 in towns had a criminal record, as opposed to only one in 1,044 in the country. He also found that disease caused a much higher mortality rate in towns than in the country.[3] In the fetid courtyards of London's East End and the cellar dwellings of Liverpool the industrial revolution had begotten a proletariat whose misery, ill health, marital infidelity, and drunkenness shocked the genteel. Macaulay told his Edinburgh constituents that civilization was threatened by the barbarism it had engendered. Charles Greville, clerk of the Privy Council in 1832, recorded, after reading reports of the Sunderland slums, that "the condition of the people of Sunderland . . . is more suitable to the barbarism of the interior of Africa" and added, "We who float on the surface of so-

2. Cecil Driver, *Richard Oastler, Tory Radical* (London, 1940), p. 42.
3. James Kay, *The Moral and Physical Condition of the Working Class Employed in the Cotton Manufactures in Manchester*, London, 1832. P. Gaskell, *The Manufacturing Population of England, Its Moral, Social and Physical Conditions* (London, 1833), p. 286.

ciety know but little of the privations and sufferings which pervade the masses." [4]

Yet very little was done to protect the laboring poor. Children tending looms in the cotton mills or dragging coal carts in mines were at the mercy of capitalists. The police were inadequate, and the prisons too undisciplined to deter or reform the criminals. The local jails, said the *Westminster Review,* were hardly better in 1833 than in 1818 when the Quaker philanthropist, Elizabeth Fry, found them filthy and crowded, mere schools of crime, the probable ruin of all who entered them.[5] The *Westminster Review* looked to education as the answer, but education was everywhere wanting. The Manchester Statistical Society undertook in 1837 a study of schools in Manchester, Liverpool, York, and Salford, and offered to the people of England the first accurate survey of education. The findings of the Society showed that about one-third of the children between the ages of five and fifteen attended no school at all, while the others received either the negligible instruction of a Sunday school or of common day schools. London's East End offered less than the northern towns. In Monmouthshire three out of four children received no education, and rural instruction lagged behind the meager offerings of the new towns.[6]

The abuses of child labor, unsanitary dwellings, and widespread ignorance appeared all the more flagrant because of the general improvement in English life. To the Evangelicals the mounting profits earned by cotton manufacturers made child labor the more shameful. To the Utilitarians the advance of knowledge and the creation of a cheap press made widespread ignorance the more inexcusable. And the philanthropists found cruelty to lunatics more reprehensible than ever, now that its proper treatment was known.

4. R. H. Mottram, "Town Life," *Victorian England,* ed. G. M. Young (London, 1935), *1,* 168. *The Memoirs of Charles Greville,* ed. Lytton Strachey (London, 1938), 2, 219.

5. *Westminster Review,* 23 (1835), 221–24. Elizabeth Fry, *Memoirs* (London, 1847), *1,* 278–374.

6. *A Report of A Committee of the Manchester Statistical Society on the State of Education in the Borough of Bury, Lancashire* (London, 1835), and similar reports on Manchester, Salford, Birmingham, and York (1835–36). For Monmouthshire, PP, *40* (1840), 618 (211). Anon., *Recent Measures for the Promotion of Education in England,* London, 1835.

The Quakers at the York Retreat Hospital, for example, had discovered a humane treatment of insanity, free of mechanical restraints and hardship. Yet superintendents of provincial madhouses, in whose cells so many of the insane were chained, persevered in their belief that porridge, potatoes, and beds of straw were all that those possessed of the devil deserved. Most asylums for the insane, as also most prisons and many poorhouses, were overcrowded, badly staffed, and filthy. There was little attempt to classify the inmates. The food was poor. No one thought to cure the mentally sick or reform the criminal. Usually the governor of a prison or workhouse was arbitrary, hard, and all-powerful.[7] Abandoned to local government and private efforts the institutional care of the insane, the criminals, and the poorhouse paupers seldom rose above mere incarceration.

In many other ways England's much-vaunted liberties led to neglect. The wide freedom allotted capital certainly promoted technological progress. Its most conspicuous success was in transportation, where the locomotive and the steamship astonished contemporaries. The age was intoxicated with mechanical progress, yet no one thought to apply a governor to its acceleration. Railway lines were hastily built; vast projects were impulsively planned. Rail stocks flooded the market, while private bills to secure a right of way flooded Parliament. Overnight, once-quiet hamlets were cut through by steel lines. In the frenzy of railroad building not many paid attention to the confusion of gauges, the numerous accidents, the fraudulent speculations, and the exploited railroad hands.[8] Accidents and exploitation of labor were after all part of progress. At sea 1,000 lives a year were lost because ships were shoddily built, their masters and mates untrained, and their crews undisciplined. The seamen lived in wretched fo'castles and suffered

---

7. In the larger asylums, particularly those under the supervision of the Metropolitan Lunacy Commissioners, improvements in the treatment of the insane were being made. The deplorable conditions mentioned above were to be found in the unlicensed and private asylums and some neglected county houses. Kathleen Jones, *Lunacy, Law and Conscience, 1744 to 1845* (London, 1954), pp. 145–87.

8. John Francis, *A History of the English Railway* (London, 1851), pp. 80–100. *PP, 10* (1839), 130–42 (iii–xv).

from the tyranny of masters some of whom were fonder of the bottle than of seamanship. Among the great shipping countries in the world, England alone had no unified maritime code and no system of licensing mates.[9]

These abuses in the railroad and shipping industries, like those in the management of prisons and asylums, were by no means isolated grievances. Oppression was the lot of apprenticed paupers (such as Oliver Twist) as well as of the women in collieries, and distress bore as hard on the Spitalfields hand-loom weaver and the Leicester knitter as it did on the displaced farm hand. Even the owners of property had their complaints. The farmers smarted under the necessity of paying tithes in kind to the church, and the manufacturers protested the burdensome excise regulations. Wherever one went in England, there might be a dearth of bread but never of social and economic abuses demanding reform.

Any review of social abuses in 1833 is bound, by its selective nature, to give undue emphasis to them and thus to distort the picture. Such in part is the fault of the histories of this period by Barbara and John Hammond and Sydney and Beatrice Webb. Their passionate descriptions of the condition of the laboring class are true but need qualification. Many of the social abuses were not new, but existed before the industrial revolution; such abuses were by no means universal and in some places were exceptional; and the industrial revolution brought not only child labor and unsanitary towns but substantial improvements in the standard of living of the laboring class and the amenities of their life. These improvements must not be forgotten. But the greater the social improvements and wealth, the more the old abuses of pre-industrial England and the new abuses of industrial England became unnecessary.

LOCAL GOVERNMENT

Were not these matters, however, the concern of England's local government? What of the distinguished magistracy of the county, of the parishes whose ecclesiastical origins went back to Anglo Saxon times, of the historic boroughs whose charters carried the

9. PP, 17 (1836) 376–88. Thomas Clarkson, *The Grievances of Our Mercantile Seamen, a National and Crying Evil*, London, 1845.

solemn seals of past kings? What were they doing in 1833 to reduce pauperism, regulate child labor, educate the working classes,
or cleanse pestilent slums? These and other questions increasingly
discussed in 1833 had no simple answers. The authorities of local
government were too numerous and diverse for neat judgments.
There were some 15,500 parishes of varying sizes and kinds that
managed poor relief, maintained highways, and policed the villages
and countryside. The Crown appointed some 5,000 justices of the
peace to supervise the parishes, as well as administer justice, license
public houses, manage jails, superintend asylums, and reform the
manners of the poor. The mayors, bailiffs, and aldermen of more
than 200 chartered boroughs administered to the wants of their
towns. There were also approximately 1,800 special authorities
established by Parliament in order to remedy the failures of parishes, justices of the peace, and boroughs to perform their tasks.
There were authorities for managing poor relief, turnpike trusts
for building highways, and improvement commissioners for polic-
ing, draining, and paving the new towns. Courts leet, courts barons,
and the ancient courts of sewers—remnants of a feudal age—added
more confusion to this tangle. Together they formed that chaos
of authorities that constituted England's local government. They
composed, said Sidney and Beatrice Webb, "no system at all, but a
confused pattern of decay and growth," of old courts leet and new
paving commissioners, of antiquated parishes and reforming magistrates.[10]

The parish dealt most immediately with the problems of the
poor. Since 1601 the law had required each parish vestry to appoint an overseer for the administration of relief, but they were
appointed annually, were unpaid, and thus learned little about the
duties of their office and had no zeal for fulfilling them. Some, in
fact, were a terror to the paupers; others fell in with jobbery. The
parish vestry itself seldom had a policy. Its main desire was to keep
rates low, though occasionally the vestry fell into the hands of publicans and shopkeepers who encouraged easy relief in order to promote trade. The chief fault, however, was not venality but ignorance and indifference.

10. Sydney and Beatrice Webb, *English Local Government: Statutory
Authorities* (London, 1922), pp. 353–54.

The parish administered its roads no more efficiently than its poor relief, and so neglected police duties that more often than not it appointed no constable. Even when it did draft a constable, it paid him no wages.[11] The countryside went largely unpoliced. Such negligence might do no irreparable harm in rural parishes where the problems of government were few and traditional. But parish government was quite inadequate for the towns. Unpaid, untrained parish officials could not cope with the problems arising from crowded slums, an ignorant populace, and a disorderly working class. They had no means to put an end to the undrained courtyards and muddy thoroughfares. As a result, many of London's closed vestries (those chosen by co-option) fell into the hands of jobbing tradesmen and corrupt contractors, while her open vestries (attended by all rate-payers) spawned such turbulent factionalism that the able were repelled and the petty politician attracted. The absurdity of an open vestry governing a new town appeared most vividly in Manchester, where much of the government devolved on a parish vestry at which, if they wished, 30,000 rate-payers could attend. The resulting confusion led the citizens of this cotton metropolis to look instead to the paving commissioners for good government.[12]

Parliament had long known of the incompetence of the parish and had therefore sought for over a century to increase the powers of the justice of the peace. By 1833 the JP's were the true rulers of the country. They exercised, for one thing, almost autocratic power over poor relief. Not only could they decree policy, as at Speenhanland in 1795, but they could arbitrarily order relief to any pauper who they believed needed it, a power they exercised with more charity than economy. If, in the distribution of poor relief, the parish stands culpable of negligence and mismanagement, it is the JP's who gave indiscriminate relief most freely, and often to the importunate more than the needy. The result was the growth of a large pauperized class.

By and large the JP's exercised their other powers with the same good intent but limited vision. Appointed by the Crown on the nomination of the Lord Lieutenant, they included peers, coun-

11. Ibid.: *Parish and the County* (London, 1934), p. 69.
12. Ibid., p. 101.

try squires, and clergymen, the select of the county. Many of them possessed the honesty, dignity, and patriarchal kindness exhibited by Squire Allworthy in *Tom Jones,* but they were still amateurs at government. They knew little about the treatment of insanity or the management of prisons. They neglected their county jails and allowed roads to deteriorate. They left insane asylums either unbuilt or in scandalous condition. They made no effort to improve drainage in the towns or to enforce the factory acts protecting child labor.[13] The new problems of police, prisons, roads, drainage, and child labor demanded energy and new ideas. But the justices numbered too few, and had too little imagination and often too little power to attend to them. The once proud ornaments of England's local government faced in 1833 problems beyond their abilities and powers.

Whatever their faults, their record shone beside that of certain municipal corporations. The mayors and aldermen of England were far oftener defenders of ancient abuse than pioneers in municipal government. The Penzance and Liverpool corporations, with their efficient, honest officials and clean, improved streets were exceptions. More typical were the indolent, do-nothing aldermen of Bristol, the corrupt burgesses of Berwick-upon-Tweed, the disreputable corporation at Leicester. They were narrow, Tory oligarchies that were not only undemocratic in an age agitating for democracy but administratively ineffective in an age of acute social problems. At Leicester they feasted royally on their historic revenues while streets went unrepaired. In the City of London the proud councilors observed ancient ceremonies while prisoners at Newgate Prison festered in idleness and corrupt disorder. The Coventry corporation embezzled charity endowments while the poor went uneducated.[14] Faced with the failure of the corporations, energetic citizens pushed through Parliament special acts establishing lighting, paving, and police commissioners. These improvement commissions, with their elected committees of rate-payers

13. *PP,* 20 (1833), 1–74; *11* (1835); *35* (1836), 5.
14. Sidney and Beatrice Webb, *English Local Government: Manor and Borough* (London, 1924), 2, 405–81; *PP, 11* (1835), 273. A. Temple Patterson, *Radical Leicester* (London, 1954), pp. 198–215.

and their professional staffs, proved far more effective than the old corporations and parishes. They set new standards in efficient administration and carried out their assigned tasks with energy and skill. Birmingham's paving commissioners made that city one of the cleanest in the kingdom, and the energetic police commissioners of Manchester not only fought crime but built a town hall and managed the gas works.[15] Yet these *ad hoc* commissions could not meet the challenge of an industrial society; created to remedy a single evil, their scope and powers were too narrow; representing rate-payers who prized economy over improvement, they were held back by lack of money; diverse and anomalous, they became enmeshed in jurisdictional conflicts. St. Pancras had nineteen separate paving boards, and Dover had one with 105 commissioners.[16]

These improvement commissions suffered from the same defects as the parishes, JP's, and corporations. As units of administration they were too small to carry out general reforms. Their great diversity precluded any uniformity of action. Their unpaid officials were neither checked nor inspected by any outside authority, and the way was thus left open to irresponsibility, negligence, and corruption. The proud traditions of voluntary public service and local self-government, important as they were, could not in 1833 overcome the basic structural defects of English local government.

Not only did the chaos preclude good government but the temper of the times placed severe limits on all government. Public opinion did not, for example, consider education a responsibility of government, whether parish, county, or national; education was left to private effort or charity, neither of which met the need. The working class had no money to pay fees at private schools and the schools built by the British and Foreign School Society and the Church of England's National School Society were few and ill staffed. Not only in education but in every field of endeavor voluntary societies proved ineffective and on occasion corrupt. Under

15. Webbs, *Statutory Authorities*, pp. 252, 261–63. Conrad Gill, *The History of Birmingham* (London, 1952), *1*, 155–99.

16. Samuel Finer, *The Life and Times of Edwin Chadwick* (London, 1951), p. 306. Robert Rawlinson, *Report for the General Board of Health on Dover*, London, 1850.

the spur of Lord Brougham's speeches Parliament established a commission to inquire into charitable activities. It devoted twenty-six volumes over fourteen years to exposing abuses; the inquiries showed that voluntary effort could boast no better a record than local government in meeting the social problems of the new England.[17]

The proudest accolades of all in 1833 went to commercial enterprises—models of efficiency and initiative. Leave social problems to the self-interest of the citizen, argued journalists, economists, and politicians: let parents pay for education, water companies provide water, manufacturers fence their machinery, and railway companies run their trains; each in his way will promote the common good. But unfortunately for the public, commercial institutions were not free of abuses either. The spirit of commerce provided no answer to the education of the working class. Privately-run day schools and the dame schools (conducted at home by ill-educated though well-meaning ladies) did, to be sure, teach more of the poor than did the endowed schools; but the instruction they offered was dull and mechanical and hardly worth the twopence a week it cost. Neither was the tap water of London—uncertain in its flow, impure and tepid—worth the high rates the private monopolies charged.[18] These failures, and others, suggested rather clearly that business could not meet all the problems of an urban society, that these problems demanded the intervention of government. Yet local government did not have the trained men or the powers or the desire to intervene. What of the central government then? Did it have the men, the powers, and the purpose to reform what was amiss in society?

THE CENTRAL GOVERNMENT

By Continental standards England's central government seemed absurdly small. A French Minister of the Interior, accustomed to extensive powers and a staff of 200,000 employees throughout France, would have been humiliated to sit at England's Home

17. *PP*, 7 (1838), 42–53, 62–66, 83. *House of Commons Papers, General Index* (1801–52), p. 140.
18. Manchester Statistical Society, *Report on Salford, Manchester*, 1837. Anon., *Memorandum on Metropolitan Water Bills* (London, 1852), pp. 10–11.

Office with its limited power and twenty-nine officials.[19] The same economy of personnel and paucity of powers characterized all the departments of the government, with the exceptions of the courts, the Treasury, and the Army and Navy. England's central administration did little in 1833 besides administer justice, collect taxes, and defend the realm. It rarely touched the life of the ordinary individual and showed little concern for his well-being. It failed even to supervise those local authorities and voluntary institutions that did concern themselves with the individual's welfare.

Small as the government appeared by Continental standards, it seemed to the average tax-paying Englishmen large and extravagant. He was frankly confused by its many offices, both necessary and unnecessary, and by its many powers, both prerogative and statutory. He was offended by its wasteful sinecures and innumerable pensions, and he hated the meddling intervention of excise and customs officers.[20] He certainly had no reason to doubt that England was a centralized state—he had only to look at her historic institutions: the Crown, the Parliament, the Courts of Law, the Navy, the Army, the Treasury. In these was concentrated the dominant power of the state, and chief among them was Parliament. The Crown, to be sure, still exercised some influence on the choice of ministers, determination of policy, and formation of public opinion, but it was an influence far short of that exercised by Parliament, which had supreme authority in the realm. Few were the local authorities who did not derive their powers from an act of Parliament, and no local authorities could disobey a Parliamentary statute. Futhermore Parliament could create any judicial or administrative authority it desired and legislate on any matter it wished. Acts of Parliament prescribed the quality of bread and the size of wagon wheels, imposed rules for apprenticeship, and made laws for the Sabbath.[21] Since the Elizabethan age it

19. In 1846 France's Ministry of the Interior numbered 203,900 and the grand total of government employees was 932,000: *Times* (London), April 10, 1847; *PP, 23* (1833), 439.

20. For Tory indignation at the enormous expenditure see Hansard, *19* (1833), 673–703. For the Radical's critical view see John Wade, *The Extra-Ordinary Black Book,* London, 1832.

21. 6 & 7 William IV, c. 37. Webbs, *The Story of the King's Highway* (London, 1913), p. 202.

had never tired of passing economic and social legislation. But Parliament had never wished to create the central agencies to enforce its decrees. It left the enforcement to the parishes and the justices, superintended and aided by those branches of the central government that had emerged over the centuries. The Normans had created the Exchequer and the Treasury, the Angevins had organized a system of Royal Courts, the Tudors had developed the Secretaries of State and the Privy Council, while the Stuarts had fashioned a modern naval and army administration. The Hanoverians, to pay for their wars, expanded the revenue departments. Thus in an empirical fashion the central government grew, the modern overlapping with the medieval, in the same pattern of decay and growth that characterized local government. Classified by their function these central departments, employing 21,305 civilian officials, presented the following picture in 1833: [22]

PUBLIC DEPARTMENTS

I. *The Revenue Departments*
   Treasury (115)
   Customs (9,459)
   Excise (6,377)
   Stamps (458)
   Taxes (276)
   Hackney Coach Office
   Post Office (1,817; both a revenue and service department)
   Office of Woods, Forests, Land Revenues, Public Works, and Buildings (91)

II. *The Military Departments*

   A. Army Departments (separate and uncoordinated)
      War Office (87; under the Secretary at War)
      Secretary for War (legal and fiscal affairs)
      Ordnance Department (824)

22. Compiled largely from "Report on Finances and Accounts," *PP, 23* (1833), 439–653. The numbers in parentheses indicate the number employed in each department.

Quartermaster General's Office (28)
Army Pay Office (24)
Comptroller of Army Accounts (28)
Commander in Chief Offices (26)
Other small offices (such as Chelsea Hospital)

B. The Naval Departments (coordinated under the
Admiralty)
The Admiralty (723, the total for all subdepartments)
Surveyor of Navy
Navy Pay Office
Victualling Office
Royal Marine Hospital
Coast Guard

III. *The Courts of Justice* (no returns of personnel)

Kings Bench
Common Pleas
Chancery
Court of the Exchequer

IV. *External Affairs*

Foreign Office (39)
Consuls and Ambassadors
Colonial Office (33)
Registrar of Colonies (4)
Irish Departments (also handled by regular central
departments, such as the Customs and Excise)
Alien Office (18)
Board of Control for India (12 Commissioners)
East India Company and Indian Civil Service

V. *Management of Crown Properties*

Office of Woods, Forests, Land Revenues, Public
Works, and Buildings (91; also listed under
Revenue Departments)
Auditors' Land Revenue Office (11)

VI. *Government Services Departments*

> Audit Office (95)
> National Debt Office (32)
> State Paper Office (32)
> Stationery Office (36)
> Privy Seal Office
> Signet Office
> Attorney and Solicitor General
> King's Remembrance Office
> Four Tellers of Exchequer Offices (22)
> Clerk of the Pells (23)

VII. *Domestic Affairs*

> Privy Council (17)
> > Inspector General of Quarantine
> Board of Trade (25
> > Statistical Department
> > Corn Office
> Home Office (29)
> > Penitentiaries
> > Metropolitan Police
> > Metropolitan Commissioners in Lunacy
> > Commissioners of Metropolitan Turnpikes
> > Holyhead Road Commissioners
> > Temporary Commissions of Inquiry
> > > Poor Law Commission
> > > Factory Commission
> > > Municipal Corporations Commission
> > > Handloom Commission
> > > Charity Commission
> > > Common Law Commission
> Lord Chancellor
> Surveyor of Quarantine
> Post Office (listed also under Revenue)
> Mint (30)

Central Government

Among the oldest of the many departments, older even than Parliament, were the Royal Courts. Their expansion in the twelfth century made England a centralized monarchy and in time a national state. In 1833 they alone of all the central departments possessed the power to superintend local authorites. All JP's, all parish officers, and all local commissioners were answerable to the courts for failing to enforce the law of the land. In 1833 the Central Courts gave judgments in sixty cases concerning the duties of magistrates and parishes.[23] But sixty cases count very little against 15,500 parishes, 5,000 justices, and innumerable local commissioners, and suggest that the courts—notoriously slow, cumbersome, and costly—posed little threat to irresponsible local officials. The Chancery especially, with its interminable delays, incurred the hostility of all but fee-coveting barristers. Even the Duke of Wellington rejoiced that the Whig's irascible reformer Lord Brougham had become Lord Chancellor and would reform "that damned court." [24]

The largest and most expensive departments were not the courts but the Army and Navy. Of the fifty-two million pounds spent by the British government in 1833 twenty-seven million was for the servicing of the national debt and thirteen million for the maintenance of the Army and Navy. But the military departments, though they occasionally repressed disorders, had little to do with domestic affairs. It was in fact neither the Army nor the Navy but the revenue departments that touched most directly the life of the average Englishman, who after all did not sit in Parliament and seldom found himself before a Central Court, but could not escape the tax collector. Of the many departments constituting the civil administration the largest and most active devoted their energy to the collection of revenue and were organized under the Treasury. These were the Board of Customs, Board of Excise, Commissioners of Stamps, Commissioners of Taxes, Post Office,

23. *Law Journal Reports,* new ser. (1833), pp. 1–111.
24. Geoffrey Garrat, *Lord Brougham* (London, 1935), p. 232; *PP, 14* (1833), 1–7. For the most vivid picture of Chancery delay and inefficiency, done in 1850, see Charles Dickens, *Bleak House.*

and Office of Woods, Forests, Land Revenues, Public Works, and Buildings. Formerly three separate agencies performed the duties of the latter office. In 1835 Parliament also combined the Commissioners of Stamps and Commissioners of Taxes into one department.[25] It did so because it insisted on efficient and economical management. The administrative reformers, led by that untiring advocate of retrenchment Joseph Hume, criticized the prodigal waste of the fee system, whereby unsalaried public officials earned large incomes from fees charged for services rendered. Such a system all too often led to extravagance, corruption, and inefficiency.

Administrative reformers also censured other glaring defects of England's central administration: the hundred useless sinecures, the hopeless confusion of courts, the incompetence of patronage appointees, and the antiquated methods of the Exchequer.[26] The Court of Exchequer was indeed a museum of fossilized specimens from an antediluvian age. It had a clerk of estreat, a clerk of hanaper, and a clerk of nichills. It paid a fine salary to a cursutar baron and even more generous salaries to four aristocratic tellers, each of whom hired deputies to sit in wooden pews making reports in Roman numerals. Meanwhile the Bank of England and the Audit Office conducted their business in quarters adjoining the Tellers. The Exchequer had just given up the use of tally sticks but held tenaciously to parchment, Latin, and thirteen sinecures.

The newer departments, such as the Boards of Excise and Customs, were more efficient than the Exchequer, but to many Englishmen they were no more useful. The Customs and Excise, badly organized and staffed by patronage, were the subject of much complaint. The establishment in 1815 by the Commissioners of the Customs of a system of closer central inspection failed to end occasional corruption.[27] But more irritating to men of commerce than these custom frauds were the vexatious interventions of the excise

25. *PP, 38* (1848), iii; 4 & 5 William IV c. 60.

26. Hansard, *20* (1833), 705; *PP, 23* (1833), 553–54. Wade, *Black Book.* *Westminster Review, 21* (1834), 56–65. *PP, 17* (1840), 187.

27. Ibid. *PP, 29* (1843), 158–73 (1–16).

officers—"wretches," said Dr. Johnson, hired to collect that "hateful tax." In 1833 thousands of excise men swarmed over the land, inspecting eight times each year every tea seller and tobacconist in the realm and laying down exact regulations for the brewing of spirits and the manufacture of glass and paper.[28] Certainly neither central inspection nor the regulation of commerce were strange to the English in 1833. Quite the contrary, they were known only too well, and for that reason deeply hated.

Englishmen criticized the central government not only for its meddling excisemen and the anachronistic methods of the Exchequer but also for the lack of effective coordination between departments. Each department followed its own routine, made its own policy, and committed its own blunders. And all the time the cabinet discussed Catholic emancipation and foreign affairs. Men as various as the great Whig peer Lord Holland, the Privy Council's Charles Greville, and the Colonial Office's literary aspirant Sir Henry Taylor testified to the virtual autonomy of each department and the Cabinet's indifference to ordinary business.[29] As a result, ministers gave conflicting orders, the jurisdictions of various departments were allowed to overlap, and cautious officials evaded decisions. The efficiency and policies of each department varied greatly. The administration of the Army suffered from the confusion of many separate offices, a fault the Navy escaped because its new First Lord, Sir James Graham, had placed all offices under the direction of the Admiralty. The Foreign Office worked industriously under the stern rule of Lord Palmerston, the Board of Trade endured the mediocrity of Lord Auckland. Other departments, like the Customs and the Excise, had no single head but a board of commissioners. There were fifteen departments administered by boards, usually with twelve members. A dozen persons at the head of a department scarcely promoted efficiency, and to Bentham they were merely a "screen to hide abuses."[30] Other departments suffered from too few officials.

28. *PP,* 21 (1833) 421–59 (5–43); 24 (1834), 1, 87, 157, 205.

29. Lord Holland, *Memoirs of the Whigs* (London, 1854), 2, 84–89. Greville, *Memoirs,* 2, 345. Sir Henry Taylor, *The Statesman* (London, 1836), p. 155.

30. John Bowring, ed., *The Complete Works of Jeremy Bentham* (London, 1843), 9, 214–19.

Even the Treasury, which superintended all expenditure and distributed most of the patronage, was understaffed and overworked, and only the work of a few able men made that key department one of the more efficient. Able men were indeed finding their way into many public departments. Mostly from the middle ranks of society—industrious, talented, and full of the zeal of reform—they brought, as best they could, to uncoordinated and routine-ridden departments a new standard of intelligence and efficiency. Rowland Hill, the son of a schoolmaster, won prominence in the Post Office by laying the basis for the penny postal service, while William Huskisson's great tariff reforms owed not a little to James Hume, in 1791 only an indoor clerk in the custom house in Thames street, by 1828 a joint secretary of the Board of Trade.[31] The civil servant in 1833 was making himself felt, and was raising the administrative competence of the central agencies well above the standards of local government.

But as promising as was the future efficiency of the central government, it did very little in 1833 about the social problems which beset England. The Courts, to be sure, dealt with crime, disorder, and disputes over property; and Parliament passed laws on countless matters. The central government even had a few agencies touching directly upon social problems. But they were unimportant. The problems of waging war, more than social problems, had defined England's central government before 1833. In the mid-eighteenth century, in full reaction to Stuart despotism, the central government was severely limited, but after a series of wars culminating in the immense effort to overthrow Napoleon, England found herself burdened with an expensive military force and a huge debt. The cost of supporting these forces and servicing the debt forced a great expansion in the revenue departments. In 1833 the revenue and military departments together spent over four-fifths of the government's income and employed over four-fifths of its personnel.[32]

Though smaller in size, the departments dealing with domestic

31. *PP, 18* (1848), 151. Howard Robinson, *The British Post Office* (Princeton, 1948), pp. 258-72. *DNB, 28,* 228.
32. *PP, 23* (1833), 455-543 (1-89).

affairs had a venerable tradition, the Secretary of State for Home Affairs and the Privy Council, for example, had their origins in the late middle ages and the early Tudor period. In 1833 they were beginning to play a more active role in government: an order of the Privy Council had established the temporary Central Board of Health in 1831, with inspectors to supervise local boards and with powers to issue regulations. The Privy Council disbanded it in 1832 with the clerk of the Council, Charles Greville, recording his indignation at "vestries and parishes [who] stoutly resisted all pecuniary demands for the purpose of carrying into effect the recommendations of the central board or the orders of the Privy Council." [33] This resistance boded ill for future sanitary reforms. The disbanding of the Central Board left the Privy Council Office with nothing more than a Surveyor of Quarantine to stave off future cholera epidemics, and a Statistical Department to record its ravages should it return. The Statistical Department was a new department of the Board of Trade. Its creation in 1832 was at least a recognition of the need for knowledge about the economic and social health of the realm. The Board of Trade—itself a committee of the Privy Council—formulated tariff and navigation policy but did little else.

The Home Office concerned itself more actively than did the Privy Council in social problems. The Home Secretary, as His Majesty's leading servant, was enjoined to keep the king's peace, a duty that implied some concern for the well-being of society. But Parliament had long given such functions to the justices, over whom the Home Office had no direct control. Infrequent correspondence between JP's and the Home Office availed little; the local magistracy disregarded the Home Office's regulations on prisons and neglected or violated the law requiring them to visit asylums.[34] In only two matters had the Home Office some power: Sir Robert Peel in 1829 had persuaded Parliament to form the Metropolitan Police force under the direction of the Home Office. In the same year Robert Gordon, an Evangelical and reformer,

33. Public Record Office (PRO), P.X. 1/93, 14, 114. 2 & 3 William IV c. 10. Stachey, Greville *Memoirs*, 2, 279.

34. Webbs, *English Prisons under Local Government* (London, 1920), pp. 110–11; *PP*, 6 (1841), 241 (6); 26 (1844), 1–203.

succeeded in carrying a measure through Parliament establishing the Metropolitan Commissioners in Lunacy. These were placed under the direction of the Home Office but were, like the police, limited to the metropolitan area.[35]

Two permanent commissions, one to administer the metropolitan turnpikes and the other to administer the Holyhead Turnpike through Wales, formed part of the very limited efforts of the central government to administer domestic affairs. The roads of the metropolis and the road to Ireland were too urgently needed to tolerate the incompetence of parish management.

More important for the future growth of a centralized administration in England were the temporary royal commissions of inquiry, which in 1833 worked under the direction of the Home Office. Commissioners and assistant commissioners traveled throughout England investigating the operation of poor laws, the exploitation of child labor, the poverty of the handloom weavers, the misuse of charities, and the faults of municipal corporations. Their investigations revealed a need for a permanent supervision over local authorities and private institutions. Three of these commissions recommended the creation of central agencies able to command the available skill for needed reforms and endowed with power to carry them through. The local authorities, they concluded, were incompetent to make such reforms. The commissioners' reports, vivid in detail and comprehensive in scope, presented strong arguments for central supervision of local authorities. All that needed to be done was for Parliament to establish such agencies, but unfortunately Parliament reflected not the views of the commissioners but the sentiments and political theories of the electors.

OPINIONS AND THEORIES

Most Englishmen in 1833 looked with disfavor on a large central government. They wished no new agencies, no expensive commissions, and no bothersome interference. To Tories and conservative Whigs, heirs of Blackstone and Burke, England's local institutions—its magistracy, parish, and corporations—enshrined the wisdom of centuries. To liberal Whigs and modern re-

35. 10 George IV c. 18, 44.

formers, "enlightened" by theories of political economy, governmental intervention was harmful and vexatious. To Radicals, ever mindful of sinecures and Home Office spies, a large government was extravagant and oppressive. And to all tax payers, Tory, Whig, Liberal or Radical, an expanded government meant higher taxes. Thus jealousy of strong government became ingrained in the political attitudes of all parties.

The source of this jealousy, hence its strength, came more from special interests than political philosophy, more from attachments to local offices, property, and low taxes than from Adam Smith and Edmund Burke. The Tories above all, as magistrates and mayors, parsons and squires, defended the ancient rights of local government; but they had loyal allies in Whig aldermen and radical vestrymen. They all resented any encroachment by central government on their much prized autonomy. The two sheriffs of Norwich flatly refused in 1833 to receive the municipal corporation commissioners; and the town's council, also threatened with investigation, charged that such a commission violated their common law rights. Their brethren of the London corporation fought with equal zeal and more success to keep their police, and the patronage it afforded them, free from Sir Robert Peel's new force. In 1830 a proposed northern road bill evoked a storm of protest from local turnpike trustees.[36] In 1832 local parishes, despite the presence of cholera, resisted the orders of the Central Board of Health for improved sanitation. Whether they were turnpike trustees or municipal councilors, justices of the peace or parish vestrymen, England's innumerable local officials were dedicated to the preservation of their ancient constitutional rights —rights they believed the very bulwark of English freedom. The leading Tory journals, the *Morning Post,* the *Standard,* and the *Morning Herald,* defended these ancient prerogatives as part of a perfect constitution. The *Standard* used the analogy of a spider web to show the cruelty, rapacity, and oppression of centralization.[37]

36. Webbs, *Manor and Borough,* 2, 557. Chadwick Papers, anonymous pamphlet: *Charles Pearson and the City Corporation.* Webbs, *Highway,* p. 179.

37. *Standard,* July 25, 1834. *Morning Herald,* May 28, 1834. *Morning Post,* May 20, 1834.

Allied with local authorities in resisting central interference were the voluntary institutions, the asylums, hospitals, schools, and various charities. A pamphlet in 1828, defending the rights of St. Luke's hospital against a proposed Metropolitan Lunacy Commission, demanded full respect for "the rights and independence of every voluntary and charitable institution," and warned that any government interference "would dry up these wellsprings of voluntary munificence." Faith in voluntary institutions—in endowed charities for the sick and in private benefactions for the homeless and unschooled—ran deep in the English mentality. The laureate Robert Southey extolled it and the church viewed it as part of the Christian fabric of society. Such voluntary effort in the field of education had inspired the efforts of the British and Foreign School Society and the National School Society, and in doing so created an almost insurmountable barrier against a much-needed system of public education. Churchman and dissenter alike zealously guarded his sectarian truth against the secularism of the state.[38]

As important as local and voluntary interests in breeding suspicion of a strong central government were the manifold and substantial interests of property. The most articulate defenders of property in 1833 were the cotton manufacturers. They considered Michael Sadler's Ten Hour Bill, which he introduced into Parliament in 1831, an uncalled-for, harmful, and improper interference with the free exercise of capital. To prevent its passage they employed the arguments of political economy.[39]

Political economy, though solemn humbug to Coleridge, held a highly respected position among the intellectual disciplines of the age. Its favorite doctrine of free trade had even been ac-

38. Anon., *Observations on the Bill for the Regulation of Lunatic Asylums*, London, 1838. Francis Close, *National Education and Lord Brougham's Bill* (London, 1838), p. 12, condemned Brougham's plan because its primary evil was centralization. The most extreme presentation of the voluntarist position on education came between 1846 and 1850 in Edward Baines' *Leeds Mercury*.

39. The *Leeds Mercury* and *Manchester Guardian* represented the enlightened manufacturers. They would accept protection for children but not for adults. The political economists' objections to any factory act is best expressed in Nassau Senior's *Letter on the Factory Act*, London, 1837.

cepted by the liberal Tories, whose leader, Huskisson, practiced it at the Board of Trade. The great Whig lords, Viscount Palmerston, Lord John Russell, and the Marquis of Lansdowne, had—along with that ardent reformer Lord Brougham and Lord Jeffrey of the *Edinburgh Review*—learned its truths from Dugald Stewart, Edinburgh's eloquent professor of moral philosophy. In 1833 Miss Harriet Martineau, as yet unknown, won fame by popularizing the rigorous deductions of Malthus and the iron laws of David Ricardo in a series of domestic tales. Political economy was taught in Lord Brougham's "mechanic institutes," and at Oxford and Cambridge. The *Edinburgh* and *Westminster* Reviews ardently espoused its leading tenets, teaching men to be trustful of economic laws, jealous of the rights of property, and suspicious of government interference.[40] By 1833 laissez faire, its sovereign principle, had become one of the ruling dogmas of the age.

To those forces opposing the growth of a strong central government, to localism, voluntary effort, and laissez-faire interests, the radicals added a fourth: hatred of a wasteful, oppressive, oligarchical government—of sinecures, pensioners, and corruption, of game laws and the "Six Acts" repressing free meetings and free speech. The most vehement and widely read of the Radicals was William Cobbett, who condemned the government for its placemen, its expensive army, its profligacy, and its giant debt, all of which served not the people of England but a narrow oligarchy of boroughmongers and fundholders. These views were re-echoed, though more rationally, in the *Extraordinary Black Book,* which in 1822 ran in periodical form and in 1832, as a book, sold over 14,000 copies. Its author, John Wade, listed in 600 interminable pages every pension and every sinecure to be found in church and state; and though its tone was shrill and its conclusions exaggerated, and though sinecures and pensioners were fast becoming anachronisms, its evidence cast doubts on the value of government bureaus. Richard Oastler, the Tory Radical, exemplified the Radical's suspicion of government. Though his greatest passion was for the

40. *DNB, 43,* 1172. Harriet Martineau, *Illustrations of Political Economy,* London, 1833. *Edinburgh Review, 111* (July 1832), 52–73. *Westminster Review, 16* (Jan. 1832), 1: *17* (July 1832), 1–34, (Oct. 1832), 267–311.

legislative protection of child labor, he attacked the royal commission investigating the abuses of child labor as "unconstitutional and inquisitorial." Even the philosopher Jeremy Bentham, to whom Oastler and Cobbett were anathema, agreed that "everywhere the whole official establishment is a corruptive establishment" and concluded that "in itself Government is one vast evil." [41] Only a few among the Radicals, as indeed only a very few Whigs or Tories, saw in government an instrument for active reform. Government, though necessary, was still a costly nuisance. The less it did and spent, the better.

Equally pervasive of public opinion and in many ways conflicting with this sentiment was an active spirit of philanthropy and an eagerness for reform. A desire to ameliorate the distress of the lower classes animated generous minds in all parties, but the most prominent among these advocates of reform were the Evangelicals and the Utilitarians. The Evangelicals reflected the growth of Christian humanitarian sentiments, the Utilitarians, the continual advance of rationalism, knowledge, and science. The philanthropy of the Evangelicals had not died with its great leader William Wilberforce or with its victory over the slave trade. In 1833 two Evangelicals of a more radical temper than Wilberforce, Michael Sadler and Richard Oastler, attacked on the platform and in the press the cruelties of child labor. In the House of Commons their cause was espoused by a third Evangelical, Anthony Ashley Cooper, the future Lord Ashley and Earl of Shaftesbury. In 1833 he was a young man of 32, an earnest Christian to whom there was no greater figure in modern history than John Wesley. In the next two decades he was to urge governmental protection for the weak and the oppressed, the children in mines, chimney sweeps, pauper lunatics, young criminals, and the sick and ill-housed.

In urging those reforms Lord Ashley allied himself with the Utilitarians. The evils and abuses of industrial England offended the dictates of reason as much as of religion, and contradicted the guiding principle of the Utilitarians: the greatest happiness to

41. William Cobbett, *Political Register, 67* (1829), 17, 658. Alfred Power, *Letter to Michael Sadler* (Leeds, 1833), p. 6. Bowring, *Works, 9,* 24, 67.

the greatest number. They therefore busied themselves in very good cause, established schools, formed societies for the reform of the law, advocated factory legislation, and urged poor-law reform. Above all they championed a state system of education.

The Evangelicals and the Utilitarians had no monopoly on the spirit of philanthropy, nor did this wave of humanitarianism stem from any one school; its intellectual tributaries were many, ranging from the logical reflections of Scottish moral philosophers to the generous sentiments of the Lake Poets, from broad church sensibility to the piety of the Quakers. It was Dugald Stewart who impressed upon leading Whigs a moral earnestness about reform, and it was the Quakers who mitigated the hardships of prison life and helped found the Prison Discipline Society, typical of dozens of other philanthropic associations,[42] whose extent suggests that the desire for reform lay in the very social processes of the age, above all in the increase of wealth, growth of cities, and advance of knowledge. These facts persuaded Englishmen in 1833 that conditions of life were improving, and that they could be further improved. Indeed such improvements were as inevitable as the advance of knowledge.

The need for reform was most evident in the cities. The growth of crowded, dismal manufacturing towns ("fungous excrescences on the body politic," said Southey) brought to a sharp focus the problems of poverty, disease, ignorance, and crime. The social abuses of the great metropolises persuaded the ordinary citizen as well as the earnest Christian and the philosophic reformer of the need for reform. Both philanthropic and governmental reforms started in the cities. The first voluntary societies for popular education on a wide scale began in London and Glasgow. The first government inquiry into education and prisons occurred in London, just as the first attempt to reform the police and care for the insane came in that growing city.[43] The demand for factory legislation arose in the towns of the North, and the first sanitary investigations were carried out in Manchester and London. Everywhere the serious evils of large towns excited the concerns of

42. Thomas Fowell Buxton, *Memoirs* (London, 1848), p. 64.
43. *PP, 4* (1818); *4* (1809), 214; 10 George IV c. 18, 44.

all responsible men. The Tory *Quarterly Review* vied with the *Edinburgh* and *Westminster* Reviews in propounding schemes of social betterment. Political economists relaxed their doctrine of laissez faire to recommend governmental interference, John Ramsay M'Culloch to recommend legislation for the protection of children and women in factories and mines, and Nassau Senior for the improvement of the conditions of town life and the education of the poor.[44] Indeed no demand was more universal than that for the education of the lower classes. To Lord Brougham and Harriet Martineau, to Robert Owen and Samuel Taylor Coleridge, in fact to nearly everyone but Cobbett (who thought it "despicable cant and nonsense") popular education seemed the only salvation for a troubled society.

The necessity to reform society, though widely felt, nevertheless gave rise to perplexing questions. Who should educate the lower orders, the state or the church? And who should reform the prisons, local magistrates or a central bureau? However earnest the governing classes were for social betterment, however zealous they were for reforms, they could not proceed to them until they had answered these questions. And to answer them they had to acquire some knowledge of public administration and to rethink the problem of government.

Few English thinkers in 1833 had a comprehensive theory of government and fewer a systematic awareness of the problems of public administration. There were, to be sure, pragmatic reformers, men such as Patrick Colquhoun, the able London magistrate and author of schemes for social reform. There were also imaginative philosophers, of whom Coleridge, with his Christian paternalism, was typical. But Colquhoun had no comprehensive view of the problem, while Coleridge had no faith in what he disdainfully called "Act of Parliament reform." He would rely instead

44. The *Quarterly Review* urged licensing, tithe, church, common-law, and poor-law reform and government aid to emigration: *42* (Jan, 1830), 105, 181, 228; *43* (May 1830), 242; *46* (Jan. 1832), 349, 410; *48* (Dec. 1832), 320, 542. The *Edinburgh Review* urged church, prison, poor-law, education, and law reform: *53* (March 1831), 43; *56* (Oct. 1832), 203; *58* (Oct. 1833), 1, (Jan. 1834), 336. Marion Bowley, *Nassau Senior and Classical Economics* (London, 1937), p. 257. Leslie Stephen, *Utilitarianism* (London, 1950), 2, 234.

upon a powerful church and the preaching of the gospel to the poor.[45] It thus fell upon the Utilitarians—upon Jeremy Bentham and the youthful Edwin Chadwick—to offer a plan of reform both comprehensive and practical. They understood the necessity of "Act of Parliament reform," and they saw the need for a strong, benevolent government and an efficient, uniform administration.

"Most assuredly," said Bulwer Lytton in 1833, Jeremy Bentham is "the most celebrated and influential teacher of the age." Posterity has confirmed that judgment.[46] Through his writings and his disciples this retiring philosopher of Queens Square taught his age the importance of rational criticism and systematic reform. He taught Englishmen to ask if an institution was useful and efficient and conducive to human happiness, not whether it agreed with custom, tradition, or a mythical natural law. It was this spirit of rational, common-sense criticism rather than any particular doctrine that worked as a catalyst in the administrative growth of the next two decades. Bentham had, of course, outlined an elaborate, minutely detailed scheme of central administration in his *Constitutional Code*, but it was not published in full until 1841, nine years after his death. Furthermore the *Code* reflected only a later phase of his thinking. In his early writings he shared with many radicals their strong suspicion of the central government, with its wastefulness and corruption. In his scheme for *Pauper Management* and in his *Panopticon* he urged the management of workhouses and prisons by joint-stock companies. By this means, he wrote in his terse, dry style, "jealousy and influence are avoided and the benefit of a distinct check on the superintending power of government" is obtained. For management by the government Bentham would substitute the "duty and self-interest principle" of a private entrepreneur, a principle which expresses not only his

45. Patrick Colquhoun, *The State of Indigence and the Situation of the Casual Poor*, London, 1799. *DNB, 4,* 859. R. J. White, *The Political Thought of Samuel Taylor Coleridge, a Selection* (London, 1938), pp. 38, 153.

46. Bulwer Lytton, *England and the English, 2,* 106. George M. Trevelyan, *British History in the Nineteenth Century* (London, 1937), p. 181. A. V. Dicey, *Lectures on the Relation between Law and Public Opinion* (London, 1905), pp. 302–9. Elie Halévy's *Philosophical Radicalism* (London, 1928) is the most penetrating study of Bentham's ideas.

adherence to a laissez-faire economy but also his sanguine belief in an administrative laissez faire.

Bentham of course realized the dangers inherent in such an administrative policy. He was too shrewd to allow joint-stock companies to go completely unchecked. In his manuscript notes on police and prison authorities, drawn up as early as 1789, he provides for superintendence of these authorities by the central government. He expanded this idea in 1832 and made it the basis for a centralized state: his *Constitutional Code* outlined a precise and symmetrical plan of central administration.[47] The legislature delegates to a Prime Minister and twelve other ministers the supreme executive power. In addition to ministers of interior, trade, and finance (ministers already part of English government, though under different names) Bentham proposed a minister of health, a minister of education, a minister of indigence, and a minister of preventive service (that is, for floods and disasters). Each minister had the power to dismiss the locally elected chief official, inspect local authorities, collect facts, issue reports, and suggest policy. The central administration could thus dominate the local. But its powers in the economic sphere were small. The minister of trade could do little beyond collect statistics and advise on legislation, and the principal qualification of the minister of indigence was an acquaintance with political economy. Two principles warred against each other in Bentham's mind: a belief in the merits of centralization and a hatred for governmental interference in the economy. Fortunately his economic orthodoxy did not prevent him from realizing the usefulness of social planning. He proposed that the health, education, and preventive ministries have the powers to make mines safe, inspect schools, and see that towns were healthy. They should have those powers that would bring the greatest happiness to the greatest number. The belief that a strong efficient government would improve the well-being and happiness of society was one of Bentham's legacies to England, or more properly to those young Utilitarians who gathered around him.

The number of such disciples, as indeed those who read Bentham

47. Bentham Papers (University College, London), Boxes 154, 158: "Scheme for Central Police." Bowring, *Works, 8,* 127; *4,* 129; *7,* 380 ff.; *9,* 428–52.

at all, were very few in 1833. But they were men of energy and intellect—an important part, according to Bulwer Lytton, of the "minute fraction who think." They edited the *Westminster Review*, the *Morning Chronicle*, and the *Examiner;* they wrote in the *Globe* and the *Scotsman;* they taught jurisprudence at Cambridge and political economy at Oxford; they founded University College in London; and they won seats in Parliament and positions on the new investigating commissions.[48] The most energetic was a 34-year-old barrister named Edwin Chadwick, who had served as private secretary to Jeremy Bentham.

Chadwick had grown up in the Lancashire manufacturing town of Longsight and had spent his youth in London. While there he entered the Inns of Court, but he spent as much time discussing epidemics with medical students as judgments in tort with law students. A growing interest in social problems soon led him to write articles exposing social abuses, the first of which attacked the faulty statistics of the life insurance companies, the second and third exposing the inadequacies of parish police in London and the faults of French charities. The careful marshaling of facts and the sound and original reasoning displayed in these articles won Chadwick a position as Bentham's private secretary.[49] The sources of his social philosophy were therefore many and varied. It was not Bentham's tutelage alone that formed his mind but the early years in a manufacturing town, his studies in London, and his acquaintance with the legal, scientific, and philosophical thought of his age. He owed much to Bentham but even more, as he confessed later, to his own investigations and independent thinking. According to his friend John Stuart Mill, he possessed "one of the organizing and contriving minds of the time." [50] Chadwick could

48. Bulwer Lytton, *England and the English*, 2, 108. Stephen, *Utilitarians*, 2, 28–32; 3, 26–30. John Bowring edited the *Westminster Review*, John Black the *Morning Chronicle*, and Albany Fonblanque the *Examiner;* M'Culloch wrote for the *Scotsman* and Chadwick for the *Globe* (Chadwick Papers); Charles Austin taught at Cambridge, Senior at Oxford, and in Parliament were George Grote, John Roebuck, William Molesworth, and others. Southwood Smith was on the Factory Commission with Chadwick.

49. Finer, *Chadwick*, pp. 1–37.

50. Bentham Papers, Box 155: Chadwick to the President of the Law Amendment Society, Sept. 13, 1866. Chadwick Papers, John Stuart Mill to the editor of the *Scotsman*, Aug. 22, 1868.

never have constructed the comprehensive and logical systems of a
Bentham, nor would he have hazarded to draw up laws good for
all countries at all times. His genius was of a different kind. As
early as 1829 he had displayed in an article on preventive police
a prodigious zeal for collecting facts and a keen grasp of particular
social conditions and efficient administrative techniques—an article
that clearly showed him to be a practical reformer and not a
theorist. Not that he ignored the importance of general principles.[51]
Like all Benthamites he had a passion for uniformity. His genius
was to combine a flair for social investigation with an understanding of the general principles of administrative organization. He
knew at first hand the weaknesses of local government and the
seriousness of England's social problems, and he realized the need
of central authorities with paid experts. But he did not favor
centralization on the French model. He would give the central
agencies no more power than the particular situation demanded.
He believed that the best administration would arise from a
balance between local and central authorities, the local authorities
to carry out the details as the situation varied from day to day,
and the central authorities to determine a general, uniform policy.
This view arose not from abstract reasoning but from intensive investigations, which is why his proposals were so effective.
It was his power of social research and administrative planning,
far more than Bentham's *Constitutional Code*, that influenced
the administrative growth of the next two decades.

The central control of administration was certainly no innovation in 1833. In England there were Metropolitan Commissioners in Lunacy and police commissions, the temporary inspectors of the Central Board of Health, and the excise surveyors; in Ireland there was a comprehensive system of police,
education, and lunatic asylum inspectors; and in America, Holland, France, and Prussia there were efficient systems of prison
and education inspection. All these foreign models were studied
by the English.[52] The administrative reformers had no need to

51. Edwin Chadwick, "Preventive Police," *London Review* (1829), pp. 252–
307.

52. The Irish prison inspectors served as a direct precedent to the prison

enunciate the idea of central supervision, but only to argue its necessity—to show convincingly that local authorities could neither educate the poor nor regulate factory labor, neither distribute adequate relief nor keep their towns clean unless they received financial aid, considerable prodding, and much supervision from an intelligent and informed central agency.

For the administration of prisons and asylums, the prevention of child labor, the promotion of education, and a reformed poor law, the Benthamites, occasionally joined by the Evangelicals, urged the establishment of central agencies. But however cogent their arguments they always remained a minority. A desire to proceed slowly in redressing these grievances, and not a wish for radical change, possessed those with power, the Whig ministers and the majority in Parliament. Lord Grey wished to "work out necessary reforms . . . upon safe and moderate principles," and Lord Palmerston would "redress admitted grievances." Both their colleagues Lord Melbourne and Lord Althorp, and their Tory opponents led by Sir Robert Peel, shared this cautious, practical attitude toward reform, as did the majority in Parliament, whom Lord Brougham styled "on the whole, moderate men . . . friends of safe and rational reform." These men of the reformed House of Commons wished to remedy particular abuses. But to carry out even this moderate wish, the Whigs, because of the complexity of the problems facing them, had to turn to the keener, more industrious Benthamites.[53] They put Southwood Smith on the Factory Commission, Nassau Senior on the Poor Law Commission, and Edwin Chadwick on both. The Benthamites better than any other group of men could collect facts, draw up reports, and outline useful reforms. The evidence and reasoning of their reports were impressive, but what gave them most strength were the underlying facts. They had only to

Act of 1835, *PP, 36* (1835), 381; and the education inspectorates of Holland, America, and Prussia were subjects of much comment by many Englishmen. Leonard Horner publicized these schemes in his *Report of M. Victor Cousin's on the State of Public Education in Holland,* London, 1839.

53. PRO 30/22/1, Russell Papers, Grey to Melbourne, Feb. 1, 1835. Sir Charles Webster, *The Foreign Policy of Lord Palmerston, 1830–1841* (London, 1951), *1,* 358. Lord Brougham, *Memoirs* (London, 1871), *3,* 437.

describe the chaotic administration of the poor law, the exploitation of children, the disgraceful state of prisons, the increasing crime, the unhealthiness of slums, and the profound ignorance of the working classes to convince of the need for reform. As Macaulay said, these abuses threatened the very industrial civilization that created them. By 1833 it was increasingly evident that England needed that which Bulwer Lytton called for: "a directive government; a government always strong . . . a government educating your children, encouraging your science, and ameliorating the condition of the poor." [54]

54. Bulwer Lytton, *England and the English*, 2, 308.

2.

SOCIAL REFORM AND ADMINISTRATIVE GROWTH

JOHN STUART MILL observed of Bulwer Lytton's *England and the English* that it was "greatly in advance of the public mind." [1] Such a plea was indeed quite alien to the spirit of the times. It ran counter to the interests of the rate-payers; it offended the liberal doctrines of the Whigs; it outraged those traditions of local self-government prized by the Tories, and it aroused the fears of the Radicals.

The ordinary MP wanted no directive government. The Conservatives, weak and unnerved by the Reform Bill, shuddered at the mention of further reforms. The most vocal Radicals would suffer no such Prussian notions, and the Whig peers, such as the judicious Lord Grey and the indolent Melbourne, possessed neither the imagination nor the energy to cope boldly with the problems of an industrial society. They and their supporters were wedded, either consciously or unconsciously, to an attitude of laissez faire. Their preoccupations in 1833 were to reform municipal corporations and assuage the troubles in Ireland; and what they desired most of all were lower taxes and fewer sinecures and placemen. They had no intention of establishing in the next twenty-five years an extensive administrative state. They did not even intend to centralize the poor-law administra-

1. John Stuart Mill, *Autobiography* (London, 1924), p. 139.

35

tion, or to establish central factory inspectors. And yet the reformed Parliament did just this, and by so doing established precedents for two principles pregnant with future development: that government might interfere in economic affairs in order to protect the individual and that Whitehall might supervise local government in order to ensure administrative efficiency.

The contradiction between Parliament's political intentions and its actual performance arose from no accidental twist of history. Behind this contradiction lay two intractable facts, the urgent need of social reform and the inadequacies of local government. Whenever social distress and local abuses became intolerable and the resulting agitation for reform loud and clamorous, the safe and moderate men in Parliament took some action—action which usually demanded, of necessity, the extension of the powers and functions of the central government.

FACTORY AND POOR-LAW REFORMS

Such was the case with child labor in the textile factories. Three evangelical reformers, Richard Oastler, Michael Sadler, and Lord Ashley, supported by the widespread agitation of the workers and the awakened sympathy of the public, forced Parliament to consider reform. Sadler's Select Committee of the House of Commons had made public in 1832 the grim story of children working long hours in unhealthy factories. The report told a one-sided story, but it won the sympathy of the English people for these neglected children and it further aroused the fierce indignation of Richard Oastler. In one stormy meeting after another he organized, harangued, and incited the workers in the northern towns. In Parliament Lord Ashley pressed forward a ten-hour bill and won for it increasing support. The prospect of a ten-hour restriction for all textile workers alarmed the manufacturers, the adherents of political economy, and the timid conservatives. To head off this threat the Commons in April 1833 created, by the narrow majority of one vote, a Royal Commission, and ordered it to make a further inquiry.[2] Two of the three commissioners appointed to make the inquiry

2. Driver, *Oastler,* pp. 125–222. Hansard, *17* (1833), 79–114.

were Edwin Chadwick and Southwood Smith, and the secretary to the Commission was James Wilson. All were friends of Jeremy Bentham. The factory question thus fell to the utilitarians.

With the help of sixteen assistant commissioners they made a rapid investigation, published their report, and stated their recommendations. The report, fairer than Sadler's but not without bias toward the tenets of political economy, confirmed the fact that young children worked twelve and often more hours, and that this resulted in fatigue, physical deterioration, and a total want of education.[3] The commissioners made four recommendations for removing these evils: no child below nine should work in textile factories, children below the age of thirteen should work only eight hours a day, these same children should receive three hours of schooling, and factory inspectors should be appointed to enforce these provisions. The Evangelicals had imparted the impulse to factory reform; the Benthamites now defined its form. They insisted on the provisions for three hours of schooling and for central inspection, and they insisted that child labor alone be regulated. They had no wish to limit the hours of labor for those over thirteen, an interference in the labor market which Chadwick thought pernicious.[4] On this point Lord Althorp differed, adding to the bill a provision limiting to twelve hours the labor which those between thirteen and eighteen should perform each day. Althorp introduced his measure on the fifth of July; by August it was a law. There was no great opposition, either in Parliament or in the press. The main protests in Parliament came from those who advocated a ten-hour day, and who were more often Radicals than Tories. A few were Whigs and Liberals. The manufacturers, thankful that their machinery could run more than twelve hours, accepted

3. PP, 20 (1833), 7–29, 34. Manchester Statistical Society, *Analysis of the Evidence Taken before the Factory Commission* (Manchester, 1834), does much to dispel the exaggerated notions of cruelty, immorality, and ill health in factories, though it admits the long hours and the great fatigue.

4. Chadwick Papers, memo to Marquis of Salisbury, 1886, on the employment of children in factories; Chadwick to Lord Russell, July 10, 1838, says his suggestions on schooling and restriction of adult labor were so modified that he felt no responsibility for the act.

the bill as a necessary evil; the majority found it an acceptable answer to a scandalous abuse.[5] The factory commissioners' report had caught the prevailing temper of Parliament, though objections were voiced to the establishment of central inspectors. The *Leeds Mercury* and *Morning Chronicle* found it cumbersome, and the radical Joseph Hume said one might as well send inspectors into kitchens to prevent little girls from scalding themselves. The larger manufacturers themselves supported the idea of inspection. If there was to be a law, they wished it enforced on all alike.[6] Thus Parliament, taking its cue from the disciples of Bentham, established its first central agency.

The significance of the act lay not in the shift of administrative power from local authorities to a central department but in the insistence that the central government can regulate private enterprise for the public's welfare. The central government promised that children would not be overworked, that they would receive some schooling, and that they would work in clean and safe factories. It marked the beginning of that centrally directed collectivism which increased in the nineteenth century with each new social reform and which, combined with the need for the efficient supervision of local government, caused the growth of a large, powerful, and benevolent central government. In the factory act the central government extended its control over private manufacturers. But the real revolution in local and central relations came in 1834 with the New Poor Law.

By 1834 dissatisfaction with the evils of the old poor law seemed universal. Its administration by local parishes had broken down. Poor rates, now totaling over seven million pounds, imposed a heavy burden on the rate payers. Pauperism, encouraged by the allowance system, demoralized the agricultural laborer. Some magistrates ordered relief as irresponsibly as other overseers administered it. Many parishes fell into the hands of shopkeepers and publicans who were not above granting relief to encourage

5. Hansard, 1833: *15*, 1160; *16*, 642, 1002; *17*, 79–114; *20*, 449, 527, 576, 583.
6. *Morning Chronicle*, Aug. 12, 1833. *PP*, *20* (1833), 68. Hansard, *20* (1833), 583

business. Other parishes had fallen to small farmers who used parish money to supplement their low wages. These abuses had disturbed the English for some time. Seven select committees in the past fifteen years had examined the operation of the poor laws, finding in their investigations a chaos of inefficient authorities and malpractices, the whole of which seemed to defy any single scheme of reform. William Pitt had despaired of the problem and Sir Robert Peel confessed that "the more it was studied the more difficult it was to come to a positive conclusion"; Wellington spoke just as diffidently.[7] The conservative mind did not have the boldness to envisage those radical reforms which alone could bring order out of confusion. The problems were indeed too great even for such experienced poor-law reformers as George Nicholls of Southwell and William Day of Sussex.[8] Their practical reforms, adapted to meet the problems of the moment, resulted in patchwork improvisations.

Even the schemes of theorists, like Bentham and Senior, failed to deal effectively with the morass of local authorities. Bentham would have poor relief administered by a joint-stock company; and Senior's first proposal was to give greater powers to a magistracy, a provision which he later repudiated.[9] Neither of these proposals solved the main problem, namely how to persuade 15,500 parishes to carry out a uniform, enlightened policy with an improved efficiency. The parishes, according to chance whims or their limited knowledge, or their peculiar situation, had neglected or badly administered whatever laws Parliament had passed to stem the tide of pauperism. So apparent had their failures become that the establishment of a central board became a necessity.[10] But it was also a radical idea. It called for a far greater shift in administrative power than

7. *Quarterly Review*, *48* (Dec. 1832), 32. Hansard, *23* (1830), 533; *28* (1828), 1544.

8. William Day, *An Inquiry into the Poor Laws and Surplus Labor*, London, 1832. George Nicholls, *History of the English Poor Laws* (London, 1898), *1*, xi–xxxiv.

9. Bowring, *Works*, 7, 380 ff. Chadwick Papers, Senior's memo to the Lord Chancellor, Jan. 1833.

10. PP, 27 (1834), 157.

had the Factory Act. It would certainly meet opposition from a timorous ministry and from a Parliament jealous of large government. To overcome such opposition its advocates would have to be well-informed, persuasive and imaginative. Yet of such qualities were Nassau Senior and Edwin Chadwick, the two men whom Lord Brougham persuaded Lord Melbourne to appoint as poor-law commissioners. Melbourne, the Home Secretary, thought all Benthamites were fools, but confronted with the imposing problems of the poor law, he philosophically relinquished to them this burdensome task.[11]

Chadwick had no sooner accepted his post than he began his exhaustive investigation. Never renowned for modesty he boasted that he collected more information than all the other assistant commissioners together. He then collaborated with Senior to write the Commission's report; a report full of Chadwick's contempt for parish "jobocracies" and Senior's disdain of autocratic magistrates; full, too, of cogent arguments for consolidating parishes into district boards and for placing these boards under the supervision of a central board.[12] Lord Brougham had it printed in cheap octavo editions and widely distributed.[13] Its evidence, though selective, was indubitably true, and its broad recommendations, though revolutionary, could not be easily disregarded.[14] The report proposed four radical changes: consolidation of parishes into districts to be managed by elected guardians, formation of a central board with large powers of supervision, the establishment of workhouses and the prohibition

11. Greville, *Memoirs, 3,* 88.

12. Chadwick Papers, Chadwick to Russell, July 1838: "I drafted the remedial measures and wrote the exposition of principles . . . Senior wrote of the evils of the old system and on settlement and vagrancy"; Chadwick to Lord Spencer April 30, 1838: "I worked out the principle of the law and sustained it by so large a mass of evidence. . . . I drew up the exposition of the measure proposed to the government"; Chadwick in another memo to Lord Spencer, around 1838: "Mr. Senior wrote the part concerning settlement and the parts after the conclusion as to the machinery."

13. Ibid., Chadwick to Lord Brougham, June 1849.

14. The unpublished reports of the more intensive investigations of the poor law assistant commissioners in 1835 and 1836 support the picture of widespread abuses shown in the 1834 inquiry. PRO, Ministry of Health Papers (MH), 32/1, 12, 26, 28.

of outdoor relief to the able-bodied, and finally expanded provisions for pauper education and the improved care of the aged and the ill.[15]

To prove the need for such changes the report was accompanied by seven bulky folio volumes telling of incompetent parishes, beneficent but injudicious magistrates, wretched poorhouses, and indolent and demoralized paupers. The selective nature of the facts reported served only to give greater force to the revolutionary recommendations. Even the *Times*, at first glance, seemed impressed by their lengthy recital of abuses and looked with an open mind on their proposals. But so revolutionary was the idea of central control and so severe was the workhouse test that the *Times* quickly became the loudest opponent of the measure. The Whigs' less influential *Morning Chronicle* countered with uninhibited praise of the bill. The *Quarterly Review* judged it more thoughtfully.[16] They considered the workhouse test too severe and the report's picture of abuses too biased, but they also realized that it presented an able analysis of a serious problem. Many parishes were grossly inefficient and profuse allowances did make paupers out of once independent workers.

Englishmen of all parties admitted the truth of the report, even though it was not the whole truth. There could no longer be any excuse for delay. Lord Althorp presented a bill, based largely on Chadwick's and Senior's proposals.[17] It evoked immediate opposition in and out of Parliament. But the opponents of the bill did not attempt to exonerate the parish and the magistrates nor refute the report's picture of maladministration. Instead they concentrated their attack on the establishment of a central board. The *Times*, the *Standard*, and the *Morning Herald* assumed an attitude of astonishment at such a monstrous innovation. So extravagantly did they denounce its unconstitutional and un-English principle of centralization that the *Morning*

15. *PP*, 27 (1834), 127–207.
16. The *Times* began on Feb. 24, 25, and April 19, 30, 1834, a criticism that did not end till the late 1840's. See also the *Morning Chronicle*, Feb. 25, May 9, and throughout June and July. *Quarterly Review*, Aug. 1834.
17. Chadwick Papers, Lord Althorp to Chadwick, April 28, 1838: "You framed the measure, I was only the instrument of carrying it out."

Chronicle accused them of using the cry of centralization to obscure the real issue.[18] The *Chronicle,* knowing the depth of the prejudice against centralization, explicitly disavowed any liking for it but confessed that in this case circumstances demanded a measure of centralization. Very few English journals in 1834 dared argue, in abstract, for the merits of centralization. This was even true of John Black, editor of the *Chronicle* and an admirer of Bentham. All the papers which supported the New Poor Law, whether the Radicals' *Examiner* and *Globe* (for which Chadwick wrote) or the *Spectator,* dwelled on the overwhelming need for reform. They stayed clear of theory and of the explosive issue of centralization.[19]

But the opposition would not tolerate any reticence on such an issue. The more the bill was debated in Commons the more the Tory journals, despite their party's support of the measure, fulminated against its centralizing tendencies. Especially resentful of these tendencies were the local parishes of London and of twenty-five of the largest towns in England, which protested against the idea of a central board. Angry at any interference in their local affairs, they sent petition after petition to Commons, where they knew the final decision would be made.[20]

In the House the bill progressed easily. Lord Althorp when introducing it argued its sheer necessity. The failure of parish administration made necessary, he said, the creation of district guardians and central commissioners. Lord Melbourne told the Lords he had no liking for this Benthamite measure, but could see no other answer. With a shrewd understanding of conservative interests he emphasized that the poor rates were "the heaviest direct tax on the country" and would continue to rise, if nothing were done. To allay the fears of government interference with the Englishman's liberty, Lord Brougham argued that the measure actually meant less government interference in

18. *Times,* May 5, 1834. *Standard,* May 5, 1834. *Morning Herald,* May 28, 1834. *Morning Chronicle,* April 21, May 12, 1834.

19. *Globe,* May 3, 1834. *Examiner,* May 24, 1834. *Spectator,* May 3, 1834. Chadwick Papers, Chadwick to Lansdowne, April 7, 1834.

20. Hansard, *24* (1834), 1027–32.

a man's private business than before.[21] In this he was partly right. The Poor Law Amendment Bill called for a shift of power from local to the central government, but not for an increase in the power of the government to intervene in private affairs. There would no longer be some 15,500 uncontrolled petty tyrants. Furthermore the bill's emphasis on strict relief agreed with the current dogmas of political economy. The Government would in the future be less solicitous and bountiful to the poor. If the Factory Act had been more collectivist in its tendencies than centralist, the New Poor Law was more centralist than collectivist. It brought a shift in existing administrative power, not its extension. For this reason economists such as Poulett Thompson of the Board of Trade and Philosophical Radicals such as the banker George Grote gave it their unqualified support. On its third reading the bill received an overwhelming majority, one which included almost all the Conservatives. Only two Conservatives opposed it on its second reading and only eleven on the third.[22] They had many reasons to wish its passage. It relieved them as magistrates of onerous duties from which they frankly wished to be free; and above all it meant lower rates. If their newspapers expressed their prejudices correctly, they clearly voted against their prejudices and in favor of their purses.

The minority in Commons who opposed the bill, led by William Cobbett, the most unphilosophical of the Radicals, certainly did not keep silent. They magnified the powers of the new commissioners; called them irresponsible, arbitrary, and tyrannical; raised the specter of patronage; inveighed against the appointment of assistant commissioners who would inspect the districts; and tried on every occasion to excite local prejudices.[23] Their agitations had some success. They forced the Government to drop the clause giving assistant commissioners immunity from court proceedings and the clause giving the com-

21. Ibid., 22 (1834), 874–89; 25, 272, 444.
22. Ibid., 24 (1834), 1061. *Manchester Guardian*, April 26, 1834.
23. Hansard, 24 (1834), 314, 318, 345, 430, 1046–53; 23 (1834), 1298, 1341.

missioners the power to abolish poor law incorporations created by local acts. They also limited the term of the commission to five years, thus hanging over them a Damocles sword. William Cobbett thought this unnecessary for the English people and would not even allow the introduction of the measure.[24]

The New Poor Law was no party measure and no party had a monopoly of the opposition. Whigs and Conservatives alike joined in every minority vote, though the Reformers and Radicals usually predominated. Locality, in fact, meant more than party. Lord Kenyon was a Conservative and Colonel Evans a Radical, yet both objected strenuously to the idea of a central board. They were both defending the interests of a large, wealthy, well-organized, politically articulate parish, that of Marylebone in London. The representatives from Birmingham and Leeds also protested. Edward Baines, the nonconformist reformer of Leeds and the editor of the *Leeds Mercury,* proposed that all efficiently run parishes, those with rates below 2s. 6d. on the pound, be exempt from any central control. Baines wished a stern law for the poor, but local independence for Leeds.[25] The representatives of strong urban parishes were in a minority, the majority representing smaller, weaker, and less efficient parishes, in other words weaker centers of administrative power.

Only one county member voted against the Bill on its second reading. When it is remembered that most of the 3,000 parishes under fifty inhabitants and most of the 8,000 under one hundred inhabitants were in the countryside, the reason for the vote becomes evident. Small parishes poorly managed could offer neither arguments nor resistance to measures for central supervision, nor could they find allies in county magistrates overburdened with work and a gentry overburdened with rates. With pauperism increasing and rates rising, the members of Parliament were far more disposed to accept the central control of consolidated districts than to espouse the traditional localism of John Walters and the Tory press. Local autonomy meant the continuance of high rates and widespread pauperism; con-

24. Ibid., *23* (1834), 973–74, 1335.
25. Ibid., pp. 314, 806, 1289; *25* (1834), 469. *Leeds Mercury,* July 5, 1834.

solidation meant lower rates and declining pauperism. The New Poor Law thus passed with large majorities, even though it effected a profound change in English public administration. It established a central department with extensive powers—to inspect workhouses, to report on their administration, to confirm appointments, to audit accounts, and to issue rules on a multiplicity of matters. But this great increase in the power of the central government did not mean that local government was supplanted. It merely ended its autonomy and irresponsibility. Indeed, in one sense it promoted its growth by establishing a new unit of local government, the poor-law union. For the next two decades the chief problem in administering the poor law would be to establish these new unions under central control and enforce in them the hard policy of workhouse relief. It was a problem of formidable proportions.

PRISON, TITHE, AND CHURCH REFORMS

The zeal for reform of the 1830's touched upon lesser abuses as well as the larger problems. And it was by means of these minor reforms as well as by the more fundamental, hotly debated ones that the central government grew larger and more powerful. In 1833, for example, Parliament established a commissioner to confirm the constitutions of savings banks and friendly societies, and in the same year it voted money for an agent to inspect ships carrying emigrants to the new world, an agency which by 1839 had become part of the Colonial Land and Emigration Commission.[26] Neither of these acts ruffled any Parliamentary tempers or caught the eye of a news-hungry editor. The Prison Act of 1835 met with a similar indifference. The press gave it no attention and Parliament passed it with scarcely any debate. But behind this minor reform, which established another central inspectorate, lay the work of dedicated Christian reformers. From the year 1777, when the nonconformist John Howard first published his detailed description of the sordid and miserable prisons of the day, until the year 1835, when the London Prison Discipline

26. Fred H. Hitchins, *The Colonial Land and Emigration Commission* (Philadelphia, 1931), pp. 26, 37.

Social Reforms

Society demanded reforms, it had been primarily men and women of deep religious convictions who exposed the deplorable conditions in prisons and urged their amelioration. Miss Elizabeth Fry, a Quaker, devoted her life to ministering to those unfortunate persons who found themselves in London's wretched prisons. Sir Samuel Hoare, her brother-in-law, and Thomas Fowell Buxton, the heir to the mantle of the great Wilberforce, founded in 1816 the Prison Discipline Society. Their efforts had brought improvements, many of them incorporated in the Prison Act of 1824.[27] That Act, the first attempt ever made to formulate a national policy for prisons, provided for the classification of prisoners, hard work for convicts, and regular reports to the Home Office on committals and prison discipline. Parliament, having established no machinery to administer it, saw the act go largely unenforced.

At Leicester inmates received inadequate diet and were put to hard labor, while in Newgate, despite its cold, damp, crowded chambers, prisoners drank, gambled, and boasted to the young of great crimes. At the Cambridge House of Correction hardened prostitutes mixed freely with young girls imprisoned for their first offense. These schools of crime, along with industrial dislocation and an inefficient police, had their inevitable effect. Crime rose 140 per cent from 1817 to 1831, an increase considerably greater than the rise in population.[28] The chaos of prison disciplines, varying from prison to prison, could not prevent this turn to lawlessness. The Prison Discipline Society, represented by its chairman Samuel Hoare and two secretaries, William Crawford and George Bullar, presented to the House of Lords' Select Committee of 1834 the full story of these evils. To confirm the truth of their story the Lords' Committee, led by the Duke of Richmond, initiator of substantial prison reforms,

27. Buxton, *Memoirs*, p. 64. Fry, *Memoirs, 1*, 428–42. Webbs, *Prisons*, pp. 107–9.

28. Population increase from 1817 to 1831 was less than 33 per cent. From 1800 to 1831 it was from 8,900,000 to 13,900,000. The crime increase was much larger. *PP, 35* (1836), 4–14, 40, 69; *11* (1835), 373, 517–19. Prison Discipline Society, *Report of the Select Committee on Secondary Punishments* (London, 1833), p. 2.

visited the dismal and grubby jails of London.[29] In Committee hearings they questioned many magistrates about these evils, most of whom quickly confessed their failures and admitted the complete lack of uniformity in prison discipline. Most of them agreed that there was a need for inspectors who could enforce a uniform policy. The only person who opposed the idea of inspectors was Sir Peter Laurie, Lord Mayor of London. Sir Peter, unembarrassed by the notorious reputation of Newgate, said that the very idea of "such government spies" was an insult "to the honour of the magistracy." [30]

But the majority in Parliament differed from the Lord Mayor and established central inspectors, though they very carefully limited their powers. In particular they granted the inspectors no control over the spending of money raised from the county rate. The magistracy of England did not mind surrendering irksome duties and cooperating with central inspectors—they had made such sacrifices in the Factory Act and the Poor Law Amendment Act—but they jealously guarded their control over the county rate. The Duke of Richmond's bill, which called for little beyond inspection, thus passed easily. The only opposition came from Sir Robert Inglis, the most ardent advocate of Robert Southey's Tory paternalism.

The very calmness of its passage allowed the Whig Viscount Howick to announce to the Commons the basic principle that was to define the administrative growth of the state in the nineteenth century. The Prison Bill was like the Poor Law Amendment Act, he said, because it intended to leave "the actual detailed administration to local authorities, but to subject them to the supervision and control of some central authority, who should see that the duties were efficiently performed." [31] The effectiveness of this balanced system of public administration depended, however, upon who possessed the dominant power, the central or local authorities. In the case of the Prison Act the

29. *PP, 35* (1836), 1–48. *Morning Chronicle,* Aug. 17, 1835. *PP, 11* (1835), 16–46, 67–71, 469–78.
30. Ibid., *11* (1835), 20, 68, 123, 129, 177, 290, 463–65, 479.
31. Hansard, *30* (1835), 401–4.

real power remained with the local authorities. They controlled all expenditures, appointed all officers, and drew up all rules and regulations; the Home Office could merely sanction the rules and appoint four inspectors to make reports, and if the reports were adverse, the Home Office could do no more than deliver a verbal reprimand. Edwin Chadwick scoffed at the measure as "rude and defective." What else, he added, could be expected from a measure which arose from "the impulse and sentiment of a voluntary society." [32] Such was the Benthamite disdain for the unscientific measures of dedicated Evangelicals and patriarchal peers.

The Prison Act of 1835 was the only reform in that year which added a new agency to the central government. The really important administrative reform of the year was the Municipal Corporation Act, creating an efficient local government that was to offset the growth of the central government. The new boroughs enjoyed complete autonomy. Only over loans and the sale of property, which needed the Treasury's sanction, could the central government interfere. The year 1835 brought mostly advances in that reformed local self-government which paralleled in the nineteenth century the expansion of the central government.

In 1836, however three acts further increased the power of the central government. Each infringed on the power of the Established Church, which had long incurred the severest strictures from reformers in all parties. Even its most loyal defenders admitted the need of improvement. The abuses were too obvious to be further countenanced. The enormous difference of income separating the lowly paid vicars from the wealthy bishops encouraged more ill feelings than religious zeal. The size and wealth of bishoprics were anomalous, Lincoln having 1,234 benefices and a handsome revenue, while Bangor had a meager 124 benefices and empty coffers. Indolent ecclesiastics mismanaged their wealth, while the Church was too poor to meet the spiritual needs of the masses in the new factory towns. The Church had its full share of absentee rectors, nonresident prebendaries, and leisure-loving

32. Chadwick Papers, memo on central administration, around 1840.

canons, but it did not have enough preachers to bring the gospel to the laborers of Manchester, Liverpool, and Birmingham.

The spread of nonconformity in these great metropolises threw down a challenge which only a Reformed Church could meet.[33] Even Tories admitted the need for reform. The Duke of Wellington had urged it supported by no less a person than the Archbishop of Canterbury. In 1835 Sir Robert Peel, during his brief ministry, appointed a special commission which brought to light many of the inequalities and inefficiencies that blunted the effectiveness of the Church. In 1836 Lord Russell proposed a bill for a permanent Ecclesiastical Commission that would end abuses even if it had to rearrange the bishoprics and redivide and manage the Church's wealth. The Commission was to number thirteen, including the Archbishop, the Bishop of London, three Bishops appointed by the Crown and the eight Crown-appointed laymen. The Crown was thus responsible for eleven of the commissioners, eight of whom were laymen. It was an administrative agency with a majority of lay members. The High Church party saw its dangers and fought it vigorously. "It would render the clergy mere stipendiaries of the state," warned the Bishop of Hereford, while the Bishop of Exeter feared such a commission would encourage a tendency to perpetual change. In the Commons Sir Robert Inglis, who thought the Bill a "monstrous and atrocious presumption," warned the House that, "it sought the overthrow of the whole system of the Church." [34] The protests that the Commission was unconstitutional and unprecedented carried little weight in a nation where the bishops had long been state appointees, and at a time when the Church desperately needed reforming. The Bill passed, 175 votes to 44, and the ecclesiastical commissioners began the difficult task of making the Church more efficient.[35]

Parliament supported them in this task in 1836 by two measures designed to remedy two outstanding injustices, the payment of tithes in kind, and parish registration. Men still paid, as they

33. Hansard, 1833: *17*, 179–87; *15*, 298–301; *32* (1836), 126–36; *35*, 13–52.
34. Ibid., *35*, 661–64, 13–52, 344, 534. *PP*, 24 (1846), 185–200.
35. Ibid., *24* (1846), 548.

had time out of mind, one-tenth of the fruits of their labor to the Church, and still registered at the parish church the death of their parents, the birth of their children, and their own marriages. But to a capitalistic society tithes in kind were an anachronism and the parish register a very faulty statistical record. Futhermore, the law requiring marriage in the parish church rankled with the dissenters. The demand for commutation of tithes and for a better system of registration became widespread. Even the *Quarterly Review*, the Church's most loyal friend, recommended tithe reform, and the *Times*, the oracle of safe reforms, announced that the existing registration law "is imperfect and requires not merely partial amendment but real fundamental reform." To effect such a reform a Select Committee had urged in 1833 a national civil registration of births, marriages, and deaths, a proposal applauded by the utilitarian *Westminster Review*.[36] Edwin Chadwick, now secretary of the Poor Law Commission, suggested that the clerk of the poor law unions fulfill this task, but Lord John Russell, now Home Secretary, disregarded his wise advice. He proposed instead a Registrar General's Office with many local registrars, all of course appointed by the Home Office and all, the *Times* feared, sure to be Whigs. The fear of patronage was far from dormant in the 1830's and it forced the ministry in this instance to delegate the appointment of local registrars to the poor-law guardians, thus strengthening the local authorities' control over registration. But supervising these local registrars was the Registrar General's Office.[37] So once again the Government resorted to the pattern of local administration under central supervision.

The tithe question, more controversial and complicated, posed greater difficulties. The amount of tithes paid to the local rector or deanery varied from parish to parish. Who was to determine what rent payment should replace one-tenth of the gross produce, the clergyman or the squire? Or perhaps the state? Sir

36. *Quarterly Review, 42* (Jan. 1830), 105. *Times,* Jan. 3, 1834. *PP, 14* (1833), 5. *Westminster Review, 21* (July 1834), 115–19.

37. Chadwick Papers, Chadwick to John Russell, July 3, 1836, and notes on the multiplication of agencies, around 1840. Hansard, 1836: *32,* 1087; *31,* 367–85; *35,* 79–89, 693. 6 & 7 William IV c. 86.

Education

Robert Peel hoped that it might be arranged by private voluntary agreements, and in 1835 drew up a bill, which never passed, to promote this solution. Lord John Russell's bill in 1836 took a more realistic view. If it could be done voluntarily, excellent, but if by 1840 the clergy and the local owners had reached no agreement, then a government agency would enforce one. The government, to promote these voluntary agreements and to enforce the compulsory ones, would send down an assistant tithe commissioner. Three commissioners in London, two appointed by the Home Secretary and one by the Archbishop, would sanction the agreements. The bill establishing this new administrative department passed easily, though not without protests from the defenders of the Church's ancient rights.[38] To many their arguments appeared shrill, illogical, and anachronistic, yet in their vain attempt to hold back the tide of secularism they were loyal to the ideals of Coleridge and Southey, the ideals of an ecclesiastical society. They understood only too well the trend toward secularism. In 1836, for instance, they witnessed the establishment of three new departments of the state, the Ecclesiastical Commission, the Registrar General's Office, and the Tithe Commission, all of which marked the further recline of the Church and increased ascendency of the state. And by 1839 this wave of secularism threatened to engulf the Church's control of education.

THE EDUCATION CONTROVERSY, 1839

The Whig proposals of April 13, 1839, to establish a state normal school and provide for the inspection of all schools receiving state aid was the first measure of centralization to evoke a political dispute along party lines. Neither the New Poor Law nor the Factory Act, nor any of the minor reforms, had divided the House of Commons strictly on party lines. But the inspection of schools did. All parties, to be sure, wished to see the schools of England improved, wished to end the lamentable want of education among the working class; but just what solution should be adopted led to deep disagreement, the cause of which was

38. Hansard, 1836: *27*, 173–82; *31*, 185–94; *33*, 510, 979.

the problem of Church and State. And the pressure which brought that dispute to a head was the crying need for education. It thus seemed in 1839 as if the irresistible demand for popular education had met the unyielding claims of the Church.

Widespread ignorance was not new to England. From time immemorial the English peasant had lived in quiet illiteracy, unperturbed by broadsides and handbills, schools, and mechanic's institutes. The bailiff explained his daily work to him, the clergyman instructed him in his religious duties, and old wives' tales were an important source of general knowledge. The industrial revolution and the growth of cities made impossible this luxury of an uneducated proletariat. Crowded into slums and resentful of abuses, the proletariat could no longer be safely left in ignorance. "When we contemplate," said the *Edinburgh Review* in 1833, "the vast mass of manufacturing population congregated in our large towns . . . and their power, we may well be apprehensive." The agitations of the London Workingman's Association and the growth of chartism in the northern towns heightened these apprehensions and gave force to the warning of the *Edinburgh Review*, "We can no longer defer the great education question." [39] From these cities came the movements that argued most zealously for public education. The statistical societies of Manchester, Birmingham, and London made the first reliable inquiries into the want of education; the Manchester Committee for National Education and the Central Society for Education (established in London) were the first to demand government action to alleviate this want; and large public meetings in Bolton, Sheffield, Leeds, and Liverpool passed resolutions urging a system of national education.[40] The demand for public education was almost solely an urban movement.

The investigations and the reports of the Government's new inspectors strengthened and gave point to these urban agitations. The reports and investigations made by the new inspectors of

39. *Edinburgh Review, 58* (July 1833), 2.

40. Manchester Statistical Society, *Reports on the State of Education in the Borough of Bury* (1835), *York* (1837), *Salford* (1835). *Journal of the Statistical Society* (April 1840), p. 25. *PP, 7* (1838), 62–66. *Manchester Guardian*, June 5, 1939. Hansard, *43* (1838), 710–38.

Education

factories, prisons, and the poor law mark a new force for social reform. They represented the new power of the bureaucracy, well informed, keen in argument, intimate with ministers, and able to publicize their opinions through printed reports. On the question of education the new inspectors fully availed themselves of these advantages. Leonard Horner, a factory inspector, spoke out bluntly (in his special report of 1839 on education) on the failure of the schooling provisions of the Factory Act, on the complete lack of good schools in manufacturing towns, and on the need of legislative action. William Day, an assistant poor-law commissioner, supported Horner's plea for legislative action but for his part demanded the formation of pauper, not factory, schools. Frederick Hill, a prison inspector, argued hopefully that the chief preventive of crime was "the general and enlightened education of the people."

Other factory, prison, and poor-law inspectors filled their reports with the same refrain: crime, destitution, industrial unrest, drunkenness, immorality—all these had their roots in the deep and widespread ignorance of the working classes.[41] None of these inspectors supplied more evidence or argued more persistently for educational reform than the assistant poor-law commissioner, Dr. James Kay. His vivid study of the unhappy conditions of the Manchester working classes and of their profound ignorance had already stirred English opinion. As Secretary of the Manchester Statistical Society he promoted the first investigations into the educational destitution of industrial towns. In 1835 he became the assistant poor-law commissioner for Norfolk and East Kent, where he diligently investigated the problem of rural pauperism. He found it greatest among those with the least education; and he found that the schooling of those in workhouses—the very center of pauperism—was the most inadequate of any in the community. He argued in his reports that education was the "most important means of eradicating the germs of pauperism from the rising generation."[42] Kay's

41. *PP, 31* (1837), 63 (10); *42* (1839), 353 ff.; *31* (1838), 309 (10); *18* (1838), 459–90 (1–31). PRO, 30/22/2, Russell papers of 1839, on a proposed scheme for education includes extracts from Hill's prison reports and Horner's factory reports.

42. *PP, 20* (1839), 95–103; *28* (1838), 147–52.

53

wide knowledge of education, rural and urban, English and continental, brought him before the House of Common's Select Committee on Education.

For week upon week in 1837 and again in 1838 this Committee heard from Dr. Kay and others that most children from the lower classes were educated either badly or not at all; that in Bethnal Green only one child in four went to school; and that in northern towns the majority of children who went to school at all went only to Sunday schools or to some dame or common day school held in a stuffy garret or damp cellar. The teachers in these schools, poorly paid and untrained, were mostly those who could not succeed in any other occupation: one of them had ordered two globes, one for each hemisphere; another would not take the roll, since King David had got into trouble trying to count the Children of Israel. To this gloomy picture the secretaries of the voluntary societies, the Church of England's National Society and the British and Foreign School Society could add only a few rays of light. Their schools, though the best offered to the working classes, were bogged down in the dull routine of the monitorial system, where eight-year-old monitors had seven-year-olds read aloud the Church catechisms or Scripture, neither of which they understood. Furthermore these schools were very few in number and attendance at them was brief and irregular.[43] Voluntary exertions, however well intentioned, did not produce teachers or money.

The bulk of the laboring class thus remained, as Henry Dunn, secretary of the British Society, told the committee, "in utter and hopeless ignorance." [44] The reports of the inspectors and the findings of the Select Committee only publicized a condition that had long been obvious and as far back as 1820 had inspired Lord Brougham to present a bill for a national system of education. In 1838 that redoubtable Scotsman was still pressing a bill for government aid to education. Tempered by past defeats and sobered by

43. *PP*, 7 (1838), vii, 1–42, 275. For the best summary of educational conditions in 1839 see James Kay, *Recent Measures for the Promotion of Education in England*, London, 1839.

44. Henry Dunn, *National Education, the Questions of Questions* (London, 1838), p. 7.

an awareness of religious opposition, he reduced his demands to the barest minimum: government grants to voluntary schools and a Board of Education to guarantee their efficiency. The Church still did not like the plan—it savored too much of state control. It was, they said, only a little better than Arthur Roebuck's frankly Prussian scheme for district, rate-supported schools, inspected by the central government and offering nondenominational religious instruction. Roebuck, a Philosophical Radical and a follower of Bentham, was a pugnacious debater. Along with George Grote, Charles Buller, and Joseph Hume, he helped form a coterie of Benthamites which never relented in its demands for a system of public education.[45]

The Whig ministry finally took action. On April 13, 1839, the recently formed Committee on Education of the Privy Council recommended a teacher's training school, grants to other than National and British Society schools, and the central inspection of secular instruction in all schools receiving grants. To the Philosophical Radicals the proposals reflected the usual compromise of the overcautious Whigs; to High Churchmen, blasphemy. The recommendations had in fact been drawn up by James Kay, whom Lansdowne and Russell henceforth kept as their chief adviser.[46] It was indeed a compromise, and a compromise which became even more tepid when the proposal to establish a normal school was dropped. The grants to Church schools totaled only £30,000, only £10,000 more than the annual grants given in the past for school building and, said the indignant Brougham, £40,000 less than was voted to build the Queen more stables.[47] The wealthiest country in the world, with a laboring class in "utter and hopeless ignorance," voted to spend only £30,000 on education and to hire but two inspectors! Yet even this token remedy aroused the fury of the *Times*, the Tories, the Lords, the Church, and the Methodists.

The sources of this hostility were the unresolved problem

45. Hansard, *39* (1838), 435–65; *20* (1833), 139–66. Lord Brougham, *A Letter on National Education*, Edinburgh, 1839.

46. Thomas Adkins, *The History of St. John's College, Battersea* (London, 1901), p. 27.

47. Sir Spencer Walpole, *A History of England* (London, 1910), *4*, 184.

of Church and State and the religious jealousies of the Methodists. The position of the Church in English society was highly ambiguous. To Tories and High Churchmen the Church and not the state had exclusive right to educate all children. Was not the historic Catholic Church of England legally recognized as the national Church, and its doctrines approved by Parliament? Low Churchmen and Whigs considered the demand for such a monopoly unwise and unbearable. Most Tories, ominously aware of the encroaching secularism and still mindful of the tithe and ecclesiastical commissioners and the new civil registrars, resolved to fight for Church control of education. William Gladstone, recently from Oxford, and famous alike for his brilliance and his piety, warned all good churchmen of the state's encroachment on the Church's power and urged them to fight it in every quarter.

On the floor of the House of Commons, on June 14, 1839, they responded to the ancient cry, the Church in Danger! Lord Stanley rose to denounce the new Committee of Education as "despotic, irresponsible, unconstitutional," and to warn them not to be beguiled by the modesty of their demands, for the Committee would be a "fertile source of new plans." Gladstone was more temperate, but no less convinced that the plans were insidious, and insisted "that the State had never yet recognized the principle of teaching all forms of religions indifferently, and of placing truth and falsehood on a footing of equality." Since to Gladstone the English Church possessed the truth, and the state was its guardian, the state should see that the Church controlled education. His arguments followed logically from earnestly felt convictions. His future rival, Disraeli, felt no such inhibitions in regard to either logic or piety. Grandly and eloquently he paraded forth the specter of centralization. To vote for this Committee, he told Commons, meant a return to "the system of a barbarous age, the system of a paternal government."

To the ecclesiastical argument was thus added the constitutional argument and the fear of centralization, a fear which the Tories fully exploited. Even Lord Ashley, who looked to a paternalistic state to prevent child labor, protested against the indefinite, unlimited, and inordinate powers assumed by the Committee on Education, and warned that to accept state aid meant the end of all Church control of education.[48] The Tories greatly exaggerated the powers of the Committee on Education. The Committee, to be composed of the President of the Privy Council, the Home Secretary, the Chancellor of the Exchequer, and the Lord Privy Seal, would be answerable to Parliament for every penny spent and every order given; and their inspectors could give advice only if asked. Dogmatic churchmen and Methodists could not endure this encouragement of popery and heresy. The Tory *Morning Herald* called the plan a trick perpetuated by papists and radicals to introduce popish scriptures into the schools, while the Methodist's *Watchman* decried the opening of the door to heretical and popish teachings.[49]

But what really gave strength to the opposition was the threat to the Church's power. It was that which moved the Oxford Convocation, the Cambridge Senate, and thousands of petitioners to condemn the measure, the Tory press and the *Times* to call it alien, despotic, unconstitutional, and unchristian, and the peers to proceed in their carriages and robes down the Mall personally to ask Her Majesty to withdraw the order.[50] They all feared the loss of the Church's power and the ascendancy of the State. Since all grants went to voluntary schools, their fears seem greatly exaggerated; yet in the long run they were justified. The Committee of Education, as Lord Stanley warned, would be "fertile in new schemes," and each scheme would increase the power of the State.

The Tories tried heroically to stem this tide of secularism, to defeat the measure, and to save for the Church the right to educate the poor. But the Church's efforts through their own schools did not begin to meet the educational needs of the lower classes. Noble as was the vision of Gladstone and Lord Ashley, Coleridge and Southey, of a Christian society held together by one Church

48. Hansard, *48* (1839), 227–59, 268–75, 578–89, 622–34.
49. *Morning Herald,* May 20, 1839. *Watchman,* May 29, June 5, 1839. *Standard,* May 22, 1839.
50. *Times,* May 2, 21, 28, 30, 1839. *Standard,* June 5, 1839. Adkins, *History of St. Johns,* p. 30.

and one doctrine and suffused with Christian charity, it did not fit the realities of 1839.

The Whigs and Radicals in arguing for the measure never tired of describing those realities. They showed how impossible was a Church-dominated scheme of education in a land of nonconformity and they enlarged upon the great dangers of an illiterate laboring class. They opposed the Tories' ecclesiastical argument with an imposing social argument. England's towns and cities would never be free of crime, pauperism, drunkenness, infidelity, and chartism unless England gave the working people moral and religious instruction. This the Church could not do without the help of the State, whose aid, in the name of equity, must go to all voluntary schools, nonconformist and Church alike. And if this aid was to be effective, there must be Government inspection. These arguments, compelling as they were, barely sufficed to carry the measure in the Commons. The necessary appropriations for the aid were voted by a majority of only two.[51] Without the support of the Irish and a few dissenters, the measure would have been defeated, a fact galling to all good anti-Irish, antipapist Englishmen and embarrassing to those dissenters who six years later took up the fight against State aid to voluntary schools. The House of Lords passed six resolutions condemning the measure as unwise and unconstitutional, complaining that the ministry, by an order in council and by a provision in a money bill, had by-passed the Lords.[52] A weaker ministry would have capitulated, but Lord Lansdowne, an enlightened Whig who cherished memories of Bentham's visits to his father's Bowood estate, wrote privately to Lord John Russell to persevere even if defeated, since "we are so decidedly right!"[53] Lord John and Lord Lansdowne, along with the acquiescence of Lord Melbourne—then more preoccupied with the education of the young Queen than with the education of the nation—held firm. They appointed Kay secretary to the Committee on Educa-

51. Hansard, *48* (1839), 261–68, 296–301, 529–70, 589–92, 793. The *Morning Chronicle, Globe, Courier, Sun, Spectator, Manchester Guardian,* and *Leeds Mercury* supported the scheme.

52. Hansard, *48* (1839), 1234–1336.

53. Rollo Russell, *Early Correspondence of Lord John Russell* (London, 1913), 2, 269.

tion and appointed two inspectors. Meager as was this initial measure, the State now had assumed a responsibility for educating the people and had added another department to its expanding central administration, a department which would be fertile in new schemes.

CONSERVATIVE REFORMS AND TORY PATERNALISM

The year 1841, which saw the Conservatives triumphant at the polls, also witnessed continued economic distress and the mounting seriousness of the condition-of-England question. At the hustings the Conservatives had attacked the evils of factory labor, the harshness of the New Poor Law, and the inhumanity of political economy, promising in its place a concern for the well-being of the lower orders. Peel, as early as 1835, had set the tone for the new conservatism in his Tamworth Manifesto. In it he not only accepted the Reform Act but promised the "redress of real grievances." Disraeli in 1841 told his constituents: "There is no subject in which I have taken a deeper interest than the condition of the working class," and Gladstone and Ashley, the disciples of Coleridge and Southey, came to the election filled with a spirit of Christian philanthropy.[54] Ostensibly freer than the Whigs from mercantile interests and less bound by the doctrines of political economy, the Conservatives boasted a greater sensitivity to the moral and social conditions of the urban proletariat. And with a majority of 81 they possessed the opportunity to make Tory paternalism an effective answer to the problems of an industrial society.

Two of the most acute problems facing the Conservatives in 1841 were the exploitation of women and children in the coal mines and the primitive treatment of the insane in private and county asylums. Such inhumanities by man to man had long existed and had long been forgotten or overlooked. A public either indifferent or preoccupied with political reform took little notice of conditions in the darker recesses of the earth, or in

54. W. Cooke Taylor, *Life and Times of Sir Robert Peel* (London, 1851), 2, 406–7. W. F. Monypenny and G. M. Buckle, *Disraeli* (London, 1912), 2, 231. John Morley, *Gladstone* (London, 1921), *1*, 238. Edwin Hodder, *Shaftesbury* (London, 1886), *1*, 339–41.

the secluded halls of asylums. But by 1841 ardent reformers, among them the young Conservative member of Parliament, Lord Ashley had made the public aware of these evils. Ashley's evangelical faith persuaded him to take earnestly to heart Christ's injunction that "even as ye do it unto the least of these ye do it unto me." The suffering of one pauper lunatic or one child in an isolated mine counted with Ashley as much as the weightiest questions of constitutional reform or the grandest calculations of the greatest happiness to the greatest number. In 1833 he had helped to emancipate children from long, fatiguing labor in the factory, and in 1840 he had labored to gain protection for the miserably exploited chimney sweeps. In 1842 he successfully led the fight for a new lunacy act and for an act excluding women and children from the mines.

The plight of women and children in the mines constituted a continual refutation to any claim that England was civilized. The worst hardships of the overworked factory hands could not compare to the miseries of mine labor. Yet not until 1836, when a hand loom commissioner voluntarily investigated and reported on child labor in the mines, did the Government learn of these oppressive conditions; and not until Lord Ashley in 1840 told the House of Commons of this exploitation did the Government appoint a Royal Commission to investigate their distress. The Commission, made up of the economist Thomas Tooke, the utilitarian reformer Southwood Smith, and two factory inspectors, Robert Saunders and Leonard Horner, compiled, in three ponderous volumes, such a compendium of abuses and sufferings that government interference became inevitable. The Tories' *Quarterly Review*, which acknowledged that a new and barbarous world had been revealed, found itself in agreement with the *Westminster Review*: they both described the evils of mine labor and both argued for the need of government protection. The *Leeds Mercury*, as did many other papers, ran pictures, copied from the commissioners' reports, of small boys and girls pulling heavy sacks of coal through narrow seams.[55] Lord Ashley, on June

55. *PP, 15* (1842), 255–57. *Westminster Review, 38* (June 1842), 46–69. *Quarterly Review, 70* (June 1842), 86–105. *Leeds Mercury*, May 14, 1838.

7, 1842, citing throughout from "this awful document," provided Commons with even further stories of abuse, of women worked as beasts of burden, of foul air, dangerous explosions, long hours, fatigue, indecencies, and immorality.

With only 16 dissenting votes the Commons passed a bill prohibiting mine employment of women, apprentices, and children below the age of thirteen.[56] A more practical member than Ashley added a provision for government inspection of mines, and the bill went to the Lords. The peers of the realm were not so deeply moved as the members of Commons. Led by Lord Londonderry, a great mine-owner, they reduced the age of exclusion from thirteen to ten and allowed apprentices between the ages of thirteen and eighteen to work in mines. Lord Warncliffe, the Government's leader in the Lords, did nothing to combat these concessions. Back in Commons, where the coal interests had grown bolder and the Government more timid, the compromises were accepted. Never a government bill, it won from the ministry only a quiet assent. Peel spoke only once, and then for acceptance of the Lords' amendment. Gladstone voted against it, and Disraeli was silent.[57]

The disappointment which Ashley recorded in his diary over the timidity of Peel, Warncliffe, and Graham, and the opposition of Gladstone and the Tory peers, grew even greater in 1844, when he returned to the battle for the ten-hour day. On this issue he fought his own party. Both Peel and Graham insisted that the Government limit women and young children to a twelve-hour rather than a ten-hour day, a position they incorporated in the Factory Act of 1844. They mustered their conservative forces and defeated by three votes Ashley's amendment to limit the labor of women and young people to ten hours.[58] The *Economist* decried the fact that so large a portion of the Liberals supported Ashley, and added regretfully that the manufacturers must now look to the Tories to defend their interests. Lord Ashley, deserted

56. Hansard, *63* (1842), 1320–64; *64* (1842), 936.

57. Ibid., 1842: *63*, 1329–64; *64*, 936, 538–44, 1166–68; *65*, 84–85, 101–23, 571–88, 1094–1101.

58. Ibid., *73* (1844), 1073–1155, 1241–66, 1371–1462. *Economist*, 2 (April 24, 1844), 722–23.

by his party, lost another battle in his campaign to establish a more protective government. But undismayed, he applied himself to the removal of another social grievance, a minor one to be sure but one that inflicted unnecessary suffering. He set out to end the cruel treatment of the insane.

Lord Ashley's interest in the care of the insane began in 1828 when he spoke for the bill establishing the Metropolitan Commissioners in Lunacy. He subsequently became a commissioner himself, visiting asylums, inspecting patients, studying the newest methods of treatment, and writing official reports. Through the diligent labors of these commissioners improvements were made in the metropolitan asylums and by means of their published reports public opinion was awakened from its torpor. But their work did not extend far. Outside of the London houses, and a few enlightened country asylums, life for most lunatics was dismal and hopeless. An assistant poor-law commissioner, William Gilbert, in a long memorandum to the commissioners, told them that the enlightened care of the insane in such asylums as Lincoln and Hanwell, with their warm rooms, good meals, clean clothing, and kind treatment, was exceptional, and that the smaller asylums hung on to their chains and cribs.[59] The great nineteenth-century movement for a humane and intelligent treatment of the insane had never penetrated these small asylums, where uninformed managers thought the insane vicious and incurable. Conditions in them went largely unnoticed until 1842, when Lord Ashley secured an act of Parliament empowering the Metropolitan Commissioners in Lunacy to visit all asylums in England.

Two years later the commissioners published their report. Only twenty-five of England's forty counties, it pointed out, had county asylums, and most of them needed improvement. Conditions in the private asylums varied greatly. Some were quite comfortable. Most of them, however, were mere houses for incarceration, and a few were a nightmare of cribs, chains, damp rooms, and brutal attendants. The pauper lunatics, who numbered some 18,000 out of the 23,000 persons considered insane, suffered

59. MH, 37/26, Jan. 1835. D. A. Tuke, *The History of the Insane* (London, 1882), pp. 173–231.

an equal misery. They were consigned to the back room of a poorhouse and were made the butt of vulgar derision.

The findings of this report provided the press and journals with good copy and aroused the public to demand reform.[60] The Government, on Lord Ashley's urgings, introduced two bills, one to extend government inspection to all houses for the insane and the other to require every county to build an asylum. Lord Ashley spoke at length for their acceptance, and the Commons passed them with near unanimity.[61] The obstacles to the improvement of asylums had been not vested interest but public ignorance and apathy. For centuries that apathy remained unchallenged, but when nineteenth-century humanitarianism joined with a more scientific understanding of insanity it diminished. Yet neither humanitarianism nor science would have availed much had not government officials investigated the abuses and had not Commons placed asylums under the surveillance of government inspectors.

Lord Ashley contributed one more measure to the reforms of this era of conservative government: the Calico Print Works Act. The same Royal Commission that investigated the exploitation of children in mines had exposed their employment in these humid, overheated factories. As a result, Ashley recommended for them the same protection given to children in textile factories. Parliament passed the Act in 1845, thus placing them under the supervision of the factory inspectors. Imperceptibly, by a quiet process of accretion, a strong central administration was rising.

The reforms in mining, lunacy, and print works received their impulse from Lord Ashley and not from the activities of Peel's ministry. The ideal of a strong government protecting the weak and ameliorating abuses did not inspire Peel, Graham, or Gladstone with quite the fervor it did Ashley. Evidence of their paternalistic outlook is not too abundant. Peel and Graham in 1843 did attempt to establish an educational scheme for factory children, but the scheme so decisively favored the Church that

60. Jones, *Lunacy, Law and Conscience*, pp. 145–96. *North British Review,* 3 (Aug. 1845), 398. *Quarterly Review, 74* (Oct. 1844), 224–29.
61. Hansard, *81* (1845), 180–202.

it had no chance to pass. Gladstone in 1842 secured the passage of a bill empowering railroad inspectors to postpone the opening of unsafe lines, to require proper signals and fencing, and to investigate all accidents. But this act, just as the 1840 act, only sought to ensure public convenience and safety; neither touched on matters of rates, or tried to end the chaotic system by which various special committees of Parliament passed on the many bills designed to aid railway construction. Clever speculators, like Undecimus Scott, the crafty member of Parliament in Trollope's *Three Clerks,* used financial rogueries and managed committees to defraud the public. Such frauds, according to a select committee of Commons, occurred far too frequently, and not only in financing railways.[62] Gladstone in 1844 had the courage —some felt brazenness—to seek a remedy by asking all joint-stock companies to register with the Board of Trade, and empowering the Railway Department, instead of sundry Parliamentary committees, to report on the merits of proposed lines. He also asked Parliament to give the Government the power either to revise a company's rates if after fifteen years its profits exceeded 10 per cent, or to purchase the line itself. The measure, with its threat of nationalization, raised a furor among financial and railway circles and among the advocates of an unfettered economy. What else could be expected, asked the *Economist,* when an "ingenious and abstract metaphysician" sat at the Board of Trade! To Mr. Bernal, a Whig member, the Government's right to purchase a railway was a victory for the principle of "centralization." To the Tory member, Mr. Colquhoun, the bill would open the door to "power and patronage," a view which the radical John Bright echoed in warning the house against "the entering wedge of government interference." Peel himself joined the critics, saying "it was precisely by the vigorous, judicious, and steady pursuit of self-interest that individuals and companies ultimately benefited the public at large." [63]

62. *PP, 10* (1839), 130–42; *PP*, 21* (1844), 15–33 (iii–xix); *PP*, 26* (1846), 168 (6).

63. *Economist, 2* (July 6, 1844), 962, 974; (July 20), 1066. Hansard, *76* (1844), 630, 638, 644; *72* (1844), 250.

Gladstone, abused and intimidated, met with the railway companies and agreed to a provision that if the government did revise rates it would guarantee the company a 10 per cent profit —the very same profit, the *Economist* wryly noted, that in the first place called for governmental interference.[64] The clause was as nugatory as that which allowed the Railway Department to make suggestions to the sundry private bill committees which still clung firmly to their power to pass, in helter-skelter fashion, on future railway construction. The only substantial check on the freedom of the railways came from the clause requiring daily third-class trains, covered, convenient, and cheap. This provision and an act requiring future joint-stock companies to register all relevant documents and information formed the principal measures proposed by Gladstone that called for more active government regulation of the economy.[65] An opponent of Ashley's Ten Hour Bill and Mining Act, Gladstone distinguished himself at the Board of Trade more for his sympathy with the proprietors of mines, factories, and railways than by a paternalistic concern for the laboring classes. His background, like Peel's, was mercantile, and he was a believer in political economy. Disraeli on the other hand represented the landed aristocracy and the new ideals of Young England. But Disraeli in this era of conservative reform showed little practical interest in the building of a benevolent state. He gave a silent vote for the Ten Hour Bill of 1844 and one speech against the New Poor Law, and that alone constitutes his record of support for social reforms.[66]

The reality of Tory paternalism, in fact, rests almost solely on the greatness of Lord Ashley, certainly a firmer foundation than that of the sentiments found in *Sybil* and *Coningsby*, both published during this period. From 1841 to 1846 it was Lord Ashley's bills, supported as much by Whigs as Tories, that mark the continued and expanding role of the central government. And on the two most serious questions confronting England— the unhealthy and unsanitary condition of the laboring classes

64. *Economist*, 2 (July 27, 1844), 1035.
65. 7 & 8 Victoria c. 85, 110.
66. Hansard, *73* (1844), 1462.

and their widespread want of education—the Tories, despite the urgings of government officials, Lord Ashley, Carlyle, and the press, accomplished very little. All they did about sanitation was to pass the Metropolitan Building Act, a measure whose 120 clauses empowered the Board of Works to appoint surveyors and referees and to lay down specifications on a host of matters from the height of chimneys to the size of cellars. But the Act was designed, as Chadwick told Graham, more to ensure proper buildings for London's upper classes than to bring badly needed sewerage and good water to the poor.[67] Improvements in public health as in public education had to wait until the Whigs resumed office, for the Whigs were willing to push these in the face of bitter outcries they evoked against the growth of centralization.

67. 7 & 8 Victoria c. 84. Chadwick papers, Chadwick to Graham, May 12, 1843.

3.

THE ISSUE OF CENTRALIZATION

THE QUESTION OF centralization had entered English politics with the New Poor Law of 1834, but it did not in the next decade become a prominent issue. Parliament passed the Prison Act quietly. The Education Order, though evoking a lecture against centralization from Benjamin Disraeli, involved primarily the issue of Church and State. The Railway and Mining acts never brought questions of administration to the fore, and the Lunacy Act, like the Prison Act, touched upon too few interests to provoke great opposition. The issue of centralization was kept alive, in fact, only by the persistence of the agitation against the New Poor Law, the measure that first introduced the controversy into English politics. The opponents of this law never ceased to condemn its centralizing tendency and never tired of applying to its three commissioners such epithets as heartless, tyrannical, arbitrary, and un-English.

But the noise of their clamor far exceeded its effectiveness. The agitation against the law, for all its humane impulses and despite the blessings given it by the *Times,* lacked respectability. For one thing, the names of such anti-Poor Law agitators as Raynor Stephen, Fergus O'Connor, and Richard Oastler sounded much too revolutionary; for another, the rank and file conservatives shied away from any real opposition to a law and an agency

67

that had substantially lowered the poor rates. In 1842, when Peel's government renewed the Poor Law Commission for five years, they simply confirmed what they had previously sanctioned silently; and by 1846 a centrally controlled administration of poor relief was an accepted English institution. Not even the Andover workhouse scandal of that year, exploited to the fullest by the *Times,* could end the central control of relief for the poor.

The year in which the issue of centralization first achieved national prominence was 1847. In December 1846 the Whigs, concerned over the widespread lack of education, had issued an education order expanding the activities of the Committee in Council on Education. In February 1847, in order to meet the problem of unhealthy towns, they introduced the Health of Towns Bill. Both measures raised a storm of protest against the increasing power of the central government. The recommendations of the Committee on Education provoked the first outburst. These recommendations proposed to give voluntary schools additional grants to raise teachers' salaries and employ and train student teachers, and to provide scholarships for students at teacher training schools. In order to make sure that the money was wisely spent, the committee would have its inspectors test the qualifications of both teachers and student teachers.[1] Because the largest share of the government grants would go to the Church of England schools, the new proposals would further strengthen the Church's dominance over English education—or, in the dissenter's minds, would have the effect of proselytizing the children of the working class with false doctrine!

Nonconformity, growing stronger every year and feeling its new strength, had its reasons to fear further state aid to education. Was not Peel prepared in 1843 to exclude nonconformist teachers from factory schools? Would not most of the grants now proposed go to Church schools? Would not the nonconformists be neglected? The more radical of the dissenters, especially the Congregationalists and Baptists, condemned the measure outright.[2] Their leading papers and journals—the *Patriot,* the *Non-Conformist,*

1. *PP, 45* (1847), 1–8.
2. Edwin Hodder, *The Life of Samuel Morley* (London, 1888), p. 79.

Evangelical Magazine, and *Christian Witness*—protested against this encroachment of the state over matters of conscience. John Bright told the Commons that education was a matter for the churches and individuals and not for the government.[3] And Edward Baines, Jr., the most powerful and untiring advocate of the nonconformist cause, denounced in his *Leeds Mercury* all inspection of schools. He did so with the same vigor with which he had earlier deprecated the inspection of factories. Both meant centralization, which for Baines was the greatest evil of the day. In the columns of his paper he set forth a philosophy of complete liberalism, one which approached as near as any man of property would allow to the position of philosophical anarchism. The individual alone was responsible for earning his living, schooling his children, choosing his religion, running his factory, working his children in mines, and draining his house. Liberty he thought "the chief excellence of man"; law, in itself, "a beggarly thing."[4]

The radicals of the nonconformist world welcomed this uninhibited individualism. In a series of lectures in London by Congregational ministers and laymen, later published as the Crosby Hall Lectures, and in the *British Quarterly, Record,* and *Eclectic Review,* the dissenters expounded this theme, forming it into a clear and consistent theory of opposition to all centralization. They felt, in the words of the Reverend A. Wells, that "State power in religion, state power in education, state power in inspectors, state power in Whitehall, reaching over England, are all, as kindred influences, against Dissent, against liberty, against national spirit, against allied interests of self governed and self acting people."[5] Such a doctrine appealed to the puritan jealousy of secular authority and the puritan pride in the self-

3. *Times,* April 21, 1847.
4. *Leeds Mercury,* April 1, 1848, and any issue from 1847 to 1850. The attack by the *Leeds Mercury* on the Committee on Education never flagged.
5. A. Wells, *On the Education of the Working Class* (London, 1847), p. 66. B. Parsons, *Education, Natural Birthright and the Unconstitutional Character of the Committee on Education,* London, 1847. Edward Miall, *On the Non-Interference of the Government with Popular Education,* London, 1847. Richard Hamilton, *On the Parties Responsible for the Education of the People,* London, 1847.

reliance of the elect. It strengthened the Victorian nonconformists' hostility to the central government; and when combined with the new triumphant economic dogma, as it was in the *Leeds Mercury*, it gave to the opponents of a strong central government the clear, rational dogma of noninterference.

The *Economist*, whose faith in political economy went as deep as the dissenters' belief in a free conscience, expounded at great length the truth of that principle. Avowedly neutral on religious questions, it reached the same position as the *Leeds Mercury* by reasoning from economic principles. It opposed all mischievous meddling, all interference with economic laws, all commissions, and all bureaucrats; in short that "engrossing centralization which was dwarfing the whole nation to the poor standard of ministerial capacity." [6] It castigated Ashley for his false philanthropy and condemned the factory acts as "shackles on England's prosperity." It was supremely confident that the effort of free individuals and not state interference would promote progress; so it condemned factory, mining, and railway legislation, state aid to education, and the inspection of asylums and prisons.[7] It saw no use whatever in any state action not solely limited to keeping order, administering justice, and defending the realm. Its liberalism was more absolute than that of Adam Smith.

THE PUBLIC HEALTH ACT

The *Leeds Mercury* and the *Economist*, in complete agreement in denouncing factory inspectors and education grants, found no reason for not condemning Lord Morpeth's sanitary reform Bill. They opposed the Bill in 1847, when it failed to pass, and in 1848 when it became, with some changes, the Public Health Act. Lord Morpeth's Bill, even more than the education grants or factory inspection, demanded an exact definition of the relations of local and central government, the key question to the problem of centralization. The Bill, like the Poor Law Amendment Act of

6. *Economist,* 5 (July 10, 1847), 780.
7. Ibid., *1* (March 23, 1844), 609; *3* (April 20, 1845), 697 (June 8), 869 (May 25), 811 (July 6), 961 (May 31, 1847), 488 (July 19), 680; *6* (March 27, 1848), 335 (April 3), 381. *Leeds Mercury,* Feb. 12, March 11, 1848.

1834, compelled the English to decide what part local authorities and what part the central government should play in public administration. The sanitary reform movement in 1847 and 1848 and the growing squalor of English towns would not permit further evasions.

The forces and events involved in the passing of the Public Health Act of 1848 were not unlike those behind earlier reforms. In many respects it provided a classic example of the manner in which social reform over these two decades caused the expansion of the central government. The problem of sanitation was peculiarly the problem of the densely populated manufacturing towns that had sprung up in the last half century. The unhealthy life of the lower classes, dwelling in the filthy, overcrowded slums of these towns, became one of the main causes for the general distress of the areas. Cholera widows burdened the poor rates and orphans turned to crime. These evils of slum life first attracted the attention of the medical men in Liverpool, Manchester, Chester, and other factory towns.[8]

Not until the officials in the new central agencies had investigated the evils and published their findings did they become widely known. Assistant poor law commissioners like Dr. Kay and E. C. Tufnell helped expose the ignorance of the lower classes; now Edwin Chadwick, secretary to the poor law commissioners, and Southwood Smith and Niel Arnott, two special inspectors, exposed the wretched slums in which the lower classes lived out their suffering. Edwin Chadwick in 1834 first noticed the appalling sickness and fever in the crowded and dirty slums. In 1838 and 1839 Southwood Smith, a close friend of Jeremy Bentham, joined with Dr. Niel Arnott and Dr. Kay, both Utilitarians, to draw up a report on the sanitary condition of London as a cause of pauperism.[9]

The report painted a picture of unrelieved misery. It shocked the Bishop of London, who moved that the Poor Law Commission

8. Robert Lewis, *Edwin Chadwick and the Public Health Movement* (London, 1952), p. 36.
9. *PP, 20* (1839), 91–106; *PP, 28* (1838), 212–339 (67–94). Chadwick Papers, Chadwick to S. Smith on the origin of the Public Health Act, undated.

make such a survey for the whole country. Chadwick at once set to work with his singular industry and compiled a grim record of undrained streets, impure water, airless, crowded tenements, vice and immorality, and general sanitary negligence that cost England dearly in lives, disease, poor rates, and crime.[10] The 1842 report on the sanitary condition of the laboring population awoke the public to the need of reform. It sold eight times as well as any other official document and led to the organization of many associations for the reform of the unhealthy conditions of English towns.[11] The government itself was forced to appoint a royal commission to make a full inquiry. As often before—with education and lunacy and print work, for example—the initial impulse for reform came from the investigation and reports of government inspectors. The larger the government grew, the more it found to reform. An enlarged bureaucracy, in short, tended to further its own growth.

The importance of the new agencies in pressing for reform and expansion should not be exaggerated. Government inspectors could expose abuses but could not pass laws; they could give the impetus but could not carry through the reform. Edwin Chadwick and Southwod Smith needed the powerful support of that humanitarian and reforming zeal in public and Parliament that had carried factory, education, and prison reforms. This support it received after the famous report of 1842. Lord Ashley, whose persevering and moving pleas had persuaded the Commons to pass factory, mining, and lunacy reforms, joined with two Benthamites, Chadwick and Smith, to champion the cause of healthier towns. Southwood Smith and Lord Ashley helped form the powerful Health of Towns Association—a pressure group in many ways similar to the Anti-Corn Law League—into which were channeled much of the humanitarian energy and scientific skill of England. Membership was varied and distinguished. Whig noblemen like Lord Morpeth and Viscount Ebrington, liberal reformers like Edward Bulwer Lytton, economists

10. Poor law commissioners, *Report on the Sanitary Condition of the Labouring Population of Great Britain,* London, 1842.

11. Chadwick Papers, Chadwick to Lord Morpeth, May 10, 1848.

like Thomas Tooke, Radicals like Joseph Hume, and even Young Englanders like Benjamin Disraeli all lent their prestige to the sanitary cause. Indeed, the *Economist* expressed astonishment to see so many gentlemen active in a reform movement.[12]

Distinguished though the movement was in its honored list of members, not peers and baronets but doctors and engineers undertook the active work of investigation and propaganda. The secretary of the Association was an engineer, Henry Austin, later to become the chief inspector of the General Board of Health. He, others of his profession, and many eminent physicians brought to bear on the sanitary problem the most advanced knowledge then attainable of drainage, water supply, and the combating of epidemics. Their published findings made it plain that where drainage was defective, refuse unremoved, ventilation bad, and water impure disease was sure to strike. To improve such areas they proposed to establish local boards of health that would construct combined drainage and water supply systems and ensure closer inspection of cholera cases. To establish and supervise these local boards the Health of Towns Association recommended a central board of health.[13]

These proposals agreed with the earlier and more detailed recommendation of the Health of Towns Commission of 1845, a royal commission appointed by a Conservative ministry and headed by a Conservative peer, the Duke of Buccleuch. The commissioners' report recommended that local authorities carry out, under the supervision of a central board, comprehensive schemes of improvements. The commissioners who urged these proposals, later to form the basis of Lord Morpeth's Health of Towns Bill, were not theorists of the Benthamite school but practical men such as Sir William Cubitt, a Conservative member of Parlia-

12. John and Barbara Hamond, *Shaftesbury* (London, 1923), pp. 156–57. Health of Towns Association, *Report on Lord Lincoln's Sewerage and Drainage of Towns Bill* (London, 1847), p. 1. *Economist*, 5 (Dec. 11, 1847), 1420.

13. R. D. Grainger and Hector Gavin, both physicians and both to become inspectors of the Board of Health, worked actively for the Association and published private works. Grainger, *Unhealthiness of Towns,* London, 1845. Gavin, *Sanitary Ramblings,* London, 1848, and with Sir Henry Austin, *The Report of the Health of Towns Association on the Sanitary Conditions of the Metropolis,* London, 1847. Lewis, *Chadwick,* p. 166.

73

ment, and Robert Stephenson, a railway engineer. The idea of a central board had been suggested earlier in reports by Smith and Chadwick, but its wide acceptance came not from their theories but from actual conditions. Local authorities, with some exceptions, did not have the power, knowledge, and energy to improve sanitary conditions. The Commission realized the obvious fact that they could not be improved throughout England without the stimulus and guidance of technically informed agents of central departments.[14]

If acute sanitary evils called forth support for the Public Health Bill, the threat of centralization contained in it provoked opposition. The establishment of another central agency aroused local magistrates, property-owners, and traditionalists to oppose the Bill in the same spirit as they had opposed poor law commissioners and education inspectors. They wanted no Board of Health and no meddlesome inspectors. Among these powerful and vocal forces opposed to the Bill were the staunchly independent municipal corporations, the firmly entrenched sewer commissioners, and the many parish vestries. For them it was a matter of patriotism, self-interest, and idealism to fight at every turn the establishment of a central board. And to their aid came tenement landlords, factory owners, proprietors of butcher shops, and water companies for whom regulations and the expensive improvements demanded by them would mean a curbing of their freedom and a lessening of their profits. There were also the rate-payers, who opposed all costly improvements; Parliamentary agents, who would lose their lucrative fees for drawing up local acts; and local engineers, who wished to earn a profit from building the traditional and expensive systems of drainage and water supply.[15]

The power of these various interests was considerable, especially

14. *PP, 17* (1844), vii–xv, 510–55; *11* (1840), 245–46 (xviii–xix). Chadwick Papers, Chadwick to Lord Campbell, July 26, 1848, disavows responsibility for the Public Health Act, claiming that after the first meeting with Lord Morpeth he took no part; and a letter from Chadwick to C. May, July 20, 1852, suggests the Health of Towns Commission report served as a guide for the Act.

15. Chadwick Papers, Chadwick to Lord Ellenborough, July 21, 1848, and Chadwick to Russell, May 14, 1848. *Standard,* May 20, 1848. *Globe,* May 11, 1848. *Leeds Mercury,* March 18, 1848. *Spectator,* April 17, 1847.

since they could call to their support Tory hostility to a Whig measure, the jealousy of the Dissenters at the growth of the state, and the reigning creed of political economy. And, as always, they could fall back on the Englishman's pride in local self-government. The municipal corporations led the fight against the Public Health Bill. The small landlords who dominated their common councils feared that the central government would order expensive improvements for which they must pay. The City of London, for example, printed hundreds of copies of pamphlets against Lord Morpeth's Bill, sent them to other corporations for distribution, and organized the opposition of local paving commissioners and water companies. They also distributed copies of the *Morning Chronicle,* a paper which, though once an advocate of reform, had now fallen into the hands of the Corporation and was the loudest in condemning centralization.[16] The Conservative press—the *Standard, the Morning Advertiser,* and the weekly *John Bull*—gave the *Chronicle* spirited support.[17]

None of these papers dared fight the Public Health Bill on the issue of sanitary reform. The disease and bad drainage of the great towns were incontestable. These papers dwelled instead upon the threats offered to English liberty by the creation of another powerful central board. They were for sanitary reform, but it must be administered by local not central authorities. The central government, they asserted, would only make things worse.

The arguments against centralization were numerous, some clever and ingenious, some containing a modicum of truth, yet many more tiresome, clichéed, or irrelevant. They repeated the arguments of the *Leeds Mercury* and the *Economist,* extolling the virtue of individual action and decrying the effects of government interference. They dragged up the old fears of government tyranny, of wasteful expenditures, and of Whiggish corruption and patronage. They also resurrected the charge that commissioners appointed by the Crown were irresponsible while local

16. Chadwick Papers, Chadwick to John T. Delane, Nov. 27, 1850, Chadwick to Russell, July 17, 1848, and unaddressed, undated letter of 1847 on change of ownership of the *Morning Chronicle.*

17. *Standard,* May 9, 1848. *Morning Advertiser,* May 4, 1848. *John Bull,* May 13, 1848.

authorities were not, a theme they reiterated with a most persuasive monotony, though it completely disregarded the fact that the Public Health Act, as Lord John Russell said, gave nine-tenths of the power to locally elected boards, and that the central board was directly responsible to Parliament.[18] The *Morning Chronicle* exploited fully the argument that any central administration would discourage and eventually destroy local self-government. They employed J. Toulmin Smith to expound this view. He was a clever, energetic barrister and had written a book entitled *Centralization or Representation.* He provided for the forces hostile to centralization historical and constitutional arguments rooted in the grand principles of Anglo-Saxon self-government. From the folk moot of Alfred's time to the municipal corporations of 1848, local government formed the traditional bulwark of English liberty, while Whig commissioners, like the Stuarts' Star Chamber, promised only patronage, corruption, and continental despotism. Centralization, Smith claimed, was unconstitutional, un-English, and alien to self-government. It was "only communism in another form." It would only destroy the aptitude for independence.[19]

The belief that too much central government discourages local self-government and lessens individual self-reliance was widely held. John Stuart Mill, among others, believed it. Like Bentham he considered government interference in itself evil. Persuaded by de Tocqueville of the dangers of centralization and ever concerned for the freedom of the individual, he preferred the principles of local rule and laissez faire to those of centralization and collectivism. His discussion "On the Limits of Government" in his *Principles of Political Economy,* published early in 1848, reflects a real distrust of government. "In all the more advanced communities," he wrote, "the great majority of things are worse done by the intervention of the government, than the individuals most interested in the matter would do them . . ."[20]

18. *Morning Advertiser,* May 4, 1848. Hansard, *98* (1848), 799.

19. Joshua Toulmin Smith, *Centralization or Representation* (London, 1848), p. x, and *Government by Commissioners, Illegal and Pernicious,* London, 1849. Lewis, *Chadwick,* p. 168. *Morning Chronicle,* April 22, 1848.

20. Mill, *Autobiography,* p. 135, and *Principles of Political Economy* (London, 1866), 2, 565, 558–603.

Mill's distrust of increased centralization was always judicious and reasonable. It had little in common with the rigid dogmas of the *Economist* or the extreme fears of the *Leeds Mercury* or the grandiose theories of Toulmin Smith. And it was certainly far removed from the passionate attachment to the ways of the past that prompted the pugnacious and eccentric Tory Colonel Sibthorp to refuse to ride on railways, to vote against all government commissions, and to tell the Commons in a debate on the Health Bill that "he disapproved of the new patent water closets and much preferred the old system." [21] Unyielding Tories, hating centralization, opposed it not with arguments but with heat and prejudice. The editors of *John Bull* bluntly asserted that England needed corporations not bureaus, and that "it is wasting ink to write about the matter. The national character is formed and there is an end to it." And the *Standard* echoed this appeal to prejudice by denouncing the Health Bill as "quackery" and recommending that the lower classes be left alone, "for their Anglo-Saxon instincts will lead them to clean and dry and comfortable dwellings." Indignant at the Poor Law Commission and fearful of the Board of Health, the *Standard* asked shrilly, "How much farther are we to go with centralizing? . . . It is to come to the supply of raiment and food? Is there to be cobbling and baking boards at Whitehall?" [22] Loyalty to ancient ways and a dislike of expensive bureaus made many a Tory a foe of the Public Health Bill, an ally of radical dissenters with whom they had little else in common.

To counter these arguments and dispel passions, the journals that supported the Health Bill sought to justify the central control of local government. Most of them simply amplified the principle Lord Howicke had announced in 1835 in defense of the Prison Act, namely that local authorities should administer the law in its particulars, but subject to the supervision of a central department. This principle, common to the administration of the Poor Law, prisons, and lunatic asylums, was flexible and reasonable. The *Daily News* and the *Times* both argued that in order to improve sanitary conditions there must be local and

21. Hansard, *118* (1848), 711; *76* (1844), 515.
22. *John Bull,* May 13, 1848. *Standard,* May 9, 1848.

central government. They even recommended that the central board have the power to compel the local boards, whose interests were usually adverse to reform, to make the needed improvements.[23] But most of the arguments for the Public Health Bill dealt not with the virtues of a balanced system of central and local administration but with the immediate problems of sanitary improvements, preferring the palpable facts of dirty streets to dull and not very popular ideas of public administration.

For any discussion of administrative theory sympathetic to the growth of a strong central administration the English had to turn to the utilitarian theories found in the *Westminster Review* and the *Edinburgh Review,* or to the paternalism of the *Spectator.* The *Westminster Review* had consistently looked to the central government for social reforms. It had given its blessings to the Poor Law Commission, the factory and mining inspectors, the Lunacy Commission, the Registrar General, and the Ecclesiastical Commission. In October 1846 they roundly condemned the liberal dissenters on the *Leeds Mercury* and *Eclectic Reviews* for opposing state aid to education. They regarded such opposition as "destructive" and they insisted that the government could be a source of good as well as of mischief. The Utilitarians were embracing a mild collectivism, one which the liberal *Spectator* in 1844 called the New Faith. This New Faith envisaged a well-ordered society ruled over by a paternalistic government. The *Economist,* which took offense at the *Spectator's* strictures on laissez faire, dismissed the New Faith as misguided sentimentalism and false philanthropy.[24] Thus after the great triumph on the question of free trade the Liberal camp was split in two. The Liberals of the *Spectator* and the Utilitarians of the *Westminster* and *Edinburgh* reviews found themselves at odds with the *Economist,* the *Leeds Mercury,* and the *Eclectic Review.* The dissenters hostile to state education found themselves divided from the Philosophical Radicals, who enthusi-

23. *Daily News,* May 8, 1848. *Times,* May 9, 1848.
24. *Westminster Review, 46* (Sept. 1846), 87–107; *47* (April 1847), 141. *Economist, 2* (April 20, 1844), 697. *Spectator* (May 13, 1848), p. 465, and (April 13, 1844), p. 346.

astically supported it. And the social reformers of London favored a health bill opposed by the Radicals of Manchester.

Cobden traced back to the education controversy of 1847 the division among middle class Liberals,[25] but the split ran even deeper than this, for it involved the larger question of the role of the central government. The northern Radicals, proud of their growing cities and tenacious in their advocacy of laissez faire, took a much more hostile attitude to central government than did the London Liberals, who were more philosophical and more mindful of the whole nation's welfare. Northern papers such as the *Leeds Mercury,* the *Macclesfield Chronicle,* and the *Sheffield Independent* opposed the Education Order, the Public Health Bill, and a centralized police, all of which reforms were championed by the *Spectator* and the *Westminster* and *Edinburgh* reviews.[26] The issue of centralization had quite decisively divided the English Liberals.

The opponents of centralization wrote with fervor, confidence, and a tone of infallibility. Whether Tory localists like Toulmin Smith or nonconformist Radicals like Edward Baines, they had no doubts whatever of the unimpeachable soundness and universal applicability of localism and laissez faire. The utilitarian supporters of centralization wrestled more seriously with deep contraditions between the need of society and the principles of their political philosophy, and as a result suffered more doubts and tensions. More sensitive to abuses in society, they expounded collectivist tendencies; but wedded to political economy and a distrust of government, they could not work out a clear and consistent theory. The *Westminster Review,* in its articles on police reform, factory legislation, mining conditions, school aid, and the regulation of asylums, looked on the government as an instrument of benevolence. In answer to the nonconformist Liberal who regarded government as a parish constable paid to keep order, the *Review* argued that its chief aim was "the reconstruction of the social edifice on sound principles." [27] But the *Westminster Review*

25. John Morley, *Life of Richard Cobden* (London, 1896), 2, 30.
26. *Macclesfield Chronicle,* March 13, 1847, May 20, 1848. *Sheffield Independent,* March 3, 1847, May 10, 1848. *Spectator,* May 1, 1847, p. 420.
27. *Westminster Review, 46* (Sept. 1846), 97.

still opposed any regulation of adult labor, still adhered to the principle of noninterference in economic matters, and still warned against the abuse of the power of patronage, continuing to echo Bentham's fear of a powerful government.

So also did John Austin, an intimate friend of Bentham. Austin, once professor of jurisprudence at London University and Bentham's neighbor at Queens Square, published in the January 1847 issue of the *Edinburgh Review* the first systematic analysis of the problem of centralization. In his article he argued that centralization was not incompatible with popular or local government. It did not, he said, mean excessive government, and to say that it did was to be deceived by current fallacies. Centralization on the contrary only meant a more efficient government, one in which central boards established a general policy and local boards carried out the details. The local authorities, Austin openly admitted, were subordinated to the sovereign power of the central government, but this frankness did not make the truth any more palatable. In the *Quarterly Review's* article "Centralization" (July 1851) the author insisted that English public administration arose from two independent and equal sources, local government and central government. The problem of an indivisible sovereignty, which led Austin to place local government in a position subordinate to Parliament and the Crown, did not bother the advocates of ancient tradition and corporate power.

Austin's main argument that centralization would mean not more government but less may have been good Benthamism but it fitted ill with administrative fact. The education, mining, and factory inspectors and the poor law, lunacy, and ecclesiastical commissioners brought more not less government to England. But Austin could not admit this, because he still feared a meddling government. The same fear influenced John Stuart Mill, who likewise wrote in 1847 on the problem of centralization. Mill's regard for individualism and local government was high enough to lead the arch localist Toulmin Smith to cite extensively from Mill's *Political Economy*. But Mill also urged the central government to promote education, regulate railway fares, and provide good drainage and pure water. The contradiction between a belief in natural economic laws and the usefulness of positive legislation and administrative centralization, a contradiction inherent in Bentham's social philosophy, persistently created a tension in the social philosophy of Austin, Mill, and the writers of the *Westminster Review*.

The greatest happiness of the greatest number in fact often seemed to be better promoted by government action than by natural economic laws. Even the *Times*, the voice of England and the declared enemy of political and economic theory, expressed in 1845 an attitude that could only encourage social reform and the growth of the central government. "It is a settled principle of every constitution," it declared, "that the legislature is not merely empowered but obliged to interfere at times with the private rights of individuals, where the general advantage of the community requires it."[28] Such a principle, unconsciously a paraphrase of Bentham, persuaded many a member of Parliament to vote for further government interference. Just how and when the government should interfere had to be decided in a thoroughly pragmatic fashion. If abuses were serious and the local government had failed to end them, the central government should intervene. For this reason the most telling arguments for greater government control of sanitary authorities were not the theories of Austin and Mill—theories quite contradictory in themselves—but concrete descriptions of the failure of local government to clean up England's filthy towns.

All manner of journals gave publicity to unsanitary conditions. Among daily papers there were the *Times*, the *Daily News*, the *Globe*, and the *Examiner;* among weeklies the *Satire* and the *Douglas Jerrold's Weekly;* and among specialized periodicals the *Journal of the Statistical Society*.[29] Never had the press described

28. Smith, *Government by Commissioners*, pp. 165, 176. Mill, *Political Economy*, 2, 558–603. Metropolitan Sanitary Association, *Memorials on Sanitary Reform, Including the Correspondence of John S. Mill* (London, 1851), p. 21. *Times*, Dec. 26, 1845.

29. *Douglas Jerrold's Weekly*, May 13, 1848. *Examiner*, Aug. 5, 1848. *Satirist*, May 13, 1848. A committee of the Royal Statistical Society made an investigation to confirm the accuracy of the 1842 and 1844 official reports. The conditions which they found were just as appalling. *Journal of the Statistical Society, 11* (Jan. 1848), 1–25.

so vividly the alleys of London, and never had they debated with such animation the purity of the water and the size of drains. Never had they condemned so roundly, each according to his bias, local authorities or central boards. Never in fact had any social abuse, and the failure of local government to redress it, convinced so many London papers of the need of centralization; never before had the proposed central agency provoked in other papers such vehement criticisms of centralization. But Parliament and not the press would make the final decision.

In 1848, with cholera threatening England, Lord Morpeth again introduced a Public Health Bill. It passed—though not, to be sure, without considerable opposition and harmful changes.[30] The opposition to the Bill came largely from the Conservatives and consisted largely of repetitious attacks on centralization. In the Commons David Urquhart, the Conservative member from Staffordshire, condemned any central interference of any kind in local affairs. His colleague, Lewis Buck of Devonshire, took the same dogmatic stand, asserting that he was opposed to every kind of commission, whether poor law, railway, or health. The railway magnate George Hudson opposed the Bill on the same grounds, boldly proclaiming that centralization was repugnant to the people. When the Public Health Act was to be applied to Newcastle, the conservative Lord Lonsdale joined in the chorus against centralization. [31] The Bill was clearly repugnant to Tory sentiments.

More than sentiment lay behind these diatribes against the central board. Definite interests were at stake, involving, for example, the control of local patronage and the preservation of low rates and private property. Urquhart's denunciation of centralization reflects the strength of special interests. He represented the borough of Stafford, but when he denounced centralization he spoke for the Corporation, which was against the Public Health Act, and not for the majority of the inhabitants,

30. Chadwick Papers, memo on the multiplication of agencies: "not until cholera hit hard were sanitary measures taken, and then under the impulse of terror."

31. Hansard, *98* (1848), 711–27, 739, 796–99.

who were for the Act.[32] Rate-payers, fearing that expensive improvements would raise rates, were frequently in opposition. Lord Lonsdale, owner of the ground rents for slum tenements in Gateshead, knew that expensive sanitary improvements in the tenement sections would mean higher rates, which, with rents already at a maximum, would have to be paid by the owners. Lonsdale successfully opposed the application of the Public Health Act to Gateshead by pushing through a local act. But the local act commissioners made no improvements. In 1854 cholera ravaged Gateshead, as it had in 1849.[33]

The Public Health Act threatened yet other private economic interests. Water companies making comfortable profits feared that a central board would encourage the towns to build their own water systems. Economic interests of all sorts looked with jealousy upon this intrusion of the central government into economic activities.

Opposition to the Public Health Bill, though supported by municipal corporations, rate-payers, and private water companies, was not sufficient to defeat the Bill: the condition of English towns was too serious for that. Members of every political persuasion and representing every interest insisted on the creation of a central authority that could order newly created local boards to improve drainage and supply better water at cheaper rates. No single class had supported previous measures of social collectivism; in almost every instance it was the community as a whole, voting according to its conscience. The measure of that conscience is found not only in the zealous work of the leaders of sanitary reform but in the affirmative votes of such men as Joseph Hume and Sir William Clay. Clay, despite his chairmanship of a London water company, voted for the Act, as did Hume, the veteran Radical and longtime opponent of the factory acts who now expressed his belief that "the government should be prepared to

32. Chadwick Papers, unaddressed letter by Chadwick, May 14, 1848. Chadwick made an investigation at Stafford and found that the corporation, but not the people, were against the Public Health Act.

33. Ibid., unaddressed letter by Chadwick on Newcastle, Sept. 28, 1833: "Lonsdale from the first was the most active opponent of that measure. He told me that he was an enemy of centralization."

put down all self-interested parties and consult alone the interests of the many." [34] It is this Utilitarian social ethic, far more than Benthamite schemes for central inspection, that caused the growth of central government in England in these years.

Only forty-seven members dared oppose the passage of the Health Bill, and they were the angry, unyielding protectionists and those with special interests to protect. Yet few of the 345 voting for the Bill were zealous advocates of centralization, and on particular clauses they showed their localist bias. They amended, for example, the clause permitting the General Board of Health, on a petition of any number of rate-payers, no matter how small, to establish a board to recommend improvements. The change made necessary the signatures of one-tenth of the rate-payers, a stipulation that raised a definite obstacle to the administration of the Act, since most rate-payers did not cherish expensive improvements. To compensate for this loss the Bishop of London, showing a greater concern for the poor than the rate-payer, succeeded in inserting a clause requiring the General Board of Health to order an inquiry if the mortality of any town rose to over twenty-three in 1,000 per year.[35] The opponents of the measure also succeeded in limiting the duration of the Board to five years, thus seriously weakening its efficiency.

But the defenders of the powers of the General Board did preserve its right to confirm the appointment and dismissal of local surveyors and health officers, and the Bill which finally became law was, as were the other agencies of central control, an acceptable compromise between the advocates of central control and the defenders of local government. Once the Board of Health was established, it had only limited powers of supervision. In times of epidemic, to be determined by the Privy Council, it could, according to the Nuisance Removal and Disease Prevention Act of the same year, send out inspectors to organize the board of guardians and town councils for the prevention of cholera. But its powers even in such instances were limited to the making of

34. *DNB, 4*, 466. Hansard, *98* (1848), 1248; *91* (1847), 644.
35. *Examiner,* Aug. 5, 1848.

suggestions.[36] It did not possess, for instance, the powers of the Poor Law Commission. The opposition had forced the government to begin its program of sanitary improvement with an administrative machine barely adequate. Chadwick was exasperated, and told Lord Campbell that the "final act is only a wreck of the original bill." [37]

The issue of centralization, forced on the English by unsanitary towns, incompetent local authorities, and the possibilities of improvements was thus met by a dubious compromise which was not to last more than six years. There were too many interests opposed to the Board; in an outburst of anticentralism in 1854 they would destroy it.

FURTHER ADMINISTRATIVE GROWTH, 1849–1854

The social evils consequent upon England's industrial revolution allowed the Victorian governing classes no rest. Their pride in local government and their faith in laissez faire kept stumbling over social grievances and conflicting with the spirit of reform. In 1849, though on the threshold of the prosperous fifties, they still faced many unpleasant problems. Mining accidents exacted an appalling toll of lives. In 1849 some 756 out of 200,000 miners lost their lives. Explosions of "fire damp" in badly ventilated mines caused most of the accidents—cave-ins and shaft accidents most of the others.[38] Equally as miserable and almost as dangerous as the miners' lot was the fate of the merchant seamen. They lived in holds more wretched than the cellar dwellings of the Glasgow and Liverpool slums. They suffered the cruelty and tyranny of incompetent officers, unhindered by fixed maritime laws and tribunals. In 1836 a select committee reported that 894 lives a year were lost in shipwrecks caused by defective vessels and by officers ignorant of navigation. By 1847 conditions were no better.[39]

36. 11 & 12 Vict. c. 63, 123.
37. Chadwick Papers, Chadwick to Lord Campbell, July 26, 1848.
38. *Mining Journal*, March 23, 1850. PP, 27 (1849), 373–85 (i–xii).
39. PP, *17* (1836), 376. Thomas Clarkson, *The Merchant Marine, A National Crying Evil*, London, 1847.

Centralization

Another national disgrace in 1849 was the East End of London, exempted from the Public Health Act but not from hastily built tenements, undrained streets, stagnant cesspools, and overcrowded cemeteries. Impure water, a continuing source of disease, made life expectancy in the East End one-half that of the West End. It was also a center of crime, most of which was committed by juveniles. The *Times* reported that out of 28,000 committals in the country, 17,000 were youth under seventeen years of age. Upon conviction, most of the juveniles went to prisons, not to the few reformatories.[40] These reformatories, furthermore, depended entirely upon the charitable efforts of philanthropists. Yet donations to voluntary charities of any type were seldom sufficient and were seldom well administered. In 1850, despite half a century of humanitarian work, the many endowed charities of England were still under attack as useless and corrupt. They enjoyed an income of over a million pounds, but aside from hospitals put it to little use. The charity commissioners found some trustees applied charitable funds more diligently to their own needs than to those of society. Most charities were honest and well intentioned, but anomalous and inefficient.[41]

All these abuses—the fearful toll of lives in mines, the misery of merchant seamen, the unsanitary metropolis, juvenile crime, and the wasteful charities—were evils of long standing. They had existed in 1833 and were undiminished in 1850. The more remote, such as mining accidents, lay hidden from the Victorian conscience; others became the subject of inquiries and patchwork reforms. Four royal commissions, thirty-two annual reports totaling thirty-eight folio volumes, two select committees, the dogged criticisms of Lord Brougham, the solemn chastisements of the *Times,* and the satirical pen of Anthony Trollope—all, with extravagant criticism, told of the failings of endowed charities. From 1844 to 1853 Whig and Conservative ministries introduced nine bills calling for reform, but each failed to overcome the conservatism of lawyers such as Lord Cottenham, the jealousy of

40. *Edinburgh Review, 91* (April 1850), 385. *Times,* Aug. 2, 1853.
41. *Westminster Review, 59* (Jan. 1853), 32. MH, 32/28. *Times,* Aug. 4, 1853. J. P. Fearnon, *The Endowed Charities* (London, 1856), pp. 1–83.

ecclesiastics such as the Bishop of London, and the public's apathy.[42] Merchant marine reform fared little better, though Parliament applied patchwork measures. From 1835 onward it gave powers to various departments to end the chaos of merchant shipping: the Customs could register and inspect ships, the Emigration Commission could check passenger accommodations, and the Admiralty could register ships and seamen. None of these reforms removed the more serious evils. They did not end crimpage (by which owners of seamen's lodging houses lured the men into debauched houses, into debt, and then into the service); nor did they improve the dismal living quarters of the sailors. In 1850 a thousand accidents would occur as a result of ignorance and neglect.[43]

The Victorians had a capacity for enduring evils, and not merely remote ones. At their very doorstep, in the capital of the realm, they had long found in the common lodging houses, the streets, and the tenements vice, degradation, and disease. In 1853 Dickens called it a "cinder heap" and the *Times* an inferno. Intimidated by the majesty of the City Corporation—to Dickens the worst old government in England—and cowed by the hundreds of sewer commissioners and vestry officials, Parliament refused to intervene to end these abuses.[44] And after all, why bother? Were not these evils, along with juvenile crime, mining accidents, and corrupt charities, merely minor blemishes in a society preparing to celebrate, in the exhibition of 1851, the triumphs of capitalism and the march of scientific progress?

Yet between 1850 and 1854 Parliament finally set to work to remedy the situation. In 1850 it passed a Mining Inspection Act, a Merchant Shipping Act, and a Burial Grounds Act; in 1851 an Act to regulate London's common lodging houses; in 1853 an Act

42. *Westminster Review*, 59 (Jan. 1853), 32–46. PP, 27 (1843); *18* (1845), 7. *Times*, Jan. 27, 1834, May 10, 1853. Lord Brougham, *Letter to Samuel Romilly on the Abuses of Charities*, London, 1818. Anthony Trollope, *The Warden*, London, 1855.

43. Sir Hubert Smith, *The Board of Trade* (London, 1926), pp. 100–4. 5 & 6 William IV c. 53; 9 & 10 Vict. c. 100. *Mining Journal*, Nov. 23, 1850.

44. Charles Dickens, *Hard Times* (London, 1912), p. 184. *Times*, Jan. 4, 1853. Dickens, "Metropolitan Sanitary Association Speech of Feb. 6, 1850," *The Nonesuch Dickens* (London, 1937), 2, 384.

for the suppression of smoke in London and an Act to regulate lighthouses and pilot authorities; and in 1854 an Act to aid juvenile reformatories, an Act establishing a permanent charity commission, and a comprehensive Merchant Marine Act. The result of this outburst of reform was the creation of two new central departments: the Merchant Marine Department and the Charity Commission. These also served to give additional powers to the General Board of Health, that it might establish government-managed burial grounds in London; to mining inspectors, that they might better prevent accidents; to prison inspectors, for the inspection of juvenile reformatories; and to the Metropolitan Police, for the inspection of common lodging houses and smoky chimneys.

The supporters of these measures so disrespectful to the rights of property and the creed of the economists justified themselves by appealing to the spirit of the age. Joseph Hume, who had long defended the rights of the corporation of Trinity House to manage the country's lighthouses expensively and inefficiently, now defended his vote for Board of Trade supervision of that ancient body by saying, "the spirit of the age in which we live requires an entire change in the system under which these matters are now managed." The *Times,* in arguing for the Merchant Marine Bill, spelled out the main features of that spirit. "The solicitude of the public and the government" said the *Times,* "for the physical and moral well being of every class of the labouring population . . . is one of the most humane and distinguishing characteristics of the present time." [45] Such solicitude—first awakened in 1832 over the plight of factory children, aroused again in 1839 because of the need for schools, and fully engaged in the public health movement in 1848—now left its imprint on a host of minor reforms. This spirit of reform, so real to Joseph Hume and the editors of the *Times,* so vague to the historians, was no impersonal mystique; it arose from the intense feelings of a few individuals acting on the sensibilities of a governing class increasingly accustomed to change and reform, increasingly persuaded of the possibility of progress, and increasingly alarmed by

45. Hansard, *124* (1853), 1251. *Times,* Aug. 2, 1850.

industrial and urban misery. Although the humanitarianism which defined that spirit found its most energetic expression in the Evangelicals and Utilitarians, it was far more widespread.

The reform of the merchant marine, for example, began with the early experiences of James Silk Buckingham as a fourteen-year-old merchant seamen. He saw at first hand floggings, drunkenness, and misery. He did not forget these evils when he became, inspired by the radicalism of the time, a talented lecturer and writer and an ardent reformer. He was a rationalist, a humanitarian, and a friend of the Utilitarians. In 1836 he headed the select committee investigating the merchant marine. In 1837 his Bill to make the needed reforms was summarily defeated by the Commons.[46] The spirit of the age was not ripe for reform; but it could not, after these disclosures, long overlook the evils of the merchant marine. Thomas Clarkson, earlier a member of Wilberforce's Clapham sect, next took up the cause of the seamen. His *The Grievances of Our Mercantile Seamen* presented a compassionate picture of their suffering. He sent the pamphlet, along with a prodding note, to Lord John Russell, a man who was always sensitive to grievances. Russell turned the matter over to Henry Labouchere, who in 1839 had condemned Buckingham's measure as "vexatious interference." [47] Labouchere, who had also read the reports of James Murray of the Foreign Office on the inferiority of English seamen to American seamen and on the need of a central department, drew up and presented a measure. The shipowners condemned it as vexatious. He altered the measure to meet their objections, giving them the dominating role over the local shipping office and allowing the Board of Trade only limited supervision.[48] Even at that, the *Liverpool Chronicle* and the London shippers objected to its "centralization." But by 1850 either the members felt more humanely toward seamen than in 1837 or the rivalry of the American merchant

46. Ralph Turner, *James Silk Buckingham* (London, 1934), pp. 60–73, 287–93. *PP, 17* (1836), 374–80, 580, 775.
47. Smith, *Board of Trade,* p. 103. Hansard, *112* (1850), 108–11. PRO, 30/22/7, Labouchere to Russell, Jan. 1848, and PRO, 30/22/5, Thomas Clarkson to Russell, Sept. 9, 1846.
48. Hansard, *112* (1850), 1372.

marine and the advent of steam posed more serious challenges, for Parliament passed the Bill.[49]

In the same year, in an empty House and with little debate, Commons passed the Mining Act; the only real opposition in the House of Lords came from the Tory coal magnates Lord Lonsdale and Lord Londonderry. In Commons hardly anyone but Benjamin Disraeli opposed it. The impetus for the Mining Bill had come from two Radicals, Joseph Hume and Thomas Duncombe. Duncombe, though one of the loudest foes of centralization, was always ardent for the welfare of the laborers. Supporting Hume and Duncombe in urging the reform were the editors of the *Mining Journal* and men of the mining trade, such as Matthias Dunn, an obscure coal viewer who had turned publicist, organizer, and reformer. Dunn led the agitation organized by the South Shields Committee and was a chief witness before the select committee of 1849 on mining accidents. Well informed on the progress of mining technology, above all on improved means of ventilation, he knew that accidents could be reduced. The government, persuaded by Sir Henry de la Beche and by Lyon Playfair, a friend of Chadwick, came to the same conclusion, and in 1849 recommended a bill for inspection.[50] The spirit of reform in this instance originated with practical men, aware that advances in mining technology had made accidents much less necessary.

The roots of society's solicitude for the poor ran in many directions. In the case of the mining reforms it originated in the Radicals' concern for the plight of the worker, in the coal-viewers' knowledge of mining conditions, and in the scientists' awareness that accidents could be ended. In the quite different field of preventing juvenile crime it came from bishops, eminent lords, Utilitarian philosophers, town dandies, and poor-law and education inspectors. Active in the Society for Juvenile Delinquency Reform were the liberal Bishop of Norwich, the Duke of Richmond, Lord Brougham, the recorder of Birmingham, Matthew Hill, the Earl of Harroby, Lord de Talby, the Marquis of West-

49. *Liverpool Chronicle,* May 11, 1850. *Times,* April 18, July 9, 1850.
50. Hansard, *106* (1849), 1335. *PP,* 7 (1849), iii–ix. *Mining Journal,* Jan. 12, 19, 1850. *Newcastle Chronicle,* March 23, 1849, May 10, 1850.

minster, and members of Parliament from all parties, including that dashing social figure and political aspirant Monkton Milnes. They all attended the conferences held in Birmingham, London, and Chester—cities where the problem of juvenile crime was the greatest; and they all sought for the answer to that problem in those industrial schools so gloriously praised by E. C. Tufnell, a poor-law inspector, and Seymour Tremenheere, a mining inspector. In Parliament the cause of juvenile reformatories was espoused by Lord Ashley and Charles Adderley, both Evangelicals. Lord Ashley, now the Earl of Shaftesbury, led the fight in the House of Lords and Adderly in the Commons. Their Bill, introduced by Lord Palmerston, called for government aid and inspection of the reformatories that accepted young criminals. In 1854 the Bill finally passed.[51] No common doctrine, no one religious persuasion, no single philosophy, no one party inspired the movement for juvenile reformatories; it was the response of men of various sensibilities to an acute problem who had become convinced that society, through its government, could solve such problems.

The spirit of reform, widely diffused as it was among different parts of the governing class, was often faint-hearted and faltering. It could not carry a really effective mining bill or create an efficient charity commission. And on the question of cleaning up the "national cinder heap" it failed completely. Parliament continually refused to give the Metropolitan Sewers Commission the money or power to deal with London's drainage, and the Whig ministers who passed the Act empowering the Board of Health to build and manage cemeteries near London refused them the money to carry it out.[52] They also dared not interfere with the water companies further than to inspect the sources of water supplies. Yet these same members, despite all the laws of supply and demand, restricted to 6d. a mile the fares which London's hackney carriage could charge. London cabbies did not have the power

51. *Macclesfield Courier*, March 9, 1850, Feb. 4, 1854. *Morning Chronicle*, Dec. 21, 22, 1853. *PP**, 7. (1845), 180–92. *Times*, July 15, Aug. 2, 1854. Hansard *129* (1853), 1099–1104; *131* (1854), 782; *135* (1854), 232.

52. 13 & 14 Vict. c. 52. Chadwick Papers, memo. of 1853 on Lord Seymour and burial grounds.

and influence of the water companies, parish vestries, and local sewer commissioners.[53] "Solicitousness toward the poor," that distinguishing characteristic of the age, had its limits. The Victorian governing class wanted improvements, but they wanted no trouble; they wished the government to end scandalous evils, but not to increase its powers and expense or infringe on vested interests. Henry Labouchere proudly told the Commons when he introduced the Merchant Marine Bill that "he had fallen on a plan which would prevent a system of undue centralization and yet insure an effectual check on local abuse." [54] This tension between an earnest concern for social reform and a deep respect for property, local government, and liberty defined the reforms from 1850 to 1854. It prevented the new Charity Commission from appointing new trustees and ordering reform, and it denied the mining inspectors the power to compel improvements. Burial inspectors could only close cemeteries and water inspectors could merely report that the river sources were impure.[55] The central government thus grew in the number it employed far more than it did in the powers it could exercise. It was a situation that reflected both the diffuseness and the shallowness of the high tide of reform in the early 1850's.

Very few were the institutions untouched by this tide, which had been rising since 1833. There was no stopping the spirit of progress and the moral passion of the Victorians to keep their house in order. The advancement of science and art required (especially at a time when English markets were threatened with continental goods and manufactures) a Department of Science and Art to promote technology and design. It was duly established in 1852. The advancement of learning and new standards of efficiency demanded the reformation of Oxford University. Parliament created, in 1854, a central commission to help in this reformation. The advancement of medicine gave rise to anatomy inspectors whose duty it was to prevent any illicit trade in corpses

53. Hansard, *119* (1852), 215-25. 15 & 16 Vict. c. 84. Hansard, *127* (1854), 422-29, 834, 1018.
54. Ibid., *112* (1850), 1116.
55. 13 & 14 Vict. c. 100; 15 & 16 Vict. c. 84, 85; 16 & 17 Vict. c. 137.

needed by schools of anatomy. Yet another commission had been established to prevent the exploitation of the whippers unloading London's coal barges.[56]

The *Westminster Review* in 1853 argued that a firm conviction of moral and rational progress underlay these widening demands for improvements. "We are receding fast," they boasted, "from the barbarism of former times and as a community we are awakening to a far stronger and more general sense of the claims and dues of all classes. We are beginning to estimate our objects and possessions more according to rational principles . . ."[57] The *Review*, and many others in Victorian England, believed that reasonable men in an age of technological and moral advance could create a more humane and just society, and they believed that the central government was one instrument by which it could be done. Forced by the failure of local authorities to deal with striking social evils, the English, from 1833 to 1854, established those central agencies whose total functions added up to an administrative revolution. In an unintentional manner they had created Bulwer Lytton's directive state. A list of the agencies active in 1854 and created after 1833 shows at a glance to what extent the early Victorians built a centralized administration concerned with the well being of Her Majesty's subjects.

I. *Permanent Departments for General Administration*

    A. Independent Commissions
        1. Poor Law Commission (1834)
        2. Ecclesiastical Commission (1836)
        3. Lunacy Commission (1842)
        4. Charity Commission (1854)
        5. Registrar of Births, Deaths, and Marriages (1836)

    B. Home Office Inspectorates
        1. Factory inspectors (1833)
        2. Prison inspectors (1835; after 1854 they also inspected reformatories)

56. *Economist, 11* (April 9, 1853), 390. HO, 45/189. Hansard, *71* (1843), 402–7.
57. *Westminster Review, 59* (Jan. 1853), 32.

3. Anatomy inspectors (1839)
4. Mining inspectors (1842 and 1850)
5. Burial inspectors (1854)
6. Constabulary inspectors (1856)

C. Colonial Office
  Colonial Land and Emigration Commission (1839)

D. Privy Council Departments
  1. Committee on Education (1839)
  2. Board of Trade

  a. Merchant Marine Department (1850)
  b. Department of Arts and Sciences (1852)
  c. Railway Board (1839)
  d. Commissioners of Patent and Invention (1850)
  e. Office of Registrar of Joint-Stock Companies (1833)
  f. Design Registry Office (1839)

II. *Permanent Departments for the Metropolis*

A. Home Office: Metropolitan Police
  1. Inspectors of common lodging houses (1853)
  2. Inspectors of noxious trade (1854)

B. Office of Woods and Forests and Public Works: expanded powers over Thames embankments, parks, and numerous streets

C. Board of Trade
  1. Inspectors of London water sources (1852)
  2. Commissioners to regulate London's coal whippers (1843)

D. Metropolitan Sewers Commission (1847)

E. Metropolitan Building Commission (1844)

III. *Temporary Commissions*

A. Administrative
  1. Oxford University commissioners (1854–58)

2. Commissioners of Tithes, Enclosures, and Copyhold (1836, Tithes; 1841, Copyhold; 1845, Inclosure; 1851, consolidated)

B. Commissioners of Inquiry into:

1. Statute law	6. Charitable donations
2. Cambridge University	7. Three election disputes
3. Fine arts	8. Mercantile law
4. Newcastle cholera	9. Registration and conveyance
5. London Corporation	10. County courts

The powers granted to these agencies were largely designed to regulate social not economic matters. Economic freedom was infringed only to correct scandalous social evils, such as child labor or distressing living conditions. The early Victorian collectivism was thus social and not economic in its emphasis.

After 1854 this increasing collectivism, with its attendant centralization came to a halt. The event that checked this growth in the powers of the central government was the defeat of the General Board of Health in 1854. That event ushered in an era of localism, marred only in 1856 by the creation of the constabulary inspectors. In the 1860's, as the *Pall Mall Gazette* later wrote, local interests held their own. The years 1833 to 1854 thus remain the formative period for the *ad hoc* construction of the Victorian administrative state. From 1870 to 1911 the imperfections, the confusions, and the weaknesses of that administrative state forced Parliament to pass consolidating measures: the Education Act of 1870, the Local Government Act of 1871, the Mining Act of 1877, the Prison Act of 1877, and the Factory Act of 1878. This was a great era of consolidation. After 1905 a new era began, with government consciously intervening to remedy economic abuses. In the early Victorian period it intervened mainly to remedy social evils. In remedying these evils, it laid the basis for the British administrative state.

Political Attitudes toward Centralization

The early Victorian governing classes had never intended to transform the English government in this fashion. In 1854 as in

95

1833 they viewed a strong central government with hostility. Eager localists in 1854 petitioned against the Poor Law Board, defeated the County Police Bill, and threw out the General Board of Health. Even Bulwer Lytton, once a Radical but now a Conservative, earnestly hoped that England should never part with "the vital principle of self-government in contradistinction to centralization." [58] The latter was still an evil word. For two decades the central government had increasingly impinged on private interests, insulted local patriotism, abolished local jobs, and threatened higher taxes. Opposition to it was widespread, deep, and unreasoning. At the very mention of the word Mr. Podsnap, the English patriot of *Our Mutual Friend,* exclaimed, "Centralization. No. Never with my consent. Not English."

To that sentiment both Benjamin Disraeli and John Bright would have agreed. In 1854 Disraeli led his Tories into the lobby against the General Board of Health and John Bright headed the deputation protesting Palmerston's centralizing Police Bill. Of the two men, Disraeli could claim for himself and his party the longest record of hostility to a centralized administration. The Conservative's traditional loyalty to old institutions and his vested interest in low rates and the sanctity of property made him look with suspicion on all innovations promising a change in social and political power. The most ardent defenders of the Church and the corporations were Sir Robert Inglis; David Urquhart; George Hudson, the railway king; and Lord Lonsdale, the colliery magnate and proprietor of the tenements of Gateshead.[59] Between 1841 and 1846 one-half the businessmen who came to the House of Commons chose to sit on the Conservative side. They and their landed friends in the Conservative party had in the two decades since 1833 successfully opposed the central supervision of police and highways. They had unsuccessfully opposed the Education Order of 1839 and the Public

58. Bulwer Lytton, *Speeches of Edward, Lord Lytton* (London, 1874), p. 181.

59. Charles Dickens, *Our Mutual Friend* (London, 1953), p. 132. *Manchester Guardian,* June 24, 1854. Anon., *Liberals and Conservatives and Their Policy towards the Working Class,* London, 1855.

Health Act of 1848.[60] Only when their immediate interests were involved, as in the desire for lower poor rates—or when their consciences were aroused, as by Lord Ashley over mining evils —did they look to a stronger central government. Conservatives voted for the New Poor Law, the lunacy acts, the mining acts, and other minor reforms. Their traditionalism was not doctrinaire.

The Manchester Liberals, on the other hand, prided themselves on adherence to doctrine. They worshiped not the venerable and traditional but the new and the rational, above all the principle of laissez faire. The John Brights and Edward Baineses of the northern towns—manufacturers and nonconformists, and proud citizens of progressive boroughs—felt only jealousy of Whitehall and its bothersome interference. They opposed all factory regulations, all interference with their church schools, any meddling in their town affairs. They were men of property, faith, self-reliance, and civic pride, could manage their own police and sanitation, and could run their own mills and schools. Their new theories and new wealth, no less than the conservative's old loyalties and interests, strengthened that political jealousy against an expanded central government which Mill in his *Autobiography* said "is the subject not only of rational disapprobation but of unreasoning prejudice." [61]

In the extremists of both parties, in the Tory's Colonel Sibthorp and Colonel Ferrand and in the Liberal's Thomas Duncombe and Sharmon Crawford, this unreasoning prejudice reached its highest point. Strong-willed, antagonistic toward a government of entrenched interests, and the champions of the poor, they expressed the most violent feeling against the most centralizing of all reforms, the New Poor Law, and they had the greatest suspicion of expensive and corrupt commissioners.[62] But only in Colonel Sibthorp, the enemy of railways, water closets, and commissions,

60. *Stamford Mercury*, Aug. 1, 1839. Hansard, *50* (1839), 356–58; *45* (1839), 1319–26.
61. Mill, *Autobiography*, p. 135.
62. Hansard, *44* (1839), 364; *59* (1841), 925–55; *81* (1845), 1414–16; *78* (1845), 707; *91* (1847), 978–1002.

did this prejudice nearly reach consistency. Yet even he tarnished his record of unbending opposition to centralization by urging government inspection of railways.[63] Duncombe agitated for a mining act, Crawford and Ferrand for the Factory acts.[64] The Radicals hated a strong central government, but upon occasion there were some things (railways and mills) which they hated more, and to check these they would turn to a stronger central government.

The Whigs also disliked centralization. Their pleas for social reform invariably emphasized the practical need of government action and de-emphasized its centralizing tendencies. The Whig journal the *Morning Chronicle,* in supporting the Poor Law Act of 1834, disavowed any liking for the principle of centralization. The Duke of Richmond viewed the Poor Law Commission's power with great alarm, yet introduced the Prison Bill in the following year; and Lord John Russell and Lord Lansdowne, when they urged a grant for education, were careful to point out how limited would be government interference. Henry Labouchere in 1850 and Edward Cardwell in 1853 both specifically disclaimed any preference for centralization. Labouchere told the Commons he had no "abstract love for centralization," and Cardwell told them "the government desires nothing so little as centralization in this matter." [65] Yet the result of both men's speeches was a Merchant Marine Department and a stronger government.

That the Whigs spoke against centralization at the same time they promoted it has its explanation. They believed that it was the function of government to redress admitted evils and remedy acknowledged grievances. Being in office for fifteen of the twenty-one years that followed the passage of the Reform Bill, they felt the pressure of these evils and these grievances. And bearing the tradition of compromise and responsible statesmanship, they sought to remove them by *ad hoc* reforms that inevitably ex-

63. Ibid., *76* (1844), 515; *98* (1848), 711.
64. Ibid., *74* (1844) 637; *98* (1848), 876; *106* (1849), 1335.
65. *Morning Chronicle*, April 21, 1834. Hansard, *25* (1834), 273; *48* (1839), 791, 1255–74; *112* (1850), 111; *124* (1853), 1247.

panded England's central administration. Their real inclination was to let things alone, and their closest interests lay with the protection of property rights and the maintenance of county, parish, and municipal autonomy. They preferred the easy-going localism of the eighteenth century, but the nineteenth century would not allow it. Instead they had to follow that new canon of Whig rule and pass those reforms which circumstances (and the prodding of Radicals and humanitarians) forced upon them. Confronting the social problems of an industrial society and the demands of the Evangelicals and Utilitarians for their solution, the Whigs became the improvising architects of that most rambling of structures the Victorian administrative state.

The only group with a political theory that favored a strong benevolent government was the Utilitarians. The Evangelicals, no doubt, looked to the central government to redress those wrongs which lay deepest on their conscience, and it was their great leader, Lord Ashley, who prodded his indifferent Conservative ministry to pass mining and lunacy reforms. But Ashley had no definite political philosophy, only a clear and consistent Christian philanthropy. He forgot, when drawing up his Mining Bill, to propose inspectors for its enforcement. The Utilitarians would never have overlooked such an important point. Inspection was a cardinal principle of Bentham's *Constitutional Code,* and a profession for Dr. James Kay and Edwin Chadwick. Indeed it was more than a profession for them; it was a vocation, a calling, which led them to produce reports so cogent and informative that education and health reform became a necessity. It was the Utilitarians alone who spoke explicitly, in government reports, in the *Edinburgh Review* and *Westminster Review,* and in Parliament of the merits of centralization; and they possessed the most consistent record in support of factory, poor-law, prison, Church, educational, mining, lunacy, sanitary, and merchant marine reforms. Their belief in legislation for the greatest happiness to the greatest number—and their awareness of the uniformity and effectiveness of central agencies and the anomalies and inefficiencies of local authorities—made them the most zealous advocates of a strong, centralized, benevolent government.

Centralization

Only the Benthamites possessed a political philosophy which admitted the necessities of social and administrative reform. But even so, they held in theory that government was in itself a mischief, albeit often a lesser mischief than no government. Utilitarian members of Parliament, such as Arthur Roebuck and Joseph Hume, opposed any interference with adult labor (as indeed did Chadwick); and their leading philosopher after Bentham's death, John Stuart Mill, praised local self government and individual self-reliance.[66] Very few in the two decades after 1833 embraced wholeheartedly a centralized, paternalistic state, one that would regulate labor, clean towns, educate the poor, control the Church, commute tithes, supervise asylums, and manage lighthouses. And yet from 1833 to 1854 Parliament created such a state.

It was above all the *Times,* the voice of England, which exhibited these contradictions between sentiment and performance. In 1838 it roundly denounced government by commissions, in 1843 it said centralization had been carried too far, in 1845 that centralization was a purely French notion and a danger to commercial liberty.[67] Yet it supported nearly every social reform, including the Education Minutes of 1847. The *Times,* like the governing class it represented, did not adhere too firmly to its announced opposition to centralization.

J. Toulmin Smith, the arch localist, realized this fact, and realized the reason for it. "We are losing sight daily," he complained in 1849, "of principles and allowing ourselves to be made the dupes of presumptuous empiricism." [68] Presumptuous empiricism, the meeting of every problem on its own merits, was the mood that explains the growth of administration from 1833

66. Hansard, *74* (1844), 107–8; *20* (1833), 584. The Utilitarians of this period were, in general, considered Radicals. Not all Radicals, of course, are Utilitarians, not even most of them. The term "Radical" is a wide one, referring to such different personalities as George Grote and Richard Oastler. The term Utilitarian is narrow; I use it to refer to those influenced by Jeremy Bentham and the Mills. For the best discussion of them see Leslie Stephen, *The English Utilitarians,* London, 1900.

67. *Times,* May 14, 1838, Nov. 2, 1843, Feb. 19, 1845, July 7, 1853.

68. Smith, *Government by Commissioners,* p. 367.

to 1854. Each reform was passed to meet an observed fact not to accord with a principle. The result, most naturally, was a helter-skelter series of statutes and agencies, unrelated and uncoordinated. The *Edinburgh Review* in 1853 lamented the irregularity of that legislation, "so empirical, tentative, unsystematic, and irregular. . . . What is forced upon them, they do, what is not forced upon them they ignore or postpone." And the author added very perceptively, "Our national maxim is one thing at a time." [69] It is not, then, in the political theories of the time, not in any party platform or philosopher's dreams, that the reasons for the growth of England's central government can be found, but only in those forces economic, social, scientific, and governmental that arose from the transformation of English society in the early nineteenth century.

The great transforming event was the industrial revolution. It brought large factories, expanded mines, railways, the steamship, and crowded, dirty cities; and it created the wealth that made poverty and misery and ignorance unnecessary. The abuses of child labor in factories demanded restriction on hours and inspection; railway accidents forced the government to inspect new lines; the advent of steamships (and with it boiler explosions) meant government examination of boilers, hulls, and officers; and the growth of towns led to prison reform societies, clamor for public education, and the public health movement.

The industrial revolution did not create abuses where none existed before; it concentrated them and brought them into the open. Conditions on sixteenth-century frigates, in seventeenth-century mines, and in eighteenth-century cottage industries were as harsh and miserable as work in the new factories; and the life of agricultural laborers was as trying and hard, and less relieved by amusements and schools, than the life of Manchester workers. But the abuses of the countryside were more dispersed, less threatening, and more customary; and the agricultural laborer was much less articulate and revolutionary. The evils of town life, on the other hand, were apparent to all, and the discontent of the new proletariat alarmed the governing classes. In 1840

69. *Edinburgh Review, 100* (Oct. 1854), 290–91.

the *Quarterly Review* spoke of the urban working class as "that vast inflammable mass which lies waiting to explode into mischief"; the *Edinburgh Review* in 1851 called the physical and moral evils "in the very heart of our towns . . . an open and fearful account against society." [70] The growth of factory and town posed the greatest challenge to society and forced the ruling classes to turn to the government for an answer, even if it meant being presumptuously empirical.

In thus turning to the government Englishmen had to choose between central agencies or local authorities, a difficult and disconcerting choice. The frequent failures of local government and voluntary societies forced them, no matter how strong their love of local autonomy, to accept some central control. Where local administration was the weakest and most inefficient, as in the rural parish and magistracy, resistance to centralization was the least; where local administration was energetic and able, above all in the towns, there was strong resistance to centralization. In 1833 the strongest opposition to the New Poor Law came from Leeds, Birmingham, and Marylebone, centers of civic pride and civic ability; and in 1854 the mayors, aldermen, and members of Parliament of the northern towns opposed and defeated the centralizing Police Bill. "The jealousy of English liberty," wrote Homersham Cox in his discussion of the English constitution, "is nowhere more strikingly illustrated than in the sedulous preservation to the municipal bodies of their rights to self-government." [71] But equally striking were their failures in cleaning and draining streets, managing prisons, establishing schools, and building asylums for the insane—failures that forced the central government to intervene. Local administrators did not have the knowledge or will to construct efficient units of local administration, and there was no possibility that they could bring into being that national uniformity which a growing national consciousness demanded.

It was not the existence of abuses alone that promoted the

70. *Quarterly Review, 67* (Dec. 1840), 97. *Edinburgh Review, 94* (Oct. 1851), 208.
71. Homershan Cox, *The British Commonwealth* (London, 1854), p. 454.

growth of the central government: there were other forces working to that end, such as the advance of science, the rapid increase in wealth, a deep humanitarianism, and a growing belief in progress. All these forces were intertwined and interdependent. The humanitarianism of the period, so important in inspiring men to press for social reform, had deep roots in England's Christian faith, pre-eminently in the evangelical movement inspired by John Wesley. But it also had its source in the humane ideals of the rationalists, the eagerness of the Benthamites to reform the laws, and a Whig aristocracy still inspired by the philosophy of the enlightenment. The advance of science also created a demand for social reforms and a centralized administration. "Business accumulates year by year," said the *Times* in 1853, "new departments arise as science develops new capabilities, and society becomes aware of fresh wants and shortcomings." [72]

The increase in scientific knowledge made possible the reform of abuses formerly accepted as irremediable. Engineers, educationalists, doctors, and administrators constantly developed better drainpipes for streets, better ventilators for mines, more scientific means of preventing cholera, better methods of treating the insane, improved methods of teaching, and surer ways of reforming juvenile offenders. Each new advance not only made reform possible but made it all the more necessary. And the moment reforms were undertaken, there was the employment of paid experts carrying out a uniform and enlightened policy and the rise of central agencies supervising local authorities. Advances in science made the amateur, unpaid administrator—the local justice of the peace or town bailiff—an inefficient servant. He had to be replaced by paid professionals employed by a central agency.

The effective use of public servants to propose yet further reforms was characteristic of England's growing central administration. The poor-law inspectors discovered the desperate need for more education, the metropolitan lunacy commissioners looked into the need for closer supervision of local asylums, and the

72. *Times,* July 26, 1853.

mining inspectors reported that their own powers should be increased so that they might ensure proper safety. The growth of these agencies brought into being a new and powerful means of social investigation and a new source of political pressure. These investigations and the pressures, in turn, accelerated the growth of the central government. Numerous inspectors brought social problems to the nation's attention, turned local abuses into a national concern, and so hastened the growth of the central government. This is not to say that they were alone in ferreting out and publicizing abuses. Improved mails, the growth of a national press, easier travel, greater internal migration—all helped make England a more self-conscious and uniform society, demanding a more integrated public administration.

It was this convergence of many causes, economic and social, intellectual and technological, that led through the confused avenue of political conflict to the expansion of the central government. Special interests and the dominant political attitudes hampered that expansion, but in the end the ruling classes decided that the social abuse must be ameliorated, even if it meant more government.

4.

POWERS AND ORGANIZATION

HAD JEREMY BENTHAM constructed England's administrative state it would have been uniform, well ordered, and powerful. Each department would have possessed definite powers to inspect, report, issue directives, plan policy, and remove local officers; and each department, placed neatly under one of thirteen central ministers, would supervise clearly delimited districts and subdistricts. There would be no large, unwieldy boards of unpaid dilettantes and paid favorites, no confused jurisdictions, no disorderly array of local authorities, and no crippling inadequacies of personnel and power.

The central administration of 1854, with no such Benthamite symmetry or strength, was ramshackle and weak. The diverse powers of the new central departments were jealously limited; and their organization within the central government fell far short of even the most rudimentary principles of administrative responsibility and departmental efficiency. The architects of the Victorian administrative state, improvising to meet the problems of the day, faced a difficult task. They had to build an administrative state in an era when few wanted one; they had to wrest powers from a jealous Parliament; and they had to fit their new agencies into a central administration that had evolved not from a philosopher's mind but from a medieval king's household. It is little wonder that the powers were often insufficient and the organization inept.

THE POWERS

The sixteen new departments of Her Majesty's government, despite the marked diversity of their functions, did possess certain powers in common.[1] All, for example, could inspect local authorities and publish reports on them. Most could order prosecutions if local officials or industrialists violated those laws established for their regulation. Three of the central agencies could draw up and enforce their own rules and regulations, and nine of them could confirm the rules and regulations drawn up by local officials. The power to confirm local appointments fell to only one agency, the Poor Law Commission, though three other agencies could prevent local authorities from making unjust dismissals and the Merchant Marine Department could appoint four of the ten members who made up the local boards. Ten of the departments could hold hearings and pass judgments on matters in dispute, and three could license or certify local institutions, such as hospitals for the insane and prison cells for the criminal. Only three agencies enjoyed the power of dispensing grants of money to local authorities. Six could insist that local authoritites keep registers of pertinent information, and almost all could demand that the local authorities send in periodical returns on their activities. The right to call for returns, like the right to inspect and report, was common to every department.

This uniformity reveals the dominant theme of the Victorian's administrative philosophy, the belief that exposing abuses and

1. In 1854 the sixteen most clearly defined departments with nationwide power to supervise local government and private institutions were the Prison Inspectorate, the Mining Inspectorate, the Factory Inspectorate, the Anatomy Inspectorate, the Burial Inspectorate, the Poor Law Board, the General Board of Health, the Charity Commission, the Lunacy Commission, the Railway Department, the Merchant Marine Department, the Emigration Office, the Tithe, Inclosure, and Copyhold Commission, the Department of Science and Art, the Ecclesiastical Commission, and the Education Committee.

106

giving advice would be quite enough to persuade local authorities to mend their ways, obey the law, and adopt uniform practices. It was a belief in persuasion and knowledge as the best administrative devices. It reflected the profound faith of Victorians that in a society of free men an increase in knowledge will bring progress in its train. Let the prison magistrates or the school teacher know about improved disciplines and new techniques and they would surely follow them.

The Victorians were not wholly wrong in placing their faith in the powers of inspection, reporting, and the dissemination of knowledge; they proved the most useful of all powers. Given the right to visit local authorities, summon witnesses, demand testimony on oath, and examine local documents, there was little an inspector could not find out and publicize. He was an official to be reckoned with, just as he was an official to be listened to. He knew a great deal about prison discipline, education, or mining, and it was usually in the interest of prison governors, teachers, and mine-owners. to hear what he had to say. Matthew Arnold, poet, literary critic, and school inspector, believed that immediate personal contact with local authorities was the most effective means of supervision; and Edward Strutt of the Railway Board and Sir Joshua Jebb, inspector general of prisons, insisted that both railway-owners and prison officials welcomed and accepted the recommendation of the inspectors.[2]

Other officials questioned this sanguine faith in persuasion. Sir Frederick Hill, a colleague of Jebb's, doubted seriously if inspection and advice alone were adequate.[3] The mining inspectors, who could inspect mines and give advice but could not order improvements, not even in the most dangerous mines, shared this skepticism. In 1853 they pleaded with the Home Secretary for more stringent powers. The *Mining Journal* supported their plea, expostulating that "the inspectors do not have the power to enforce the simplest and most reasonable rules."[4] Yet Parlia-

2. H. E. Boothyrood, *A History of the Education Inspectorate* (London, 1923), p. 24. *PP, 17* (1850), 7; *18* (1848), 168–69.

3. *PP, 18* (1848), 398; *26* (1849), 180 (xiii).

4. HO, 45/4105. *PP, 15* (1855), 660–71, 675 (90–92, 96). *Mining Journal*, May 7, 1853, March 11, 1854.

ment was always chary of granting powers to those departments which supervised the workings of capital. Railway inspectors, for example, could inspect lines only to sanction their openings or inquire into fatal accidents. At all other times the companies enjoyed perfect freedom to hire incompetent engineers, use the shoddiest equipment, and follow the most dangerous schedules. Until 1844 the subinspectors of factories could not even enter a mill without begging the owner's permission, and the mining commissioner appointed in 1842 to prevent women and children from working in mines could not summon witnesses.[5] In an age sensitive to the inviolability of private property Parliament wished to preserve maximum freedom.

The power to inspect, report, and advise depended at all times on the cooperation of the local authorities. If these authorities merely scoffed at the inspector and threw his circulars in the waste basket the inspector's advice meant very little. Only if a department could order prosecutions or issue rules with the force of law could it compel a mill-owner to fence his machinery or a poor law union to build a workhouse. The power to order prosecutions was relatively common. The factory and mining inspectors, the poor law and railway boards, the lunacy and charity commissioners, and the Merchant Marine Department could all institute court actions whenever they learned of a violation of the law. The threat of court action gave force to their investigations and suggestions. Unfortunately the old historic courts of law acted slowly, and with great care not to allow the agencies to exceed the narrow and occasionally ambiguous limits to their powers set forth in the statutes. There was always apt to be a flaw. Even in the Factory Act of 1844, drawn up with such care and filled with such a wealth of detail about hours of work, lunch time, whitewashing, and the fencing of machines, there were oversights. The factory inspectors, for example, found

5. The principal acts defining the Railway Department's powers are 3 & 4 Vict. c. 97 and 5 & 6 Vict. c. 55, and for the powers of the Railway Commission, 7 & 8 Vict. c. 85. For the best summary of their powers see Cleveland Stevens, *English Railways, Their Development and Their Relations to the State* (London, 1915), pp. 135 ff. For mining, HO, 45/1490, and 5 & 6 Vict. c. 99.

that their right to order prosecutions was frustrated by the magistrates' right to impose the fines. In areas where the magistrates were also mill-owners the small fines blunted the effectiveness of the law and vexed the patience of the inspectors.[6]

The law courts moved slowly and not always surely. The poor law commissioners swore out many a writ of mandamus in order to compel reluctant overseers to follow their orders, but the overfull docket of the Queens Bench caused interminable delays in serving the writs, and the Board of Health did not consider common law prosecutions of nuisances worth the time or expense. Yet as awkward, costly, and unwieldy as was court action, it remained the principal means of compelling local institutions, whether factories or charities, to obey the law. The power to order prosecutions was pre-eminently the power that defined the work of the factory and mining inspectors. They were in a sense administrative policemen commissioned to enforce a clear-cut law.

The Poor Law Commission faced more complicated tasks than the enforcement of industrial regulations. Parliament thus gave it more formidable powers. No other agency, except the Merchant Marine Department of 1854, possessed such a vast accumulation of powers, legislative, judicial, and administrative. Besides the regular powers to inspect, advise, report, and order prosecutions, it could issue rules and regulations on every phase of poor law management, could order rates raised for building a workhouse, could confirm the appointments of paid officials, and could order that parishes combine into unions and elect a board of guardians. After 1844 it could also appoint auditors, grant money to school teachers and medical officers, and help set up schools and asylums for the education and care of pauper children and pauper lunatics.[7] Of these many powers, the right to issue regulations with the force of law was the most radical, though even it was not unprecedented. The Excise Commission had long laid down rules for the manufacture of glass, spirits,

6. 7 & 8 Vict. c. *15*. *PP, 31* (1837), 59 (6); *PP, 33* (1840), 9. In 1854 Palmerston complained of such evasions, HO, 87/3.
7. 4 & 5 William IV c. 76; 7 & 8 Vict. c. 37, 101.

and paper and the sale of tea and tobacco; and the factory inspectors could (until 1844) issue rules and regulations on such matters as keeping registers and the use of time clocks. But neither of these departments had such extensive legislative powers as the Poor Law Commission. Whatever the subject—management of workhouses, education of pauper children, or dispensation of relief—the commissioners laid down the rules and the guardians had to obey. Defiance brought a writ of mandamus from the courts, the stern reminder that local guardians had best heed the commissioners' rules. To prevent the abuse of these extraordinary powers Parliament insisted that all general rules (those applicable to more than one union at a time) had to be sanctioned by the Home Office and sent to Parliament. Special orders to a single union needed no such confirmation, a fact which the hard-pressed commissioners, anxious to avoid delay, exploited to the fullest, issuing general regulations individually as special rules.

In addition to the right of issuing regulations, the Poor Law Commission possessed another efficient and infrequently granted power—the right to confirm the appointment of all local paid officials, from the workhouse governor to the assistant overseer. No other agency could do this.[8] The factory inspectors could appoint certifying surgeons, and the General Board of Health could prevent the unjust dismissals of local surveyors, but that was all. Under Chadwick's strict surveillance the Poor Law Commission used this power to force guardians to appoint men by merit not by political favors, thus introducing principles of civil service reform into local government for the first time.

Besides issuing regulations and confirming appointments the commissioners could also order taxation for the construction of workhouses, grant money to workhouse teachers and medical officers, order the formation of unions, and insist on the fair assessment of property for rating. These powers made the Poor Law Commission the strongest of the central departments and the prototype for the administrative bureaus of the future, with their discretionary powers to legislate, grant aid, and sanction

8. 17 & 18 Vict. c. 104, 123.

appointments. It was an exceptional department, the work of "one of the original and contriving minds of the age" grappling with one of the most urgent and formidable of problems. Only the dire need of reform explains why Parliament accepted Edwin Chadwick's pioneering scheme, and its array of discretionary powers.

Parliament treated much more harshly Chadwick's plans for a General Board of Health. The powers of the General Board of Health, once Parliament had restricted them, can scarcely stand comparison with those of the "three bashaws of Somerset House." The Board which met at Gwydyr House in July 1848 to improve England's public health felt little elation over the powers the Public Health Act vouchsafed them. Chadwick called the Act "a mere wreck of what was intended." The *Morning Chronicle,* the bitterest enemy of sanitary reform, rejoiced at its crippled state. "One hardly sees at the moment," it wrote, "how the General Board of Health will manage to pass the time." Their optimism was too great. Chadwick, recovering from his initial dejection, concluded that the Act was at least a working measure.[9] The Act gave the Board four main powers. It could, on the petition of one-tenth of the rate-payers or if the mortality of the town exceeded a yearly average of 23 in 1,000, order a full inquiry. It could sanction long-term loans made on the town's rates for sanitary improvements. It could prevent the dismissal of locally paid surveyors and medical officers. And it could settle disputes between aggrieved rate-payers and local boards.

The first two were the most effective powers. Once a petition was sent in or a high mortality rate discovered, an inspector came down from London ready to expose every bad sewer or disease-ridden tenement in town. Witnesses would be summoned, cesspools and water mains examined, hearings held, and inexorably there followed a full report and a provisional order for the establishment of a local board of health. By its power

9. 11 & 12 Vict. c. 63. Chadwick Papers, Chadwick to Sir George Sarpent, June 20, 1848. Lewis, Chadwick, pp. 171–74. *Morning Chronicle,* June 8, 1848. Finer, *Chadwick,* pp. 319–31.

to sanction all loans for engineering works, the central Board could insist on proper drainage and water works. But after the provisional order was issued and the plans sanctioned, the central Board's powers practically ceased.

Neither the power to protect surveyors from unfair dismissals nor the power to hear aggrieved parties really bothered the local boards. Once established, they were autonomous. The General Board of Health could not even inspect local boards. Only if the Nuisance Removal and Disease Prevention Act was invoked could the central board exercise any interference. And that Act —which allowed the board to draw up regulations on the prevention of cholera and issue them to local boards of health and poor-law unions—could be invoked only when the Privy Council deemed cholera to have reached epidemic proportions;[10] it was invoked in 1849 and 1854. But the powers gained from the Act proved largely illusory. Chadwick and the inspectors complained bitterly at the ease with which local boards of health and poor law unions neglected these orders. The General Board of Health was not the autocratic board its critics claimed; it could act effectively only with the cooperation of local officials. The real power of the Act of 1848 went to the local boards.

The principle of granting greater administrative power to local authorities than to the central departments characterized the Victorian administrative state. Parliament wished the local people to have the privilege of managing themselves and the right to pursue policies of their own choosing. The power of the Poor Law Commission to issue regulations was exceptional: the power to draw up regulations for the management of prisons and asylums was given to the local justices, and the owners of mills, mines, and railways were entrusted with drawing up regulations for their safe management. Charity trustees had powers to manage charities, and local pilot officials to license pilots.

But to prevent these many officials from promulgating a chaos of differing and ill-advised rules and to gain that uniformity which was one of the aims of the new central administration, Parliament gave to the central departments the right to sanction

10. 10 & 11 Vict. c. 123.

these regulations. The Secretary of State through mining and factory inspectors confirmed the regulations for collieries and mills, and through prison inspectors and commissioners of lunacy the rules for managing jails and asylums. The Merchant Marine Department checked on the rules of the local marine boards, lighthouses, and pilot authorities, and the Railway Board passed on all bylaws that concerned the treatment of passengers.[11] These powers were negative: they checked abuses, instead of creating new policy; and in the end they proved less effective than many hoped. Rules for the management of prisons, asylums, charities, and mines remained varied and inefficient.

Another power common to most central departments and designed more to check abuses than encourage positive planning was that of giving judgment on matters in dispute. The Poor Law Commission, after 1851, could decide (if the parishes agreed) all disputes between parishes about the cost of union relief. This provided an excellent opportunity for the parishes to avoid the quarrels that once led to costly and litigious court battles. The General Board of Health assured all persons who felt injured by the rates of a local board a fair hearing and a just ruling.[12] The Railway Board could judge on a multiplicity of questions that arose between companies and the public. The Merchant Marine Board mediated between ship-owners and pilot authorities, judged disputed elections to local marine boards, and settled conflicts between seamen and their masters.[13] In all these matters the central departments sat as judicial boards, much as did regular courts of law.

But the line between the judical and administrative was never clear. For example, was the right of the Tithe Commission to arrange for the commutation of tithes judicial or administrative? And what of the right of the Inclosure Commissioners to sanction the inclosure of common land? To the members of both Commissions, and to their assistants who went out into the country-

11. 4 & 6 William IV c. 38, 3 & 4 Vict. c. 97, 7 & 8 Vict. c. 15, 8 & 9 Vict. c. 126, 13 & 14 Vict. c. 93, 13 & 14 Vict. c. 100.
12. 11 & 12 Vict. c. 110, 63.
13. *PP**, *47* (1848), 227 (33). 13 & 14 Vict. c. 93.

side with powers to summon witnesses, make surveys, hold hearings, help select valuers of tithe and property, and arrange commutations and inclosures, such functions appeared administrative.[14] But to the parson angry at the tithe settlement or the farmer disappointed at a new inclosure, the final decision, made by a board far off in London, appeared judicial. It could just as well have been handled by the Queen's Bench. From time out of mind disputes over tithes or inclosures came before the historic courts of law; now an administrative board had the temerity, and the power, to tell the parson and the squire how to settle their affairs.

In like manner the Ecclesiastical Commission and the Masters in Lunacy could sit in judgment on disputes over the property of bishops and lunatics.[15] The central administration was asserting itself. Gradually, and for the most part unnoticed, they were gaining judicial powers as well as legislative powers, thus laying the basis of the modern administrative state, with its characteristic and wholly necessary extension of wide discretionary powers.

The powers accruing to the new central departments were more numerous and varied than effective. The statutes defining them are long, detailed, and comprehensive, but the powers actually granted were almost always carefully limited. Parliament displayed a scrupulous economy in the granting of general powers of compulsion. The number of statutes giving power to the Railway Board, for example, are very great. Hundreds of private acts and some dozen general acts empowered that Board to allow railway companies to change their plans (initially spelled out in a local act) for the radius of curves or the gradients of inclinations, or to make settlements with other companies for junctions, amalgamations, or leasing rights on their lines. The Railway Board could also settle gauge disputes, regulate mail trains, and see that third-class trains were covered, comfortable, and ran faster than twelve miles an hour. The list could be

14. *PP, 28* (1838), 37. 6 & 7 William IV c. 71, 8 & 9 Vict. c. 118. By 4 & 5 Vict. c. 35 the Tithe Commission could also settle copyhold leases, and by 14 & 15 Vict. c. 53 the Tithe and Inclosure Commissions were merged.
15. 6 & 7 William IV c. 77; 16 & 17 Vict. c. 70.

spelled out at great length, but this would not make up for lack of power in crucial matters: the Board could not review and pass on railway legislation, could not inspect established railway lines, could not summon witnesses, could not insist on safe equipment—in fact had nothing whatever to say about railway equipment, schedules, and rates.[16] The railway companies valued the Board as a useful authority that would arbitrate their disagreements or sanction changes in their plans, but they would tolerate no serious regulation by the Board.

Little has been said of the Education Committee of the Privy Council. It alone had no statutory existence and so no statutory powers. A Privy Council Order established it and gave it the right to appoint inspectors. A Parliamentary vote of supply gave it money to grant aid to worthy schools. This power did not seem much, compared to those Boards with extensive statutory powers. An education inspector could not summon witnesses, nor even, as a legal right, inspect a school. Furthermore the Privy Council told them explicitly to leave religious instruction alone and to make no suggestions about improved pedagogical techniques unless asked.[17] Yet despite a lack of specific powers and these counsels of circumspection the Education Committee possessed the most effective power of all, that of the purse. To schools too poor to hire an able teacher or rent a good building money meant everything: accept it and the school thrived; have it denied and bills went unpaid. Through this power the Education Committee in 1847 expanded its control over the schools of England, certifying and paying pupil teachers and school masters, providing more and better books, and improving the quality of instruction. Few schools could reject such aid, even if their autonomy was jeopardized by inspectors.

The power of granting money, so disarming in appearance, was in 1846 extended to the Poor Law Board and in 1854 to the Inspectorate of Prisons under the Home Office. Parliament gave the Poor Law Commissioners £60,000 to distribute to auditors, medical officers, and school teachers in the various unions. It

16. *PP**, *47* (1848), 219–31 (25–36).
17. *PP*, *41* (1839), 255–65; *40* (1840), 400–5 (11–16); *8* (1844), 400–3.

115

gave some £5,000 for the maintenance of reformatories that were certified by the prison inspectors. In later years this power to grant money came to be one of the most efficient and popular means of supervising local authorities. But at first the power was extended very slowly, for though it proved effective as an administrative mechanism, it also proved corrosive of that local independence to which the early Victorians were closely wedded.

One last power was the right to license, and to revoke the licenses, of local institutions. It was the paramount power of the Commissioners of Lunacy, and it was absolute.[18] The revoking of a license simply ended the existence of any private or county asylum. It was a power so sudden and complete in its effect that Parliament seldom granted it to a central department. Like grants in aid to schools, the licensing of institutions was novel and experimental, a clear departure from the more general rule that the powers of inspection, reporting, advising, arbitrating quarrels and sanctioning self-imposed regulations would be sufficient to establish an equitable balance between local and central authorities—a balance that stood as the ideal of early Victorian public administration.

Was this a workable ideal? Were the powers given to the central departments adequate to balance the entrenched interests of the local agencies? Were they sufficient to allow for efficient administration? These are key questions; the answers to which depend on one's standard of administrative efficiency and one's view of government's rightful role in society. To many Tory localists, or to those who believed in an undeviating application of laissez-faire principles, the vast heterogeneous powers of the expanded central administration seemed unprecedented, uncalled for, and un-English. To the more sanguine, the Whig adherents of compromise and the more liberal-minded adherents of laissez-faire principles, they seemed adequate. To the practicing administrators they were entirely inadequate. Frederick Hill, a prison inspector, told the Home Secretary it would be impossible to establish a good system of prison discipline without a new act. The mining inspectors in one voice insisted in 1853 on the

18. 8 & 9 Vict. c. 100, 126.

need of new powers. Both prison and mining inspectors had reason to complain; neither group had the power to enforce its own recommendations. Being the two weakest departments in the government, their complaints are not surprising.

More surprising are the protests of the poor law inspectors. William Day, an assistant commissioner, wrote the commissioners in 1836, "I am daily becoming convinced that neither we nor you have the power to carry the guardians beyond their convictions." The commissioners, ten years later, voiced the same complaint: "We constantly remonstrate with the Board of Guardians [to abandon their old workhouses], but have little success in carrying into effect the only sound remedy." [19] Despite the Commission's large panoply of rights and powers, belligerent guardians could defy its orders, challenge its inspectors, and even defy its writs of mandamus. If they could defy such a Commission, the poor law guardians had even less trouble with the Board of Health. In 1849 they simply neglected the Board's orders for meeting the cholera epidemic. The Board of Health could do nothing to enforce the order. Neither could it enforce its orders upon those local boards of health that it had helped establish. The General Board of Health's powers depended, as did the powers of so many agencies, on persuasion not compulsion.

The early Victorians had two main reasons for denying these agencies coercive powers. In the first place, they were reluctant to interfere with the rights of property, whether mines, railways, or factories; and in the second place, they held tenaciously to their faith in the virtues of local self-government. Almost all acts defining the relations of central and local authorities gave the lion's share of the power to the local authorities. The visiting justices who supervised prisons and insane asylums enjoyed an immediate and direct control over these institutions, and they could easily evade the suggestions of the prison inspectors or the commissioners of lunacy. The board of guardians could do the same, for to them alone belonged the power to judge how, in each individual case, relief should be dispensed, and to them alone belonged the supervision and payment of overseers and work-

19. MH, 32/21, Oct. 16, 1836; *PP**, *36* (1846), 361.

house governors. Local boards of health once established were autonomous. Local self-government remained the ideal of the English; the use of central control was only an unhappy necessity, adopted to prevent serious evils and to gain a modicum of uniformity and efficiency. Hence it was that the English, between the years 1833 and 1854, established those ad hoc departments which had powers useful enough if local authorities cooperated but hardly adequate if they did not. These departments could encourage and stimulate local improvements, but they could not enforce them. Their effectiveness therefore depended on the tactful and intelligent use of the few powers they had. In a well-organized agency this tact and intelligence might be effective. In an ill-organized department they could be wasted. For this reason much of the success of the new central departments in meeting England's social problems depended on the very unromantic and mundane problems of administrative organization.

THE ORGANIZATION

The problems of organization which confronted the new central departments were neither few nor simple. The area of administration was large, staffs were small, internal workings ill-defined, and incorporation into the central government ill-considered and hasty. Each department faced roughly the same questions: how to supervise local authorities scattered from Lands End to Berwick with only a few inspectors, how to plan and carry out uniform and clear policies, and how to coordinate those policies with the conflicting intentions of Ministers, Parliament, and public opinion. The answers found to these problems were a mixture of time-worn customs and innovating experiments, of blunders and happy accidents, of ineptitudes and wise insights. On the whole these answers were awkward and reflected both the rudimentary state of administrative planning among Victorian reformers and the difficulty of working under the surveillance of an economy-minded Parliament, suspicious of all bureaucrats.

In the organizing of systems of inspection, for example, each agency suffered from Parliament's hostility to large and expensive departments. From 1839 to 1844 it allowed the Education Committee only three inspectors. The number was obviously inadequate and the Committee on Education demanded more. By 1848 they had sixteen inspectors—a gratifying increase, but still insufficient, since the number of schools requiring inspection now totaled around 4,000 and the pupils around 800,000. Furthermore, the minutes of 1846 had greatly increased the duties of the inspectors, who now had to test pupil teachers, certify schoolmasters, examine every classroom, check over the finances, inspect normal schools, and write lengthy reports. All this simply could not be done for the 200 and more schools assigned to each inspector. A minute of 1844 had set down 140 schools as the most an inspector could visit. In 1848 the average was over 240. In 1852, with over 20 inspectors, the average had not improved. Inspector of schools Henry Moseley had to leave 103 of his schools unvisited, while his colleague Douglas Tinling failed to visit 194 of his 356 schools. As it was, he traveled 7,069 miles and examined 17,877 children. By 1854 the staff had increased to 24 inspectors and nine assistants, but the increase of schools continued unabated. Inspection remained much as it had been in 1848, when the manager of Kings Somborne school described it as "vagrant and desultory." [20]

The inspectors of other departments had to make even more desultory visits. From 1843 to 1854 a single mine commissioner, Seymour Tremenheere, was deemed sufficient to ensure that no women and children worked in the 2,000 collieries in England and Scotland. The *Mining Journal* doubted if he ever descended into a mine. Six mining inspectors after 1850 had to guarantee the safety of thousands of miners, and two charity inspectors supervised 40,000 charities. One mining inspector estimated that it would take him four years to visit each colliery. The

20. *PP**, *8* (1844), 25; *18* (1848), 471; *37* (1850), 5–7; *40* (1852) 11, 206. Richard Dawes, *Observations on the Working of the Government Scheme of Education*, London, 1849. The *Westminster Review*, *16* (Sept. 1846), 106, compared the parsimony in hiring education inspectors with the parsimony in hiring poor law assistants and predicted the same lamentable fate.

Times estimated that the charity inspectors, visiting one charity each day, would need one hundred years to make their first rounds.[21] Such were the herculean labors an unthinking and economy-minded Parliament expected of its civil servants. There is no doubt that many a child was worked in mines, that many a remote and dangerous recess in a mine never saw the lamp of an inspector, and that corrupt managers of charity funds had great license. They were all beneficiaries of Parliament's keen wish for economy.

Other departments, it seems at first sight, enjoyed a more respectable ratio of inspectors to local authorities. In 1854 the Poor Law Board had twelve inspectors for some 600 unions. The six commissioners of lunacy supervised, in 1848, 176 county and private asylums. The three prison inspectors in England in 1853 visited 275 prisons. These tasks at least seem possible, when compared to those of the education and mining inspectors or to the duties of the four chief factory inspectors who, with fourteen assistants, watched over, in 1839, 4,654 factories.[22]

But the job of examining a poor law union, a lunatic asylum, or a prison entailed far more detailed investigation and the giving of much more counsel than did the enforcement of a child labor law or the certifying of a class room, and the number of inspectors assigned to such work never proved sufficient. The famous Andover Union workhouse scandal in 1846 reflected this want of careful inspection. For several years the inmates of the workhouse suffered from a very sparse diet and were put to the repulsive task of crushing bone. The cruelty practiced on prisoners in the prisons of Birmingham and Leicester continued for many years because of this same want of inspection. There simply were not enough inspectors, and Parliament continued its persistent desire to cut expenditures. Sir Robert Peel in 1842, in response to the poor law commissioners' demand for more than the then nine assistant commissioners, answered that "it is material to the satisfactory working of your own measure to keep the

21. *Mining Journal*, Feb. 2, 1850. *Times*, Oct. 26, 1835. HO, 45/4921.
22. MH, 32/47, April 1853 memo. HO, 12/7889. *PP**, 27 (1847), 19 (11); *PP*, 52 (1853), 116 (3); 26 (1854). 3.

public and Parliament with us on the score of economy." Sir James Graham, who in 1842 spoke loudly of the need of assistant commissioners—"they are the eyes and hands of the Commission" —and Sir George Lewis, who in 1842 ruled the Commission, timidly followed Peel's cautious advice and carried on with nine assistant commissioners.[23] They disregarded Edwin Chadwick's warning that fifty unions were too many for one assistant commissioner, and they ignored the repeated memos of the previous commissioners that the number of assistants ought not to be reduced.[24]

In 1837, to perform the heavy work of forming unions, the Commission employed twenty-one assistants. From 1842 to 1846 there were only nine, each one vainly visiting seventy-one unions, spending half their time in post chaises going from one to the other. The were able to return to a union only after a year or more had elapsed, and so were unable to keep the guardian on his toes and ensure that the workhouses were clean and neat. Henry Parker could not keep up this pace. Faced with seventy-nine unions and 1,653 parishes, he could not keep the guardians at Andover from starving the inmates into gnawing (so it was reported) at the very bones they were to crush.[25] The *Times,* chief enemy of the New Poor Law, exploited this scandal for all it was worth. Much was said in the press and in Parliament against the harsh features of the New Poor Law and the commissioners who administered it, but few newspapers saw (or at least published) that the real error was to allow the guardians their own way, and that this negligence was due to insufficient inspections. The *Times,* which in 1838 had called assistant commissioners a waste of money, turned a blind eye. The scandal rebounded to the disfavor of the bureaucrats of Somerset House, bureaucrats who, many said, formed a sad contrast to the efficiency of private enterprise. But few realized, as the *West-*

23. British Museum (BM), Add. MS, 40,413, Peel to Nicholls, Feb. 3, 1842. *PP, 27* (1846), 561 (519), 557 (515), 681 (639).

24. Chadwick Papers, Chadwick to Russell, Feb. 7, 1841. MH, 1/2, April 27, 1835; 1/18, April 5, 1839, HO, 73/56, July 31, 1840.

25. *PP, 45* (1843), 95. MH, 32/40, Sept. 30, 1844; 32/7, Feb. 19, 1844. *PP*, 28* (1846), 185, 502-3, 519, 681.

minster Review pointed out in 1841, that there were dozens of commercial houses in London that hired more traveling agents than the Poor Law Commission did assistant commissioners.[26]

The fate of John Perry, the prison inspector for South and West England was like that of Henry Parker: the government assigned him far too many institutions for reasonable supervision. Sir George Grey, pursuing economy with the same diligence as Peel, reduced the number of prison inspectors in England in 1849 from four to three. Perry was required to visit 103 prisons in twenty-eight counties, and they included Leicester and Birmingham, where local magistrates tolerated gross abuses. Not until the newspapers exposed the whippings and punitive diets did these abuses come to Perry's notice.[27] Like Parker he was too overworked.

The Andover exposures of 1846 and the disgraceful conditions at Leicester and Birmingham fell under the bright glare of publicity. Many other abuses did not. Many a lunatic pauper suffered in his workhouse because the six commissioners of lunacy could not visit his dreary quarters: It was all they could do to visit the 176 hospitals under their surveillance, let alone the lunatics in 750 workhouses and twenty prisons. From August 1845 to August 1846 they visited only 340 workhouses.[28] The authorities of the rest were free to treat the lunatics as they saw fit, which was miserable indeed.

The General Board of Health was also overwhelmed with work. It had too few engineering inspectors to investigate the many towns applying for help in 1848, and far too few medical inspectors to combat cholera in 1849 and 1854. The six superintending inspectors simply could not handle the 246 applications for help from unsanitary towns. Each examination took over a week, with a myriad of culverts and cesspools to examine, topographical surveys for drainage to make, boundaries to determine, water possibilities to investigate, aggrieved parties to meet,

26. *Times,* May 14, 1838, March 6, 1846. *Westminster Review, 36* (July 1841), 48.

27. HO, 12/7889; 45/ os 2581. *Birmingham Mercury,* May 21, 1853.

28. PP*, *36* (1847), 19 (11), 244 (236), 265 (257). Lewis, *Chadwick,* p. 340. Finer, *Chadwick,* p. 346.

hearings to be held, and elaborate reports to write. The two medical inspectors faced even more formidable tasks in combating the cholera epidemic, and despite the Board's repeated memoranda to the Treasury they remained woefully undermanned.[29]

The Treasury, watch dog of spending, was timid about giving grants to Boards as unpopular as the Poor Law Commission and the Board of Health. Parliament scrutinized the vote of supply of these agencies more closely than those for the Army and Navy or the Colonial, Land, and Emigration Board. The latter board had the luxury of twelve officers, each in a major port. These officers supervised matters infinitely less extensive than the transformation of English poor relief.[30] Such a luxury was exceptional. The paramount rule was economy, and the principal defect in the organization of the new central departments remained the fact that too few inspectors were employed for the inspection of too many local authorities.

The second defect was the want of efficient planning in the London offices. The early Victorians had not been schooled in the rationale of administrative planning; they either did things in the old way or improvised. The Home Office was a case in point. Its office in Whitehall had not changed much from the indolent days of the eighteenth century, with the single exception that much work was now pressed into its busy office. They had the same permanent undersecretary, the same Parliamentary secretary, and the same clerks chosen more for reasons of political favor than merit. By 1850 that office was overburdened. In addition to its extensive and busy correspondence with magistrates, the governor of the Channel Islands, and the Irish Lord Lieutenant, it had to supervise the factory, mining, and prison inspectors. Easygoing and negligent, it allowed each inspector to become king of his own district.

The indolent Lord Melbourne had set the pattern in 1835 by rejecting the idea of an Inspector General of Prisons because he could not abide the prison philosophy of the man most qualified

29. Ibid., 345. MH, 4/6, Sept. 3, 1852; 5/2, Sept. 18, 1849; 5/10, Sept. 1, 1854. *Times,* Aug. 27, 1853.
30. Hitchins, *Colonial, Land and Emigration Commission,* pp. 159–70.

for the job, William Crawford. Crawford was the protagonist of separate confinement and an inspector of prisons. Melbourne neither had the courage to dismiss Crawford nor the desire to allow him to extend separate confinement to all the prisons of England; so he appointed four equal and autonomous inspectors, each with his own favorite policies. Sir James Graham in 1844 held a meeting to end this diversity and draw up a set of uniform rules. It was their first meeting, it was marked by disagreement, and it was their last for quite some time. Thereafter the old rule of diversity held sway.[31] Captain Williams believed in enforced silence, Frederick Hill in industrial training, and William Crawford in separate confinement. John Perry, in contrast to the above three, felt it was not the job of the prison inspector to push any single policy.[32] Such was the gentle anarchy of the prison inspectorate under the negligent reign of a busy Home Secretary.

The mining inspectors enjoyed a similar reign of freedom in their districts. Each managed his own fief. Until 1854 they never met together, and the Home Secretary, being no authority on steam jet ventilation or mine buttressing, gave them no central guidance. Each went his own way, unencumbered by an inspector general and not bothered by assistants. Herbert Mackworth wrote caustically that until there was some coordination the present system didn't deserve the name of inspection. His colleagues did not agree. Deeming the job of inspection too sensitive and skilled for assistants and believing the Home Secretary quite able to coordinate their activities, they objected to a single inspector general with numerous assistants. They had a jealous regard for their own freedom and power and would protect both even if it meant uncoordinated policies and a want of uniformity in their execution.[33]

Compared to the prison and mining inspectorates the factory inspectorate, after 1844, appeared a model of order and efficiency.

31. HO, 12/4130; 45/541. *PP*, 25 (1843), 1–14.
32. *PP, 31* (1838), 1; *30* (1838), 1–14. HO, 12/1042, 8546.
33. HO, 45/5377, 4105. There was an Inspector General of convict prisons, Sir Joshua Jebb. His functions were mainly to supervise the construction of prisons. He had no power over the inspectors: HO, 45/541.

Organization

They met half yearly, they wrote joint reports, they consulted the Home Secretary together, and they possessed a central office with a secretary and common records. Yet even the factory inspectors enjoyed an autonomy that would have surprised a continental theorist. The Whig Horner, but no other inspectors, urged millowners to employ children half-time to allow for more schooling, while the Tory Saunders, again with no other inspectors agreeing, wanted children below nine to work in mills. In 1846 Horner differed with the Home Secretary, George Grey, on whether the use of "relays" to work children after 6 o'clock was legal. Horner said it was illegal and prosecuted all who use relays in that manner. Grey was too timid to make a pronouncement. He was, moreover, too busy to inquire into all the details,[34] and turned over such business to the permanent undersecretary, who prepared agendas, answered the ordinary requests for information, and abstracted in brief marginalia the essence of all important letters.

Neither the permanent undersecretary nor the Parliamentary secretary could determine mining and prison policy or dismiss and appoint burial inspectors; nor could they reshape prison districts, call the mining inspectors to joint meetings, or meet delegations of millowners. All these matters belonged to a Home Secretary burdened with Irish troubles and caught in the vortex of Parliamentary debates and party politics. The *Westminster Review* in 1837 considered such a busy officer "utterly incapable" of supervising the Factory Act. An experience of Lord Palmerston in 1854 illustrated the confusion of that office. Only recently appointed its Secretary, he entered the Commons to defend Shaftesbury's chimney-sweep bill. To his surprise and embarrassment he found that the Home Office's Parliamentary secretary was violently attacking the measure, which, as Home Secretary, Palmerston intended to defend. Palmerston was an energetic administrator and a hard worker, yet in 1853 he wrote from the

---

34. Hansard, *74* (1844), 337. *PP*, 27 (1844), 584 (19). Chadwick Papers, memo. on central administration (in which he takes a dim view of the efficiency of the factory inspectorate). HO, 45/1851. *PP*, *31* (1837), 60 (7), 53 (31). *Westminster Review, 26* (Oct. 1837), 105.

Home Office, "I despair of ever reading these [prison] reports."
Only by diligent efforts did Lord Palmerston bring some order
to an office marked by a confusion of responsibility, insufficient
staff, and inadequate coordination.[35] But not many Palmerstons
appeared at the Home Office in these years.

Five of the sixteen new departments were subdepartments of
the Home Office and looked for their efficient direction to its
single executive. Most of the other new departments, on the other
hand, were semi-independent boards with plural executives. The
use of boards was traditional and universal in English government,
both local and central. Magistrates in Quarter Sessions and
parishioners in vestry meetings had long met as boards. The
greatest of the central departments, the Treasury, was a board,
which in turn supervised the boards of Customs, Excise, and
Stamps, all of them with more than three commissioners,
most of whom were chosen for reasons of patronage. The English
trusted boards but distrusted single executives, who could threaten
arbitrary rule. A board meant deliberations, discussion, and
mutual checks. Faith in boards fitted the pluralistic and corporate
sense of public administration, a system in which mutual checks
and open proceedings would efficaciously prevent autocratic
administration. It also multiplied the high offices to be dispensed to friends. Boards might not ensure quick and efficient
decisions, but they promised both considerable patronage and
mature deliberations.

The use of boards to administer the New Poor Law, promote
sanitary improvement, regulate railways, supervise lunatic asylums,
and manage ecclesiastical property met with mixed success.
Much depended on the commissioners in charge and the efficiency
of their secretaries. The Poor Law Commission in the thirties
promised to be a model board. The many difficulties raised by a
single board processing thousands of letters, issuing hundreds of
orders, and making detailed decisions rapidly were solved by
means of fixed agendas, explanatory memos, and standard orders,
all carefully prepared by the diligent secretary and his assistants.

35. *Westminster Review*, 26 (Oct. 1837), 113. Hodder, *Shaftesbury*, 2, 479.
HO, 12/7201.

The supervision of the assistant commissioners was to be facilitated by weekly diaries, and magistrates and guardians were to be kept informed by official circulars. Edwin Chadwick had planned the whole scheme and promised to make it work with dispatch.[36] In every board, as indeed in every office, the secretary's position was pivotal. Lord Palmerston, in discussing the India Control Bill of 1854, spoke at length on their importance:

> It was impossible to overrate the advantage to the public service of having in each department of the government a permanent secretary, not belonging to any political party, not swayed by passion or feeling . . . but a man who, being the depository of the lore and knowledge belonging to the particular department was able . . . to give the newcomer into that office that information as to past events, as to the principles regulating the department, as to the knowledge of individuals, and as to the details of transactions, without which it was impossible for any man, let him be ever so able and ever so expert, to perform his duties with satisfaction to himself and advantage to the public . . .[37]

James Kay was such a man at the Education office, and James Stephen at the Colonial Office. Edwin Chadwick hoped to fulfill that position at the Poor Law Commission. But his chief employer, the proud baronet Sir Thomas Franklin Lewis, had no such intention. He viewed Chadwick's erudition, zeal, and hard efficiency with jealousy, and was discomforted by his very presence. In part to evade Chadwick's zeal and in part from their own notions of efficient administration, the commissioners took to answering correspondence and making decisions in their separate offices. The scheme was not lacking in merit, and three efficient commissioners, meeting occasionally, even if only for tea, could have made it work passably well.[38] But two of the three original

36. Chadwick Papers, Chadwick to Grey, 1846, on the transactions of the poor law commissioners; Chadwick to Coode, June 19, 1847; Chadwick to Normanby, May 12, 1841.

37. Hansard, *129* (1853), 825.

38. *PP, 49* (1847), 1–8. Finer, *Chadwick,* pp. 243–93, gives a brilliant description of the personality clash between Lewis and Chadwick.

commissioners, Franklin Lewis and John Lefevre were anything but paragons of efficiency and industry, nor were their successors, George Cornewall Lewis and Sir Edmund Head, any better. Affairs became worse, correspondence fell into arrears, local boards grew impatient, two secretaries resigned, and the assistant commissioners, consulted much less frequently, grew disgruntled. The commissioners worked either alone or in pairs, a procedure at variance with the statute and not only violently attacked by Chadwick but successfully contested by the Rochdale Union. The Andover scandal and the unjust firing of Parker and Day by personal letter and not by board decision revealed the commissioners' confused management.[39]

The debacle of the Poor Law Commission only furthered the mounting criticism of administration by boards. Even the ancient boards were under attack. A report of 1835 on the three-man Excise Board revealed marked inefficiencies, and in 1843 serious frauds in the Customs exposed the negligence of its thirteen commissioners and evoked sharp criticism in the Commons on the inefficiencies of boards. By 1847 Joseph Hume, one of the most outspoken of the Radicals, in contemplating the Poor Law Board, admitted that "he began to have doubts indeed of all boards." At the same time the three-man Commission of Woods and Forests fell into such a state of mismanagement that further criticism was made of the board system. More and more critics came to agree with the *Westminster Review,* that "administration by boards deprives the public of the security of personal responsibility." Even the Tory Sir James Graham confided privately to Peel in 1845 that he distrusted boards because he found their division of responsibility quite objectionable.[40]

Board management still had its defenders. Officialdom, for

39. Chadwick Papers: memo to Lord Spencer, April 25, 1838, Tufnell to Chadwick, May 28, 1847; Chadwick to Roebuck, March 24, 1845; 1846 memo. to Grey. Chadwick even had a Professor Möhts of Prussia give his views on the procedures of the poor law commissioners—procedures Möhts found "impossible on the continent": Möhts to Chadwick, July 30, 1847.

40. *PP, 30* (1837), 141–339 (5–200); *PP, 29* (1843), 158–73 (1–16). Hansard, *71* (1843), 394, 398–99; *92* (1847), 349. Sir James Graham Papers (Netherby, Cumberland), Graham to Peel, Dec. 28, 1845.

one, held to old ways. The Treasury had a high opinion of boards. Its secretary, Charles Wood, told a Parliamentary committee that board decisions are "sounder and fairer than those of individuals." The Customs continued to be managed by thirteen commissioners, even though the *Times* in 1854 again denounced its inefficiencies. Even Edwin Chadwick found some merit in boards, though at heart and as a good Benthamite he considered boards screens for evading responsibility, and suggested so to his friend Slaney in 1848 when he wrote that "unless there can be well defined division of labor, boards are most difficult and dangerous as instruments for executive work." But in his feud with the poor-law commissioners he sharply criticized them for abandoning board procedures and spoke glowingly of the value of such deliberations. At a board, he wrote the Home Secretary, minutes were carefully kept; at a board there was open discussion, publicity, and no secrecy; at a board arbitrary and capricious actions were impossible. He even insisted that "board procedure would have prevented Andover." [41] As arguments of a neglected secretary of a board, they had an *ex parte* tone.

Superficially the proceedings of the General Board of Health seemed to prove the truth of Chadwick's arguments. The board meetings were always conducted properly and efficiently, as was all the business of the small office in Gwydyr House. The superintending inspectors sent in weekly diaries, attended the board, and had all their policies and plans checked by a chief inspector. But that any merit for this efficiency ought to redound to the board is doubtful. The real ruler of the office was Edwin Chadwick, a fact he admitted in a private memo: "Notwithstanding its collective style, the Board of Health consists virtually in a single individual." [42]

In the same manner the Railway Board until 1845 was subordinate to a single executive, the Board of Trade's president,

41. *PP, 18* (1848), 363–65. Chadwick Papers, Chadwick to Slaney, May 16, 1848, Chadwick to Grey, 1846 memo. on poor law commissioners, and in 1845 a memo. on board management versus individual. In both memos. he argues for the merits of boards.

42. Ibid., Chadwick's memo. of 1854 on the *Morning Chronicle's* attack on the Board of Health.

just as the Merchant Marine Department after 1850 obeyed the same officer. Many boards had in reality a single chief and not a plural executive. The most powerful board in the central administration, the Treasury Board, according to the candid opinion of its secretary, Charles Trevelyan (who had only disdain for board management), was under the effective control of the Chancellor of the Exchequer.[43] The Poor Law Board after 1846 was a board only in name; its management was entirely in the hands of its president.

In general the boards with the fewest executives worked the best. The three tithe commissioners and the six lunacy commissioners managed their departments with creditable efficiency, while the lavishly staffed Ecclesiastical Commission managed its affairs with discreditable negligence, and the thirteen metropolitan commissioners of sewers after 1849 fell into disreputable squabbles between those for and those against Edwin Chadwick. Forty-four men, honorary and unpaid, sat on the Ecclesiastical Commission, a strange assortment of ex officio, lay, and ecclesiastical members. The two archbishops, the five ministers from the government, all the bishops, three deans, and six judges sat as unpaid but interested parties. There were eight permanent commissioners. Few attended the meetings, no one kept any records of their decisions, business fell into confusion and the bishops, unless their dioceses were threatened, into somnolent indifference. Their paid secretary felt free to invest ecclesiastical funds in railway stocks, which he did to the cost of all. After a series of failures, he absconded in 1849 to the Continent, leaving the pious bishops outraged and the delighted critics of ecclesiastical administration demanding reform.

To placate them, John Russell proposed abolishing the board. Large boards were falling from favor, and especially unpaid honorary commissioners—"dilettantes" said the *Daily News* in 1850, "who follow their own whims" and whose substitution for paid officials was "tantamount to the substitution of the less efficient for the more efficient." The Ecclesiastical Commission was an obvious absurdity. But the early Victorians, though

43. *PP, 18* (1848), 143, 356.

suspicious of unpaid commissioners, clung firmly to a belief in boards, if only to allow a compromise of interests or a dual administration. To ensure a fair administration, representative of both State and Church, Sir George Grey proposed a board of three ecclesiastical commissioners, two of the men paid and one unpaid. The Archbishop of Canterbury could appoint one of the paid commissioners. Grey felt such a board would protect the interests of both parties.

A few agencies enjoyed a single executive, though usually under the disguise of a board or committee. James Kay was a mere secretary to the Committee on Education of the Privy Council who could not even hire his own clerks, and his salary and status were far inferior to the nature of his work and his singular abilities. Yet by the grace of an enlightened President of the Council, he was granted full power over his committee and achieved an internal organization whose efficiency spoke well of the Victorian's growing sense of administrative planning.[44]

The cost of this efficiency was the overworking of Kay himself. He answered a voluminous correspondence, interviewed numerous deputations, conferred with schools trustees, bargained with religious societies—and all this as a mere assistant secretary, underpaid and unheralded. Yet despite these handicaps Kay made the education office one of the finest of the new central departments.[45] It was indeed through men like Kay, Chadwick, and Rowland Hill that a new sense of administrative planning brought new standards of efficiency. By experimenting with official circulars, weekly diaries for inspectors, and carefully recorded minutes, the new departments were improving their internal organization; and by a similar process of trial and error they slowly learned of the need to coordinate their respective agencies more effectively into an integrated central administration.

Traditionally, all administrative departments of Her Majesty's

44. 3 & 4 Vict. c. 113. Hansard, *118* (1850), 351–65, 627; *110* (1850), 938–43. *PP, 7* (1848), iii–xvii, 525–34. *Daily News*, May 11, 1848.

45. Frank Smith, *Life of Sir James Kay Shuttleworth* (London, 1923), pp. 213–16.

Powers and Organization

Government came under the surveillance of a responsible minister, and according to constitutional convention it was the job of the Cabinet and Prime Minister to coordinate their policies. It was a sound theory but one not always followed in practice, or followed only as an afterthought and in hasty and contrived fashion. The key minister for coordinating the new departments of central control was the Home Secretary. Directly under him came the factory, prison, mining, burial, and anatomy inspectors, while indirectly he watched over the commissioners of lunacy, the Poor Law Commission (until 1846), the Tithe and Copyhold Commission, the General Board of Health, the Charity Commission, and a host of minor commissions of inquiry, including in 1854 the important Oxford University Commission. It was an arduous job simply to supervise these agencies; but taken in conjunction with his other duties, his management of convict prisons, his control over the Channel Islands, his concern in Irish affairs, his superintendence of the metropolitan police, and his communications with the country's magistrates, such a task of coordination proved to be beyond the capacities of any ordinary Home Secretary. In the morning he might have to write magistrates concerning bathing privileges on a beach or permission for a performer to walk a rope between two balloons high over Battersea. In the late afternoon he would have to debate the great political questions of the day. When could he meet with the prison inspectors or plan factory policy? "I am" said Graham in 1845, "on duty about 14 hours every day in the House of Commons, the labor of which is rapidly becoming too great for human endurance." Edwin Chadwick in 1841 and again in 1855 protested against the pratcice of burdening a busy secretary, more sensitive to political than administrative pressures, with the task of supervising innumerable agencies. In 1847 Lord John Russell, in recommending that the New Poor Law Board be separated from the Home Office, repeated in essence Chadwick's complaint.[46] Yet Parliament went on

46. Graham Papers, Graham to Lord Anson, July 13, 1845. Chadwick Papers, 1841 memo. on central administration and 1855 memo. on accountability. Hansard, 92 (1847), 355–56.

granting the Home Secretary loose and ill-defined jurisdiction over new departments, especially over those semi-independent boards it wished to create as nonpolitical bodies but over which it wished to retain some control. The result was a structure full of ambiguities and uncertainties; no one knew exactly where the center of administrative responsibility lay.

The Victorians' experiments in semi-independent, nonpolitical boards reflected their fear that administrative decision would be made the handmaid of party bias or be caught in the maelstrom of factional politics. The Poor Law Commission was the classic and tragic example of such an attempt. Nassau Senior had persuaded Lord Althorp to give the Poor Law Commission a real measure of autonomy so that it might escape the influences of party politics. Its three commissioners were to be permanent and nonpolitical, free from Parliament's volatile opinions. In their offices at Somerset House they were to remain aloof from the criticism that thundered from St. Stephens. Only one avenue of communication was to remain open between the two, and that was to run through the already crowded mazes of the Home Office. Yet no one quite knew for certain whether the Home Secretary was or was not responsible for the Poor Law Commission. The *Times,* furious as always at the New Poor Law, was certain by 1845 that the Home Secretary's responsibility for the commissioners was a mere "juggle." Sir James Graham, the Secretary in 1845, shared this feeling. To Lord de Grey he wrote in the same year, "I possess influence but no power. All the acts of the Commission are quite independent of the executive government. They appoint the assistants . . . there is no appeal from their decisions, the sole power in the hands of the executive is power of removing all, or any one of the three . . . which is applicable only in cases of flagrant misconduct."

The Board thus enjoyed—in theory and in the view of the *Times* and Graham—relative immunity from party politics. In actuality it suffered more from political pressures, from the *Times'* intimidating editorials, and from Graham's own influence than many of the other agencies. Its commissioners yielded to the angry cries of MP's and newspaper editors, and sometimes they yielded against the advice of their own assistants.[47] The New Poor Law was a political issue, and the commissioners could not escape the intensity of feeling, no matter how great their theoretical independence. The final breakdown of the Commission did much to dispel the chimera of an agency acting free of political influence. In 1846 Parliament insisted that the president of the new Board be a member of Parliament and answerable to it. The new Board, managed by frankly political appointees, was, according to one of the former commissioners, an entire success.

The belief that boards should be free of political influence did not die with the demise of the Poor Law Commission. Suspicion of political appointees ran deep. In 1846 Charles Buller, a radical, praised the Tithe Commission as a "body free from objections on the score of political or party bias . . . one not responsible on a change of government." The *Leeds Mercury* expressed alarm at "a system which changes the government Board of Education with every change of administration," and decried Lord Lonsdale's arrival at the Privy Council, "a man well known on the turf but never before heard of in any connexion with education." [48] Only two years after the change in the Poor Law Commission, Parliament unwittingly established another semi-independent department, the General Board of Health. At first the Commissioner of Woods and Forests and Lord Ashley sat at the Board, thereby furnishing a direct link with the Commons. But with Lord Ashley's elevation to the Lords in 1851 and the persistent absence of the busy Commissioner of Woods and Forests, the Board became, as Palmerston said in 1854, "to all intents and purposes an independent body of the state." [49]

The results show how hasty and confused was the construction of the Victorian administrative state. The General Board of Health did not, in the first place, control all sanitary matters; The Privy Council still controlled matters of quarantine. The Board had a confused relation with the Metropolitan Commission

47. Graham Papers, Graham to Lord de Grey, Dec. 12, 1843. Bentham Papers, Box 154, 607, Tufnell to Chadwick, 1845. *Times*, Sept. 7, 1844.
48. Hansard, *82* (1845), 33–34. *Leeds Mercury*, Jan. 17, 1853.
49. Hansard, *135* (1854), 973.

of Sewers, which Chadwick tried, to his own injury, to control. From 1850 to 1851 the General Board of Health was in charge of burials in London, but could do nothing before the obstructive policies of the Treasury. Parliament therefore gave the control over the cemeteries to the Home Office. The Board made extensive studies of London's water supply, but Parliament gave control of this matter to the Board of Trade. The Board of Health was in charge of preventing cholera epidemics, but it could not take action without a Privy Council order and unless the Treasury approved the employment of medical inspectors. If these were granted, the Board had then to work through the Poor Law Commission. Its own chief commissioner ran the Office of Woods and Forests, refused to attend meetings, and attacked the Board in Parliament.

The final mistake was to place the supervision of this chaos of conflicting responsibilities and functions in the Home Secretary, who was already engulfed in other duties. Lord Palmerston, as Home Secretary, fought the Board's battles against the Treasury and defended the Board in Parliament, but he confessed that he was powerless before the Treasury's control of the purse. All, in short, was confusion.[50] The lines of responsibility were obscure and ambiguous and there was little coordination of policy.

This confusion was not entirely due to the administrative structure. There was a rough scheme defining the lines of responsibility. The Home Office supervised the semi-independent boards and could plead their cause in the Cabinet. The Privy Council proved successful in managing the Committee in Education, and the Board of Trade managed very ably the Railway Board and the Merchant Marine Department. There existed considerable central superintendence over most departments. The Law Office passed on bills drawn up by the central departments and gave opinions on legal questions; the Commission of Audit checked the accounts of all departments; and the powerful Treasury, by its check on all expenditure, dominated the entire structure.

50. Chadwick Papers, Chadwick's memo. on Lord Seymour, 1854, and vindicatory memo., 1854. HO, 45/4485. Lewis, *Chadwick*, pp. 211 ff.

Powers and Organization

Contrived though it was, the administrative state was not therefore without some order and efficiency. If there were no great conflicts, no great negligence, and no incompetent ministers, it could work well. But its lines of responsibility were not clear enough for the strains of jealousies, conflict, and incompetence. Had Lord Morpeth remained Commissioner of Woods and Forests and Lord Ashley remained in Commons, the history of the General Board of Health might have been one of harmony and efficiency, but with Lord Seymour as Commissioner of Woods and Forests and Charles Wood, an opponent of the Board's burial scheme, in the Treasury, the necessary cooperation was not forthcoming. The paralysis that resulted was another reflection of the defects of ad hoc and timid legislation.

The Englishman's flair for improvising and compromising allowed for a considerable expansion of central administration in a period hostile to it, but it did not result in the best-organized administration. Despite some genuine progress in administrative techniques in particular offices, there remained in 1854 many serious flaws. The new agencies lacked adequate powers and staff and often suffered from inefficient internal organization or ill-defined relations with the Cabinet and Parliament. There were occasions, then, when policies were uncoordinated and administration was slipshod. In the society of the 1830's and 1840's this too often meant badly managed prisons, overworked children, dangerous mine explosions, poor schooling, unhealthy towns and miserable insane asylums. Averse to a powerful bureaucracy and disinclined toward regimented planning, the Victorians put their faith not in statutory powers and strict regulations but in men. This meant that in the administrative state personality and intelligence were all-important. Only tactful, vigorous, and artful inspectors and shrewd and able commissioners could make these agencies effective and so make Victorian England a well-governed society, increasingly enlightened, civilized, and humane. The achievement of this goal depended ultimately on the quality of men who served in Her Majesty's government.

5.

HER MAJESTY'S PUBLIC SERVANTS

AT THE BEGINNING of the nineteenth century the aristocracy and its friends held the governing positions in England's public administration; by the end of the century those positions had fallen into the hands of the middle class. In local government stipendiary magistrates and elected county and town councils replaced the Lord Lieutenant and the appointed and unpaid magistrate; in the central administration career men scoring high on civil service examinations replaced the unpaid honorary commissioners and the recipients of patronage. Noble lords may have continued to sit in the cabinet in the nineteenth century, but their friends ceased to dominate the lesser boards. They were forced to give way to the expert.

The period from 1833 to 1854, with its expansion of new central departments and its reforming administration, forms a crucial part of this century-long change, a time when the sons of earls rubbed shoulders with the sons of barristers, when the great landed gentry cooperated with self-made bureaucrats in the administration of education grants and prisons. The Lansdownes, Russells, and Melbournes worked at Whitehall and Somerset House with the Chadwicks, Horners, and Kay Shuttleworths; and staffing the inspectorates, doing the immediate task of supervision, were men from all sectors of the governing classes, a few even drawn from those lower classes once far removed from the pale of government. Men of various classes had of course long associated together in government departments, a few of the ablest rising to positions of power, but such association and mobility was largely vouchsafed by the grace of the great landed families. In 1833 these families, above all those who held peerages, occupied the chief offices of state.

MINISTERS AND COMMISSIONERS

Between 1833 and 1854 King William IV and Queen Victoria invested with office six First Lords of the Treasury, ten Home Secretaries, six presidents of the Privy Council, and nine presidents of the Board of Trade. These were the men charged with the responsibility of directing the domestic affairs of the nation and grappling with the pressing social problems of the industrial revolution. They were men of wealth and titles. Five of the Prime Ministers, six of the Home Secretaries, and all six of the presidents of the Privy Council came from the peerage; most of the others were members of the finest country families or the most respected mercantile families.[1] The Reform Bill notwithstanding, the aristocracy occupied the top administrative positions and gave to England a rule of patricians.

That rule was in general conscientious, honorable, and enlightened—the virtues in short of the eighteenth-century grandee, or as some of them fancied, of Roman senators. To these virtues were added a love of industry and efficiency, qualities born of the nineteenth century.

They also had their faults. They were timid and lacked imagination in meeting the irksome, bothersome challenges of an industrial society. They faltered before problems of jerry-built slums and crowded prisons, bad sanitation, and widespread lack of education. They preferred to evade and postpone any real so-

1. The five Prime Ministers were Lord Grey, Lord Melbourne, Lord Russell, Lord Derby, and Lord Aberdeen; the six Home Secretaries were Lord Melbourne, Lord Russell, Viscount Duncannon, the Duke of Wellington, Lord Palmerston, and Lord Normanby; the Privy Council Presidents were Lords Lansdowne, Wharncliffe, Lonsdale, Granville, Rosslyn, Buccleuch, and Queensberry.

lutions rather than depart from old ways, disturb vested interests, or raise taxes. They were not, of course, a homogeneous lot. There was very little in common between Lord Melbourne, Sir Robert Peel, and Lord John Russell, the three Prime Ministers from 1834 to 1852. Melbourne was grandly eccentric. "He is certainly a queer fellow," wrote the astonished Charles Greville in 1834, "to be Prime Minister." He was charming, indolent, and bookish, a man who loved wit and pleasure and could accept no dogmatic truth. He thought that Benthamites were fools and that "the whole duty of government is to prevent crime and to preserve contract." [2] Under his direction the government became merely a collection of self-acting departments.

He was not, however, as many charged, an inefficient administrator. When he put his hand to it, as he did at the Home Office in 1834, he could astonish his contemporaries by his dispatch and assiduousness. It was after all part of the accomplishments of men of the grand manner, whether in Quarter Sessions or Whitehall, that they could manage governmental matters. But as Prime Minister he lacked any fixed convictions or any deep interests. While he educated the Queen, Palmerston ruled at the Foreign Office, Lord John Russell at the Home Office, and Lansdowne at the Privy Council. That singular freedom which the loose organization of England's central administration gave to poor-law commissioners and prison inspectors was thus reinforced by Melbourne's lax rule. Each department in pleasant autonomy went its own way.

Sir Robert Peel ended this laxness. In Peel the Victorian virtues of industry, orderliness, and efficiency found full expression. Though not of the landed class, he attended Harrow and Oxford and acquired some of their manners and beliefs. By his staunch Toryism and superior capacity he assumed the leadership of their party. He came to the Home Office in 1822 and remained, except for part of 1827, until 1830. He brought to the Office the energy of his Lancashire manufacturing background and a paternalism tempered by a firm belief in laissez

2. Greville, *Memoirs*, *3*, 59; David Cecil, *Lord M* (London, 1954), p. 124; Brougham, *Memoirs*, *3*, 380.

faire. He established the Metropolitan Police, made reforms in criminal law, and won a reputation as a first-rate administrator. It was, then, with high expectations that he became Prime Minister in 1841.

His industry was at once apparent. He corresponded frequently with the heads of each department and kept a watchful eye on all matters. But the results were, paradoxically, less happy than those resulting from Melbourne's genial indifference. Under Peel's rule the administration of the poor law became indecisive, the railway policy a muddle, and the Ecclesiastical Commission a confusion. The railway panic of 1845, the Andover scandal of 1846, and the growing ineptness of the Ecclesiastical Commission revealed a far from sure hand at Number 10 Downing Street. Nor was there any sign of the boldness of the Tamworth Manifesto in the continued and unreconciled differences among prison inspectors, the illegal working of women in mines, and the failure to expand public education.

Peel, of course, was not entirely responsible for these failings. Preoccupied with the issues of the day—the distress of 1842, the discontent in Ireland, and the struggle to abolish the corn laws —he had to delegate much to mediocre administrators, not all (as for example, G. C. Lewis) of his own choosing. But it was Peel who asked the Poor Law Commission to employ nine instead of twelve assistants. It was Peel who told the Commons that self-interest and competition should regulate railway construction. It was Peel's passion for economy that helps explain why so little was done to expand the Committee in Council on Education and why the Home Office employed only one mining inspector to see that some 2,000 collieries employed no women. It was Peel's government that delayed sanitary reform by unneeded and redundant in-vestigations.[3] His administration shows the difficulties and trag-edies of an able but overcautious mind in a period of rapid social change. He displayed great capacity for management and

3. BM, Add. MS 40,446, Sept. 22, 1841, Peel to Graham. In 1841 the policies and personnel of the Poor Law Commission were subject to personal conferences between Graham and Peel: Hansard, 72 (1844), 249–53. From 1841 to 1845 education grants rose from £30,000 to £75,000: Hansard, 87 (1845), 1233.

deep sincerity, yet hampered by his own party, bound by his stern belief in political economy, and isolated from subordinates by his coldness and reserve, he could not give the new central departments the power, personnel, money, and new ideas they needed.

Nor did he appoint able men to head the departments. Lincoln at the Board of Works was, according to Greville, "worse than useless"; Wharncliffe at the Privy Council was unimaginative; and Edward Strutt, head of the Railway Commission in 1846, was a sheer embarrassment.[4] Separated from his party by his reserve, Peel was even more isolated from the working classes, for whom he distantly and earnestly cared but whose needs and passions he could not really understand, even after reading Chadwick's sanitary report. Peel was a reformer only when conditions weighed exceedingly heavy on his slow though sincere conscience. He lacked that boldness which the "hungry forties" demanded of the chief administrator.

Lord John Russell, Peel's successor in 1846, was a scion of a great Whig family and combined an aristocratic sense of *noblesse oblige* with the ardor of a reformer. He believed that old institutions must change to meet modern needs. He championed Catholic Emancipation, the Reform Bill, the Factory Act, the New Poor Law, and ecclesiastical reform. As Home Secretary from 1835 to 1839 he showed himself not only an attentive administrator but sympathetic to social change. With Lansdowne and against great opposition, he fought for government grants to voluntary schools. He believed in the New Poor Law and gave the Commission clear and firm supervision, as well as some twenty-one assistants. He encouraged Chadwick's sanitary investigation and established a reformatory prison for young criminals. He viewed political economy as a dreadful thing and had a tempered faith in the benevolent role of an active government.[5]

4. Greville, *Memoirs*, 5, 202, 456–57.
5. MH, 10/1, Sept. 1835. HO, 73/52. MH, 1/12, June, 17, 1837. Russell, *Early Correspondence*, 1, 97–98. C. B. R. Kent, *The English Radicals* (London, 1889), p. 374.

Civil Servants

Yet Russell's years as Prime Minister were not marked by inspired administrative efforts, nor were they free from serious failings. As Home Secretary he appointed factory inspectors for purely political reasons and not for merit. He could never forget his aristocratic connections with the Whig oligarchy; and possessing immense self-confidence, he could be most obstinate. Edwin Chadwick and Lord Ashley both suffered from this obstinacy; in the great battle between Chadwick and George Lewis, brought to a head by the Andover scandal and the unjustified dismissals of Parker and Day, Russell found himself bound by marriage connections to defend Lewis and speak disparagingly of Chadwick.

He perpetrated a similar injustice in 1854 when he accepted and repeated some of Lord Seymour's irresponsible charges against Chadwick's management of the Board of Health. Seymour had after all been Russell's appointee as Commissioner of Woods and Forests and head of the Board of Health. Lord Ashley had urged the appointment of the sympathetic Viscount Ebrington, but Russell, stubborn as ever, insisted on Seymour. To the very end he stuck by his fellow Whig and peer. And when Seymour and the Treasury sought to thwart Chadwick's burial scheme, he did nothing to defend Chadwick.[6] But then, to a Prime Minister busy mediating between Palmerston and the Queen, burial grounds were trivial. Prime Ministers occupied themselves with party politics, foreign affairs, finance, and Ireland—not burial grounds and drains and solitary confinement. Such matters belonged to the Home Office.

From 1841 to 1854 (after the rule of Melbourne and Russell) three men dominated the Home Office: Sir James Graham, Sir George Grey, and Lord Palmerston, all men of landed property and all adherents to paternalism. The two baronets—the Tory Graham and the Whig Grey—each administered the Home Office for over five years. Graham acted with vigor and strength and won unpopularity. He was a vain, outspoken country gentleman of undoubted talents. He had improved his own estates in Cumber-

6. Chadwick Papers, Chadwick to Gulson, 1847. Hansard, *135* (1854), 999–1003. Greville, *Memoirs*, 5, 458, and 7, 33. Brougham, *Memoirs*, 3, 468. Lewis, *Chadwick*, p. 243.

land, written thoughtful pamphlets on currency, spoken out for reform, and improved the efficiency of the Admiralty. By 1841 hostility to the Whigs' Church reforms and an awakened fear of democracy brought him to the Tories and, by Peel's choice, to the Home Office. There he demonstrated the industry and efficiency of a Peel, and somewhat the same narrow social outlook. His was a hard efficiency. He insisted that the prison inspectors meet together, but only to agree that the "hope of reforming prisoners by gaol discipline is visionary" and that "the first object of imprisonment is terror to evil doers." [7] He spoke against the Ten Hour Act and failed to enforce the provisions for fencing shafts in textile mills. He drew up the Factory Schools Bill of 1843 with admirable skill in matters of detail, but its insistence that all teachers and a majority of trustees be members of the Church of England made it entirely unacceptable to dissenters. He supported the New Poor Law, but only if administered prudently, cautiously, and cheaply, a timidity shared by the two chief commissioners, Sir George Lewis and Sir Edmund Head. Under Graham's guidance the Commission sought to smooth over and conceal all troubles. The result was Andover and public disgrace. A believer in political economy, Graham objected to much of the Public Health Act because of its paternalistic despotism toward the workers.[8] His acknowledged administrative talents were, in short, limited by his narrow vision, sternness, and conservatism.

Sir George Grey, who succeeded Graham in 1846, was less stern and less efficient. He was conscientious and prudent, a safe and unexceptional administrator. He voted for Ashley's Ten Hour Act in 1847 and introduced Chadwick's burial scheme in 1850, but then nullified the former by not declaring it illegal to use relays to work children after 6 P.M. and frustrated the latter by not standing up to the Treasury and demanding its implementation.[9] Grey had no boldness and no great sympathy with

7. *PP*, 25 (1843), 1–14. Graham Papers, Graham to Brougham, Oct. 16, 1841.

8. Finer, *Chadwick*, pp. 243–73. *Leeds Mercury*, May 27, 1848.

9. Hansard, *90* (1847), 782; *111* (1850), 694–95. *Leeds Mercury*, Feb. 2, 1850. *Times*, March 14, 1850. HO, 45/1851.

the distressed. He opposed the Mines Inspection Act as being at variance with private enterprise, and he dutifully accepted the harsh discipline of separate confinement and the treadmill. He discouraged the introduction of useful labor at the Manchester prison.[10] He would have made an attentive and sober magistrate on some county bench, but he did not have the breadth of vision needed by a Home Secretary in an age of social reform.

Palmerston alone had the abilities requisite for a good Home Secretary. His pungent, forthright memoranda offer a sharp contrast to the cautious directives of Graham and Grey, and they express a more generous social attitude. He told the factory inspectors that all shafts must be carefully fenced, and he told the prison inspectors to reduce separate confinement, abolish the crank and treadmill, and introduce useful labor—all of which reflected his conviction that the first object of prison discipline should be the reformation of the prisoner. He ordered the mining inspectors to meet together and plan more effective measures. He was unintimidated by special interest. He lectured the brewers and tanners of London on the inequities of their smoke-emitting furnaces, reprimanded borough magistrates for their ineffective police forces, and, despite angry cries from the clergy and their archbishop over the loss of burial fees, shut down London's noxious parish cemeteries.

In a memorandum expostulating on the undersecretary's delay in prosecuting smoky Thames steamers, he made it clear that if "the Home Office simply copies out my directions and sends them on in the shape of a letter to some other office, instead of taking the necessary steps for the execution of my instructions . . . it renders the Home Office a mere repeating telegraph or worse than that, a nullity." He managed the office with vigor, and he applied its powers to ease the lot of prisoners, protect factory workers, and make England healthier and cleaner. His defense of the Board of Health in the House of Commons showed a real solicitude for the poor. Though he feared to give the working classes the vote, he nevertheless wished to mitigate their

10. Hansard, *105* (1849), 557. HO, 12/1024. Hansard, *106* (1849), 1337.

distress. He was a sincere paternalist, and able administrator, and a worthy though perhaps untypical representative of the Victorian aristocracy.[11]

The aristocratic tradition of paternalistic administration found nowhere a more kindly and negligent expression than in the rule of Lord Lansdowne and Lord Wharncliffe at the Privy Council. Lansdowne was a Whig who combined the *noblesse oblige* of the eighteenth century with the utilitarianism of the nineteenth. His father had been Bentham's patron, and upon Bentham's recommendation young Lansdowne went to Edinburgh to study, along with Palmerston and Lord Brougham, under one of Scotland's great moral philosophers, Dugald Stewart.

Lord Wharncliffe, on the other hand, enjoyed no such exposure to the earnest doctrines of reform. He was a Tory, though not a stern and unbending one. He was conscientiously devoted, as Lansdowne was enthusiastically devoted, to the government's scheme for education—a matter which, of course, constituted the principal business of the Privy Council. Neither were able administrators. Lansdowne was forever leaving town for his lovely estate at Bowood or sleeping through Cabinet meetings; Wharncliffe was more alert but had less understanding of the perplexities of the education problem. Fortunately, Lansdowne's very negligence proved a signal virtue. Too indolent to manage the details of the office, he turned them over to James Kay Shuttleworth, one of the most energetic and skilled administrators of the period.

Other aspiring officials did not enjoy such benevolent and protective chiefs. Chadwick's experience with the patricians was more varied and unhappy. He served under Lord Morpeth, who headed the Board of Health from 1848 to 1850. Morpeth was another Lord Lansdowne, easygoing, amiable, concerned for the poor, and a friend of social reform; but his successor Lord Seymour was both lazy and callous. He announced that his rule for good administration was to do as little as possible; and as for sanitary reform, "physical degradation and misery

11. See my article, "Lord Palmerston at the Home Office, 1853–1854," *Historian*, *21* (Nov. 1958), 63–81.

was not only irretrievable, but a proper necessity for the great mass of the population." [12]

Chadwick knew at first hand how different the patricians could be. He had witnessed at the Board of Health the earnestness, loyalty, and selflessness of Lord Ashley. He had seen the understanding of Morpeth and the gentle inefficiency of John Shaw Lefevre, who was a poor-law commissioner. More severe, no doubt, were his memories of Sir James Graham's implacable hostility to him during the Andover hearings, and the disdain shown him by Sir Franklin Lewis, the pompous Welsh baronet from Radnorshire. Nor was he any happier about the subsequent humiliations dealt him by Sir Franklin's scholarly son Sir George Lewis, and Sir George's university friend, Sir Edmund Head. Chadwick complained bitterly to Lord Althorp over the appointment of these young Oxford graduates, both relatively inexperienced in poor law matters. In answering Chadwick's protests Lord Althorp quite bluntly reminded him of the social cleavage which still marked Victorian society and which left its mark on the public administration. "I must frankly admit," said Althorp in 1841, "that your station in society was not such as would have made it fit that you should be appointed one of the commissioners." [13] Such remarks hurt Chadwick's sensitive nature and prompted him to judge the commissioners too harshly. Sir Franklin Lewis' arrogance was indeed unfortunate, but he could and did work hard and ably, and certainly his son, and the accomplished Oxford don, Sir Edmund Head, had a keener sense than did Chadwick of administrative contingencies. They knew that a rigorous poor law must be pliantly administered. Sir George in his subsequent career at the Treasury and Sir Edmund as Governor General of Canada both proved themselves administrators of more than average skill.

In their very acceptance of Chadwick, despite his assertiveness and dogmatism, the aristocrats revealed an awareness of the value

12. Chadwick Papers, Chadwick to Lord Russell, July 1854. Lewis, *Chadwick*, p. 244.
13. Chadwick Papers, Lord Althorp to Chadwick, May 8, 1841, Chadwick to Althorp, May 8, 1841.

of that energy and drive to be found in middle-class reformers; but in their rejection of his management of the Board of Health and in their consciousness of his humbler station, the patricians showed their narrowness, conservatism, and timidity. They were afraid to take those aggressive steps and adopt those new ideas and to support those bolder officials that the urgent social problems of a rapidly changing nation required. The governing class appointed inspectors but denied them adequate power; in the same spirit they welcomed the aid of their Chadwicks but withheld from them complete confidence.

The governing class of England was composed not only of peers and the landed gentry but also of wealthy merchants and successful professional people. Many of these won their way to the highest positions in England's expanded central administration. Five of the presidents of the Board of Trade came from the commercial world, and they brought from it high standards of planning and efficiency. They also brought with them a firm conviction in the truths of political economy. Gladstone, the most august of them, managed the Board of Trade from 1841 to 1845. He directed affairs with a strong hand but an unsympathetic view toward the protection of industrial workers. He opposed Ashley's Mining Act of 1842 and Ten Hour Act of 1844, did nothing about the deplorable state of the merchant seamen, and at the behest of the railway companies nullified the price-regulating clauses of his Railway Bill of 1844.[14]

His successors, Henry Labouchere, a Whig, and Edward Cardwell, a Peelite, dealt more firmly with these problems. In 1850 Labouchere passed the first Merchant Marine Act and in 1854 Cardwell the second. Edward Cardwell's Bill, with its 504 clauses, was a masterful blending of exacting detail and sound principle. It revealed a capacity superior to Labouchere's, and it illustrated that new talent for minute planning which the Victorian middle classes brought to the central administration. No Lansdowne, no Melbourne, no Russell could have dealt so deftly with so complicated a problem. Cardwell, like Gladstone and Labouchere, was

14. Hansard, *64* (1842), 937; *73* (1844), 1264, 1462. *Economist*, 2 (July 6, 1844), 962.

the son of a merchant, but like his two predecessors he was groomed in the public schools and educated at Oxford.[15] He belonged to the governing class and was accepted with ease at Whitehall and No. 10 Downing Street. Accredited, well mannered, polished, wealthy, Cardwell took his place in the patriciate.

It was only in the ranks below the ministry, in the ranks of the undersecretaries and commissioners that the self-made men of humbler station, the George Porters, Rowland Hills, Lyon Playfairs, Kay Shuttleworths, and Chadwicks could gain office and work in the same harness with Etonians and Oxonians. Possessing great capacity or great energy or both, they brought to these departments a passion for reform and a skill at administration that was sorely needed. On the Education Committee the patrician Lansdowne's easy tolerance blended well with Kay Shuttleworth's earnestness. At times, however, the reformer's passion and skill were more productive of conflict than efficiency. On the Board of Health Chadwick's tactless demands for continual improvement brought deep antagonisms.

Edwin Chadwick and James Kay Shuttleworth [16] represented the advent of a new type of administrator. They voiced in unequivocal words the need for social and administrative reform. Both came from Lancashire families of nonconformist faith. Neither attended a public school; neither went to the two traditional universities. Kay attended Edinburgh University on a scholarship and Chadwick studied at the Inns of Court. Both reacted strongly to the squalor of city life. Kay knew the filth and poverty of city life as a doctor in Manchester; Chadwick saw it all around him as a young lawyer dwelling near the Inns of Court. Chadwick soon found himself more interested in the problem of ill health and bad police than in torts and writs. Both men felt impelled to write about the disease, misery, and immorality of town life, and both came under the influence of Jeremy Bentham. The character of both measured up to the exacting ideals of the Victorian nonconformist conscience. Their

15. *DNB, 11,* 367; *3,* 952.
16. In 1842, by marriage, Dr. James Kay became Dr. James Kay Shuttleworth.

aspirations were elevated, sober, and dedicated. They pursued with a restless ardor the reform of all social evils. They sought to abolish a principle of poor relief that only corrupted its recipient. They sought to remove the causes of disease. They sought to extend religious and moral education. As administrators they were indefatigable, strict, and wedded to sound principles.

All this appeared very formidable to the indolent gentlemen of Whitehall, the cautious members of Parliament, and the entrenched local authorities. Some of the fault lay with the ardent reformers, who lacked grace and urbanity. To Matthew Arnold, Kay Shuttleworth "did not attract by person and manner; his temper was not smooth or genial, and he left on many persons the impression of a man managing and designing." [17] Chadwick was of even rougher texture, far more outspoken than Kay, more belligerent, and more self-confident. He irritated his colleagues by being too well-informed, too insistent on efficiency, and too often right. When wrong, he was unyielding. He alienated the established interests of Victorian society by espousing heretical ideas. Kay was a Victorian liberal, advanced in his opinions, enlightened in his views, yet prudent and orthodox. Chadwick was a more complex figure, who mixed radicalism with his orthodoxy. Connected by birth and marriage with manufacturing wealth, he was no socialist and would have no regulation of adult labor. Disturbed by the waste and chaos of parochial self-government, he even had doubts about a working-class democracy. Yet he could argue strongly for government management of burial grounds and municipally owned water works, and voice the heterodox opinion that the government should use its powers to prevent all waste and inefficiency in society, a principle pointing eventually toward Fabian socialism and one deeply disturbing to the Victorian propertied class.[18]

Kay's outlook was simpler and more respected. His career, which could not have been improved on by Samuel Smiles, was an epitome of dedication and virtue. At fifteen he was a Sunday

17. Adkins, *St. Johns,* p. · 19.
18. Samuel Finer and R. A. Lewis in their studies of Edwin Chadwick present two excellent accounts of his complex and dominant personality.

school teacher, at twenty he ministered to the poor, at thirty he organized the Manchester Statistical Society, at thirty-six he became secretary to the Committee on Education. While secretary he helped, voluntarily and at great personal cost, to found England's first teachers' training college at Battersea. He gave the best years of his life in the service of the Committee, and resigned only when his health broke under the strain of overwork. After retirement he lectured to the Macclesfield workers on the virtues of public parks and free libraries, and at Leeds told them of the evils of strikes and trade unions. He was at his happiest at his Battersea College, where, after spading the garden with the pupil teachers, he gathered them around him and told them of the virtues of frugality and simplicity and spoke about the value of the industrial arts. His students long remembered this kindly, Victorian Polonius, ever solicitous of the well-being of his flock, ever busy teaching them right morals and religion. Not even his Pestalozzian views on education, so generous and liberal and so latent with Rousseauism, could mark him as a radical. He was persuaded till his death that the moral and religious education of the working class would transform England from a land of disease, immorality, pauperism, and crime to a land of manufacturing prosperity, free trade, reform, empty prisons, temperance, and progress.[19] Kay's promises were more orthodox than Chadwick's, and his manner more conciliatory. He did not talk of expropriating profitable water companies, and he did not write severe memoranda on his colleagues' failings.

Chadwick was the more significant administrator, however. No matter how ungraciously he acted, he could not be pushed aside. His New Poor Law revolutionized England's local administration; his social investigations into the causes of disease forced the Government to concern itself with the public's health; and his fertile ideas for efficient administration together with his effective agitation in 1854 for civil service examinations make him a pioneer. He was, for all the frustrations and defeats he met, the leading figure in England's expanding central administration.

19. Adkins, *St. Johns*, p. 55. *Macclesfield Courier,* April 7, 1854. *Leeds Mercury,* Jan. 21, 1854.

There were no other Chadwicks in England's new bureaus. They would hardly have tolerated more. Kay Shuttleworth provides a more standard type of the middle-class, hard-working, and conscientious administrator, as did men like Southwood Smith at the Board of Health, Lyon Playfair at the Department of Science and Art, George Nicholls at the Poor Law Office, and Richard Jones at the Charity Commission. These men were mild-mannered, courteous, plodding, and earnest. They served diligently under aristocratic ministers.

Among them, Southwood Smith enjoyed the greatest reputation. He was reputed to be the first of sanitary reformers. He began his career as a Unitarian minister, then became a physician for a London fever hospital, and finally entered public service because of his interest in public health. Lyon Playfair also gained fame by a successful career in medicine, the study of which he had pursued under the great Liebig. His brilliance, ability, and zeal made him very acceptable to the Government. George Nicholls came from an old Cornish family, and won recognition and advancement by success at sea, in banking, and as a reformer of the poor law at Southwell Parish. Richard Jones was professor of political economy at Haileybury, where he gained a reputation as a leading critic of Ricardo's apriori school of economics and as an advocate of more empirical methods of economic analysis.[20] His practical attitude, which served him in good stead as tithe and charity commissioner, was not untypical of men like Smith, Playfair, and Nicholls.

The virtues exhibited by these men—their alertness, their strong individualism, their unusual industriousness—often conflicted with the narrowness, class pride, and conservatism of the old school of officials, whether at the Treasury or in the Cabinet. But despite these tensions, cooperation remained the rule. At the Home Office, for example, men of the lower middle class, like Henry Waddington, worked right alongside Parlia-

20. Gertrude Lewes, *Dr. Southwood Smith: A Retrospect,* London, 1878. Sir George Nicholls, *A History of the English Poor Laws* (London, 904), i–xxxviii. William Whewell, *Literary Remains of Richard Jones* (London, 1859), pp. ix–xi. *DNB, 10,* 1045.

mentary undersecretaries such as John Manners Sutton, Henry Fitzroy, and Fox Maule, each the son of a peer. Equally successful was the cooperation of those men, drawn from all sectors of Victorian society, who as Her Majesty's Inspectors did the crucial job of supervising local authorities. Their talents, ideals, and knowledge contributed much to the success of England's new administration.

INSPECTORS

The majority of those country squires, merchants, clergymen, doctors, engineers, professors, captains, and colonels—more than 140 all told—who left their secure professions to become Her Majesty's Inspectors came from the upper ranks of the middle class.[21] Only a few among them boasted any aristocratic connections, and not many rose from the lower middle class. None came from the proletariat. The large majority were sons of country gentlemen or members of the professional class or businessmen. Their families had the wealth and position to provide them with excellent educations and to find positions for them in the Church, the army, or the business world.

They represented the more successful of England's growing middle class. Twenty-three of the sixty-four (concerning whom there is information of their family origins) came from families of comfortable estates in the country, ranging from the wealthier county families to those of less repute, less income, but no less respectability. Twenty-three others came from professional families, who increasingly made up the middle class; seven were sons of clergymen; seven, sons of lawyers; six, sons of doctors; and three, sons of schoolmasters. In most cases their fathers were men who had done very well in their professions. The three schoolmasters, for example, included Thomas Arnold of Rugby; Rann Kennedy of King Edwards School, Birmingham; and Thomas Hill, of Bruce Castle, Tottenham—all headmasters. In the same way, the four who came from military families had fathers of rank, majors or captains; and the six whose fathers were businessmen enjoyed handsome incomes.

Thus out of the sixty-four concerning whom there is informa-

21. For evidence on the inspectors see references below, Appendix A.

tion, sixty-three came from families which, in all likelihood, were among the 10 per cent of the wealthiest and most respectable. Sir Robert Rawlinson, a health inspector, alone came from the artisan class. His father was a builder and could give his son only a day-school education. Of the fifty-six concerning whom there is no information of their family origins, the chances are that their families enjoyed less social prestige and smaller incomes; but the information concerning the education of eighty-two of the inspectors suggests that more than sixty-three came from the prosperous classes. Sixty-three enjoyed a university education —twenty-six at Oxford, twenty-one at Cambridge, and the remaining ones at the Scottish Universities, Trinity College, Dublin, or Kings College, London. Of those who did not go to a university, some enjoyed, as did Colonel Ash A'Court and Henry Pilkington (both assistant poor-law commissioners), a public school education. Others, such as the education inspectors Joseph Fletcher and the factory inspector Thomas Howells, secured their education at the Inns of Court. Quite a few went to professional schools—the Royal Military Academy at Woolwich and the Royal Engineering School at Chatham—or to the medical schools like St. Thomas' or the Webb School of Medicine. Even those like Edward Cresy, Henry Austin, and Robert Rawlinson (all of the Board of Health) who received no formal degrees from a university or a medical school, profited from advantages of unusual apprenticeships. Edward Cresy learned his architecture from the famous James Parkinson and Robert Rawlinson, and Henry Austin learned engineering from the master, Robert Stephenson.

With the possible exception of one or two mining inspectors, there were, then, few examples of really self-made men. They all benefited from a substantial education, and with that advantage rose to success as gentlemen farmers, clergymen, lawyers, engineer, doctors, and officers in the army and navy. At the time of their appointment as inspectors eight were gentleman farmers, twelve were practicing law, fourteen were in divine orders, sixteen were engaged in a medical practice, five were teaching school, and three were lecturing at universities.[22] Five came from the business

22. Three of the school teachers, one professor and one lecturer, were also clergymen.

world, twelve from the army, and three from the navy. Eight were engineers and three coal viewers. Almost all were successful in their profession. Favored by birth, family, and education, they were among the successful of the middle class. With the patricians they still formed the active part of England's expanding governing class.

The concept of class, either of a middle or a governing class, can of course be both useful and misleading. To say that Her Majesty's Inspectors came from the middle class and that that class was becoming a dominant part of the governing class is, in a broad sense, quite correct. But the middle class and the governing class were anything but homogeneous. The middle class formed a large and complex segment of society, including highly respected squires and ambitious coal viewers, distinguished professors and uncultured but successful builders, university men and apprenticed engineers. Her Majesty's Inspectors came from the many ranks within this varied middle class. The education inspectors, for example, were better educated than the health inspectors, and the assistant poor-law commissioners were men of greater social prestige than the mining inspectors.

Even among the assistant poor-law commissioners, however, there were great differences in family position and education. Edward Boyd Twisleton, son of the Archdeacon of Columbo, grandson through his mother of Lord Say and Sele, and trained at Oxford and the Inner Temple, had little in common with Edward Gulson, a fellmonger of Coventry, a Quaker, and a former apprentice in the business world. Nor did Colonel Ash A'Court and Charles Clement, like Twisleton the brothers of peers, have much in common with Charles Mott, a London contractor for poorhouses; yet all were assistant poor-law commissioners. Between these three younger brothers of peers on the one hand and the Coventry fellmonger and London poorhouse contractor on the other came men of varying social positions. Five were baronets and four were listed in Burke's landed gentry, giving to the assistant commissioners the most rural and aristocratic coloring of any of the new departments. Of the twenty-three inspectors who came from the landed gentry, thirteen went to work for the

154

Poor Law Commission. They served alongside men of urban backgrounds, the sons of lawyers, doctors, and businessmen. With only a few exceptions, such as Twisleton's irritation with Gulson, these men worked together in agreeable harmony. Their cooperation illustrated the fusion of the different segments of England's complex middle class that gave to the nineteenth-century governing classes its strength and its dominant social philosophy.

The education inspectorate enjoyed a greater uniformity of social background than did the assistant commissioners. None of the former was a baronet and none had connections with the peerage, but they were, as Kay Shuttleworth told a Parliamentary committee in 1848, gentlemen either of university training or with a liberal education.[23] Although twelve of the poor-law assistants attended no university, only one of the education inspectors, Joseph Fletcher, was denied that privilege. Fletcher, however, read law at Lincoln's Inn. The education inspectors came from the professional ranks—six from clerical families, the others from the homes of doctors, solicitors, and schoolmasters. Only two were of country families and none from the competitive world of business. They were men of culture and learning if not country families and titles.

The factory and prison inspectors had varied backgrounds. Some came from the urban and mercantile world. Three of the prison inspectors, William Crawford, Bisset Hawkins, and Frederick Hill, were from London, being the sons respectively of a wine merchant, a surgeon, and a schoolmaster. Among the factory inspectors, Leonard Horner's father was an Edinburgh linen manufacturer, T. J. Howell's a barrister and judge, and James Stuart's a Glasgow doctor. These men knew at first hand the urban problems of the day, and their education was of a practical bent. Only two of the ten prison inspectors and only one of the seven factory inspectors were graduates of either Oxford or Cambridge. Both Stuart and Horner attended Edinburgh University, the latter to study chemistry. The most enlightened of the prison inspectors, Frederick Hill, brother of Rowland

23. *PP, 18* (1848), 472.

Hill the post office reformer, began life as a teacher in his father's school at Tottenham. He was then only thirteen years old. John Perry studied medicine at St. Bartholomew's hospital; two other prison inspectors, Captain Williams and Captain Kincaid, went straight from grammar school to the army. Their social standing and their education were not as distinguished as those enjoyed by assistant commissioners and education inspectors, but they came from stations in life that ensured an adequate education and guaranteed them entry into the world of army commissions, business opportunities, professional advancement, and finally government service.

The same generalization holds true for the lunacy commissioners and the inspectors hired by the Board of Health. Few went to public schools, few entered Oxford or Cambridge, and none is listed in Burke, but all enjoyed the advantage of a good education. Even Robert Rawlinson, who later boasted that his schooling never cost over 3½ d. a week, profited from apprenticeships served under Jesse Hartly, Liverpool's ablest dock engineer, and Robert Stephenson. Five of the health inspectors and eight of the lunacy commissioners received a medical education, six at famed Edinburgh University. Those who did not attend a university, like Richard Grainger, learned their medicine in schools like the Webb School, of which Grainger was later the head. Oxford and Cambridge shunned, for the most part, such practical studies as medicine, just as they shunned altogether the science of engineering. None of the engineers hired by the Board of Health and none of the Mining Inspectorate came from those cloistered halls. The one engineer who did go to college went to the new Kings College, London. Engineering commanded a much less favored status in society than even medicine. It was a trade for builders and coal-viewers; upper-class men learned it only if they chose a military career, in which case they were taught at the Royal Military Academy or the Royal Engineers School at Chatham. Sir Francis Bond Head, a poor-law assistant, learned his engineering at Woolwich, and the Railway Department obtained all its inspectors from the army's Royal Engineers. Henry Labouchere, at the Board of Trade, had a high estimation of their abilities: "Whenever the government was in difficulty of finding an officer of high capacity for civil administration," he told a Parliamentary committee, "the right man was sure to be obtained among the officers of the Royal Engineers." [24]

Chadwick, however, looked elsewhere for the engineers he wished to enlist in the battle for sanitary reform. These men he found in the ranks of those who had received their education in the trade itself. Along with the railway and mining inspectors—all engineers—they constitute the one group concerning whom little information on family background can be found. They possessed neither the social prestige of most poor-law assistants nor the university training of the education inspectors. Yet the social position of the few concerning whom there is information suggests a status not without solid advantages. James Smith's father was a well-to-do manufacturer, Herbert Mackworth's father a naval lieutenant, Captain Laffan's a doctor, and Rawlinson's a private builder. Their homes, like those of the other inspectors, were ones in which earnest parents taught the virtues of hard work and the usefulness of knowledge.

Less disparate than family origins and education was the choice of a career made by the inspectors and their success in it. Seventy took up some profession, while only eight remained gentlemen farmers and only five entered the business world.[25] The very function of some of the new departments naturally demanded trained experts from the fields of law, medicine, and engineering. The Board of Health needed medical inspectors and the Lunacy Commission was required by law to employ doctors and barristers. The railway, mining, and health departments needed engineers; and to assuage the suspicion of the Church all inspectors of Church schools were clergymen; hence the large proportion of doctors, lawyers, clergymen, and engineers staffing these new inspectorates. The poor-law, factory, and prison departments enjoyed greater leeway, and as a result employed journalists, country squires, and merchants as well as clergymen and lawyers.

Whether they were lawyers or journalists, engineers or clergy-

24. Whitworth Porter, *History of the Corps of Royal Engineers* (London, 1889), *1*, 1.
25. The Army and Navy men are included as professional career men.

men, then, the inspectors were usually men of more than common attainments. The patricians of the governing class generally selected able men, sincere in the wish to alleviate social evils. They did not employ those mediocre political favorites who dominated the revenue departments and who became the objects of Anthony Trollope's satires. Among the doctors who left their lucrative practices for government service there were many of great reputation. Richard Grainger, a medical inspector for the Board of Health in 1849 and a burial inspector in 1854, had been Professor of Anatomy at St. Thomas and was a fellow of the Royal Society and an author of brilliant works on anatomy and the organic sciences. He was also a proprietor and editor of the *Medico Chirurgical Review* along with Gavin Milroy, another doctor whom Chadwick brought to the Board of Health in order to stamp out cholera. As a writer for that review and for *Lancet* and as author of *Plagues and Quarantine,* Milroy had won an enviable reputation among the medical fraternity.

Chadwick sought such men, who applied their energies and imagination not to bedside calls and surgery but to public medicine and sanitary reform. Dr. John Sutherland and Dr. Hector Gavin, like Grainger and Milroy, were active in the cause of sanitation. Sutherland was editor of the *Health of Towns Advocate* of Liverpool and Gavin was a lecturer on medicine, an author of numerous books, and editor of the *Journal of Public Health.* These were not merely professional doctors, and the same was true of the medical men of the Lunacy Commission. Posterity has forgotten the names of Edward Seymour, Samuel Gaskell, Bisset Hawkins, and James Cowles Prichard, but to the London medical world in 1848 they were well known. Seymour, Gulstonian lecturer, physician to the Duke of Sussex, and physician to St. George's Hospital, had written many works, among them *Observations on the Medical Treatment of Insanity.* Samuel Gaskell had won his fame as head of the Lancaster asylum, where he pioneered in modern and humane methods of treating insanity. Bisset Hawkins (who later became a prison inspector) and James Prichard attained distinction as scientists. The Royal Society honored both with membership, a tribute in part to their wide

158

interests. Hawkins, first professor of medicine at Kings College, had not only written on medical statistics and cholera but had authored a distinguished work on the history and culture of Germany. Prichard, a Bristol physician, wrote on insanity and also on Egyptian mythology and the natural history of man, his works helping to form the beginnings of the science of anthropology.

The achievements of those engineers who joined the early Victorian bureaucracy were more modest and practical but within their own fields nonetheless substantial. They were not authors but builders and inventors. Rawlinson won fame by constructing (with the use of hollow bricks) the magnificent vaulted hall of St. Georges, Liverpool, reputed to be the largest hall in Europe. His fellow engineering inspector at the Board of Health, William Ranger, was the inventor of concrete hollow bricks, and in 1848 was professor of civil engineering at Putney school and at the Royal Engineers Academy at Chatham. Chadwick liked inventive, imaginative engineers, not mere mechanics wedded to traditional methods. James Smith of Deanston was an inventor of note, developing new techniques for land drainage; and Edward Cresy, author of the *Encyclopedia of Civil Engineering* and other works on English and continental architecture, pioneered new techniques of bridge engineering.

The engineers of the Railway Department had, upon their entry into government service, less reputation. All were captains in the army, but later two became full generals, one a major general, and a fourth, J. L. A. Simmons, attained the highest possible rank, field marshall. The only one not to attain such high military rank, Douglas Strutt Galton, won many honors in his long career in government service, ultimately becoming Director of Public Works and Buildings, President of the Senate of London University, and a fellow of the Royal Society. The men who first traveled over England's changing countryside to test railway bridges and examine fill-ins and toll gates were military engineers of more than passing competence. Her Majesty eventually bestowed upon all the Knight Order of the Companions of the Bath.

None of the twenty-eight education inspectors and only two of the thirty-four poor-law assistants were granted such an honor, but at the time of their joining their respective departments they were no less successful in their callings. Lord Lansdowne and the Archbishop of Canterbury did not use the Education Committee as a reserve for inept clergymen, nor did the Poor Law Commission, as its violent critic Peter Grimsditch told the Commons, hire "mostly barristers at law and of very short standing and no experience of the social feelings and habits of the country." [26] The education inspectors came from prosperous Church livings, and many had experience in education. Both the Reverend John Allen and the Reverend Henry Moseley had taught at Kings College, London. Allen had been a lecturer on the New Testament and Moseley a professor of natural history. The Reverend Joseph Morell and the Reverend William Brookfield had been private tutors, the latter to Lord Lyttleton's son. The Reverend Alexander Thurtell was a tutor at Caius College, Oxford, and Edward Woodford was head of Madras College, St. Andrews. The Reverend W. J. Kennedy and Scott Nasmyth Stokes both worked as secretaries to school societies, Kennedy for the National Society, and Stokes for the Catholic Poor School Committee. Henry Longueville Jones, once a lecturer at Magdalen, founded a college at Manchester.

Nine of the education inspectors therefore had previous experience in education. The others came directly from curacies or, if inspectors of poor-law schools, from the practice of law. All were men of scholarship and learning who moved in a cultivated and genteel society and were intimate with many of London's literary personages. Lord Lyttleton believed that the Reverend William Henry Brookfield of St. Lukes, Berwick Street, London, had "as a preacher to a cultivated metropolitan congregation of English churchmen, no superior in his own day." [27] Brookfield was a close friend of Tennyson, Hallam, and Thackeray and was much admired by Thomas Carlyle. F. C. Cook, a contemporary of Brookfield's at Cambridge and a friend of Tennyson and

26. Hansard, *49* (1839), 353.
27. Lord Lyttleton, "Preface," *The Sermons of William Henry Brookfield*, ed. Mrs. W. H. Brookfield, London, 1886. Brookfield is described in Thackeray's *Curate's Walk* as Frank Whitelock.

Hallam, won a first in the classical tripos and studied under Schlegel at Bonn. He attracted the attention of Bishop Blomfield when curate at Grey's Inn and was appointed an inspector. With knowledge of fifty-two languages, he wrote voluminously on biblical criticism. He had a promising career ahead, yet at the age of thirty-four he chose to travel over England's countryside expounding the elements of writing and reading to ill-trained, underpaid schoolmasters.

J. D. Morell, by the time he became an inspector, had written a *History of Modern Philosophy*. Almost all the education inspectors published—many, like J. P. Norris, voluminously. Trained at Rugby under Dr. Arnold and receiving an M.A. at Cambridge in 1849, Norris entered directly into the Education Office. Not long afterward came the most famous of all Rugbyans, Matthew Arnold. He had been Lord Lansdowne's private secretary, an employment that no doubt led to his appointment. There were, of course, men of very average abilities among the education inspectors, but as a group they were far from being that "inspectorate of elderly half-educated school masters" described by Robert Morant in 1902.[28]

The assistant poor-law commissioners were more diverse in their professions. Among them were many country gentlemen who, Mr. Grimsditch notwithstanding, knew intimately the social conditions of the countryside. Eight were magistrates and deputy lieutenants; many others owned or managed agricultural property. Thomas Stevens owned 3,000 acres, and Henry Pilkington, though by training a barrister, managed extensive agricultural property. Grimsditch was correct, no doubt, in asserting that there were barristers on the Commission, and they were barristers of no little account. The most able in Graham's judgment was Edward Boyd Twisleton, a man of keen intelligence who had taken a first at Oxford and who had met with success on the circuit.[29] He was a member of London's most fashionable intellectual circle, dining at Holland House, visiting the Carlyles, and taking his young American wife to breakfast at the Grotes' and to dinner

28. Boothyrood, *Education Inspectorate*, p. 114.
29. BM, Add. MS 40,447, Graham to Peel, Nov. 4, 1842.

Civil Servants

at Nassau Senior's. At Senior's they met Lansdowne, Sir Charles Trevelyan, and Edward Carleton Tufnell. Edward Tufnell, the brother of the Whig MP Henry Tufnell and son-in-law of the Earl of Radnor, was also a barrister and an assistant poor-law commissioner. He was an ardent reformer and in 1839 helped establish the first teachers' training college in England. Alfred Power, another barrister, was, like Twisleton, a first at Oxford and a success at the bar. He then joined the Royal Commission which inquired into the Old Poor Law, for which he wrote one of the fullest reports.

The list of capable assistant commissioners could easily be prolonged. There was Thomas Graves, who, before he went to the poor law office, was a professor of jurisprudence at University College, London and a fellow of the Royal Society. There was Sir Francis Bond Head, army officer, engineer, Andean explorer, man of science, and author of the urbane and charming *Bubbles of Nassau,* a book which Coleridge commended.

There were, of course, men of little distinction on the Commission, country gentlemen like William Day and W. T. H. Hawley and Richard Earle, but on the whole they were not merely Whig barristers hired for a job; like the inspectors of the other new departments they were well known and successful. Perhaps at no other time did abler men enter the British civil service to do the drudgery of mere itinerant officials, bringing their great talents to bear on improving workhouses and prisons, promoting better schools, urging better care of the insane, inspecting such varied items as railway switches, mining shafts, and textile machinery.

The entry of such men into the government service raises two questions: why were they chosen, and why did they accept? In an age moving from a belief in political patronage and favoritism to one of civil service examinations there can be no simple answer to the first question. All inspectors were chosen by one of the principal ministers or by important commissioners. The appointments were personal and not dependent on tests. The Home Secretary appointed the factory, prison, mining, and burial inspectors. The president of the Council (with his secretary's help and the approval of the archbishop) appointed the education inspectors. The Poor Law Commission appointed its own assistants.

The opportunities for political patronage and favoritism were very great, especially since it was the accepted practice of the age. Lord John Russell confessed privately to Lord Melbourne that the Whigs should reward those who deserved well of their party. Such a risk Russell took appointing James Stuart, editor of the staunchly Whig *Courier*, as a factory inspector. Stuart, a choleric figure, had an unsavory reputation which included killing James Boswell's grandson in a duel and embezzling money from a widow's savings association. Brougham called him an "unworthy wretch" but allowed Russell to make him a factory inspector—a job he performed, in Lord Ashley's judgment, most negligently. His negligence was hardly surprising, since he had called the clause for central inspection "a great blunder." [30]

Not all political appointees proved as poor. Stuart's colleague, Leonard Horner, brother of the ardent Whig reformer Francis Horner, had few equals in vigor and efficiency. As one of the founders and one of the first wardens of London University, as a fellow of the Royal Society, and as a successful manufacturer, he commanded great respect even before he became an inspector. The subinspectors were also political appointees and, according to Chadwick, of dubious competence. In an article in the *Westminster Review* Chadwick attacked their appointments, along with the selection (over his own application) of George Lewis and Sir Edmund Head as poor-law commissioners.[31]

The nepotism and favoritism demonstrated in the appointment of Lewis and Head were not, however, at variance with eighteenth-century standards. Even Sir James Graham, who boasted that there was no political favoritism during his rule of the Admiralty, practiced it in making his brother-in-law Registrar General and in appointing his close friend and private secretary

30. PRO, 30/22/2, Brougham to Russell, Nov. 28, 1838, July 1, 1836. *DNB*, 25, 91.

31. Chadwick Papers, memo. on central administration, 1841. *Westminster Review*, 26 (Oct. 1836), 113–15; 46 (Sept. 1846), 109–12.

to the Railway Department. The *Economist* roundly attacked the latter appointment because the ex-secretary's brother had stock in the South Eastern Railway Company.[32] Patronage and favoritism from 1833 to 1854 undoubtedly guided the appointment of most officials. According to James Stephen of the Colonial Office the large majority of officials were picked "to gratify the political, the domestic, or the personal feelings of their patrons." [33]

But this was a practice increasingly under the fire of reformers and rapidly in retreat. In the newer central departments it was being supplanted by considerations of merit. The factory inspectors in 1833 were political appointees; the assistant poor-law commissioners in 1834 were not. A memorandum from Nassau Senior to Lord Melbourne set the new tone by insisting that he pick first-rate men. They should be, he said, men who possessed "diligence, impartiality, decision, discretion, knowledge of human nature . . . invention, and resource"—a very tall order indeed, but not enough for Senior, who added that they should also be men able "to conciliate prejudice and to persist in those measures of which they foresee the ultimate success." The three commissioners, with the help of Senior and Chadwick, proceeded to pick such men from over two thousand applicants. They read countless letters of recommendation and interviewed dozens of candidates, finally employing those with the most experience and proven ability. Of the twelve chosen, only two were known to them before their appointment.[34] On the whole, they chose well. Senior, writing in 1840, was surprised at the "perfect purity and sagacity" with which the commissioners had made their appointments, and at the absence of government interference. The result, he said, was "a body of assistants such as . . . no board ever possessed." [35] Other agencies also selected men by merit

32. Ibid., p. 113. Chadwick Papers, memo. on Graham, 1847. Hansard, *78* (1845), 288. *Economist, 3* (Feb. 8, 1845), 120.

33. Emmeline Cohen, *The Growth of the British Civil Service, 1780–1939* (London, 1941), p. 101. *PP, 20* (1855), 75.

34. *Quarterly Review, 53* (April 1835), 284.

35. Chadwick Papers, Senior to Melbourne, June 30, 1834, Senior to Home Secretary, 1840.

and not by favoritism. Chadwick, an early and tireless advocate of civil service reform, used what power he had to persuade local poor law authorities and boards of health to choose men by their capabilities and not by their political loyalties. At the General Board of Health Chadwick was as exacting as Senior, demanding the employment of engineers and doctors with experience, reputation, integrity, and a belief in reform. Chadwick was, in fact, guilty of favoritism, a favoritism for men who shared his ideas of sanitary reform. But this never blinded him to the picking of talented men to espouse his cause. He valued his cause too much to endanger it with incompetence. He knew that the delicacy and complexity of the work demanded administrative skill.

Lord Lansdowne and Kay Shuttleworth—the men who (with the approval of the archbishop and, in some instances, the British Society) chose the education inspectors—also realized the need for skill. The task of inspecting Church schools involved equally great difficulties. Religious jealousies and suspicions had to be conciliated and untrained school masters told how to teach. To do these delicate tasks, Lansdowne and Shuttleworth chose the best of the available clergy. Lansdowne told the Reverend John Allen, whom he employed as the first inspector, that the government, in view of the public's suspicions toward state aid, "was anxious to find a person *omni exceptione major*," and that "for their own sake the government would appoint [as his colleagues] men of unblemished reputation." [36] In truth all the new departments faced delicate and difficult problems. Substantial administrative powers were generally denied them, and they therefore needed men of tact, intelligence, energy, and firmness, men truly *omni exceptione major*. To gain such men careful consideration was given to character, talent, and experience. Usually such consideration was informal, though at the Home Office formal examinations were given in 1850 to determine the appointment of mining inspectors. The emphasis on merit in these new agencies and their avoidance of patronage form a forgotten chapter in the civil-service reform movement of the 1840's and 1850's. That movement aimed principally at bringing

36. R. M. Grier, *John Allen* (London, 1889), pp. 83–84.

examinations to the thousands of Treasury and Custom officials —to clerks and secretaries. In a different manner and in a higher sphere, consideration of merit was already supplanting favoritism. It was an informal development but no less effective, and it reflected those new standards of efficiency that Victorian England, facing imposing administrative and social problems, could no longer avoid.

The caliber of men who joined these new departments was high, their jobs were difficult and trying, and they were not always well paid. The factory inspectors received the largest salary, £1,000 a year. The education inspectors were paid £450 a year plus 15 shillings *per diem* when traveling, and the assistant poor law commissioners £700 plus one guinea a day. Their annual earnings were about £850 and £1,000 respectively.[37] The prison inspectors received only £700 a year, with no expenses except railway and coach fare, and the mining inspectors only £600. These men received less than their professions generally paid. The mining inspectors wrote many memoranda to Lord Palmerston complaining that £400 and 12 shillings a day expenses was much less than they could earn as coal-viewers and managers. Some of the poor-law assistants, as William Day and Colonel Ash A'Court, received less than they would have earned managing their estates.[38] Both said they joined the service at a monetary sacrifice because they wished England's poor law improved. Most of the assistants no doubt made no such sacrifices, but on the whole the pay was never commensurate with the arduous nature of the employment and the great abilities demanded of these itinerant officials. The Victorians, with a passion for cheap government, kept the salaries of public officials low.

Why, then, did squires like Daniel Goodson Adey and clergymen like William Henry Brookfield choose to leave their comfortable estates and secure livings to argue with workhouse masters and examine children on reading? And why did able doctors and engineers like Richard Grainger and William Ranger leave

37. *PP, 18* (1848), 276, 469.
38. HO, 45/4105, 4921; 12/16,018. *Times,* Aug. 17, 1844. MH, 32/1, Nov. 7, 1834.

professorial chairs to visit the cholera-plagued slums of Gateshead and travel many miles and work many long hours? The answer to these questions can be found only in a closer examination of the social philosophies and personal attitudes of these lesser Victorians.

6.

THE INSPECTORS' OUTLOOK AND CHARACTER

BEFORE HER MAJESTY'S INSPECTORS joined the government, their basic beliefs did not differ greatly from those held by other members of the early Victorian middle class. The inspectors came from the same sort of homes, of the successful and well-to-do; they attended the same schools, matriculated at the same universities, and joined the same clubs. They thus reflected the same orthodoxies. Their families, often of the professional class and of evangelical faith, taught them industry, purpose, discipline, and a sense of moral duty; and at their chapels and churches they learned a sturdy Christianity.

As witnesses of England's marvelous commercial and industrial expansion, and as readers of Adam Smith, David Ricardo, and J. R. McCulloch, many of them gained an unquestioned belief in political economy. Some of them studied moral philosophy at Edinburgh under the famed Dugald Steward; many more attended Oxford and Cambridge, where they learned the manners of gentlemen and the obligations of a ruling class. Only a few came under the direct influence of Bentham. A moderate liberalism and a Christian morality rather than a political radicalism set the dominant tone. As orthodox liberals they looked for prosperity and social improvement from the unimpeded operation of the laws of laissez faire, as Christians they expected it from the moral and religious reform of the working man, and as gentlemen they looked for it from the paternalism of a benevolent ruling class. Beneath these three convictions lay a belief that social progress depended not on a powerful state but on energetic, educated, and morally upright individuals. Though circumstances led the inspectors to a more collectivist social outlook, they never forsook the firm foundations of Victorian individualism.

The factory inspectors expressed this individualism most noticeably in their adherence to laissez faire. To Leonard Horner, a deep admirer of his fellow Glaswegian, Adam Smith, and a lifelong friend of the economist McCulloch, the protection of children was the only justification for government interference with capital. Adults were "free agents." They could bargain freely for hours and wages, and their well-being lay in their skill and industry as laborers.[1] Three of Horner's colleagues—Rickards, the shrewd and practical East India Merchant, Saunders, the Tory reformer, and Howells, the austere ex-judge—agreed. At first they all opposed the ten-hour day or any regulation of adult labor. They respected property rights and the law of supply and demand. Other inspectors also held to these principles. Two mining inspectors, Matthias Dunn and Herbert Mackworth, cautioned Lord Palmerston against undue interference with the rights of property; and James Smith, the health inspector, preached that "self-interest was the never failing law of nature." The inspectors almost to a man disapproved of trade unions.[2] The most radical-minded of them, Frederick Hill the prison inspector, condemned unions for their interference with the free and salutary working of the labor market. He also criticized any legislation that excluded women from labor in the mines or prohibited company stores. His own home had resembled, said his older brother Rowland Hill, a "political economy club."[3] Hill, like his good friend Horner and

1. *Memoirs of Leonard Horner*, ed. Katherine Lyell (London, 1890), *1*, 158, 177. Nassau Senior, *Letters on the Factory Act* (London, 1837), appendix, "A Letter by Leonard Horner."

2. HO, 45/4105. James Smith, *Report of the General Board of Health on Lancaster* (London, 1894), p. 22.

3. *Frederick Hill, An Autobiography*, ed. Constance Hill (London, 1894), p. 76. PP, *37* (1846), 479 (xviii). Frederick Hill, *Identity of Interests of Employers and Work People*, London, 1870. Rowland Hill, *Life of Rowland Hill* (London, 1880), p. 23.

like James Smith the Scottish manufacturer, grew up on a political economy which taught that the worker was a "free agent" and would prosper most in the freest economy.

The poor-law assistants, even more than other Victorians, believed in a stern individualism. Not only should the government grant the individual the right to bargain freely over wages and hours of labor, but it should guarantee that he use that right by denying him an easy, corrupting, and enslaving relief. The factory inspectors' "free agent" became the assistant commissioners' "independent laborer." The chief aim of the assistant commissioners was the liberation of the pauper from the corruption of easy relief, a conviction that rested upon a variety of presuppositions running from the rigid economic assumptions of the liberals to the harsh moral conceptions of the rural squires.

Among Chadwick's friends, liberals such as E. C. Tufnell and Alfred Power, economic reasoning predominated. Tufnell was convinced that "those who rule the destinies of nations might perform their duties more efficiently if they were acquainted with the science of political economy." Alfred Power interpreted that science to mean opposition to the ten-hour day and support of the workhouse test. In favoring the workhouse test, Power concurred with the opinions of Nassau Senior and Edwin Chadwick that the Old Poor Law had disturbed the labor market, flooding it with paupers receiving relief in aid of wages.[4] If the allowance system were ended, the market would right itself, would indeed become a free market, one governed by supply and demand.

William Day, a squire proud of his economic learning, could have explained all this. Along with many others he believed in the wage-fund theory and considered easy relief simply a withdrawal of money out of that fund from which wages were paid, wages that would make the worker an independent laborer. Easy relief, then, would not end destitution. Only reformed individuals working in a free economy could do that. The poor-law assistants took an optimistic view. There were no Malthusians among

4. *PP, 20* (1833), 531–35. Thomas McKay, *A History of the English Poor Law* (London, 1904), p. 204. *Journal of the Society of Arts* (May 1875), p. 610.

them. The wage fund was an expanding fund. The means exist, said Charles Mott, "for the absorption of surplus labor, when the natural process is not interfered with by the administration of the poor laws." [5] The liberal assistant commissioners had a faith in the natural harmonies of a capitalist economy.

The conservative assistant commissioners—men such as Goodson Adey, William Hawley, and Thomas Stevens, all country squires and all magistrates—shared with their liberal colleagues a belief in a strict relief. They even exceeded the liberals in their stern refusal of outdoor relief, urging the guardians to send not only the able bodied but the aged, the young, and the infirm to the workhouse. The political economists were not alone in the 1830's in espousing the hard doctrine that every individual must answer for his own livelihood. Adey, Hawley, and Stevens followed neither Ricardo nor Senior, yet Adey would apply the workhouse test to the aged and infirm, who "though partially disabled are still quite equal to obtain their livelihood." And his colleague from Hampshire, the forthright Hawley, decried that "benevolence which poisoned industry" and those "humanity mongers who corrupted paupers with easy relief" and so encouraged "idleness, riots, and debauchery." Hawley considered most paupers "parasites, knaves, and drivellers." [6] They were not much more to Thomas Stevens of Bradfield, the ardent tractarian from Oriel College, a clergyman and squire. Stevens ascribed destitution "to the wicked abandoned habits of the poor" and saw no other remedy for it than the development in them of those "habits of frugality, steadiness and industry which are necessary to excite in their employers a disposition to give permanent employment at adequate wages." In a sermon, *Poor Relief, Not Charity,* Stevens assured his listeners that the selfless charitable injunctions of Christ should not be applied to poor relief. Charity meant alms to really deserving poor;

5. Chadwick Papers, Day to Chadwick, Sept. 21, 1834. William Day, *An Inquiry into the Poor Laws and Surplus Labour,* London, 1832. *PP, 36* (1846), 301 (6). MH, 32/48, Kay to Commissioners, May 14, 1836. *PP, 36* (1846), 300.
6. MH, 32/6, Adey to Commissioners, Aug. 4, 1838. Chadwick Papers, Hawley to Chadwick, Nov. 5, 1837. MH, 32/38, Aug. 7, 1836; 32/39, Sept. 25, 1837.

it did not mean state relief, which, because it encouraged idleness and drink, should be limited to the workhouse.[7]

Behind the harshness of Adey, Hawley, and Stevens lay the traditions of a rural squirearchy that saw poverty as the offspring of mere indolence, and prosperity as the reward of sturdy virtues. It was a moral assumption which exactly suited the economic maxims of their liberal colleagues, and which gave to the assistants a unanimity which, in view of their varying backgrounds, was quite remarkable. Almost to a man they believed, as Tufnell formally put it, that "the circumstances of the individual are more dependent upon their own dispositions than any other cause." [8] Destitution, then, could only be removed by freeing him from a corrupting relief, by putting him on his own, in short, by making him a "free agent" and "independent laborer." The individualism of the assistants thus rested on moral certitudes as well as on economic theory.

The prison inspectors, believing in individual responsibility, shared the same moral assumptions. The criminal, like the pauper, is responsible for his fallen state and must be dealt with strictly. Easy prison discipline, like easy relief, corrupts. The criminal must first be deterred from crime by the dread of punishment; but if this fails and he is imprisoned, he must be separated from his compatriots in crime, and in solitary confinement be forced to reflect on his sins. William Crawford and Whitworth Russell, the most prominent of the prison inspectors, were convinced that prisons should be places of dread, that no discipline deterred men from crime more than separate confinement and hard labor. Sir Joshua Jebb, the inspector general of convict prisons, agreed; to create a severe discipline, he designed plans for separate cells and invented the crank, an instrument to be turned thousands of times for no other purpose than hard exertion. All three believed that the lonely reflections of separate confinement would convince the criminal of his guilt and so promote his reformation. It was an idea Crawford gained from the Philadelphia Quakers, and it

7. Thomas Stevens, *Poor Relief No Charity* (London, 1845), p. 12.
8. *PP, 19* (1842), 144.

was of course consonant with a stern Victorian individualism.[9] Whatever the social evils of the time, then, the inspectors explained them largely in moral terms and sought to remove them by reforming the individual. If children learned vice while working in factories, factory schools should be established to teach them virtue. If easy relief corrupted the morals of the poor, it should be ended in order to teach them to be independent laborers. Crowded prisons were schools of crime, but solitary confinement would convince the prisoner of his individual guilt. Even lunatics were pitied for their lack of a moral sense. James Cowles Prichard, a lunacy commissioner, wrote a book to show that insanity was not always due to delusions of the mind, the rational mechanical view of the eighteenth century, but to "errors actually in the moral state, the dispositions, the habits." He wanted a new category, "moral insanity." [10] Far more widespread than classical economics, far more deeply rooted in the outlook of the inspectors, was the assumption that social evils arose from the moral defects of the individual. "The cause of most social evils," said the education inspector J. P. Norris, "lie within the individual." [11] Pauperism could be checked, argued Tufnell, by "giving moral advantages to the children, by implanting in them the seeds of industry and good conduct." "If no education is given a child," said Leonard Horner, "What chance of his growing up to be a healthy, strong, intelligent, ingenious, honest, and right principled man, a useful citizen." [12] If no strict relief, insisted William Day, what "rewards for forethought, frugality, and industry" and what deterrence of idleness, improvidence or extravagance? "Unless [the convict] acquire habits of industry and a liking for work," wrote Frederick Hill, "little hope can be entertained of his conduct after liberation." [13] The inspectors' great hope lay in the growth among the

9. *Law Magazine* (Aug. 1835), pp. 53–55. *PP, 11* (1835), 113–22; *PP, 30* (1838), 2.

10. James Cowles Prichard, *On the Different Forms of Insanity* (London, 1842), p. 174.

11. J. P. Norris, *On Girl Industrial Training* (London, 1860), p. 12.

12. *PP, 17* (1840), 142 (75). Leonard Horner, *The Employment of Children* (London, 1840), p. 16.

13. MH, 32/15, Dec. 30, 1837. Hill, *Autobiography*, p. 183.

lower orders of good habits, of prudence and forethought, morality and sound religion. It was a moral view, in keeping both with the traditional rural attitudes toward the poor and with the new economics of Victorian liberalism.

The inspectors hoped for much from the moral improvement of the working class, but no more than what they demanded of themselves and the upper classes. Hard and exacting as they occasionally were, they were not hypocrites. Their character did not belie their pious sermons on middle-class virtues. They pursued their work with uncommon diligence, viewed their callings with a high seriousness, and lived respectable lives. "He was up at five," says the diary of Frederick Hill's wife, "and never retired till eight P.M." "Yesterday I was out at work before nine" wrote John Allen, "and with the exception of five minutes in a biscuit shop, I did not even find time for eating till after ten at night, and this morning I was in a fly by a quarter after six." [14]

Their industry was prodigious—and their integrity apparently incorruptible. In twenty years of government service not one of the inspectors was involved in graft or corruption. The praise their obituary notices accorded forms an imposing catalogue of the virtues most esteemed by the Victorians. Even after discounting the usual exaggerations of such hagiographical notices, the picture is formidable to an age of easier manners and more lax standards, formidable in particular because of the men's passion to do good.

Not a few had a seeming compulsion to improve society. Hill, from his boyhood at Hazel School, where his father had preached service to humanity, had possessed a strong wish to obtain some day "a useful and important part in government"; and Edward Gulson, upon applying for the Poor Law Commission, promised "at all times to do my utmost to serve our general weale." This was no idle assertion, for it came from a man who had given, with no pay, two years of full-time work as Coventry's Director of the Poor. Both Hill and Gulson came from nonconformist homes, as did Horner and James Cowles Prichard. Horner and Prichard possessed a lively missionary spirit. Horner told his wife that he revived his flagging spirits during the drudgery of his long hours

14. Hill, *Autobiography*, p. 211. Grier, *Allen*, p. 109.

inspecting factories by remembering "that I am the instrument of making the lives of many innocent children less burthensome." [15] Like Kay Shuttleworth and Edwin Chadwick (also nonconformist), Hill, Gulson, Horner, and Prichard had a puritan sense of calling, which they expressed in a secular dedication to social reform. Hill's father, headmaster of the progressive Hazel School, taught his sons to hate tyranny, champion liberty, and judge all social institutions by Bentham's rule of the greatest happiness to the greatest number. In Horner's home likewise was this combination of nonconformity and liberalism so productive of an ardent idealism.[16]

Less is known of the background of the health inspectors, men like Hector Gavin, Richard Grainger, Gavin Milroy, and Robert Rawlinson. Gavin and Milroy came from Edinburgh, Grainger from Birmingham, and Rawlinson from Chorley. All these places were centers of Calvinism. Long before joining the Board of Health, the men had devoted themselves to sanitary reform: both Gavin and Grainger had written books exposing the wretched conditions of the factory towns, and Milroy and Sutherland edited journals that championed sanitary reforms. As inspectors, they carried with them a crusading zeal. Said a friend of Grainger, "He himself regarded it as some acquittal of the obligation laid upon every man to be useful in diminishing the physical ills which impede the moral and religious welfare of his fellow men." This was the spirit that led Thomas Carlyle to praise the philanthropy of those "cholera doctors" who penetrated "into black dens of infection and despair." It was a spirit openly expressed by their colleague Robert Rawlinson in a letter to Chadwick in 1847. "It is," he said cryptically, "a matter of indifference how I serve the sanitary movement provided I serve it." [17]

Such fervor for reform did not, naturally, inspire all the in-

15. Hill, *Autobiography*, p. 113. MH, 32/28, Jan. 4, 1835. Leonard Horner, *Memoirs*, 2, 14.

16. Rowland Hill, *Life*, pp. 19–23, 193. *Memoirs of Francis Horner*, ed. Leonard Horner (London, 1843), pp. 1–2.

17. *Lancet*, Feb. 18, 1865, p. 190. Thomas Carlyle, *Latter Day Pamphlets* (London, 1850), p. 64. Chadwick Papers, Rawlinson to Chadwick, May 25, 1855.

spectors, especially those of a less evangelical background. But even among the amiable squires, the dour prison inspectors, and the cultivated Anglicans of the education inspectorate there ran a strain of reforming zeal. William Day, Colonel Ash A'Court, Thomas Stevens, and William Hawley had all abandoned their comfortable estates to carry the message of a sounder poor relief to unenlightened guardians. It was a tough job. The quarrels, long trips, and frustrations were unending. "My work is sadly irksome," said Ash A'Court, "but if any good results I shall be satisfied." [18] All five of these squires as magistrates had devoted great time and energy, without pay, to reforming their parishes, and all had been prevailed upon, without solicitation, to join the Commission. William Day had published a pamphlet in 1832 to spread the gospel of poor-law reform, and Thomas Stevens had left Oriel college a dedicated Christian and close friend of Robert Wilberforce and Henry Manning. The ideals of Newman, said a college friend, never left him, inspiring him to sacrifice his income to found a Christian college at Bradford.[19] Stevens was not the only inspector to sacrifice his income to the great cause of education. E. C. Tufnell, more interested in sound morality and good habits than the catechism and sacraments of the Holy Church, gave half his salary to found, along with Kay Shuttleworth, the first teachers' training school in England: St. Johns', at Battersea. Tufnell persistently argued for a stringent and severe poor law yet gave liberally of time and money that the condition of men might be improved.[20] It was a paradox not uncommon to the inspectors.

The prison inspectors William Crawford and Whitworth Russell were no less zealous for the progress of mankind than Tufnell. Crawford had been active in the British and Foreign School Society, the antislavery society, and the prison discipline society, while Whitworth Russell won acclaim for his earnest work as chaplain of Millbank.[21] Like Stevens and Tufnell, they

18. Chadwick Papers, A'Court to Chadwick, Nov. 20, 1834.
19. Rev. T. Mozley, *Reminiscences* (London, 1882), pp. 18–23.
20. Chadwick Papers, Chadwick to Prince Albert, April 25, 1857. *Journal of the Society of Arts* (May 21, 1875), p. 607.
21. *DNB*, 5, 57. E. G. O' Donaghue, *Bridewell* (London, 1927), p. 227.

were strenuous Christians, sensitive to its injunction to serve humanity. Yet these very men, so benevolent in their dedication to reform, insisted on the severest poor law and the harshest prison discipline. Crawford had devoted his life to the betterment of English prisons, yet from his ardor came the agony of solitary confinement. The error was one of understanding more than impulse. "No one," said G. L. Chesterton, Governor of Coldbath prison, "could question the purity of [Crawford's] motives," but "he was the prisoner of his too hastily formed opinions." [22] The same could be said of some of the assistant commissioners. Misreading human nature, they failed to see how social forces influenced its formation. To Hawley, paupers were drivelers and parasites. To Stevens they were idlers. Henry Pilkington, observing the large size of families among the poor, plaintively asked Chadwick, "Why do folks marry?" [23] The complexities of human nature escaped many of the inspectors, and for what escaped them they often substituted dogmas. They were wedded, and wedded very strongly, to their theories: the workhouse test for the poor, separate confinement for the prisoner, and the four-inch glazed pipe for drainage. Supreme self-assurance is perhaps an inevitable attribute of the reformer's character; certainly it was a source of strength and energy in Her Majesty's inspectors. "Our confidence in the decided superiority of separate confinement," said Crawford and Russell, "remains unshaken." [24] With like confidence, most inspectors held firmly to the cardinal doctrine that most of the social evils of England could be removed by the moral redemption of the individual, whether a pauper, a worker, or a criminal.

Many of the inspectors hoped that the higher orders would promote this moral reform and be the architects of a more humane and benevolent society. They looked to the individuals of the upper classes and not to the state to promote a benevolent paternalism, hoping that mill-owners would create model factories, farmers offer good wages, magistrates run model prisons, and landlords provide pure water and good sewers. And they hoped

22. G. L. Chesterton, *Revelations of Prison Life* (London, 1856), p. 171.
23. Chadwick Papers, Pilkington to Chadwick, Oct. 20, 1834.
24. *PP, 4* (1841), 3.

that the propertied class would give amply to support good schools for the poor. Leonard Horner praised those mill-owners whose clean mills, regular hours, and schools formed an inspiration for others. Strongly supported by his colleagues, Saunders and Howells, Horner pleaded with mill owners to build better schools.[25] The school, in fact, became the most concrete expression of this paternalism. E. C. Tufnell and Seymour Tremenheere urged poor-law guardians and mine-owners to establish or support industrial training schools, to be formed on the "model of the well-ordered family." Frederick Hill wished the same domestic order for small prisons, and he too wished the upper classes to take a paternal interest in establishing reformatories and schools.[26]

R. D. Grainger spoke for many of the inspectors when in 1846 he implored the press to "awaken the influential classes to a recollection of the high responsibility attaching . . . to wealth and power." The inspectors, like many Victorians, were shocked at the abuses of industrialism and the condition of the urban proletariat, and looked to the wealthy and well-bred to redress those conditions. "The root of many evils in the social state," said Horner, lay with "a want of a kind consideration of the employer for the employed . . ."[27] If the propertied classes did well by them, these evils would diminish. This was the ideal of paternalism propounded by Coleridge, defended by Southey, and preached by Carlyle.

The inspectors did not believe in egalitarian movements or statism. They were not democrats, and they shuddered at the idea of socialism. Tremenheere, though a fervent reformer and a friend of the workers, feared the universal suffrage of American democracy and, like most inspectors, deprecated all trade unions. Sir Francis Bond Head, a spirited poor-law reformer, said he would rather be a footman the rest of his life than endure "the stench of that society where all men are called equal."[28] All the inspectors feared the

25. PP*, 34 (1847), 9; PP, 26 (1848), 110–13 (5–8); 42 (1839), 353–429.
26. MH, 12/6042. PP, 32 (1846), 607 (398); PP*, 34 (1844), 748–51.
27. Grainger, *Towns*, p. 35. PP, 26 (1848), 160 (11).
28. Seymour Tremenheere, *The Constitution of the United States Compared with Our Own* (London, 1854), p. 296. Review of Sydney Jackman, *Galloping Head* (London, 1958), in the *Times Literary Supplement* (June 27, 1958), p. 358.

chartists. They would give the lower classes clean houses, a reforming poor law, regulated mills, and better schools, but they would not (except for Frederick Hill and the school inspector J. D. Morell) grant them universal suffrage. In their reports they spoke of the working class as something removed and alien to them, a class to be benevolent toward but not to share power with. A sense of moral duty and social necessity inspired their benevolence, not a warm compassion, and their utopia was not a workingman's democracy with unions and "fair shares" but a middle-class paternalism with sound social institutions, good schools, and a moral and dutiful working class.

The inspectors' belief in the paternalism of private citizens suited their strong individualism and their distrust of a large state. They hoped that voluntary action, with only the minimum of government interference, would correct the social and moral evils which so alarmed them. This paternalism as well as their political economy and their hope in the reformed individual showed them to be true sons of the early Victorian middle class.

Yet these very men, whose ideas would seem so antique to an English Fabian or an American New Dealer, entered government service, and before long were urging greater government intervention. With no conscious intent to do so, they helped lay the basis for the administrative state, and without abandoning their economic doctrines developed a collectivist social outlook. The theoretical contradiction in Bentham's thought between a belief in natural economic laws and in the positive role of the state in promoting happiness imposed itself on many of the inspectors in the form of concrete, ever-recurring problems. An awareness of the usefulness of the central government came into conflict with their political and economic philosophies. They saw the interconnections between ignorance, poverty, and crime. And they were aware that the great advances lately made in sanitation, education, railway engineering, prison discipline, and the care of the insane were going unheeded. They became convinced that the government in an age of material progress and social reform must play a greater role. To some of them a voluntary paternalism soon appeared an illusion. Leonard Horner told Tremenheere that not six mill-owners in all of Britain cared for the well-being of workers. The experience and knowledge acquired by the inspectors clashed openly with some of their most cherished theories.

Above all else it was their intimate and inescapable contact with the worst abuses of town and factory life that persuaded them to modify their economic theories and stern individualism. The theory of the "free agent" did not correspond to the worker's entire dependence on the mill. Factory inspectors who in 1833 opposed the ten-hour day soon changed their minds. Rickards found the theory of the "free agent" highly doubtful. "Human labor," he expostulated, "in union with machinery is not free." Robert Saunders went on record in 1844 for an eleven-hour day, and in 1847 for the ten-hour day.

It was Leonard Horner, the most outspoken of the inspectors, who criticized most bluntly the doctrines on which he had been bred. "It quite disgusts me," he said, "to hear the cold calculating economical throwing aside all moral considerations, and with entire ignorance of the state of the people who work in factories, talking of its being an infringement of principle to interfere . . . If I were free to write, I could from my experiences make such a statement as could shew the fallacious reasonings and bad political economy of those who with their extravagant extension of their doctrine of *laissez faire* bring discredit upon the science they cultivate." [29] Many things drove Horner to rethink the doctrine of free agents: the mill-owners' evasion of rules, their continued exploitation of children in factories, their failure to support good schools, and the failure of the Factory Act of 1833 to hinder in any way the growth of profits. By 1847 he was for the ten-hour day.

Facts similarly jarred the assumptions of other inspectors. Edward Twisleton and Alfred Power, who shared Tufnell's belief that destitution depended upon the dispositions of the poor found it difficult to explain the widespread destitution which the depression of 1842 brought to Stockport. To these highly successful barristers, fresh from the Inns of Court and Oxford, the suffering of the unemployed workers in Stockport came as a new ex-

29. R. K. Webb, "Seymour Tremenheere, A Whig Inspector," *Journal of Modern History,* 27 (Dec. 1955), p. 361. Leonard Horner, *Memoirs,* 2, 158. HO, 45/1117. *PP, 45* (1835), 155 (9).

perience. They saw at first hand thousands of millhands willing to work but unable to do so from want of jobs not personal industry. In their report Twisleton and Power admitted that the cause of this destitution was the depression of the cotton industry.

Tufnell, to be sure, clung to his belief that an individual's well-being still lay in his skills and character, but he admitted the problem was more complex and admitted too that one's skills and character reflect the surrounding social and moral conditions.[30] Factory inspectors saw that trade depressions caused pauperism and the poor-law assistants saw that crowded, unsegregated workhouses and wretched slums encourage vice and immorality. Prison inspectors found that widespread unemployment led to more felonies, and health inspectors found that cholera widows burdened the poor rates and that drunkenness and crime arose naturally from squalor. The inspectors became aware of the complex interactions between various social evils, and of the need for government action to remove their generating causes. Horner, Tufnell, Kay, Mott, Gulson, Tremenheere, Fletcher, and Hill, form a core of inspectors, all of a liberal background, who saw clearly the wretched condition of the urban proletariat and what it cost society to leave them in such misery. As a result they insisted on institutional reforms, factory schools, multipurpose prisons, and enlightened asylums for the insane. The poor-law inspectors followed rigidly the doctrines of individualism in treating the able-bodied, but toward the aged, the infirm, and the young they adopted the doctrines of collectivism. "The object of our first care," said Charles Mott, in every way an orthodox follower of Senior and Chadwick, "are the very young and their general protection . . ."

The health inspectors felt the same way about the inhabitants of unsanitary towns. To an awareness of interacting social and moral evils they added the material conditions of urban life, the slums and sewers that fostered disease, crime, and drunkenness. "There is no physical evil in the city," said Richard Grainger in his *Unhealthiness of Towns* (1845), "which is not accompanied by a moral evil." And he found "crime most rife where material degradation is most profound." His colleagues agreed with him.

30. *PP, 35* (1842), 43–46, 171–81, 193–225.

Hector Gavin in his *Sanitary Ramblings* found in the "sad scenes of wretched misery" in town life the same source of demoralization.[31] To Rawlinson, "Filth, misery, vice, and crime are inseparably connected"; and for his fellow engineer William Ranger, like Rawlinson pragmatic and direct, the "neglect of sanitary arrangement produced disease and misery which results in pauperism; crowded cottages, room tenements, and common lodging houses, filled with degradation, immorality, and misery, they foster crime, which acts and reacts upon the whole frame of society."

The whole frame of society! It was a concept directly expressive of the inspectors' awareness of the interconnections between social and material evils, evils which Captain Williams, a prison inspector, attributed to the "peculiar state of society, being felt principally in large towns." It was an awareness that led inspectors subscribing to the most austere doctrines of political economy to espouse collectivist social reforms.[32] Even Frederick Hill, whose home was likened to a political economy club and who said that the Government's exclusion of women from mines was undue interference, urged government support of reformatories, model prisons, workhouses, homes of refuge, mental asylums, playgrounds, picture galleries, and libraries—all places for rational amusement.[33] His friends Kay Shuttleworth, Chadwick, Horner, and Tremenheere agreed that the government had a role to play in the reformation of society. Poor-law and health inspectors shared the same views. The government was not to tamper with the economy, but it was to remove those "physical, moral, and social evils" that afflicted England's burgeoning cities.

A belief in progress and in the continued advance of knowledge and science also encouraged the reforming zeal of the inspectors, imperceptibly strengthening that strain of social collectivism which increasingly characterized their outlook. They were not only aware of pressing social evils and their mutual interrelations,

31. *PP, 36* (1846), 295 (12). Grainger, *Towns*, p. 37. Gavin, *Sanitary Ramblings*, p. 21.
32. Robert Rawlinson, *Further Report of the General Board of Health on Macclesfield* (London, 1851), p. 4. *PP, 24* (1845), 131.
33. *PP, 25* (1843), 443–59 (2–18); *PP*, 34* (1844), 747–51; *PP, 31* (1838), 8.

but they saw in the progress of knowledge a means for their removal. A true zeal for reform rests not solely upon indignation at existing evils but also upon a belief that these evils can be removed. The inspectors shared the Victorian's optimism about science and reason. They believed in the advance of knowledge, in the marvels of the four-inch glazed sewer pipe, in better mining ventilation, in curing insanity by scientific treatment, and especially in the possibility through education of molding human character. The evils of the past need not be. Civilization was advancing in step with human enlightenment.

A large minority of the inspectors were scientists. Eleven inspectors, coming from five different agencies, became fellows of the Royal Society. The Society elected Leonard Horner because of his geological research, Henry Moseley because of his work in hydrostatics, and James Prichard because of his pioneering work in physical anthropology.[34] Others, less honored, belonged to local societies, like Seymour Tremenheere, who was a member of the Cornwall Geological Society. The doctors and engineers belonged to the Royal College of Physicians and the Civil Institute of Engineers. The Royal Society invited neither Matthew Dunn nor Herbert Mackworth, both mining inspectors, to their august ranks, but Dunn wrote articles on steam-jet ventilation for the Civil Institute of Engineers, and Kings College offered Mackworth the professorship of geology. Richard Grainger and John Sutherland, two health inspectors whom the Royal Society likewise ignored, expressed their deep faith in science and its promises. Grainger, author of *Observations on the Cultivation of the Organic Sciences,* was certain that "We are on the eve of a great social amelioration" since "for the first time in our career science is about to be brought to bear on the various questions which exert so direct an influence on every inhabitant." His colleague Sutherland, later Miss Florence Nightingale's devoted servant and private secretary, wrote in 1850 that, "It must now be considered an established truth in science

34. The other eight members were John Graves, Sir Edmund Head, Sir Edward Parry, all poor-law assistants; Bisset Hawkins, a prison inspector; Douglas Galton of the Railway Department, Edmund Halswell and Edward Seymour, lunacy commissioners; and Capt. F. W. Beechey, of the Merchant Marine Department.

that the health, the wellbeing, and the duration of the life of man
are intimately connected with the observance of the natural laws of
the universe . . ." and he concluded on a collectivist note that
those laws could not be observed unless men acted "in their social
or corporate capacities for the protection of each other and of
the entire community." [35] The advance of knowledge in their own
time filled Grainger, Sutherland, and many other inspectors with
a buoyant confidence in the future. It made them impatient of
old ways and zealous for new, critical of local ignorance and
eager to use the central government to spread enlightenment.
They urged the new central agencies to promote new techniques
in mining, in the building of railways, and in the construction
of sewers; to encourage more enlightened means of treating
prisoners and the insane; and above all to improve the education
of the working class.

In their faith in the power of knowledge they voiced a credo
first espoused by the philosophers of the Enlightenment but never
until the early Victorians accepted with such quiet assurance.
The poor-law and education inspectors believed they could reform
paupers and refashion the character of the working class, making
them moral and hardworking, the secure basis of the good society.
The health inspectors had no rivals in that hopefulness which
excites a zeal for improvement. "The sanitary movement," said
Rawlinson, "is the greatest because the most humane movement in
ancient or modern times." [36] Sanitary cities, clean homes, and a
healthy working class would diminish disease, drunkenness, vice,
and crime, all of which Rawlinson viewed as inseparably connected.

Nowhere was the scientific spirit of the inspectors and the
collectivist strain in their social outlook more closely connected
than in their zeal for social statistics, through the collection of
which they hoped to make a scientific analysis of the interconnections of moral and social evils and so find means for their removal.
Kay Shuttleworth had helped to found the Manchester Statistical
Society in 1832. With E. C. Tufnell he established the Royal
Statistical Society in 1833. From 1833 to 1854 their membership

35. Grainger, *Towns,* p. 47. *PP*, 40* (1850), 187 (3).
36. Chadwick Papers, Rawlinson to Chadwick, Jan. 26, 1854.

included two education inspectors, Joseph Fletcher and Seymour Tremenheere, the prison inspectors Russell, Crawford, and Hawkins, the health inspectors Rawlinson and Holland, and Colonel Sykes of the Lunacy Commission.[37] Other inspectors, like Leonard Horner and Frederick Hill, were active in the statistical section of the British Association for the Advancement of Science. And Captain Williams, though a member of no statistical society, had a passion for collecting statistics on crime, finding in the numerous government returns on education, savings deposits, poor rates, and committals evidences of those social and moral forces which "acted and reacted upon the whole frame of society." Fletcher, the young education inspector and a disciple of Bentham, entitled his article on poverty, crime, and ignorance in England "The Moral and Educational Statistics of England." [38] Fletcher attributed all the social and moral ills to the widespread ignorance of the working class. Unemployment, pauperism, crime, intemperance, disease—all could be eradicated by sound moral and intellectual education. This was the cardinal faith of the inspectors. It suited their inherent individualism. Make the individual strong, morally sound, and skilled at a trade, and he could become a free agent and an independent laborer. But how to make the working class morally sound, strong, and skilled—that was the great unanswered question that lay within the province of the thirty education inspectors. It fell to them to carry out the Victorian middle-class's ideal of fashioning the working class in their own image and so creating a free, Christian, industrious, and prosperous society.

THE SCHOOL INSPECTORS

In January 1840 Lord Lansdowne appointed, as the first inspectors of English schools, the Reverend John Allen and Hugh Seymour Tremenheere. He chose them only after great deliberation. He had to be particularly careful about Allen, whose duty it would be to inspect Church of England schools. The Church wanted no importunate bureaucrat telling its National Society

37. *Annals of the Royal Statistical Society, 1834–1934* (London, 1934), p. 16. *Journal of the Statistical Society, 6* (1845), 48; *10* (1847), 37.
38. Joseph Fletcher, "Moral and Educational Statistics of England," *Journal of the Statistical Society, 10* (1847), 193–225.

schools how to teach the children of the poor. If there were to be inspectors, it wanted godly men like the Reverend John Allen. Both the Archbishop of Canterbury and the Bishop of London had, in fact, on Lansdowne's request, chosen Allen, who represented to them the ideal Anglican: pious, scrupulously virtuous, orthodox, and with unquestionable loyalty to the Church. He combined a forceful will with gentlemanly manners, and sought his daily guidance from prayer. From his youth he seemed destined to work in the Lord's vineyards. His father, the devout Rector of Burton, Pembroke, had imposed on him a severe and exacting regimen of prayer, study, and abstinence. Meat was eaten but every other day, and there could be no sketching of the countryside for young John until he had studied five hours. This strictness and piety apparently caused no revolt. Allen left his home for Westminster school equipped with an awe for what was holy and a detestation for what was evil. He was a studious, bright youngster, able to withstand the bullying of the older boys and impervious to their naughty pictures of naked women.

At Cambridge Allen's religious and moral ardor grew unabated. He entered in his diary his moral resolves and his remorse at not living up to them. He found the merry gatherings in William Thackeray's room too frivolous and so gave them up. Cards, dancing, and tobacco he forsook—dancing and cards as sheer idleness, and tobacco because it deadened his sensibility to the fact of sin. He was prodigious in study, rising at five to read Aristotle, and he took every opportunity to kneel in prayer. It was his mission in life, he felt, to follow God's will and expound Christian truth. He removed Thackeray's doubts concerning the Trinity, and in doing so moved him to tears. He even buttressed the faith of his closest friend, the urbane and witty Edward Fitzgerald, future translator of Omar Khayyam. John Allen's awesome morality was a force to be reckoned with at Cambridge, especially as it was displayed in an agreeable, even humorous personality. "He could," said one of his friends, "influence others without the least attempt at dictation." After Cambridge he served a term as schoolmaster at Pimlico then embarked on a successful career as lecturer and chaplain at London's Kings College (where one of his students was Charles Kingsley). It was from this post that he left to join the education office. His Christian zeal and his rugged morality were by then in no ways diminished. "He was simple, upright, and honest," said Manning, and Bishop Lonsdale added, "he had never known any man who feared God more and man less." [39]

Hugh Seymour Tremenheere was no less forceful a person than Allen, only it was not Christian truth which drove him so much as an inward compulsion to set society aright. His father, Major Walter Tremenheere, was of a good Cornish family and had retired in Wooten, Gloucester, after winning many honors in the French wars. He was reputed "the very soul of honor and high mindedness, and of great warmth of heart," the ideal qualities for a member of the local governing class, and the qualities passed on to his eldest son Hugh. The Major gave his son the best of educations, sending him to Winchester and to New College, Oxford, on the Grand Tour, and to the Inner Temple. Hugh responded with energy and diligence to his opportunities, winning the gold medal at Winchester, a fellowship at New College, and distinction as a barrister. He was thirty-six when he came to the education office, by then an ardent Whig, singularly sensitive to the social ills besetting England and deeply convinced that they could be removed by the diffusion of useful knowledge.[40]

Allen and Tremenheere, both Anglicans and both Whigs, agreed on many social ideals, above all on the moral value of a sound education. But their basic assumptions represented quite different philosophies, the Anglican's and the liberal's. John Allen nearly rejected the appointment as inspector because of his fear of the secular power of the state, and he was convinced that "it is the duty and by consequence the right and privilege of the Church to be the teacher of the nation." [41] Only the entreaties of the Bishop of London, who told him that if there were to be inspectors, they might as well be the best Anglicans, persuaded him to accept. The Church chose well. Allen was convinced that any education that was not Christian, and by Christian he meant Anglican, was useless. He abhorred education that was purely

39. Anna Allen, *John Allen and His Friends* (London, n.d.), pp. 1–29, 26, 58. R. M. Grier, *John Allen*, pp. 4–37, 49.

40. *DNB, 67*, 187. S. G. Tremenheere, *The Tremenheeres* (London, 1925), pp. 80–86.

41. *PP*, 8*, (1844), 283.

secular. The assiduous learning of the Holy Scripture was for him the core of all education. What after all was the aim of education but "to bring God's will to those who might otherwise go the way of sin and vice"? "Scriptures reprove, correct, and instruct in righteousness," he added. Full of this righteous zeal he told the children, "Let me ask you to be obedient to your parents, kind to one another, pure in your thoughts, true in your words, diligent in your daily tasks, then you will be happy yourselves, and make others happy around you." [42]

When Allen worried about the prevalence of sin and disbelief, Tremenheere worried about the prevalence of improvidence, intemperance, profligacy, and chartism. Where Allen believed with Coleridge that all social evils arose from sin, Tremenheere believed that they arose from ignorance. He put his faith in political economy, industrial training, and the development of all the faculties of man. If one could develop the intellectual, physical, and moral faculties of the pupils, train them in skills, and teach them the immutable laws of the economy, then England could meet the growing threat of the urban proletariat. The sensuality, drunkenness, and improvidence of the working classes and the spread of dangerous ideas by cheap literature persuaded Tremenheere that the gross ignorance of the lower orders threatened the dissolution of society. It was a fear that impelled him to plead with those "of superior station" to give their unremitting exertion to educate "the lower orders." Training in industrial arts, lessons in political economy, and instruction in morals, he argued, would end pauperism, trade unions, and immorality. He was certain that "right reason and right feeling could be substituted for wrong ones" and that the Norfolk laborers could be lured from the delights of the pub to the rational enjoyment of ecclesiastical architecture.[43]

42. Grier, *Allen,* pp. 84–87. John Allen, *Sermon in Behalf of an Infant School* (London, 1954), p. 7.

43. Webb, "A Whig Inspector," *Journal of Modern History,* 27, 361. *PP, 26* (1844), 43; *33* (1842), 213–328. Tremenheere's reports on education in Norfolk and Monmouth and on industrial and model schools give his views on society and education. He also wrote popular works designed to correct what he considered as perverse and radical ideas corrupting the working class.

School Inspectors

From 1840 to 1854 thirteen more Anglican clergymen joined with John Allen to inspect Church of England schools. Though they could not equal the heroic piety of John Allen, they did share his zeal for the Church and Christian morality. Like Allen they were men of respectable origins and of university training. None came from the aristocracy, and none from either the artisan or working classes. Their fathers were professional men, clergymen, doctors, solicitors, and schoolmasters. All but one of the inspectors attended universities, and fifteen of them attended Cambridge.

The Cambridge of the 1820's and 1830's was a different place from Byron's university of 1807 with its "din of drunkenness, and nothing but hazard and burgundy, mathematics and Newmarket, riot and racing . . . and intellects as stagnant as the Cam." By the 1820's there was, besides the perennial burgundy and racing, a revival of religion. Christopher Wordsworth had imposed daily chapel at Trinity, and Frederick Maurice and John Sterling, precocious undergraduates, had solemnly dedicated themselves to the preaching and practice of a Christianity that was at once liberal and orthodox. The curriculum itself had not improved much; but its undergraduates, according to Tennyson, read Jeremy Taylor and Livy, rated Shelly over Byron, and admired Coleridge and Wordsworth. It was not the lectures that provided the new ferment of ideas but, as Carlyle said in his *Life of Sterling,* "the manifold collision and communications of young ingenious living souls," of men like Arthur Hallam and Tennyson, and those other serious young men who, Monkton Milnes said, were "for their wealth of promise, a rare body of men such as a University had seldom contained." [44]

Two of England's future school inspectors preceded John Allen at Cambridge, Henry Moseley (1823) and Frederick Cook (1826). They were the contemporaries of Frederick Maurice and John Sterling. Moseley, the son of an eccentric clergyman who wrote on nervous disorders, missionaries, and Greek music, took a great interest at Cambridge in natural philosophy, in which he found truths as certain as those revealed in Holy Writ. His curiosity about

44. Hallam, Lord Tennyson, *Alfred Lord Tennyson: A Memoir* (London, 1898), pp. 36, 661. Thomas Carlyle, *Life of Sterling* (New York, 1900), p. 35.

189

the majestic and beautiful laws of the universe led him, after taking Holy Orders, to become the first professor of natural philosophy at Kings College, London. Frederick Cook, a friend of Moseley and later of Thackeray and Tennyson, turned his Christian devotions to biblical scholarship and philosophy. After winning a first in the classical tripos, he journeyed to Germany to study under Niebuhr and Schlegel and to prepare for his lifelong battle against disbelief and skepticism, a battle he waged not only in the schoolroom but later by voluminious scholarly writings in linguistics and biblical criticism.

John Allen and Frederick Cook were still at Cambridge when William Brookfield and William Kennedy came down from Sheffield and Birmingham. Brookfield's father was a solicitor of high standing and his mother the daughter of the vicar of Sheffield's parish Church. Kennedy's father was the Reverend Rann Kennedy, curate of St. Paul's, Birmingham and a schoolmaster at King Edward's, a poet of some reputation, intimate friend of Coleridge, and a man much praised for his moral excellences, transparent honesty, complete rectitude, and Christian humility. Each of the three sons of Reverend Kennedy attended Cambridge. Benjamin became Maurice's fast friend, Charles won innumerable honors, and William gained the Parson prize (as had his two older brothers) for Greek composition.

Little is recorded of William's stay at St. John's. Such was not the fate of William Brookfield. Handsome in appearance and talented in conversation, he became a conspicious figure among the bright wits and fashionable gentlemen. He did not forsake, as did Allen, the jollier gatherings. He possessed, his friends said, an irresistible humor and a lively mind. Yet beneath this gaiety was a sturdy common sense and a sober Christian faith. Tennyson called him a man of humorous melancholy mark. Thackeray modeled Frank Whitelock of *Curates Walk* on Brookfield, just as he had used John Allen as the original of Major Dobbin in *Vanity Fair*. As a clergyman in a fashionable London church, Brookfield impressed all with his eloquence and learning and his serene confidence in Christian truth and man's reasonableness. He called himself, despite his love of convivial gatherings and his faith in the power of reason, a Calvinist, and so vigorously did he preach God's injunctions that Carlyle praised "his manful front against a world of confusion and obstruction." [45]

A similar spirit of moderate Calvinism pervaded most of the Cambridge inspectors, including the youngest of them, John Pilkington Norris. Norris was the son of a Chester physician who had displayed in boyhood a precocious love of biblical studies which fitted him for study at Arnold's Rugby. At Cambridge he won the Latin prize, a first in classics, and a fellowship at Trinity. In 1849, at twenty-six, he became an education inspector, eager to improve the Church's religious education. Though he had some predilections for the High Church (he edited the works of John Keble), he saw the Anglican Church, as did Allen, Cook, Moseley, and Brookfield, as the *via media,* the national establishment, the conscience of the nation, the instrument whereby the children of the poor could be saved from infidelity and immorality, the cement of soceity.[46]

The Cambridge-trained inspectors won their appointments for their promising talents and their zeal for the Anglican faith. There were among them no extremists, no ardent tractarians, no zealous evangelicals, no skeptical latitudinarians. They represented the comfortable, comprehensive middle way, a comprehensiveness that infuriated the first Catholic inspector of schools, Thomas Marshall. Marshall was the son of an Anglican clergyman, a graduate of Cambridge, and a priest in the Church of England. But at twenty-seven he turned to the Catholic faith, and did so with a passion that led him to attack, in polemical writings full of sarcasm, the broad, ill-defined, easy-going faith of his colleagues.[47] But the Cambridge clergymen remained undisturbed by Marshall's ill-mannered diatribes, and undisturbed too by Lyell's geological writings, or the German rationalists. They believed in the Scriptures, the Thirty-

45. *Times,* Jan. 23, 1872. *Notes and Gleanings,* 2 (1889), 114–18. Brookfield, *Sermons,* pp. viii–xliii. Grier, *Allen,* p. 29. Charles and Francis Brookfield, *Mrs. Brookfield and her Circle,* New York, 1905.

46. *The Biograph* (1881), pp. 64–65. J. P. Norris, *The Education of the People,* Edinburgh, 1869.

47. Thomas Marshall, *My Clerical Friends,* London, 1873. *Biographical Dictionary of English Catholics* (London, 1895), p. 479.

Nine Articles, and the Catechism. Like Allen they desired that the Bible and the Book of Common Prayer form the core of education. Every parish needs, said Frederick Cook, teachers who "are well acquainted with Holy Scripture, trained in habits of devotion and reverence by bonds of affection to the Church." [48] Nowhere were these bonds of affection stronger than in the lives of Cook and Moseley, Brookfield and Norris, men who brought to the schools of England a beautiful and unruffled faith.

Moral truth, even more than theological truth, defined the educational outlook of these earnest men. They wished, to be sure, to bring the saving grace of Christ to parishes where the blessed light of the redeeming gospel had never shone, but even more intensely they wished to save the children of these wildernesses of ignorance and depravity from moral corruption. Despite their orthodoxy, the hope of moral improvement led some to assert the possibility of man's moral perfectibility, a sign both of the optimism of the age and of its preoccupation with morality. "The powers of the mind," said Henry Bellairs, "are well nigh infinite." "Man has an intellect," said Henry Moseley, "whose resources no effort would seem to exhaust." "Train up a child in the way he should go," said Allen, "and when he is old he will not depart from it." The inspectors assumed for man's character what John Locke assumed for his intellect, that it was a *tabula rasa,* upon which one could impress habits of virtue, honesty, and industry. "The philosophy of Locke," said Bulwer Lytton in 1833, "is still the system of the English." [49] The education inspectors were no exception. "Not more certainly," said Moseley, "does the metal take the form of the mould into which it is poured, than the child receives and retains the impressions of its early years." To inculcate good habits was the primary function of education and would lead to the reformation of the humbler classes. It was the same belief which dominated the outlook of the poor-law assistants.

The education inspectors indeed did not greatly differ from the

48. *PP**, *40* (1853), 42.
49. Henry Bellairs, *Sermon on Work* (London, 1852), p. 12. Henry Moseley, *Faith in the Work of a Teacher* (London, 1854), p. 5. Moseley, *A Treatise on Mechanics* (London, 1847), p. 22. *PP, 33* (1842), 277. Bulwer Lytton, *England and the English,* p. 228.

social views of their fellow Victorians of liberal persuasion. They believed in the same economic doctrines and saw the same social needs. Both John Allen and J. P. Norris, theologically the most conservative of the Cambridge group, valued political economy highly. Allen found its laws as certain as the laws of Newton, and Norris said that the more it was studied the more the "rule let alone has been adopted . . . and wisely, for what is civilization but self control." [50] But despite agreement on its basic truth they both, as did so many other inspectors, opposed its extreme forms. Allen espoused the social collectivism held by his superior, Kay Shuttleworth, and Norris preached the same paternalistic notions that Tremenheere espoused. "The let alone doctrines of the political economists," said Allen in 1857, "are wrong when applied to material doctors (hospitals) and spiritual doctors (teachers, clergy)," and Norris, who worked with Tremenheere to persuade mine owners to support industrial schools, believed that these schools should be, as Tremenheere had said, in *loco parentis* to the children of the poor. Norris was convinced that the home was "the seed vessel of society," and where such did not exist, the tasks fell to state-supported schools.[51] Their aim was to teach virtue, virtue, and more virtue. "Since each virtuous act so done tends to the formation of a habit," said Bellairs, the most platitudinous of the clerical inspectors, "the teacher must inculcate among the children habits of industry, perseverance, tidiness and order . . . and teach and see practiced the precepts of the Gospel, piety, truthfulness, gentleness, sobriety, diligence, and self denial." [52]

Underlying the orthodox faith of these inspectors, their hope of moral perfection, their laissez-faire philosophy, and their concern with social improvement lay a deep belief in the harmony and rightness of God's universe and the certainty of progress. They had no difficulty in reconciling science and religion and finding in both certainty and order. Religion and philosophy joined in their minds to assure them of the world's goodness. John Allen, the most

50. John Allen, *The Dormant Energies of Our Universities* (London, 1862), p. 8. Norris, *The Education of the People*, p. 31.

51. Grier, *Allen*, p. 246. Norris, *On Girls' Industrial Training and Education*, pp. 12–15.

52. Bellairs, *Work*, pp. 17–19.

devout of the inspectors, felt that "Everything that happens, happens well, for it is wisely ordered by our all powerful, all loving Father"; while Henry Moseley, whose particular zeal was for science, wrote a popularized picture of the Newtonian universe, *Astro-Theology*, published by the Church of England. In the book he expounds on the beauties and wonders of the stars and planets, their uniformity, their economy of motion, and the harmony of the governing laws, all of which testified so wonderfully to the Divine intelligence.[53] Scriptural truth, Frederick Cook believed, had nothing to fear from the discoveries of science, and the serene and eloquent Brookfield not only spoke rapturously of "the vast concurrence and minute operations by which the plants of the earth are brought to perfection" but assured his congregation that "reason, which God has breathed into man [was] in no way hostile to man's moral and spiritual nature." [54] Convinced of the harmony of the universe and man and the divinity of reason and intelligence, they all believed in man's progressive improvement through a Christian education. Norris was quite excited over the prospects, rejoicing that the Church, which "has gone on growing larger and larger, stronger and stronger, from that day to this, will go on until Christ comes to earth." [55] In the Cambridge-trained, clerical inspectors orthodox Christian beliefs fused firmly with the optimism of the enlightenment; confronted by the infidelity and moral anarchy of the industrial towns, they responded with a hopeful, confident, and consequently forceful Christianity. This outlook, in the hands of men of strong will, great learning, and assured position, must have made a deep impression on those more sensitive teachers and pupil-teachers who were to rise from the humbler ranks to become the schoolmasters of the working classes. The influence these exerted in the schools gave sustenance to one of the sturdier roots of middle-class Victorianism.

The eight laymen, six dissenters, and two Catholics who worked at the education office shared many of the assumptions of the Cam-

53. John Allen, *Practical Sermons* (London, 1846), *3, 273*. Henry Moseley, *Astro-Theology,* London, 1851.

54. F. C. Cook, *Modern Scepticism* (London, 1871), p. 461. Mrs. Brookfield, *Sermons,* 144, 212.

55. J. P. Norris, *Easy Lessons on Confirmation* (London, 1877), p. 14.

bridge-trained Anglicans. The secular inspectors believed with the Anglicans that education could remedy social evils. In Joseph Fletcher, E. C. Tufnell, Jelinger Symons, and other inspectors of poor-law schools, the secular, social idealism of Tremenheere (who retired in 1844) was carried on. These men believed in the creed of Kay Shuttleworth and Edwin Chadwick, in a benevolent state promoting the social good by education, sanitation, and legislation. Good workhouse education, argued Tufnell, would "make it a moral certainty that they [pauper children] shall never in after life become dependent on the rates, but always maintain respectable and independent stations." "Improved or invigorated institutions of education, police, providence, and sanitary administration," wrote Joseph Fletcher in the *Journal of Statistic,* "are essential . . . to the healthy fabric of society." [56] In Fletcher, Tufnell, and Jelinger Symons, Kay Shuttleworth found ardent disciples of this Benthamite gospel. Like Tremenheere they were social analysts and social reformers, alive to the problems of poverty, ill health, and crime and convinced of the need for a better poor law, improved sanitation, and more and better schools.

In farm schools like those of Switzerland they found their ideal. Both Fletcher and Symons wrote of the ideas of Pestalozzi and de Fellenberg, and of the utility of industrial training and farm life in reforming pauper and criminal children.[57] With these hopes, of course, the Cambridge-trained inspectors were in agreement. The differences were those of emphases, not basic assumptions. J. P. Norris, though firmly attached to scriptural education, still worked hard for farm schools based on Pestalozzi's domestic economy, while Jelinger Symons, England's most enthusiastic proponent of farm schools, wished teachers to "christianize the hearts" of the pupils and "chasten their conduct, instilling into their minds principles as well as habits of virtue, kindness, and obedience." [58] Symons' background was not unlike Allen's or Moseley's. His fa-

56. *PP, 17* (1840), 242 (75). Fletcher, "Moral and Educational Statistics," *Journal of the Statistical Society, 12* (1849), 171.

57. Fletcher, "Statistics on the Farm School System of the Continent," *Journal of the Statistical Society, 15* (1852), 1–50. J. Symons, *Popular Economy* (London, 1840), pp. 41–46.

58. *PP, 13* (1849), 287 (235).

ther was a very vigorous clergyman, wealthy enough to send his son to Cambridge. And though after Cambridge Symons chose law, not the Church, he outdid his clerical colleagues in moral fervor and sententiousness. He praised gardening because it taught forethought and economy and constantly reminded one of God; he urged the teachers to suppress evil habits and encourage all Christian virtue and to teach "truth, obedience to parents, gentleness, kindness, fidelity, courteousness, habits of attention, docility, and disinterestedness." He urged that farm schools allow no leisure, but impose upon their students "incessant industry." [59]

Symons had no doubts about the value of such a heroic regimen. If half the poor rate were spent on education, he announced, there would be no pauperism. His ideas were almost a caricature of the sanguine assumptions of the liberal inspectors. He wrote books, as did Tremenheere, to popularize the great truths of political economy, and declaimed against chartism and unions. Yet like Tremenheere he reprimanded capital for not being more paternal to its employees. He believed with Moseley that there was a great chain of being harmoniously binding the world to God's laws, and to the depths of his soul he felt that "there is no question that we are advancing in mental culture and in the mighty progress of the human weal." [60] Jelinger Symons' passionate nature comprehended all the religious, social, psychological, and philosophical presuppositions of the education inspectors, and he gave to these presuppositions an expression whose intensity and enthusiasm irritated the country squires who ran the poor-law schools. But they are a measure of the seriousness of the Victorians and a reflection of their central concerns.

The education inspectors, both clerical and lay, found themselves in agreement on the basic aims of education. But what of the methods for achieving these aims? How best to teach virtue and industry? On this problem there was also a large area of agreement. All the inspectors were sharply critical of rote learning, harsh dis-

59. *Gentleman's Magazine*, 2 (1851), 211. *DNB*, *55*, 280, 311.
60. J. Symons, *Popular Economy*, pp. 1, 44, 106, and *A Few Thoughts on Volition* (London, 1833), p. 13. *PP**, *13* (1849), 309 (257).

cipline, and a narrow curriculum; as already noted, they also embraced in varying degrees the ideas of the Swiss educators Pestalozzi and de Fellenberg. The clerical inspectors tended to draw their method from practical observations while the secular inspectors were more ardently Pestalozzian.

The clerical inspectors found the National Society schools bogged down in the mechanical instruction of Bell's monitorial system. They urged its substantial modification. Their approach was pragmatic, offering to the teachers occasional maxims gained from their wide reading and experience. "Excite their curiosity," said John Allen, citing the psychological insight of Paley, and do not use the rod. As for arithmetic, he advocated Pestalozzian exercises.[61] "In geography," said Bellairs, "use maps freely and extend the children's knowledge gradually from the known to the unknown." Teach them only a little and that well, was Norris' advice, for the important element is not the amount of information but the training of the intellect.

Moseley, too, as almost all inspectors, considered mere subject matter secondary to the disciplining of the mind. For him the physical sciences were best suited for such discipline, since they inspired the abstract love of truth.[62] The most idealistic and progressive of the clerical inspectors, he admired the Pestalozzian methods used in Shuttleworth's and Tufnell's Battersea training school. Like Pestalozzi he objected to grammar taught as a mere classification of words, history as mere chronology, and geography as mere topography, and would have instead a wide series of subjects taught, from music to science, and in a way that would arouse the pupil's curiosity, lead him to think for himself, and develop all his faculties, physical, intellectual, and moral. This was a buoyant view which his more conservative colleagues, Watkins and Kennedy (both from Cambridge) did not share. Watkins wished only a few elementary subjects more fully and practically taught,

61. Grier, *Allen*, pp. 103, 105. *PP*, 35 (1843), 301, 384.
62. Henry Bellairs, *The Church and the School* (London, 1868), p. 117. *PP*, 40 (1852), 386. Moseley, *A Treatise on Mechanics Applied to the Arts* (London, 1847), p. 26.

"by which he meant writing, speaking and reading, and a respect for the law," and not ornamental subjects like history. Kennedy expressed alarm over the growing progressivism, the phonic system of teaching reading, the failure to learn the alphabet by heart, and the abandonment of dogmatic learning in the early stages of arithmetic in favor of teaching its principles.[63] Except for Moseley's diffuse and warm-hearted suggestions, it remained for the secular inspectors to champion most consistently the new theories of the Swiss educators.

"Primary education must," said the crusading Jelinger Symons, "partake of the vital principle imparted to it first by Pestalozzi." With this opinion Tufnell, Fletcher, and Tremenheere agreed.[64] They were all acquainted with the teachings of this kindly, imaginative educator, and of his pupil de Fellenberg. Tufnell and Kay Shuttleworth had adopted many of his techniques at Battersea, Fletcher wrote of them in his book on *Farm Schools,* and Tremenheere mentioned them in his reports. The development of all the faculties of man, intellectual, physical, and moral, was to Pestalozzi the aim of education, and the method for achieving it was the evoking and training of the natural faculties. The child's curiosity should not be dulled by memorizing words and numbers, but excited by presenting it with concrete, vivid examples of the truths to be learned. From this one should move naturally to words, generalizations, and analysis. According to Pestalozzi the moral affections and mental process could be trained into "habits" of virtue and understanding, just as clay could be molded into pottery. Pestalozzi had read Locke and Rousseau, and combined a belief in the goodness of natural instincts with a belief in the ability of the mind to learn from experience. These ideas influenced Tufnell, Symons, Fletcher, and Tremenheere, as well as Lord Brougham and the editors of the *Educational Times.* Much of Pestalozzi's influence came, however, from the agreement of his ideas with the teachings of Hartley, Dugald Stewart, and the philosophers of the enlightenment. All held an optimistic, rational, and even mecha-

63. *PP, 35* (1845), 583–88; *6* (1845), 125. F. Watkins, *A Letter to the Archbishop of York* (London, 1860), p. 18. *PP, 40* (1852), 346–48.
64. *PP, 33* (1842), 327 (212). Symons, *Popular Economy,* p. 42.

nistic belief in the power of education to mold human nature.[65]
In the reports of Symons and Tufnell, as in the reports of the
clerical inspectors themselves, this Lockean psychology was dominant. It expressed itself in the repeated use of the word "habit"
accompanied by other key words: "to impress," "to inculcate," "to
instill," and "to train." "Above all," said Norris, "the purpose is
to create in children habits of order." "Characters form themselves," said Moseley, "not upon principles but upon feelings, reiterated until they become habits." And Symons talked of "instilling habits of virtue, kindness, and obedience." [66] Though they all
stigmatized mechanical learning, their zeal to train the mind and
impress Christian virtues on the moral affections was not without
its mechanistic overtones. They had an ineradicable belief in discipline and direction, a fact which marks their progressivism from
that of John Dewey.

That moral discipline which was so dear to the inspectors was
not to be physically harsh. The inspectors opposed corporal punishment and angry scolding. Allen, Fletcher, Cook, and Moseley
were themselves gentle and kind, and were exemplars of the virtues
they advocated. They urged teachers to impress habits of virtue
upon their pupils by firm rules, not sudden anger. The "habits of
obedience" said Tremenheere, should be "founded on affections
rather than fear, by appeals to reason and conscience." [67]

They also believed in a strict mental discipline. Reasonableness
as well as morality could be inculcated in the pupil. None held this
belief more firmly than the young protestant clergyman J. D. Morell, whose *History of Modern Philosophy*, written at the age of
thirty-one, had delighted George Eliot and so impressed Lord
Lansdowne that he picked Morell as a school inspector in 1846.[68]

65. H. Holman, *Pestalozzi: An Account of his Life and Work*, London,
1938. *Educational Times*, Jan. 1, Feb. 1, 1850. J. Payne, *Pestalozzi: The
Influence of his Principles and Practice*, London, 1875. *PP, 33* (1842),
327 (212).
66. Norris, *The Education of the People*, p. 187. *PP, 9* (1845), 167; *13*
(1849), 287 (235).
67. *PP, 40* (1843), 373 (156).
68. Robert Theobald, *Memorials of J. D. Morell* (London, 1891), pp. 26,
56.

In the reports that followed and in his textbooks on grammar he offered the teachers clear and systematic methods of education. He classified elementary learning into four divisions, knowledge and application of signs (reading, writing, spelling), knowledge of facts (geography, history, natural history), knowledge of abstract relations (mathematics and grammar), and the inculcation of sentiment. His treatment of the first of these was traditional. His treatment of the second was Pestalozzian, insisting that geography and history be made vivid by the concrete realities of county geography and local history. Upon the third group of studies he placed the most emphasis and thereby showed the rational bent of a philosopher. For him as for Moseley no faculty approached "the faculty for abstract learning." To promote this faculty on the elementary level he would teach grammar, for in grammar lay "all the elements of logic, and even philosophy." He found it the most ineptly taught of all subjects, and to remedy the condition he wrote an elementary grammar, excellent for its definite statements and simple rules made clear by perceptive illustrations, all of which helped to "train the mind to classify and reflect." [69]

Morell had a high estimate of man's rational faculty. More than any other inspector he reflected the rationalism of the nineteenth century. Though the son of a Congregational minister and trained at a Congregational Academy to preach its gospel, his real love was philosophy, the study of which he had pursued at Edinburgh and at Bonn, where he studied under the great Fichte. His faith was in reason. He described the Reformation as a triumph of reason, heralded the French Revolution as the advent of the modern age, and preached the egalitarian doctrine of the rights of man. He believed education "an unmixed blessing"—"every man has within him the genius of boundless faculties, of vast moral aspiration, of unlimited improvement." But rationalist as he was (and his study of religion led him to Unitarianism), he never doubted the value of moral and religious education, which he called "the head and crowning piece of the whole." He urged the teachers to use a collection of poems edited by his colleague Frederick Cook, a collec-

69. *PP, 80* (1853), 623–29; *PP**, *37* (1850), 467. P. A. Barnwell, *The New Morell: A Grammar of the English Language,* London, 1892.

200

tion filled with poems by Southey and Wordsworth.[70] Through these poems the teacher could inculcate in his pupils noble sentiments and clear moral truths. All the inspectors would have agreed that this was the ultimate aim of education. They felt it their duty to bring about the moral and social salvation of Victorian England.

The most illustrious of the education inspectors was Matthew Arnold, who joined the service in 1851. He was in general agreement with all the ideas but not with the uncritical enthusiasm with which the other inspectors espoused them. He saw in education an avenue to social order, material progress, and morality. He believed it should humanize society. His more sophisticated, more aesthetic, and more critical viewpoint put him at some distance from the pious Cambridge clergy and the ardent social evangelicalism of Symons and Tufnell. "I am a liberal," Arnold confessed, "yet I am a liberal tempered by experience, reflection, and renouncement." [71] His renouncement distinguished him from his colleagues and made his views of less practical force in the schools. He was a critic more than an educationl reformer, and his ideas were better suited to the review than the schoolroom. He took his job to gain an income for marriage, and only afterward, from that sense of duty that was an inheritance from his father, did he take an interest in "civilizing the next generation of lower classes, who as things are growing will have most of the political power." His real educational interest was in reforming the philistines among the middle class and the barbarians among the aristocracy. Civilizing the working classes remained for Matthew Arnold an onerous chore, and he remains an untypical representative of the dominant ideas of the education inspectors. He was, to sum up, a critic, not an enthusiast, and enthusiasm for industrial training and the inculcation of moral virtues lay at the core of the clerics and lay reformers of the education office.

As a sensitive critic of the sorrowful condition of the working class Arnold agreed with the other inspectors that laissez faire had

70. Theobald, *Morell*, pp. 6–23. T. Binney, *Memoir of Rev. Stephen Morell*, London, 1826. J. D. Morell, *On the Progress of Society in England as Affected by the Advancement of National Education* (London, 1859), pp. 2–11. *PP**, *37* (1850), 473–74; *80* (1853), 628.

71. Matthew Arnold, *Culture and Anarchy* (London, 1924), p. 3.

its limits, and that the state was a creative force for betterment. He advocated in his work on European education and in his *Culture and Anarchy* the social collectivism of the inspectors, and dared arouse the deepest English prejudice by "freely recognizing the coherence, rationality, and efficaciousness which characterizes the strong state action of France," and by criticizing the "want of method, reason and result" of the feeble state actions of England." [72] Arnold felt, as Horner did when he expostulated at the hard reasoning of the economists, and as did Chadwick when he declaimed against special interest, that the social ills of England demanded the intervention of the state.

Yet Arnold never spelled out the details of that intervention. Like Mill, he had read Tocqueville on centralization and had gained a fear of a strong central government. He also had, as did so many Victorians, an ambivalent attitude toward the state. He wanted state aid to schools so that they might be less feeble, yet he opposed compulsory education as undue interference. He was for the state as a creative force, yet clung to Victorian individualism. In this he represents many of the inspectors whose social outlook comprehended a deep individualism with a growing need for state action. He also represented their high seriousness and sense of duty, their abilities, and their force of character, which made them wherever they went, whether into mines, factories, prisons, or schools, effective beyond the mere statutory power they possessed as Her Majesty's civil servants.

72. W. F. Cornell, *The Educational Thought and Influence of Matthew Arnold* (London, 1950), p. 78. G. H. Bantock, "Matthew Arnold, H.M.I.," *Scrutiny*, June 1851. Much that Mr. Bantock ascribes to Arnold, such as the distinction between mechanical and vital knowledge, was commonplace among the inspectors.

7.

INQUIRY AND REPORT

THE INSPECTORS' FIRST JOB was to investigate. No report could be written, no policy formed, no order issued until they had learned at first hand what problems confronted them. It was not an easy task for undermanned central agencies. Even if they had investigated only the work of the local authorities concerned, the mere numbers of poor-law unions or schools or mills would have demanded considerable diligence. But they investigated much more. Full of the social reformer's passion, they probed into all aspects of Victorian society. They asked about the miner's drinking habits, the number of savings deposits among factory operatives, the social background of teachers, the marriage age of agricultural laborers. They collected statistics on wages and employment, and they sampled public opinion on political and social questions. Such inquiries proved invaluable to a government anxious about the social evils afflicting England. In many instances they were the beginning of an administrative process aimed at the removal of the evil in question.

The carefulness and the breadth of these inquiries varied from agency to agency and from inspector to inspector. The poor-law commissioners expected their assistants to investigate much more than did the railway commissioners. Not only were the poor-law assistants to visit the workhouses, attend the guardians' meetings, and check the overseers' books, but they were to inquire into the condition and habits of the lower classes and search out the opinions of all those who were affected by the law. The commissioners wrote to the assistants: "The peculiar nature of your office gives you opportunities belonging to no other public functionaries, to acquaint yourself with the condition of the working class." More than one government employed the service of the assistants to secure needed information. Lord John Russell in 1838 had the assistants investigate the wages, cost of living, and condition of the agricultural classes, and in 1839 he had them investigate the education of paupers and the sanitary condition of the laboring classes. In 1842 Graham sent them north to study the distress in the manufacturing towns, and in 1847 the Board of Trade had them look into the potato famine.[1] Whatever the failings of the poor-law assistants, it cannot be said that their investigations were superficial. Colonel Ash A'Court interviewed countless land surveyors to determine whether there was a surplus of laborers, and Kay Shuttleworth sent questionnaires to 247 employers of farm laborers.[2] Closer to the working class than any other agency and larger than any other agency, they had the best opportunity to make inquiries which would teach the Victorians to recognize their social evils.

But they were not, as the commissioners had said, the only public functionaries with an opportunity to inquire into the conditions of the working class. By 1836 the factory and prison inspectors had already investigated, and they were soon followed by the education, health, and mining inspectors. Kay Shuttleworth at the education office was hardly the one to limit the purview of the inquiries of the education inspectors. As a doctor in Manchester he had examined, street by street, the working men's tenements, and as an assistant commissioner he had journeyed to the continent to inquire into the education of pauper children. Many of his inspectors shared his interest in social inquiry, though only one possessed as intense a curiosity about the problems of society: Hugh Seymour

1. MH, 1/1, p. 55. HO, 73/56, p. 53. MH, 1/10, May 5, 1842; 10/6, Jan. 4, 1847.
2. Anon., *Parish and Union* (London, 1837), pp. 75–76. HO, 73/93, May 19, 1837.

Tremenheere inquired into social conditions in Norfolk and Monmouthshire; his inquiries covered a wide range of facts, about church attendance, savings deposits, the truck system, wage payments in pubs, and cheap periodicals. His colleagues, with a more subdued curiosity, asked only about the poverty and morality of the working men. The factory inspectors did the same, though occasionally they also investigated political sentiment. In 1848 they polled the factory-owners as to their opinions on the ten-hour day, a practice of sampling public opinion first used by the poor-law assistants. In 1838 James Stuart raised considerable controversy by visiting a chartist meeting to assess its dangers. His visit perturbed Lancashire's radical MP John Fielden and aroused the suspicions of Benjamin Disraeli, who both charged the Home Secretary with using factory inspectors as spies. Their charges bothered Lord John Russell very little. He reminded them that it was his prerogative to preserve the King's Peace, and he had the right, indeed the duty, to keep a watchful eye on the agitations of the working class.[3]

Local authorities did not always welcome the probings of government inspectors. The arrival of the Board of Health inspectors filled many an owner of unsanitary tenements with trepidation. Occasionally the owners organized meetings in opposition, but the inquisitions of the inspectors, who usually came armed with a petition signed by one-tenth of the rate payers, were remorseless. Accompanied by municipal officials, clergymen, doctors, journalists, and curious onlookers, they painstakingly unearthed old cesspools, visited overcrowded lodging houses, and searched out refuse littered alleys. After such a tour the inspector interviewed the local poor-law guardians and their medical officers, thus fulfilling the Board's orders to question the best qualified parties. Witnesses were summoned and hearings held. The investigations were protracted, tedious, thorough, but not without excitement. In most instances they presaged a revolution in the town's sanitary system.[4]

By 1854 England's central government possessed a network of

3. Hansard, 55 (1839), 785–808.
4. For unofficial accounts of these inquiries, *Macclesfield Courier*, May 20, 1854; *Newcastle Chronicle*, Sept. 27, 1850; *Bristol Mercury*, Feb. 23, 1850.

inspectors whose investigations left little unobserved. Not being limited to mere routine checks, they extended their inquiries into many fields, even those properly belonging to other agencies. Poor-law assistants asked about the care of the insane, education inspectors reported on bad drainage, factory inspectors examined working-class schooling, lunacy commissioners visited workhouses, and the emigration commissioners inspected the sanitary state of steamships. Everywhere the inspectors searched out the shortcomings of local officials and voluntary societies, ferreted out the abuses of private capital, questioned officials, and noted down their achievements. And as if this were not enough, they visited the homes of colliery workers and cotton operatives, in order to expose to the view of the governing classes the most intimate details of the miseries of the lower orders.

THE INSPECTORS' REPORTS

All but one of the new departments, the Merchant Marine, issued annual reports. Hansard printed the ever increasing flood, which became known as Government Blue Books. The volumes soon became a burden to the conscientious MP and were in the opinion of the *Economist* a costly waste.[5] To the general public they must have seemed an arid desert of bureaucratic detail. But to the local officials, and the owners of factories, collieries, and railways, they could be of the liveliest interest. And to the modern historian they are an invaluable source.

The reports served many purposes. They told of the willingness of industry and local authorities to adhere to governmental regulations; they explained new policies and proceedings; they described the social and moral condition of the country; they gave statistics on crime, education, and pauperism; and they espoused ideas for further reform, urging it on both local authorities and Parliament.

The inspectors' first consideration was to report the facts. If a factory violated the law, the violation must be made public; if schools were inadequate, it had to be reported. This was the view of Matthew Arnold. In his 1855 report he made it clear that "the

5. *Economist, 5* (Aug. 7, 1847), 893.

inspector's first duty is that of a simple and faithful reporter . . ."
"Inspection," he added, "exists for the sake of finding out and reporting the truth and for this above all." He was deeply concerned
at the loss of critical candor in the reports of school inspectors and
at the great temptation to reduce all to "a common flood of vague
approbation." He insisted on the "literal and unvarnished truth." [6]

Arnold's ideal was not easy to attain. Many of his colleagues
found it difficult to record gross incompetence. It pained the Reverend John Allen, a man of Christian charity, to call a schoolmaster ignorant, yet he felt it his duty to be honest, and such was
the unfortunate state of working-class schools that his reports could
only be critical. His answer was to tell the truth of the abysmal
state of education in "the spirit of love." He praised schoolmasters
when he could and pointed out their merits, but he never allowed
serious deficiencies to go unnoticed. His integrity was above reproach. On one occasion a sharp censure by Allen of a National
Society school aroused that Society and alarmed the members of
the Committee on Education of the Privy Council. They summoned the young Allen to appear before them. Sir James Graham,
after reminding Allen of his youth, asked him to remove the censure. Allen, who feared God alone, replied that it was either the
whole report or none. The Tory Home Secretary yielded and the
report was published.[7] In part because of Allen's courage, the government refused to censor the reports of education inspectors.

Allen wished to be both honest and kind. His colleagues varied
between these virtues. Ardent social reformers, such as Tremenheere and Symons, felt a compulsion to expose. "The great art is
to detail sham and expose glosses," said the pugnacious Symons in
1847. Tremenheere followed this rule so well in exposing the
failure of the British Society's monitorial system that his reports
led to his dismissal.[8] Preferring kindness to candor were Kennedy
and Fletcher. Kennedy followed the pleasant homily "Be to their
faults a little blind; be to their virtues very kind"; and Fletcher,

6. Matthew Arnold, *Reports on Elementary Schools* (London, 1910),
pp. 27, 34.
7. Grier, *Allen*, p. 141. *PP**, 7 (1845), 193.
8. *PP**, 79 (1853) 669; *PP*, 40 (1843), 655–70. (62–77).

who succeeded Tremenheere, found monitors "very respectable little agents," and praised the British school so generously that the *Westminster Review* reprimanded him for not telling the unvarnished truth.[9] The reprimand was a little severe. Both Fletcher and Kennedy, though inclined to "be to their faults a little blind," reported the more serious shortcomings. As a whole the education reports, with their strictures on dull masters and dilapidated buildings, their exposure of financial weaknesses, and their vivid sketches of the chaos of the monitorial system measured up to Arnold's ideal. It was a bleak picture, painted with warts and all.

The reports of the poor-law inspectors and the General Board of Health also preferred "unvarnished truth" to a common flood of vague approbation. Undue praise of local officials was not one of Edwin Chadwick's failings, and it was he who compiled and helped write the poor-law reports in the 1830's and the Board of Health reports in the 1850's. Many of the poor-law assistant commissioners and all the health inspectors shared his critical spirit. No timidity blunted Dr. Gavin's judgment in 1850 that many tenements were "utterly unfit to house cattle in," or Grainger's charge that London's boards of guardians were "totally unfit to supervise and enforce the ameliorations demanded for the wellbeing of the industrial classes." [10] Unpaid overseers and overpaid medical officers received equally severe remarks from the poor-law inspectors. There were, to be sure, poor-law assistants and health inspectors whose reports were perfunctory and uncritical. Perfunctoriness was the besetting sin of all bureaucratic reports and like "a common flood of approbation" was an enemy of the unvarnished truth. It did not find much place in the spirited reports of Chadwick's inspectors, but it crept into the later reports of the Poor Law Board and reduced the tithe reports to meaningless platitudes. Year after year, they monotonously repeated that all was "tranquil and harmonious"; a phrase that seemed hollow in 1843 when they suddenly demanded that Parliament give them greater powers to force recalcitrant tithe owners to come to a settlement.

9. *PP**, *37* (1850), 170; *9* (1846), 361. *Westminster Review, 16* (Sept. 1846), 106.

10. *PP**, *40* (1850), 468 (41), 479–503 (119–44); *31* (1851), 468 (42).

Perfunctoriness also invaded some of the prison reports. "All the prisoners expressed themselves happy and satisfied," read one report, a statement which, as the *North British Review* noted, one could scarcely conceive of as applying to those in England's dismal prisons.[11] The reports of John Perry in particular suffered from such clichés, and it was in his district that the worst scandals occurred.[12] But Perry was one of the most indifferent. Others were more critical. Among these were the two determined advocates of separate confinement, Crawford and Russell. Much to Elizabeth Fry's discomfort, they lambasted every aspect of Newgate Prison, exposing the beer-drinking, gambling, and undisciplined association of all prisoners that made it England's foremost nursery of crime. Captain John Williams also felt no hesitation in exposing "the scenes of real and abject misery" at Radford Debtor's Gaol, nor did Hill in detailing the mismanagement of the police jails at Durham and Newcastle.[13]

The factory, mining, and railway inspectors faced a more delicate job in reporting the unvarnished truth. The governors of the Durham and Radford jails did not have the power and influence which England's captains of industry possessed. Furthermore, most of the mining inspectors were former coal-viewers and collier managers who had every disposition to favor the owners; and factory inspectors had close ties with the mill-owners. Despite these close associations, the inspectors reported violations and negligence with remarkable candor. Only James Stuart of the Factory Office and Sir Frederick Smith and General Paisley at the Railway Board fell prey to "a common flood of approbation." Stuart never doubted the integrity and dutifulness of the mill-owners, and the reports of Smith and Paisley said little that would anger the men who ran England's railways. The railway panic of 1845 and the sharp rise in accidents that occurred after 1849 persuaded the Railway Board to report in more severe tones. Lieutenants Galton, Laffan, and Wynne discussed outspokenly the causes of railway accidents. In

11. *North British Review, 7* (1849), p. 24.
12. *PP*, 34* (1844), 167–649; *37* (1845), 207–397; *37* (1846), 673–1158.
13. Elizabeth Fry, *Memoirs*, p. 233. *PP, 35* (1836), 3–21; *26* (1843), 360 (121); *PP*, 44* (1849), 192, 199–200.

his long summary report of 1854 on these causes, Galton provoked the anger of railway-owners by stating that six out of seven accidents might have been prevented if there had been proper care by the managers of the railways and their servants.

The reports of the mining and factory inspectors for the same year were no more laudatory of mill- and mine-owners. "The majority of accidents," wrote Herbert Mackworth, "are attributable to the neglect or recklessness of the proprietors or managers of mines." Leonard Horner, whose blunt reports had long irritated the *Economist,* reprimanded the factory owners severely in 1854 for the many accidents due to unfenced shafts. Such reports, however, pleased Lord Palmerston, for whom they were intended. "It will surely be better," he wrote to his assistant, "to have the real opinion of these [mining inspectors] . . . than to have a cooked report." [14] Palmerston's advice is in sharp contrast to Graham's wish that Allen delete part of his report on schools. By and large the inspectors agreed with Lord Palmerston in wishing no "cooked" reports. Dullness and indifference existed, to be sure, but the rule was candor not reticence.

The reports of the new central agencies were not limited merely to the defects and merits of local authorities and the enforcement of industrial regulations; they sought also to describe the ills besetting Victorian society. Many of the inspectors were reformers, not routine bureaucrats, and their reports reflected this fact. They searched out abuses, described the misery of the lowest orders, exposed the social and moral evils of the new towns, and proposed no end of remedies. Though they commented on many aspects of English life, they said little on politics and political economy. Politics was too controversial and political economy too rarefied. Stuart only stirred up parliamentary criticism with his remarks on chartism, and Rickard's long essay on political economy in the 1835 factory report seemed irrelevant to the Home Secretary.[15] But though the Government wished no essays on theoretical economy, it would accept observations on the state of the national economy.

14. *Railway Times,* May 6, 20, 1854. *Macclesfield Courier,* March 11, 1854. *PP*, 42* (1854), 9; *PP, 15* (1855), 280–83 (5–8), 692 (113). HO, 45/5377.
15. HO, 43/46, p. 190.

Such observations became a regular feature of the factory reports, as they had for the poor-law reports.[16] In 1838 the Government had asked the poor-law assistants to report on the condition of the poor, wages, cost of living, and prospects for employment. In 1842 the commissioners sent Twisleton and Power to Stockport to investigate and report on the depressed state of the cotton trade.[17] But though the reports of all these men were wide in scope, including information on investments, wages, and employment, they did not offer explanations that went very deep. In explaining the depressions of 1842 and 1847 they relied on the current assumptions of the day, pointing to a sudden overexpansion of production as the cause and seeking a remedy in the free working of the market. The weaknesses of capitalism did not really concern the inspectors, who never doubted its rightness. What occupied their minds and what filled their reports with the liveliest digressions were essays on the social, moral, and physical condition of the laboring classes.

Throughout the reports there runs like a leitmotif the phrase "the social and moral condition of the laboring class." It was sometimes varied by adding to it the word "physical," or omitting "social," and often, after observing the infidelity of the workers, "religious" was included. But scarcely ever was "moral" omitted from the formula, and scarcely ever did it include "economic." These upper middle-class Victorians viewed the condition-of-England question not as did the Webbs two generations later, in economic terms of wages, employment, trade cycles, and a national minimum, but in moral terms, of habits, character, and morality. They had confidence in economic trends but only the deepest anxieties about the social, moral, and physical evils that drove the working classes into the barbarism which Macaulay feared might engulf civilized society.

The word "social" invariably preceded the others in the trilogy of social, moral, and physical evils. To most inspectors it was a vague word. In Horner's reports it referred mainly to the relation of classes, and in particular to the growing estrangement between

16. *PP*, 22 (1842), 342–45 (5–8), 360–68 (23–31); 27 (1843), 329 (40).
17. *PP*, 35 (1842), 193; 26 (1848), 108–36 (3–31); 27 (1843), 291–332 (3–43), 338–70 (3–35).

the operatives and their employers, while in the reports of Frederick Hill it had both a broader and a more detailed meaning, including the cheap theaters and absence of public parks and baths. In Tremenheere's reports it referred to the relations of various classes. He viewed with alarm the dissolution of those relations which once bound squire, yeoman, and tenant farmer in the rural village, and the advent in the towns of a wide gulf between capital and labor. In his report on Norfolk he decried the ending of the "easy gradation and social cohesion" that marked the relations of lord, yeoman, and laborer, and the growth, due to capitalistic farming and manufacturing, of that "vast interval between the classes" which lessened "social sympathies."

Bellairs, one of the Cambridge-trained school inspectors, shared Tremenheere's uneasiness. "We are at a period," he wrote, "when the distance between the different classes of society seems rather to increase than diminish." [18] Tremenheere explicitly, and the other inspectors implicitly, realized that England was in the midst of an industrial revolution, and they described quite clearly its social consequences. They regarded these vast social changes primarily in terms of the growth of a laboring class whose ignorance, immorality, and heathenism threatened civilized and Christian life.

To their lively religious consciences the social evils were at heart moral evils. They always linked together the two terms, and used them to refer to the same set of evils: improvidence, drunkenness, indolence, sensuality, and disrespect for law and order. The poor-law reports especially traced pauperism to the poor's moral failings, about which they revealed, in their private reports, considerable indignation. Gilbert found paupers addicted to "idleness, drunkenness and vice," and Gulson referred to them as "the idle and worthless." Day, too, shared these feelings when describing their "scenes of revelling and debauchery, of gambling and even fighting on the Lord's day [and] of men besot with ale, and women privately indulging in the gin bottle!" [19] By 1848 these feelings had not changed. Vagrants, said Grenville Pigott, were "idle rogues,

18. *PP, 33* (1842), 315–23 (200–8); *PP**, 7 (1845), 290.
19. MH, 32/28, July 3, 1835; 32/26, June 9, 1835. *PP, 35* (1835), 221 (114); *29* (1836), 360.

spending the day in idleness, beggary, plundering and prostitution, repairing at night to the workhouse." To Sir James Walsham they were the "lowest dregs of society . . . idle, turbulent, and filthy"; and Hawley, the stern squire of Hampshire, dismissed them as "worthless characters." [20] The assistant commissioners viewed vagrancy as another of the moral evils that afflicted the working classes.

Of all the "moral" evils which beset Victorian England the most alarming was the increase in crime. Its violence threatened both persons and property. It is not surprising that the prison inspectors sought the causes in the social and moral condition of the lower classes, or that its most liberal inspector, Frederick Hill, should— like Tremenheere, Fletcher, and Tufnell—describe them in detail. In his twelve reports he told of the drunkenness, sensuality, deep ignorance, and coarse immorality of Scotland's proletariat, of their lack of any rational amusement but the cheap theater and beer shops, and of any schooling but the dismal dame schools. Hill found in drunkenness and "the want of the habit of steady industry" the immediate cause of crime, and ignorance the ultimate cause. Economic distress he mentioned as secondary.

His colleague, Donatus O'Brien agreed with him. Not sheer hunger or want, said O'Brien, drove unemployed men to steal, but the corruptions and temptations of idleness, above all idle hours wasted in beer shops. Agreeing with all other inspectors, O'Brien singled out ignorance as the main cause of crime.[21] Where ignorance is widespread and deep it is natural to ascribe to it manifold evils. In an age like our own, one that has seen illiteracy greatly reduced, such attributions seem naive, yet it would be an anachronism to condemn the Victorians of naiveté. The reports of the education inspectors dealt directly with this ignorance, which all agreed lay at the bottom of England's ills. Tremenheere in his lengthy reports on Norfolk, Monmouth, and Cornwall revealed its striking extent. The Monmouth miner was well paid, but he saved nothing at all, married early, lived in squalor, and drank up his wages at the pub. Reckless, improvident, and given to sensuality,

20. *PP*, *53* (1848), 236,(1), 240 (5), 245 (10).
21. *PP*, *21* (1842), 375 (6), 383–84 (14–15); *25* (1843), 455–58 (14–17); *PP**, *37* (1846), 1165–81 (vii–xiv); *39* (1847), 3–25; *45* (1848), 638–85.

the miners spent their Sunday evenings in the pub not in the chapel or church. Norris also found miners sunk in moral depravity. Ten years after Tremenheere's distressing picture, the miners were still spendthrift, self-indulgent, and abandoned.[22]

Miners were not alone in these frailties. The "shameless and filthy habits" of the lower classes in Lancashire mill towns shocked the Cambridge-bred Frederick Watkins, while Henry Moseley reserved an entire section of his education report for a discussion entitled "Moral Condition of the Population." In that essay he summed up the conviction of almost all inspectors that the poverty of the people had less to do with their social degradation than was usually assumed.[23] The main source of that degradation was, of course, ignorance, and above all ignorance of religious and moral principles. The absence of any sound moral training, said numerous inspectors in countless reports, caused the intemperance, pauperism, and crime which threatened English society.

The famous reports of the Poor Law Commission on the unhealthiness of towns added the term "physical" to the "social" and "moral" evils that afflicted England. The reports of the Board of Health continued this exposure. One can almost smell the putrefying matter, open sewers, and rotten cesspools while reading them. One can see vividly the common lodging house, "huge forcing beds of vice," with eight to ten persons of both sexes inhabiting the same small room. Such pictures were designed to exploit the moral revulsion of the Victorian to sexual promiscuity. In carrying out this design the inspectors did not spare many details, or hesitate to dwell on moral consequences. In Dover, reported Rawlinson, there was a "moral plague, in its action fatal to the individual . . . the poor live together without even a show of decency or modesty." [24] In Barnard Castle, wrote Ranger, the wretched slums drive the poor to "gambling schools and to pubs . . . where drinking and smoking deprave the mind and brutalize the desires," and in these slums "fifteen and sixteen-year-olds shamelessly cohabitate."

22. *PP, 40* (1840), 615–24 (208–17); *20* (1841), 181–99 (84–97). *Mining Journal,* Sept. 24, 1843.

23. *PP*, 14* (1847) 242 (228); *9* (1846), 167–71.

24. Robert Rawlinson, *Report of the General Board of Health on Carlisle* (London, 1850), p. 56, and *Report on Dover* (London, 1849), p. 13.

From "one generation to another" he added in this report, "the lowest classes remain shameless, godless, and reprobate."

From the physical evils came some of the moral ills which afflicted the new urban centers. "Filth, overcrowding, and neglect," wrote Rawlinson, "produce vagrancy and crime. And as civilization advances, making no adequate provision for the poor in their homes and in their education, so does crime increase . . . and there will be no safety for property." [25] Ignorance, overcrowding, and bad sanitation—these were the main moral and physical evils the inspectors persistently mentioned.

The picture, however, was warped and exaggerated, colored throughout by a middle-class morality. The Monmouth miner's love of gin, the Irish vagrant's hatred of work, the Glaswegian operative's indifference to religion shocked the respectability of the inspectors. The Reverend Frederick Watkins of Cambridge could not hide his shock at "their shameless and filthy habits, and want of chastity," nor could the hard-working, self-made professor of civil engineering, William Ranger, restrain his indignation at sixteen-year-olds cohabiting. To these puritans such frightful moral transgressions lay (as Tufnell had said in his report on pauperism) in the disposition of the individual. It was not low wages, long hours, and unemployment that plagued English society, but moral error, infidelity, sin, the lazy importunate pauper, the criminal, and the drunken miner. "The evils under which [the laboring class] suffers are essentially moral," wrote Henry Moseley in 1846, "and if the renumeration of labour was doubled, they would remain unchanged . . ."

Among some of the inspectors these severe judgments were softened by an awareness that the individual was not entirely to blame. "The child," said H. G. Bowyer, one of the education inspectors, "is undoubtedly the creature of circumstances." This was a point of view implicit in the factory and poor-law reports which denied that children were free agents.[26] Robert Owen's heretical view that adults, too, are products of circumstances they could not ac-

25. W. Ranger, *Report of the General Board of Health on Barnard Castle* (London, 1851), p. 18; and Rawlinson, *Further Report on Macclesfield*, p. 25.
26. *PP**, 9 (1846), 167; 79 (1853), 583 (96).

cept. Adults were rational and free, but children were dependent and malleable; their habits were yet unformed. The fault then lay not with the child but with society's failure to give him a sound education—a failure, said Bowyer, to "surround him with such circumstances, whether physical or moral, as shall call into actions the better part of his nature." [27] The education inspectors never ceased to remind the Victorians of their failure to teach their children good habits.

Even for adults the inspectors occasionally admitted mitigating circumstances. The squalor and ill health and disease to which they were subjected were not always their fault. The reports of the Board of Health insisted again and again that disease forced many workers or workers' widows on poor relief, and that the sheer misery of slum life encouraged drink and crime. Even Tremenheere, one of the most puritanical of the inspectors, admitted in his report that the Monmouth miner sought drink as a relief from the hardships and dangers of the mines. The inspectors had no desire in their reports to insult the working classes; they decried the immorality that they saw, but they intended their exposure of the worker's ignorance and moral degradation not as a personal reprimand but as a rebuke to the upper classes who tolerated such abuses. They knew that no worker would read their reports, but they hoped that those who governed would. Horner could not hide his impatience with mill owners who failed to supply good schools, or Allen his irritation over the apathy of country gentlemen toward parish schools. The inspectors told the unvarnished truth about workhouses and mills and then rebuked those in authority for their failings. On the whole, the reports formed a stern indictment of the Victorian governing classes.

The inspectors were not satisfied merely to rebuke local authorities and factory-owners; they also set forth their own remedies. As a mere matter of official duty they had to explain official policies and aims. All the agencies did this, printing general rules and instructions. Some reports, like those of the Tithe and Copyhold Commission, did little else. The reports of other agencies went

27. Ibid.

beyond such narrow limits, first in order to disseminate useful suggestions to local officials, and secondly to argue for further reforms that would remove the moral and physical evils from which the working classes suffered.

Most inspectors had great faith in the value of reports as a means of disseminating useful information. The poor-law commissioners purposely compiled their reports to spread sound principles, and they made specific recommendations in them. The commissioners, for example, defended the value of paid officials, laid down specific workhouse rules and diets, set forth the proper methods of accounting, and argued for the superiority of the open bidding system in hiring medical officers. At the Board of Health, Chadwick and his inspectors wrote with equal detail about the virtues of consolidated water and sewer systems and the use of small-bore tubular drains. Each report of the engineering inspectors was a piece of propaganda for the Board's particular system of sanitation, laying down for the local boards the most specific rules. Just as detailed and equally propagandistic was the famous Third Report of William Crawford and Whitworth Russell on prisons. In this report they spelled out the proper size of prison cells, the right amount and kind of labor for each prisoner, the proper diet to be fed him, and the kind of moral instruction to be given him. Other inspectors lectured in less infallible tones but not with less zeal. Fletcher, Moseley, and Morell had a more gracious sense of tact than Crawford and Russell, but their disquisitions on educational methods were long and forceful. An effective way to expound one's ideas without appearing to dictate—a practice the education inspectors had to avoid—was to report on a model prison or school, hoping its efficiency would inspire imitation. Moseley's full description of the Reverend Richard Dawes' excellent Kings Somborne school and Fletcher's report on the Borough Model School provided local school committees with useful and concrete essays on pedagogical technique. In the same manner the lunacy commissioners' reports on those asylums which had rejected the use of mechanical restraints encouraged the timid governors of less enlightened asylums to follow suit. The reports of mining inspectors on the effectiveness of steam-jet ventilation in Northumberland collieries had a similar effect on the Staffordshire mine owner who wished to reduce accidents.[28]

The inspectors' eagerness for social improvement carried them beyond the mere dissemination of practical administrative suggestions. They also argued for fuller legislation, above all legislation which would remove those moral and physical evils which so preoccupied them. Horner in 1841 could not refrain from urging that "the moral condition of the working class . . . is so low it calls loudly for the interposition of Parliament" and that "no remedies can so securely be relied on as the wide extension of education." In 1849 Captain Williams, in his prison report, addressed Parliament in similar vein: "It is in the general moral and physical improvement of the humbler class that we can expect a decrease in juvenile delinquency." His colleague, Captain Kincaid, in both his factory and his prison reports, reiterated that prisons would not be empty until people attended to the moral and social condition of the poor classes.[29] Such improvements were to provide the panacea.

In spelling out improvements, many of the reports went beyond their own administrative areas. Two classic examples of this are James Kay's 1838 report on pauper education and Edwin Chadwick's 1842 report on unhealthy towns. Both championed basic social reforms, laying down two sovereign remedies for the moral and physical ills from which the working classes suffered: better education and better sanitation.

These two remedies were often echoed in the reports of other inspectors. Frederick Hill's faith in the beneficent influence of education was as sanguine as that of E. C. Tufnell, who called it "the universal remedy." Hill admired Tufnell's program for the industrial training of the children of the poor, (an enthusiam Tufnell gained from de Fellenberg, the Swiss educator) and made it the core of his theory of prison discipline. In Hill's reports good schools became an institutional answer to all the social and moral

28. *PP, 50* (1848), 5–14; *PP*, 14* (1847), 467 (449); *PP, 29* (1854), 40–53; *PP*, 29* (1850), 3 (2); *36* (1847), 74–75.
29. *PP, 22* (1842), 368 (31); *PP*, 31* (1850), 34; *42* (1850), 509.

problems of the day. Better education would reform character and improve habits. He expounded these ideas so ardently that the Home Secretary had to chastise him. "Your report," said George Grey, "is merely a pamphlet." So it was. So also was Kay's report of 1841 in which he urged a system of district workhouse schools, which would reform all paupers and thus eventually end pauperism; a report onto which the sophisticated commissioners wrote the sarcastic comment: "The renewal of the golden age. The wolf shall dwell with the lamb, and the leopard shall lie down with the kid . . . and a little child shall lead them. I fear we are not ripe for this at present." The pedestrian Grey could hardly have thought other of Hill's claim that the wisest principles of prison discipline were bound to accord with the Christian spirit of love.[30] Carlyle would have dismissed such talk as "rose water imbecility."

But the inspectors shared few of Carlyle's prejudices. They were closer to Mill's idealism and his faith in the rationality of man. They believed in the power of education to make men more perfect. Even the lunacy commissioners, who insisted that a "want of moral control was one of the commonest symptons . . . of insanity," reflected this belief in the universal efficacy of education when they urged that managers of asylums train their patients in habits of cleanliness, order, and useful industry.[31] The phrase could have occurred in a poor-law, education, or prison report. It revealed the utopian vision that made the reports of many inspectors something more than unvarnished reports of facts, made them blueprints for the reform of Victorian society and exhortations to action. Their effectiveness, of course, rested on their veracity and cogency, and on the extent to which they were actually read. They would be of little importance if unread or if dismissed as mere opinion.

Public Criticisms and Uses of the Reports

The reports of the new central agencies bore the stamp of official approval: they were the reports of Her Majesty's Government, directed to Parliament, and available in the Stationery Of-

30. HO, 12/1403. Smith, *Kay Shuttleworth*, p. 67.
31. *PP**, *42* (1849), 68 (5); *36* (1847), 228–35 (220–26).

fice. They carried weight sufficient to arouse very biting criticism on the one hand and to be invoked as unimpeachable authority on the other. Naturally, the more controversial the topic, the greater attention they aroused; few men paid attention to the reports of the Tithe Commission or the Department of Science and Art; but many closely scrutinized the reports relating to the New Poor Law, the struggle for the ten-hour day, state aid to Church schools, and the laying down of London's sewers.

Persons who were hostile to a large central government received all the reports with a jaundiced eye. The *Economist* was not too happy about the Education Committee's minutes of 1847; they found its two long volumes dry, minute, contradictory, and full of "tedious correspondence" and "frivolous letters." "We have in fact," they protested, "more big books than ever . . . to darken our minds with a vast multitude of words and frivolous things." By 1854, the addition of more central agencies and more bulky volumes led the *Times* to protest against the flood of costly reports, symbols of the growing size of England's central government.[32] Men jealous of this spawning bureaucracy could not endure its costly publications. Yet it was the public's very jealousy of the bureaucracy that made it insist on publication of reports.

Parliament and most of the press wanted reports, but they wanted them to be accurate and fair. They were not timid about criticizing them, even when they lacked the evidence to do so. The *Leeds Mercury* in 1847 and the *Railway Times* in 1854, with almost nothing to go on, roundly condemned the education and railway reports for those years. The *Railway Times* accused Galton, the author of the railway report, of deliberately making "out the worst possible case," and the *Leeds Mercury* called Henry Moseley's report "either highly overcharged or exceedingly incorrect." The *Mercury*, having little evidence to rebut Moseley's case, resorted to *ad hominem* argument, claiming that "men fresh from the refinements and external adornments in the seat of learning, or in the metropolis [were] unfit to form a true estimate of the moral condition of the seats of manufacturing and industry." Edward Baines, Jr., editor of the *Mercury*, was voicing the resent-

32. *Economist*, 5 (Aug. 7, 1847), 893. *Times*, Feb. 7, 1854.

ments of middle class nonconformists against the Anglican Church, the central government, and the universities, whose cultivated graduates now presumed to tell Lancashire and Yorkshire men that they had failed to provide schools for their own towns people. The railway-owners had a like resentment against royal engineers who told them that they mismanaged their railways.[33] In both cases the reports they attacked were among the more judicious and careful. The same could not be said of the poor-law reports of the 1830's, the prison reports of Crawford and Russell, the factory reports of James Stuart, and the reports of the Board of Health. All these suffered from prejudice and highly colored reporting.

It would, of course, be difficult to prove that the poor-law reports were "fraudulent and false," as the *Times* confidently asserted. But it would not be difficult to prove that they were highly colored. They had an argument to present—that the New Poor Law and the workhouse test would end pauperism—and they selected and colored their facts to that end. "I have been working day and night," wrote Colonel Ash A'Court in 1836 to Edwin Chadwick, "that we may have a glorious case to submit to Parliament."[34] This was the spirit behind their earliest communications. From the first, even before the law could have had much effect, they proclaimed its success. Rates were falling, wages rising, and once idle, improvident, and unruly paupers were becoming industrious, obedient, and independent workers. In the first annual report Gulson triumphantly recorded the law's wholesome results, labor depauperized, the worker's character reformed, and the rate-payers' money saved, while Adey described a moral improvement in the conduct of the workers, a rise in employment, and a falling off of the beer trade. In the second and third reports the commissioners were even more buoyant: pauperism was disappearing in the South and workers were more civil and industrious. In the fourth report Stevens maintained that he knew of no instance in which the commissioners' policy had failed to bring the most beneficial effects. In 1838 the assistant poor-law commissioner,

33. *Leeds Mercury*, Jan. 16, 23, 1847. *Railway Times*, April 22, 1854.
34. *Times*, Oct. 25, 1838. Chadwick Papers, A'Court to Chadwick, Feb. 3, 1836.

Herbert Voules, from far away Cumberland, wrote of "hereditary and habitual paupers being converted into industrious and independent labourers." [35] Across the length and breadth of England assistant commissioners reported miraculous regeneration. Their communications read like letters from missionaries describing the conversion and rebirth of the heathen.

Favored by fine harvests and a local willingness to end the costly and inefficient old system, the New Poor Law did in fact bring substantial savings, did force the importunate dole-seeker to find work, and did improve the miserable workhouses which had been the lot of the old and infirm. But it did not do all the reports claimed: it did not work a miracle of regeneration, nor, as the Webbs point out, did it solve the problem of destitution; it certainly did not work in every instance, as both Stevens and Mott claimed.

From a believer of Mott's faith fine discriminations were not to be expected. His reports on the Keighley and Bolton Unions were so critical of the guardians and poor alike that they angered the populace of both towns and led Colonel Ferrand, Keighley's member of Parliament and an ardent Tory Radical, to protest vigorously. John Bowring, MP from Bolton, wrote to Chadwick in the strongest terms concerning Mott's insulting picture of the working class. As a result of these protests Graham sent Sir John Walsham down to make another report. Walsham's report omitted Mott's wild charges that the guardians had exaggerated the extent and severity of the trade depression in order to promote their anti-corn law agitation, but he did confirm Mott's belief that the Keighley workhouse "was a nursery of filth and vice." [36] The report didn't please Ferrand at all, even after a select committee judged both reports substantially accurate, and censured Mott only for expressions "too general and unqualified." Ferrand responded with a virulent pamphlet attacking both reports, but he misunderstood his adversary's faults.[37] Mott's reports expressed in an extreme form the assistant commissioners' tendency to say only good of

35. *PP, 29* (1836), 1–35; *35* (1835), 223–29 (116–22), 268–80 (161–73); *31* (1837), 128–72 (1–45); *28* (1838), 282 (137), 177 (32).

36. MH, 12/5594. *PP, 36* (1846), 295–306; *49* (1847), 62. Bentham Papers, Box 155, p. 96, Bowring to Chadwick. *PP, 35* (1842), 69.

37. *PP, 40* (1844), 335. W. B. Ferrand, *The Great Mott Question* (London, 1844), pp. 1–30.

the new law and only bad of the old. Their fault was a strong bias, not willful misrepresentation. Certainly their reports on distress in Stockport and Rochdale showed a willingness to admit that during depressions the workhouse test was unjust and should not be enforced. By the late 1840's, when Sir George Lewis and Sir Edmund Head were poor-law commissioners, the reports had become much less prejudiced, but also less spirited, less imaginative, and less penetrating.

The prison reports of Crawford and Russell had the same mixture of bias and vigor which marked the poor-law reports. Their lengthy third report of 1838 was a learned and provoking essay on prison discipline, built around a single unquestioned premise: separate confinement was the best of all disciplines; it would reform the criminal and deter others from crime. They said of separate confinement what Stevens said of the workhouse test: it worked in every instance. They selected only evidence that would support their view, condemned all association of prisoners, and defended their own opinions with wearisome and repetitive arguments. Publication of the report excited the liveliest criticisms. George Chesterton, governor of Coldbath prison, pointed out in the *Monthly Law Review* its "unblushing partiality" for the separate system and "insulting tone toward all other disciplines." Even the Reverend Walter Clay, chaplain of Preston Gaol and a defender of the separate system, regretted that this report "was much blunted by . . . unfairness and inaccuracy." [38]

Crawford and Russell, like Mott, had a flair for pronouncing the harshest judgments on the most trivial matters. They could not, for example, restrain from pronouncing one of the books in Newgate prison indecent. The publishers of the book took them to court for libel and won. (The case did not end there. The House of Commons considered the Kings Bench review of a government report a breach of Parliamentary privilege. After five court actions and the arrest by the Commons of the sheriff who served them the libel writ, Lord John Russell settled the dispute by having Parliament pass a bill that granted all government reports immunity

---

38. *PP, 30* (1838), 1–118. Chesterton, *Revelations,* 186–88. O'Donaghue, *Bridewell,* p. 229. W. L. Clay, *The Prison Chaplain: A Memoir of Reverend John Clay* (Cambridge, 1861), p. 185.

from any libel proceeding.[39] The report of Crawford and Russell had unwittingly won a footnote in the constitutional history of England, and the ancient privilege of Parliament to unlimited free speech now extended to the inspectors' reports.)

The pronouncement of decided opinions on questions great and small characterized many of the reports of the more important inspectors. Frederick Hill exercised no detachment about the virtue of industrial education for prisoners, and his colleague Captain Williams used his fourth report to argue for the association of prisoners in silence, the very system Crawford and Russell condemned. Each education inspector openly espoused his favorite pedagogical techniques. As Morell, the philosopher of the education inspectorate, wisely observed, "Some viewpoint or other must in fact underlie every individual report." [40] The crucial question was how such assumptions were held, self-consciously and fairly, or dogmatically. Did the dogmatism of the Board of Health, for example, obscure its perception of the scientific truths of sanitation?

According to the inspectors' enemies, their dogmas distorted their statement of the truth. Captain Pechell, Brighton's MP and an opponent of centralization, called the report of inspector Benjamin Babbage on the town of Bromyard a "tissue of absurdities and misrepresentations." The Commander of the Royal Engineers at Portsmouth said almost the same of Grainger's and Rawlinson's report, calling it "a tissue of willful misrepresentation." Sir Benjamin Hall, speaking in Parliament, called the Board of Health's 1854 report "but a pamphlet written by Edwin Chadwick in laudation of his department's proceedings"; and Lord Seymour complained that the Board's reports were "all unanimous, all one-sided, and all useless." The Institute of Civil Engineers denounced the Board of Health's report of house drainage, and the Royal College of Physicians criticized the Board's report on cholera and quarantine.[41]

39. Spencer Walpole, *A History of England, 4,* 198–203.
40. *PP, 37* (1850), 463.
41. Hansard, *124* (1853), 1350; *134* (1854), 1302; *135* (1854), 985. Lewis, *Chadwick,* p. 286. Finer, *Chadwick,* p. 445. *Bromyard Petition on Public Health,* London, 1851.

Criticisms of Reports

Both groups leveled grave charges containing just enough truth to discredit the Board's reports. For Babbage to have cited three funerals in three days as evidence of the unhealthiness of a town, especially as the three who died were over sixty, provided the critics with a fine example of the inaccuracy of impressionistic reporting. And the unequivocal statement in the report on house drainage that four-inch tubular drains were far superior to all others was overly dogmatic. Chadwick's 1854 report was laudatory of his achievements, but ignored real defects in the administration of the Board of Health. The best that can be said for these defects is that they were the invariable concomitant of bold conceptions, imaginative policies, and originality of thought. The report on house drainage set forth the real virtues of tubular drainage, but it erred in defending so small a bore; and the famous report of 1850 on cholera, though it wrongly claimed that the effluvia of putrefying matter caused cholera, did mention impure water—the real cause of the epidemic—as a predisposing condition, and urged every town to provide its inhabitants with pure water.[42] With all their exaggerations and their doctrinaire spirit, the staff of the Board of Health believed fervently in inquiry, experimentation, and fact. Chadwick, compiler of the highly tendentious poor-law reports wrote the revolutionary sanitary report of 1842, just as Tremenheere, the prejudiced critic of the monitorial system, wrote reports on miners that aroused the conscience of the English governing classes. These forceful reports made a deep impression on the public mind. No amount of hostile criticism could really dissuade Parliament and the public from regarding them as authoritative.

The bulky blue books the new central agencies issued annually did not, on the whole, make exciting reading. The government in 1848 could sell only £101 worth of the poor-law reports.[43] Earnest as the Victorians were, they hardly wished to read about prison diets or the proper gradients for the Brighton-London Railway. The reports themselves did not win a wide public. Their real impact lay rather with the influential few who read them, the MP's,

42. *PP**, *40* (1850), 458–82 (83–97).
43. MH, 19/65, Jan. 26, 1849.

225

the local authorities, and the editors of the press. Through these channels they eventually altered public opinion in England.

Members of Parliament referred to them frequently. And whenever they invoked factory reports or education reports, they were heard with respect. In the battle for the 1846 education appropriations MP's cited the reports of both education and factory inspectors. They did the same in 1850 when a bill for rate-supported schools was before the House.

The reports of the prison inspectors played a similar role in Parliamentary debates, especially in the House of Lords, which since 1835 had dealt with that knotty problem. Lord Portman called the third report of prisons the most valuable ever presented. Lord Lansdowne, speaking for the 1836 Juvenile Offenders Bill, insisted "that no one who read [their] reports . . . could fail to see the necessity of something being done in this respect." Lord Brougham likewise praised the reports.[44] To men who would never visit a prison, the opinion of those who did carried weight.

Leonard Horner's influence was quite singular. Both sides appealed to his oracular pronouncements on factories. The most persistent advocate of the ten-hour day, Lord Ashley, often cited Horner's reports. In 1837 he repeated Horner's blunt charge that "factory schools were a mockery," and in 1842, Horner's criticism of the doctrine that workers were free agents. "There can be no such thing as freedom of labor," Ashley read from Horner's report, "when . . . there is such a competition for employment." The enemies of the ten-hour day, led by Graham, answered Ashley's challenge with other of Horner's pronouncements. Referring to Horner as "my excellent friend" and invoking his report as if it were Holy Scripture, Graham cited Horner's estimate that a ten-hour day would lose the average mill owner £1,530 a year and reduce the worker's wages by 25 per cent.[45] The sincere conflict in Horner's mind between social humanitarianism and classical economics found expression in his reports, thereby giving

44. Hansard, *87* (1846), 1235; *91* (1847), 1227, 1069, 1085; *89* (1847), 860–63; *109* (1850), 35–37; *44* (1838), 771; *35* (1836), 1151.
45. Hansard, *73* (1844), 1379; *33* (1836), 740–42; *63* (1844), 1109; *44* (1838), 387–88.

both sides useful ammunition. But of the two attitudes, humanitarianism predominated. In 1844 Benjamin Hawes announced that he voted for Ashley's Ten Hour Bill on "the authority of the reports of the factory inspectors"; and in the 1850's the ten-hour men repeatedly cited Horner's indictment of the mill owners for evading the 1847 Law. They exploited these reports for all they were worth.[46]

Parliament both respected and feared the reports of the government's central departments sometimes listening to their advice and other times spurning it. They asked, for example, that the Railway Commission judge which railway bills were sound. The commissioners investigated all the proposed projects and in 1845 gave its opinion, which favored the larger and more solvent companies. But the Commons did not agree with this verdict and so protested that these reports intruded upon their rights, and told the commissioners not to bother, in the future, with such reports.[47] Parliament also viewed with jealousy the Board of Health reports. Lord John Russell might say of the 1850 cholera report that "No public board ever rendered a greater service to the community than was rendered by the compilation of this report," but that did not prevent Lord Seymour or Captain Pechell from attacking it bitterly and winning the sympathy of the House.[48] The only members of Parliament who ever read the reports of the Board of Health were a few ardent sanitary reformers. For that reason the reports found their real justification in the discussions they excited in the press and the information they disseminated to the public at large.

Edwin Chadwick asked Lord Palmerston in 1853 to allow the General Board of Health to distribute 4,000 copies of the report. The Poor Law Board, he said, had distributed 8,000 copies. Lord Palmerston at once asked why so many copies were needed, and Chadwick replied that "the dissemination of such information was one of the principal purposes for which they were instituted,"

46. Hansard, *109* (1850), 925; *128* (1853), 1272; *73* (1844), 1670.
47. Hansard, *78* (1845), 941–42, 1223–26; *79*, 1061–69, 1074–83; *77*, 354–68, 1156.
48. Hansard, *135* (1854), 1000.

and that such a "dissemination of facts will tend to remove much organized misrepresentation." [49] Palmerston allowed the 4,000 reports to be distributed. The General Board of Health also distributed 22,100 copies of the engineering inspectors' reports, 1,500 of the cholera report, 6,000 on burials, and 11,000 on pipe drainage.[50] With limited powers and faith in persuasion, all central departments relied on their reports to impress and guide local authorities.

It was not always a mistaken reliance. Kennedy's education report of 1851—not very exciting—netted him fifty letters of appreciation from schoolteachers. Many more teachers and local committeemen no doubt read it and the reports of his colleagues. Just how many mine-owners read one of the 2,000 copies of Tremenheere's reports or how many guardians read the 8,000 poor-law reports will never be exactly known.[51] Their numbers may have been small, but mine-owners, poor-law guardians, and schoolmasters possessed authority and influence that cannot be measured in numbers. Richard Dawes, who knew considerable about English education, said that the inspectors' reports "have been of the most essential service in teaching those who take an interest in education to a proper opinion of that subject." Charles Dickens said he was much moved by the 1842 sanitary report. He confessed in 1851 that "it strengthened and enlarged my knowledge, made me ernest in this cause in my own sphere." [52] But most of England's enlarged governing class did not share Dickens' taste for lengthy bluebooks. Their intellectual nourishment was the daily press, the reviews, and pamphlets. It was fortunate, then, that the reports of the new central agencies enjoyed, on the whole, a good press.

The newspapers printed many of the inspectors' reports, either in whole or in part. Some were reviewed in the quarterlies. Scarcely a report of the factory or prison inspectors failed to gain a column or two in the *Times,* and to a surprising extent they

49. MH, 5/9, April 12, 19, 1854.
50. Hansard, *135* (1854), 984. *PP, 11* (1855) 151.
51. *PP, 42* (1851), 433. HO, 87/2, Aug. 5, 1853.
52. Richard Dawes, *Observations on the Working of the Government Scheme of Education* (Hants., 1849), p. 8. *Nonesuch Dickens,* 2, 393.

appeared in provincial journals. Only in an age of high serious-ness, preoccupied with moral improvement, would such bureau-cratic reports secure publication. The *Bristol Mercury* gave six columns to the health inspector's report on Bristol, and the *Hampshire and Southampton County Paper* printed in 1851 the reports of the Railway Department, the Tithe Commission, and the Board of Health.[53] The quarterly reviews dealt at great length with the inspectors' reports. The *Edinburgh Review* published three reviews on the reports of the Board of Health, three on the reports of the Education Committee, four on prison reports, and one on the poor-law reports, using these reviews to advocate liberal social reforms. It accepted the Board of Health's views on cholera, echoed the poor-law commissioners' belief that "pauper-ism arose from fraud and indolence and improvidence," and agreed with Allen and Tremenheere that there was a crying need for educational reforms. In 1847 it published an article "Crime and Popular Education," which cited both prison and education reports to prove that crime resulted from ignorance. In 1852 it linked together widespread ignorance and the want of proper sanitation to explain those moral and physical evils which led to crime, depravity, and poverty.[54] In the *Edinburgh Review* the social theories of the liberal inspectors received their clearest exposition and fullest support. But not many read that scholarly review, nor the *Westminster Review,* which also served as a plat-form for the ennunciation of the views of the inspectors. It was the *Times* that boasted of being the *vox populi.*

The *Times,* like Parliament, adopted an ambivalent attitude toward the reports of these new bureaucrats. Its attitude depended on the strong passions of its publisher and editor, Walters and Barnes. If they disliked the reports, as they disliked those of the Poor Law Commission, they called them "fraudulent and false." If they liked them, as they liked the reports of Leonard Horner,

53. *Bristol Mercury,* June 29, 1850. *The Hampshire and Southampton County Paper,* March 8, April 5, 12, 1851.

54. *Edinburgh Review, 91* (April 1850), 377; *63* (July 1836), 356; *91* (Jan. 1850), 111; *96* (Oct. 1852), 211; *75* (April 1842), 57; *86* (Oct. 1847), 270; *92* (July 1850), 94; *91* (July 1849), 1; *100* (Oct. 1854), 291; *86* (Oct. 1847), 271; *44* (Jan. 1837), 169.

they expressed a solemn respect for them. Being ardent for factory reform, they cited with approval Horner's statement in 1842 that workers during a depression were not free agents. In the 1844 debates on the Ten Hour Bill, the *Times* devoted a lengthy editorial to Horner's report, claiming for it "a much more decisive character than private advice." Strongly advocating sanitary reform, the *Times* under Delane gave full publicity to the reports of the Board of Health. "It is beyond question," it said of William Lee's *Experience in Disease and Comparative Rates of Mortality,* "that these sanitary dogmas are substantially right." It called the Board's first report very important, and in 1851 it noted that "it is plainly stated by the inspectors of the Board of Health that certain portions of some of our most popular towns must, at no distant period, become actually uninhabitable." [55] They also printed all the prison reports because of "the publicity which they give the most secret transactions." The *Times* was, in fact, delighted in 1843 that their publication inspired "our county magistrates with abject terror, with its annual exposure of abuses in our gaol." "We have no knowledge," they confessed a year later, "of the management of these prisons save the reports of the inspectors of prisons." [56]

The same was true of the reports of the mining and railway inspectors. Editors who knew nothing of the safety problems of mines or railways simply printed abstracts of the inspectors' reports. The *Macclesfield Courier* dutifully printed Galton's report on accidents, including his grave charge that management could have prevented six out of seven. The *Newcastle Chronicle* in 1849 published Tremenheere's entire report on Northumberland mines, with its exposure of wretched social conditions, its analysis of the causes of strikes, and its plea to employers to provide far more education for their workers.[57] The *Mining Journal* published all mining reports and the *Educational Times* and *Educational Record* gave ample space to the reports of the education in-

55. *Times,* Oct. 12, 1842; March 9, 11, 1844; Aug. 29, 1849; Sept. 4, 1851.
56. Ibid., Jan. 20, 1843, June 3, 1844.
57. *Macclesfield Courier,* March 11, 1854. *Newcastle Chronicle,* Sept. 7 1849.

spectors. The General Board of Health's report on water supplies in 1850 caused great excitement and was covered by the entire London press.[58] To a remarkable degree the reports of all agencies were published, in daily journals, in reviews, and in pamphlets. In the great pamphlet war over education, for example, the education inspectors' conclusions were freely used. A flood of pamphlets alternately approved and condemned the famous Minutes of 1846 and 1847. Far fewer were the pamphlets on prison disciplines, the poor laws, and factory conditions, but the authors of these were equally ready to use government reports.

In all the publications, then, whether newspaper, review, or pamphlet, the inspectors' reports opened the eyes of the decent and comfortable to the misery, ignorance, filth, crime, and degradation that was the lot of the working classes. The inspectors urged upon the upper classes the adoption of remedies which would lessen these moral and physical evils. Their reports made Victorian society more conscious of its failings, and inspired administrative actions which would remove the evils.

58. *Educational Record*, Jan. 4, 1855. *Mining Journal*, March 5, 1853. *Educational Times*, Sept. 1, 1851. Finer, *Chadwick*, p. 394.

8.

FORMULATION OF POLICY

THE MAKING OF POLICY within a large organization is of course a complicated process, and its formulation within the jumble of bureaus that made up the central government of early Victorian England was particularly complicated. Trained, well-paid civil servants did not, as the Benthamites envisioned, lay down simple, rational, and efficient policies that were at once adopted by responsible ministers. Instead there was a constant tug of war between zealous inspectors, harassed ministers, angry MP's, and indignant newspaper editors. All had their say, and from the final resolution of their opinions and interests emerged the policies which England's central administration would pursue. On matters of detail these policies reflected the zeal of the inspectors for improvement and their desire to mitigate the more acute social evils of industrial England. On the more basic issues they reflected the varying sentiments of Parliament and the public, and the timidity or boldness of the ministers. The resulting policies were thus a compound of sound reforms, judicious compromises, and inaction.

THE FIRST STEP: INSPECTORS, SECRETARIES, AND COMMISSIONERS

The central departments announced their policies in circulars, orders, rules, and regulations. But it was in the reports of the inspectors that such directives had their origin. As the eyes and ears of their department the inspectors learned about local problems at first hand, and formed ideas on how to remove them. They expressed their views in turn to the local officials through suggestions and advice and to their superiors through reports and conversation. Upon local officials the advice of inspectors often had a direct, even intimidating, impact. Upon their superiors inspectors exercised a less direct power, but because of their close contact with the facts at hand they were influential, even on basic policies. In both instances their influence depended considerably upon their intelligence, their arts of persuasion, and their firmness of character—virtues that were seldom lacking in early Victorian inspectors.

The God-fearing John Allen, for example, possessing intransigent individualism, differed considerably from Kay Shuttleworth. When in 1844 Kay Shuttleworth asked the inspectors to send in weekly diaries (a Chadwickian idea for promoting greater uniformity), Allen responded with a declaration of independence: he would make out no such diaries. Weekly diaries would only place the inspectors under the control of the secretary; "the committee," he said, "should know suggestions we make, but by our own formal reports. I object to written communications coming from this office week by week, which would have a tendency to bias the inspector as to the education he should encourage." Allen also told the secretary that Lord Lansdowne had promised him that inspectors were "not pledged to sanction views of education entertained by the government." [1] Kay Shuttleworth dropped the idea, and the inspectors, who could be dismissed only with their Church's approval, propounded freely their opinions on education.

Henry Watford Bellairs persuaded teachers to learn well their scriptural history, Christian doctrines, catechism, and liturgy; Cook urged simultaneous instruction in large galleries, a system viewed critically by Morell; Moseley insisted the master must have a separate room only for himself and those he taught; Symons wanted every school to give industrial training; and

1. Grier, *Allen*, pp. 115–20.

233

Matthew Arnold wrote eloquently on the value of girls learning needlework. Tufnell, like Allen, wished them to memorize Scripture. Morell would have them learn the logic of thought by commanding the principles of grammar.[2] In short, it lay with each inspector to fashion his own educational policy and to persuade his schools of its merits—a freedom that modern bureaucratic practices would never allow.

The prison, factory, and mining inspectors enjoyed similar freedom to express their own views. The result was an even greater divergence of opinion. The early Victorian administrator did not worship at the idol of uniformity. For sixteen years Leonard Horner and James Stuart followed opposite policies. Of 3,696 prosecutions for violating factory laws from 1836 to 1854, Horner instituted 2,761, and the other three inspectors only 935. Stuart in his first years initiated none. Horner tolerated no violators, Stuart trusted the mill-owners' good will, and the overworked Home Secretary allowed each to follow his own policy. In 1848 Stuart told Scotland's mill-owners that the employment of children in relays after 6 P.M. was legal, and his successor John Kincaid said they could leave shafts seven feet above the floor unfenced. Horner declared both illegal.[3]

The prison inspectors also had their differences. Sir Joshua Jebb, the Inspector General, believed in hard labor at turning a hand crank, because it acted as a powerful deterrent to crime; Frederick Hill condemned it on the ground that it gave prisoners a permanent distaste for labor. Whitworth Russell and Robert Crawford championed the policy of separate confinement, John Williams the method of association under conditions of silence. In view of the experimental nature of prison discipline and the strong convictions of the inspectors, such a divergence of policies was perhaps justified. Differences of opinion did not greatly disturb early Victorian administrators. Even Lord Palmerston, whose exacting demands had irritated many a Foreign Office clerk, found

2. *PP**, 7 (1845), 111, 299; 9 (1846), 98, 160. *Times,* Sept. 13, 1854. Arnold, *Reports,* p. 23. *PP**, 37 (1850), 471; *PP,* 52 (1854), 690.

3. Harriet Martineau, *The Factory Controversy* (London, 1855), p. 49. HO, 45/1851, Horner to Grey, Aug. 8, 1848, L. P. Clark to Grey, Sept. 31, 1848.

no reason to require strict uniformity from the mining inspectors. He told Herbert Mackworth that it was better to print honest reports expressing differing views than to edit them for the sake of appearing in agreement. Mackworth later confessed to Lord Palmerston that in drawing up regulations for the coal-owners, it "did not occur to me to take the opinion of other inspectors as I have no opportunity of conferring with them." [4] Like the education, factory, and prison inspectors, the men of the mining office could, within limits, define the detailed policy of their districts.

These inspectors could also influence the drawing up of whatever general regulations were deemed necessary. Despite their differences over separate confinement and crank labor, the prison inspectors met in 1843 and agreed on a set of rules for an adequate diet (including two hot meals a day), warm cells (i.e. 50°–60°), clean clothing, bedding, and quarters—more humane rules than those commonly in force. The factory inspectors also met to draw up regulations on the keeping of time books, the condition of mills, and the certification of a child's age.[5] After 1844, when these rules became statutory, the inspectors' main problem was how strictly they should enforce the acts, a matter on which they did not enjoy the closest agreement. Though partly autonomous, the Home Office inspectors—factory, prison, and mining—still had to answer to a cabinet minister. The formation of policy on particular matters thus lay with each inspector, and on crucial issues with the Home Secretary. Except among the factory inspectors, joint meetings were exceptional, and even among the factory inspectors a common policy had to wait on the Home Secretary's decision.

It was somewhat different with the education inspectors. Despite the freedom Allen had insisted on, they still had to work with a well-organized central office, one with clerks and secretaries devoted solely to educational matters. This office stood between the inspectors and the members of the Committee on Education. It drew up common examinations, book lists, and directives. Its secretary, Kay Shuttleworth, was both an apostle of a particular

4. HO, 45/5372, Mackworth to Palmerston, Oct. 27, 1854; HO, 45/5377, Mackworth to Palmerston, July 22, 1854.
5. *PP,* 27 (1843), 27–29; *45* (1836), 86 (33).

educational philosophy and an effective diplomat. The same John Allen who declared his independence from weekly reports also wrote with the deepest respect of Kay Shuttleworth's wise and consistent support of the voluntary system, with its insistence that local authorities remain the basis of England's education. Henry Moseley believed that the Pestalozzian disciplines taught in Kay Shuttleworth's Battersea training school were a model educational system.

Kay Shuttleworth was diplomatic in his advocacy of reforms. He pushed forward new policies only when they had support, something Chadwick did not wait for. He saw, for example, the necessity of replacing the utterly incompetent monitors with paid apprentice teachers. But he did not force the plan on the Committee in Council until the inspectors, in their reports of 1844 and 1845, had made it abundantly clear that monitors knew hardly more than the illiterates they policed and that schools required instead paid, trained pupil teachers.[6] The inspectors' reports were always of weight in forming policy. Kay Shuttleworth's successor, Ralph Lingen, acknowledged them as "the foundation of the entire system." [7]

A sweet harmony reigned in the Education Office. A masterly diplomat was secretary, a kindly peer who trusted the secretary was president of the Committee, and cultivated clergymen enjoying the confidence of the secretary, president, and public were inspectors. Furthermore the problems were not intractable, for everyone was against poorly paid teachers, overcrowded schoolrooms, a narrow curriculum, and rote learning. There were no deep cleavages of opinion, no bitter conflicts of personality.

The Poor Law Office formed an unhappy contrast. Its secretary was not a masterful diplomat, and its three presiding commissioners did not trust him. The public denounced the assistant commissioners, and after 1841 the commissioners became indifferent to their recommendations. Furthermore the problems faced were intractable. As a consequence the formulation of policy

6. Smith, *Kay Shuttleworth*, pp. 49, 162. *PP**, *9* (1846), 63, 105, 157, 298; 7 (1845), 275, 302, 433.
7. *PP**, *79* (1853), 15.

was at best difficult, and at worst chaotic. From 1834 to 1840 it was labored and complex, from 1841 to 1846 confused. Only after a complete reorganization of the Commission in 1847 did it become orderly and routine.

In the early period the Commission's policy reflected three contending forces: the strong convictions of the assistant commissioners, Edwin Chadwick's awesome knowledge, and the temperaments of the three commissioners. These commissioners were the imperious and stern Thomas Lewis, the patient and principled George Nicholls, and the benevolent and weak John Shaw Lefevre. On detailed matters the assistants enjoyed, at first, a wide latitude. In Norfolk and Suffolk in 1837 James Kay, without receiving any specific order from the commissioners, introduced the rigorous principles of the new law. In Halifax Charles Clements had the guardians set up an outdoor work test and a uniform system of investigating pauper cases. Thomas Stevens was quick to force on his guardians the workhouse test, while Colonel Ash A'Court proceeded slowly.[8] Gulson devised his own medical plan, and Adey worked out his unions' auditing system. Everywhere the assistants introduced their own ideas. "I too have had," William Day wrote Nicholls in 1838, "my peculiar ideas as to the way in which an assistant commissioner shall proceed. I am obliged to yourself and your colleagues for having permitted me to go on uninterrupted in my own course." [9]

Each commissioner had superintendence over one-third of the unions and one-third of the assistants, which in 1839 meant seven assistants and some 150 unions. The sheer weight of business meant that they were dependent on their assistants in the field. The correspondence between the commissioners and their assistants was copious and intimate, though varying in tone with the personality of the commissioner. With Lewis the letters were deferential, but with Nicholls and Lefevre they were more forthright and candid. Nicholls was very receptive to the assistants'

8. MH, 32/49, Oct. 1937; 32/11, Feb. 26, 1843; 32/68, March 5, Sept. 6, 1836.
9. MH, 32/50, Nov. 5, 1838; 32/4, Feb. 7, 1840; 32/6, Jan. 11, 1839, Nov. 12, 1837; 32/14, April 22, 1836.

suggestions while Lefevre was timid before their superior knowledge. William Day, an assistant commissioner, reprimanded Lefevre for his errors as sternly as had Chadwick. "Your proposed bill [on nonresident relief]," Day told his chief in 1840, "is all moonshine." Nicholls was surer of himself than Lefevre, yet he was still careful to consult the assistants. He asked Adey about accounting and in 1838 he thanked Gulson "for taking so much pains in framing medical arrangements on our English unions." [10]

The commissioners before 1840 depended on the assistants for guidance on a multitude of such questions. They took their education policy from Kay Shuttleworth and Tufnell and their medical policy from Gulson and Power. And on the vital matter of when to require a particular union to refuse the able-bodied all relief except relief in the workhouse, they followed the assistants' advice. No order enforcing the workhouse test was ever issued without the assistants' consent. The approach was entirely empirical: the test was enforced only where conditions allowed it. It was, as Chadwick told Lord John Russell, only "by successive changes of detail" that the poor law could succeed.[11] The assistant commissioners had much to say on those successive changes; they wanted them to be slow, steady, yet flexible. All of them believed that the workhouse test would reduce pauperism, but all believed that in times of great commercial distress the commissioners should set it aside.

All the recommendations of the assistant commissioners went to Somerset House for approval. It was the job of the London office to work toward a uniform policy. In that office Edwin Chadwick held the ill-defined position of secretary.[12] The ambiguous but influential role of the secretary in an administrative department had been traditional in England's central government since the time of Pepys and Downing, but to many MP's and journalists the highly informed and persuasive Chadwick was the gray eminence behind the ministry and the harbinger of a spawning bureaucracy like that of the Continent.

10. MH, 32/16, Aug. 15, 1839; 32/50, Oct. 31, 1838; 32/16, Feb. 16, 1840.
11. Chadwick Papers, Chadwick to Russell, July 3, 1836.
12. Finer, Chadwick, pp. 140–46.

The powers and the importance of the various secretaries differed greatly. Some, like R. W. S. Lutwidge of the Lunacy Commission, were only superior clerks; others, like George Porter and Samuel Liang, joint secretaries of the Railway Department, discussed and voted on major issues along with the head of the department. Kay Shuttleworth at the Education Office became the chief architect of England's educational system, an honor Chadwick hoped to emulate at the Poor Law Office. In the first years he exercised considerable influence, but after 1840 he was relegated to the task of making inquiries on sanitary conditions.

Chadwick was, when the first steps had to be taken, an invaluable man. He knew more than anyone about the Old Poor Law and had written much about the new law. It mattered little that Sir Thomas Lewis put him upstairs in an office without the plush chairs and mahogany desks which the commissioners enjoyed.[13] The plain furniture did not prevent the other two commissioners and many assistants from often dropping in on Chadwick. Walsham wrote Chadwick that he would gladly receive a lecture from him on the poor law, but not "from the gentlemen down below," and Adey, whom Nicholls consulted on accounting, wrote: "You test me too high if you expect I can offer any . . . improvements on your ideas, I am too sensible to my own in-feriority." [14] Before the imposing erudition of the secretary many were conscious of their inferiority, a situation in the long run hardly conducive to harmonious administration. Lefevre certainly quailed before the secretary's thundering denunciation of his plan to have paupers spade the lands of local farmers. "It tends," said Chadwick, "to supersede the workhouse . . . it interferes with the labor market . . . it is the allowance system in a worse form . . . it is illegal." [15] Lefevre dropped the plan.

Chadwick's superior grasp of detail and firm adherence to the logic of the new Poor Law colored the policy of the first few years. He wrote many of the Poor Law Commission's reports,

13. Ibid., p. 111.
14. Chadwick Papers, Walsham to Chadwick, June 28, 1836; Adey to Chadwick, Oct. 29, 1835.
15. Ibid., Chadwick's memo. on Lefevre's field labor plan, undated.

consulted with assistants, educated Lefevre, supported Nicholls, and fought Lewis. He swamped the Home Secretary with memoranda on sundry subjects. Chadwick wanted the quick and sure extension of the workhouse test, but never without the assent of the assistant commissioners.[16] He was a doctrinaire on basic principles, as on the workhouse test, but in carrying them out he was an empiricist. His policies were not, as his critics averred, insisted on dogmatically, but his manners implied that they were. His importunate and cogent arguments alienated Thomas Lewis and won him no great favor with the Home Secretaries.

With the appointment of Sir George Cornewall Lewis and Sir Edmund Head as commissioners, Chadwick lost all influence. The assistant commissioners also ceased to play an active role, and their correspondence lessened. The commissioners even failed to inform them of orders sent to local guardians. Nicholls, busy on the Irish Poor Law, had no influence. "George Lewis," lamented Chadwick, "holds undivided sway." Tufnell's long letter to Chadwick and the letters of other assistants testify to a general alienation between the assistants and the commissioners.[17]

The policy of the two baronets reflected the pressures of those hostile to the law in the press, in Parliament, and in the local unions. Chadwick and Tufnell objected most of all to their relaxing of the workhouse test, but a more serious fault of their administration was its unevenness and arbitrariness. William Day, peremptorily fired by Lewis and Head as a scapegoat for the outbreak of disturbances in Wales in 1843, complained not that they had relaxed the orders insisting on the workhouse but that they had too hurriedly imposed such orders on Welsh guardians. And the order for allowing bone-crushing as pauper work, which the *Times* so bitterly condemned in their exposé of the Andover Union workhouse, came from the commissioners against Chadwick's opposition. It was an exceedingly mixed picture. Tufnell even complained that Chadwick and Thomas Lewis, implacable

16. Ibid., memo. on outdoor relief, around 1840; Chadwick to Grey, Jan. 17, 1846; memo. on Lewis and Head, 1847.
17. Bentham Papers, Box 154, No. 607, Tufnell to Chadwick, 1845. Chadwick Papers, Chadwick to Roebuck, March 24, 1845.

enemies, had both pushed the workhouse test forward too rapidly. Day said the same of Sir Edmund Head when the latter was an assistant commissioner in Shropshire.[18] Yet Head and Lewis, yielding to popular clamors, allowed many guardians to give medical relief so generously that it increased malingering and pauperism.

The administration of Lewis and Head presented a discouraging picture. They did nothing to help establish district schools, they fired both Day and Parker unjustly, and, according to Tufnell, "ceased sending reasoned replies to the guardian, and never sent forth a single paper setting forth correct principles." "All their documents," he added, "might have come from the *Times* office." Their evasions finally caught up with them. Agreeing with Peel on the need of economy, they cut the number of assistants to nine. Desiring to please the Andover guardians, they allowed bone-crushing. To please the public, they fired Parker. More assistants might have discovered the abuses at Andover, a refusal to allow bone-crushing would have prevented the scandal, and standing by Parker would have prevented the select committee from condemning them for arbitrarily dismissing assistant commissioners. They chose the easy way, and it boomeranged against them: Parliament in 1847 refused to renew their Commission.

The new Poor Law Board of 1847, with a president responsible to Parliament and with George Nicholls as secretary, worked out the Department's policies more routinely—consulting the reports of the inspectors, listening to an experienced secretary, and meeting formally as a board. By now, because of the work of Chadwick, the commissioners, and their assistants, many issues had been ironed out and many general orders on accounting and medicine consolidated. The remaining questions—of settlement, rating, and the perennial one of the workhouse test—were for the president of the Poor Law Board and Parliament to work out.

In 1848 Chadwick rose in rank by becoming a commissioner. With Lord Ashley and Lord Morpeth, he was one of the three commissioners who ruled at the Board of Health. Still an em-

18. MH, 32/16, Feb. 22, 1839, Jan. 22, 1844. Bentham Papers, Box 154, Tufnell to Chadwick, 1845.

piricist in administration, he conscientiously read his inspectors' reports and listened to them at board meetings, but on the eternal truths of sanitation he continued to be doctrinaire, listening to them only to buttress his theories more solidly. He ruled the Board of Health with as undivided a sway as Lewis did the Poor Law Office—the difference being, of course, that, according to Chadwick, it was now truth not error that prevailed. Chadwick's inspectors were Chadwick men. He knew them and their ideas before he hired them. The engineering inspectors all believed in the small-bore sewer pipe, the medical inspectors knew that corrupted effluvia from pestilential sewers and cesspools caused cholera, and both groups of inspectors agreed that a consolidated system of constant flowing water and pipe sewers would bring cleanliness and health.

With such commonly shared convictions, the forming of policy was a harmonious matter. It was based in the beginning on extensive investigations and experiments, but once solidified into fixed tenents it became inflexible. Not even the engineer John Roe, on whose brilliant experiments Chadwick based his belief in the small-tubular drain, could question these doctrines. In 1854 Roe's doubts about the use of six-inch pipes for outdoor drainage and main sewers brought forth from Chadwick a papal bull: "This is a pestilent error which if again propagated must entail excommunication." [19] Heresy was not tolerated in the office on Gwydyr street.

The uniform policy of the General Board of Health, the result of enlightened despotism, was in marked contrast to the open differences within the Home Office inspectorates, the Education Office, and the Poor Law Commission. In these agencies the inspectors had a fairly large area of freedom and even secretaries could influence general policy. In the case of the Railway Department and the Lunacy Commission, a formal board laid down policy. To outward evidence—and little else is available—that policy was uniform. It was the habit of these boards to present their policies with no record of dissent.

Yet occasionally beneath such unanimity lay discernible con-

19. Chadwick Papers, Chadwick to Roe, March 30, 1852.

flicts. In 1845 the "Five Kings of the Railway Board," Earl Dalhousie, General Paisley, Samuel Liang, George Porter, and Donatus O'Brien reported favorably on the plans of the Great Western to construct a new line in preference to those of the South Eastern. In the Upper House Lord Brougham protested against the decision, pointing out that O'Brien had remained neutral, Liang and Dalhousie had voted against the South Eastern scheme and Porter and Paisley for it, and that the tie had been broken only by the chairman, Lord Dalhousie, voting twice.[20] Parliament roundly denounced the Board for recommending any scheme at all, and ended their power to make such reports. Henceforth the Railway Board dealt mainly with questions of public safety. The staff of engineering inspectors and their secretary Simmons thus assumed a more active role. Captains Wynne, Galton, and Laffan drew up braking regulations, signal arrangements, and schedule requirements, and Simmons emerged as the Board's spokesman before select committees and the author of its main report. The inspectors still wrote the reports on new lines and accidents, each voicing his own policy. Agreement was not rigidly enforced. This was the age of two gauges, one five feet, three inches, the other four feet, eight and one-half inches. Each inspector had his own preference, and the Railway Board and the Government were too timid to decide between the two.[21]

It was also an age of various prison disciplines and tests for pauperism. The lunacy commissioners protested vehemently when the Home Secretary asked for uniform regulations for all asylums. They answered that conditions were so varied, such rules were undesirable. In due course they did draw them up, expressing in them their insistence on resident medical officers, clean quarters, healthy diets, and the treatment of insanity as a malady, not a madness. But they omitted many matters. Nothing, for example, was said of the use of mechanical restraints, which as good reformers they all deprecated.[22] Because of such omissions the

20. *Economist, 3* (Feb. 23, 1845), 177. Hansard, *77* (1845), 513–14.
21. *PP, 48* (1852), 14–15, 33, 37, 44, 46, 53; *38* (1853), 281, 291–98. *Railway Times,* May 4, 1844, July 18, 1846.
22. HO, 45/1452.

definition of many policies occurred only as a result of personal visits to local authorities. The lack of definite powers and of clearly defined lines of authority left much policy-making to the personality and persuasive powers of inspectors, and gave to them a greater influence than their counterparts in continental bureaus enjoyed.

BASIC DECISIONS: THE CABINET

In determining the "successive changes of detail" that defined so much administrative policy, the inspectors, secretaries, and commissioners played a commanding role. But on the larger questions they could only send the ministers lengthy memoranda or beg for interviews. Basic decisions on these questions lay with the men who sat in the Cabinet. It was an unenviable task. Caught between civil servants bristling with facts and strong recommendations and a Parliament and press full of criticisms and entrenched sentiments, the leaders of both parties had a difficult course to steer. The Whig and Tory aristocrats who occupied Cabinet posts brought to them a wide diversity of abilities, temperaments, and political philosophies. The safest generalization that can be made about their administrative policies is that they all showed in varying degrees three qualities: a desire for social betterment, a conservative fear of radical measures, and an indifference to careful planning. In their advocacy of reforms they yielded to the pressures of the civil servants; in their adherence to conservatism they surrendered to the interests and prejudices of the ruling classes; and in their indifference to planning they reflected the ill-organized administrative structure that Parliament had constructed. In resolving these contradictory attitudes and pressures they showed a preference for compromise and a disinclination for rigid principles. Some ascribe this spirit of compromise to English character, but it is rather more obvious that the necessities of politics dictated it.

The desire for further social reform was common to all parties, although the Whigs showed a somewhat greater enthusiasm for it than did the Tories. Radicals, Whigs, and Tories were all acquainted with the vivid evils of mining disasters, cholera epidemics, and train wrecks. To meet such problems they heeded the counsels of those who knew most about them, the subordinate officials; and they depended upon them for remedies. They were usually much too busy themselves to draw up measures for reform, a fact which Lord John Russell confessed to Chadwick; [23] and if not too busy they were often too uninformed. Lord Lansdowne, for one, did not know much about the problems of elementary education, though he presided over the Committee on Education of the Privy Council. He could give scant counsel to the new school inspector William Brookfield. Aware of his inexperience, Brookfield called on his chief for enlightenment but discovered that "the old statesman knew little more about it," lost as he was "in one of those hazes of sonorous and dignified declamation."

Brookfield naturally turned to Kay Shuttleworth, who had all the pertinent details at his finger tips. Arnold's picture of Kay Shuttleworth affords a sharp contrast to Brookfield's sketch of Lord Lansdowne. "He had a clear view," wrote Arnold of the secretary, "of the road to be pursued and had a clear vision of the means to the end. By no other means than those adopted by him could a system of public education have been introduced in the country." [24] When confronted with the complicated problems of combining State aid with Church autonomy as the basis of education, "the haze of dignified and sonorous declamation" had to yield to the "clear view of the road." In 1839 Kay Shuttleworth, a mere assistant poor-law commissioner, helped draft the original minutes of the Privy Council establishing the Committee on Education. In 1846 he drew up the important minutes extending aid to teachers and pupil teachers in order to improve the quality of instruction. He conceived the plan to sell Committee-approved textbooks at a discount. He pushed forward the plan to aid normal schools. He originated the scheme of government aid to the Kneller Hall school for training workhouse and prison schoolmasters. He drew up the agreement for aid to Roman Catholic schools. And he composed the various management clauses which defined the composition of the local school committees that

23. Chadwick Papers, memo. on accountability, around 1854.
24. Brookfield, *Sermons*, p. xxiv. Smith, *Kay Shuttleworth*, p. 316.

received building grants.[25] All of these came from the mind of a man who possessed not only a clear view of the ends which he wished to attain but also a sense of the possible means to those ends, a sense which Chadwick lacked but which was requisite for administrative success. This diplomatic flair made it possible for Kay Shuttleworth to win acceptance for his ideas. He had no other power: the minor bureaucrat's station was humble; everything depended on his personal influence with his superiors. From 1841 to 1846 Kay Shuttleworth's influence came to nought; Sir James Graham and Lord Wharncliffe would have none of his schemes. In 1846 Lord John Russell and Lord Lansdowne returned to dominate the Committee. Both men wanted improvements in the education of the poor and both valued Kay Shuttleworth's ideas.

There were many inspectors and secretaries who exercised influence through persuasion; and many ministers turned to them in making the larger decisions. None of the ministers consulted subordinates more often than the Whig leader, Lord John Russell. He took his penal theories, which underlay the Prison Act of 1838 and the Act setting up Parkhurst prison, from Whitworth Russell and Robert Crawford. Both acts espoused separate confinement. He accepted the recommendations of Chadwick and the assistant poor-law commissioners that no outdoor relief be given to supplement the meager wages of the poor with large families, and did so despite the recommendation of a select committee for such aid. On educational policy he always consulted Kay Shuttleworth.[26]

Lord Russell's successor at the Home Office, Sir James Graham, accepted the prison inspectors' doctrine of separate confinement. Only his attachment to the Church of England prevented his adopting Kay Shuttleworth's new ideas. Not that Graham opposed state aid to schools; he simply wished to make certain that it strengthened the Church, which to Graham was the true educator of the people. He had introduced in 1843 a bill for the establish-

25. PRO, 30/22/2, Kay Shuttleworth to Russell, Oct., 1838. Smith, *Kay Shuttleworth*, pp. 81–84, 181.
26. Clay, *Prison Chaplain*, pp. 178, 185. HO, 73/53. Chadwick Papers, Chadwick to Grey, May 20, 1847.

ment of locally controlled, rate-supported factory schools. In drawing up the details he turned to a factory inspector friendly to the Church, Robert Saunders; the proposals that all schoolmasters and a majority of the trustees be churchmen and that the catechism be read daily were Saunders' recommendations.[27] Both Saunders and Graham failed to realize that administrative behavior, like diplomacy, is based on the art of dealing with the possible. Their bill floundered before a storm of nonconformist indignation. Graham should have heeded Leonard Horner's warning about the education clauses.

Graham, in fact, had the highest respect for this discerning and vigorous Scotsman. Though he disregarded his advice on the educational provisions in 1843, he consulted Horner at length in drawing up the Factory Act of 1844. Since 1839 both Whig and Tory Home Secretaries had called the factory inspectors to London to help draw up the amending acts that the imperfections of the original law demanded. The 1844 Act embodied many of the inspectors' technical reforms. Subinspectors could now visit mills; only water-powered mills could make up lost time by running overtime; mill owners had to fence all dangerous machinery, and if an accident resulted from one unfenced, they had to pay compensation; and the regulations on certifying a child's age and the keeping of time clocks and books were made more stringent. To these technical provisions—the result of the inspectors' recommendations—Parliament added clauses reducing the hours that children might work from eight hours to six and one-half, and that women and young persons might work from an unlimited time to twelve, reductions suggested by a select committee in 1840 and vehemently urged by Horner.

Over the years Horner's influence grew steadily. He was cited in Parliament and the press as an oracle and was consulted by ministers. Emboldened by the praise, he disregarded, in 1849, Sir George Grey's plea to be cautious in prosecuting those who used children in relays to evade the 1847 Ten Hour Act, and under Palm-

27. Graham Papers, Graham to Gladstone, March 25, 1843. *PP*, 27 (1843), 322–27 (33–38), 356–61 (21–26). Edward Baines, *A Letter to Reverend Dr. Hook*, Leeds, 1843.

erston, with a better chance to express his views on this matter, Horner drew up the Act of 1853, which finally and unequivocally ended the use of children in relays to extend the working day into the night. In addition he persuaded Palmerston to issue a circular requiring all shafts, even those seven feet above the floor, to be fenced.[28] It was through relationships such as Palmerston's with Horner and Russell's with Kay Shuttleworth, through the partnership of minister and civil servant, of the aristocratic amateur and the middle-class professional, that the central government planned an administrative policy which met the exigent demands of the new urban age.

The second characteristic of the Cabinet's administrative direction was its indifference to planning. That bureau could oppose bureau and ministers their own secretaries caused no great alarm. Edward Baines Jr.'s quarrel with Palmerston is a typical example. As president of the Poor Law Board, Baines proposed in 1854 to change the law of settlement, replacing parish responsibility for the poor with union responsibility, and thus mitigating the harsh practice of removing nonresident paupers to their old parish of settlement. Lord Palmerston at the Home Office liked the bill. In fact he liked it so well that he told a delegation of Irish MP's that it should include the Irish poor—anathema to Yorkshire and Lancashire rate-payers, who desired nothing less than doling out relief to vagrant Irishmen. Baines, who was from Leeds, reflected these sentiments. Lord Palmerston's views ran counter to Baines' policy, and the Cabinet having failed to resolve the dispute, Baines resigned. Palmerston then apologized and Baines returned. The *Times* noted, "From first to last here is a series of errors or worse than errors." [29] To Palmerston such confusion of policy was no novelty. The year before, his own undersecretary had opposed a bill on chimney sweepers that Palmerston had favored. Integrated planning on the less dramatic issues of administration did not seem of pressing importance to those who sat in the Cabinet. Chadwick said the government's policy was defined by "fragmentatious

28. Graham Papers, Peel to Graham, March 17, 1844. M. W. Thomas, *The Early Factory Legislation* (London, 1949), pp. 153–75. HO, 87/2, p. 182; 45/4770. Hodder, *Shaftesbury*, 2, 201. HO, 45/4758.

29. Hansard, *131* (1854), 1362–65; *132* (1854), 72–79. *Times*, March 30, 1854. Palmerston Papers, Russell to Lord Palmerston, March 31, 1854.

attention in departments already overburdened with business," [30] referring to the Treasury's undermining of the General Board of Health's burial policy, a classic example of the Cabinet's indifference to planning.

In 1850 an Act on Metropolitan Interments gave the Board of Health an extra commissioner and power to purchase burial grounds. There was hope of great reforms. The vagueness of the Act in determining how many of London's cemeteries the Board could buy did not dissuade the commissioners from plunging right ahead with plans to buy them all. But the Treasury, with the support of the Board of Health's always absent president, Lord Seymour of the Woods and Forest Commission, permitted the Board to buy only two cemeteries and then only with funds raised by private loans at 4.5 per cent instead of with government exchequer bills at 2.5 per cent. No one would lend a Board with only a five-year term such money, and so Parliament passed an Act in 1851 to guarantee such loans—repeating again its wish that the Board manage the cemeteries.

The Treasury continued to thwart the Board, forcing it to submit to long arbitration the price of buying up the cemeteries. The Board paid a high price for two wretched cemeteries and then, greatly in debt and burdened with useless property, had to compete with burial companies who had a much less sanitary view of the quality of service that should be offered. These delays and stipulations were excruciating to Chadwick and Shaftesbury and fatal to their plans for a unified system of publicly owned sanitary burial grounds for the entire metropolis. In 1852 the new Commissioner of Woods and Forests, Lord John Manners, without consulting the Board of which he was president, introduced a bill to repeal the 1850 Act and turn London's cemeteries over to parishes and private companies. The burial grounds remained crowded and noxious. Lord Shaftesbury concluded, "The Board has no free action, no power to effect any of its decisions, for the Treasury and the Home Office refuse or thwart every proposition."

Part of the fault of such a contretemps lay with the imperfect organization of departments, but a larger part lay with the failure

30. Hodder, *Shaftesbury*, 2, 479. Chadwick Papers, Letter on Metropolitan Interment, unaddressed, 1851.

of the Cabinet to make decisions. The Cabinet could have told the Treasury to give the Board of Health exchequer bills with which to buy up the cemeteries, and told the Board of Health to buy them all up and establish a municipal cemetery service.[31] That the Cabinet did not was only in part a result of "the fragmentatious attention of overworked departments": it was also a result of conservatism in the Cabinet and indecision of the Prime Minister. The two constantly arose to temper the government's original interest in reform.

The men at the Treasury who thwarted Chadwick's burial scheme were the Chancellor of the Exchequer, Sir Charles Wood, and the Parliamentary Secretary, William Hayter. Hayter considered Chadwick and Shaftesbury "no better than socialists" and wanted private trading companies to control London's cemeteries. Charles Wood, whom the Tory Earl of Dalhousie found "fidgety and intermeddling . . . a carping and captious critic," held the same strict laissez-faire dogmas as Hayter. To these he added an allegiance to local government, which, he wrote Lord John Russell, had to be protected, "even if it entailed a great sacrifice." [32] Seymour also opposed the socialization of cemeteries and water companies. In 1851, without consulting the Board of Health, he introduced a bill to consolidate London's water companies. His bill would not require the companies to provide constantly flowing pure water, or limit their profits, or insist on the combination, by water closets and sinks, of both the water and drainage systems. It called only for the consolidation and perpetuation of the water companies, who had long delivered impure water intermittently and at rates three times the actual cost.

Sir George Grey's bill (originating with Sir William Clay, MP and water company director) did little more to protect the consumer, and the same may be said of the bill Lord John Manners and Lord Derby introduced and which finally passed in 1852.[33] Manners and Derby believed that the delivery of water was a mat-

31. Both R. A. Lewis and Samuel Finer in their studies of Chadwick give a full account of the failure of the Board of Health.

32. J. G. A. Baird, *Private Letters of the Marquess of Dalhousie* (London, 1910), pp. 320–21. Chadwick Papers, Chadwick to Russell, around 1851.

33. Lewis, *Chadwick*, pp. 263–66, 326–27.

ter for private enterprise, yet there was an obvious need to end the sale of bad water at high rates. Their bill was therefore a compromise that sought to protect interests of the water companies, uphold laissez-faire principles, and ensure pure water at reasonable rates. It was a clumsy and inept compromise, and it failed to protect the consumer. The patrician lords who sat in the Government were torn between their humanity and their timidity, and the tension gave to their administrative decisions an uncertainty and hesitation that greatly weakened government policy and in large measure left the suffering of the people unremedied.

The planning of railway policy affords a good illustration of the great cost of governmental timidity. Sir Robert Peel refused to decide on a narrow or a broad gauge and emasculated the Railway Department's forthright report favoring the four-foot eight-inch gauge. Gladstone in 1844 hesitated to regulate railway rates, and the Whigs in 1846 created a commission to supervise future schemes but never gave it the necessary powers. They refused, for example, to allow it to audit the books of railway companies, even though the bankruptcies and frauds that led to the panic of 1845 demonstrated the necessity of such an audit. The *Times,* angry at the carelessness of the companies, their dubious finances, and the high rates they charged, condemned the Whigs' policy as "still one of patience and reluctance." [34] The *Times* was right, but reluctance, conservatism, indecision, and timidity were qualities every Government exhibited, and they, rather than pressure brought by stockholders (whom Chadwick usually singled out as the villains), explain the Ministers' failure to support the Board of Health, the Railway Department, and the mining inspectors.

Yet unlike inspectors, secretaries, and commissioners, Cabinet ministers had to please Parliament. Even its least hesitant member, Lord Palmerston, who fought mill-owners over fencing high shafts, supported the mining inspectors' every prosecution, defended the Board of Health, and closed burial grounds against the protests of a bishop—even Palmerston yielded to a delegation of MP's on the bill for a centralized inspection of local police. And he told

34. *Railway Times* (May 23, 1846), p. 745. *Economist,* 2 (July 27, 1844), 1035; *4,* (July 18, 1846), 927. *Times,* Feb. 6, 1850.

the august House of Commons, on withdrawing the Nuisance Removal and Disease Prevention Amendment Bill, that "no one was less desirous than himself to give unnecessary trouble." [35] Palmerston knew that no Cabinet could persist in an administrative policy without Parliament's support.

Parliament Has Its Say

Parliament traditionally viewed the Executive with jealousy. It had fought a civil war and deposed a ruling house to check the arbitrary actions of an executive answerable only to the King. It had impeached many of the King's servants, had audited William III's accounts, and had dictated economic reform to George III. Through select committees it had learned to superintend the Executive, and through local and private bills to invade the field of administration. But at the very moment Parliament wrested control of the Executive away from the Crown, it saw itself in danger of losing that control to an expanding and occasionally impudently independent bureaucracy.

The ardent defenders of the liberties of Englishmen saw not only the Executive escaping from Parliament's surveillance but the legislative power slipping from their grasp. They discovered that factory inspectors could, until 1844, issue their own regulations. "We will obey the laws made by the legislature," exclaimed Sir George Strickland on behalf of the mill owners, "but we do not like inspectors' law." Neither did they believe that the Poor Law Commission, the Board of Health, or the Committee on Education ought to issue regulations, provisional orders, and minutes. "During the last ten months," said Captain Pechell of Brighton, "the Board of Health has been legislating by provisional order"—orders the merit of which, he reminded the Commons, "not ten members of the last Parliament nor one of the new" understood. The Bishop of Salisbury equally feared the Committee on Education. "When the minutes have been laid on the table," he exclaimed, "they almost carried with them the force and effect of an Act of Parliament."

It was even more infuriating to realize that this was the work of

35. Hansard, *135* (1854), 689.

mere bureaucrats. The MP from Bristol, Henry Berkeley, objected that "the power given to a class of officers called inspectors was plenary and unlimited . . . education inspectors were the beginning, the middle and the end of everything in these minutes." [36] Increasingly the hand of the civil servant was replacing that of the private member. Enclosure commissioners drew up provisional orders that disposed of matters once regulated by landlords in private acts of Parliament. The Board of Health's orders replaced the local improvement acts that had once been so profitable to Parliamentary agents.

The formidable problems of a more complex society demanded public not private legislation. Private members could not be allowed to draw up bills like those of 1844 which amended the detailed provisions of former factory, poor-law, and lunacy acts; bills now originated from the recommendations of factory inspectors and poor-law commissioners. They ceased to originate in the House, the rightful province of legislative action. Private members could not cope with the intricacies of age certificates for factory children and medical relief to the poor. "It is certain," Sir George Lewis told Lord John Russell in 1847, "that the business of legislation is now more exclusively in the hands of the government than at any previous time, and that the multiplicity of the questions . . . renders the government more unwilling to trust measures to private members." To this, Lewis' arch enemy, Chadwick, added the further observation that "such is now the condition of the public business that no chief minister can attend to any new or great measures." [37] The new realities were complicated and embarassing. Neither private members nor overworked ministers could legislate on mining ventilation or sewage, on prison diets or merchant marine regulations; the job fell instead to the expert in such fields, to those with access to the facts, in short, to bureaucrats. They alone had the time, the know-how, and the zeal to grapple with the technicalities of a more perplexing age, and to Parliament's annoyance they now assumed a more active part in

36. Hansard, *128* (1853), 329–30; *124* (1853), 87; *91* (1847), 1291; *48* (1839), 1064.

37. PRO, 30/22/10, Lewis to Russell, Aug. 16, 1847. Chadwick Papers, memo. on water supply, around 1851.

legislation. The General Board of Health, for instance, from 1849 to 1853 drew up no less than eighty-six provisional orders, eighty-eight orders in council, and twenty-six bills. In 1853 it helped the metropolitan referees to draft a Metropolitan Building Bill filled with complicated rules for building.[38]

Important as was the influence of the bureaucrats on legislation, their opponents, the Pechells, Salisburys, and Stricklands, exaggerated their power. Inspectors and commissioners were indeed legislators, but only on Parliament's sufferance. Parliament could and did wreak havoc with the best of their measures. It rejected the Board of Health's proposals on metropolitan water supply and sent Chadwick and Shaftesbury into retirement. In similar manner it threw Lewis and Head out of the Poor Law Commission in 1847. Parliament's capacity to draw up detailed legislation was not striking, but it could and did exercise a firm negative voice; it showed little aptitude in drawing up a poor law, but it could establish a select committee to investigate its workings. It could also debate endlessly on the merits of amending laws, the qualification of ministers, and the justification of provisional orders. In the final count it could refuse an agency its appropriation, or abolish it. And it could still pass private and local acts.

A select committee was Parliament's best tool for intimidating an administrative department, and it used it often. Hardly an agency escaped the vigilant inquiries of these committees, which investigated the work of the poor-law commissioners and factory inspectors, looked into the problems confronting mining, railway, and prison inspectors, inquired into the care of the insane, and assessed the workability of tubular sewers. Inspectors from every agency but the Committee on Education appeared at their hearings. Not every select committee, of course, sought to criticize adversely the department whose work it was investigating; many merely sought material that would aid in writing better laws. But the select committees of 1837 and 1838 on the New Poor Law and the select committee on the working of the Factory Law had less beneficent aims. England's foremost foe of the New Poor Law—the publisher of the *Times,* John Walters—moved in 1837 for

38. *PP, 35* (1854), 108 (103). MH, 5/11, Dec. 10, 1854.

a select committee on poor laws in hopes it would expose their cruelties. Lord Ashley in 1840 hoped that his committee would prove that the Factory Law was widely evaded.

Both plans misfired. Walter's hopes were disappointed by the twenty members whom Lord John Russell appointed, the majority of whom were not hostile to the Law. Some of them corresponded with Chadwick, who had considerable influence on the committee. Among the many witnesses who testified were the assistant commissioners Hawley, Gulson, Kay Shuttleworth, and Power. Their intimate acquaintance with the Law and their intelligence and cultivation made a deeper impression on the committee than did such witnesses as the fiery anti-poor-law agitator G. S. Bull. The Reverend Bull could not substantiate any of the cases of hardship he had publicly proclaimed in order to slander the commissioners. The assistant commissioners—aided in 1836–38 by bountiful harvests, cheap corn, and prosperity—could point to the efficient management of the new unions, the great savings made, the low rates charged, and the number of paupers reduced. The select committee concluded that the New Poor Law was satisfactory, the central board necessary, and the new policy wise.[39] Their most critical comment was a suggestion that the commissioners allow guardians to issue relief in aid of wages to those large, pauper families whose many children were begot before 1832. Lord John Russell, however, rejected this suggestion, showing himself to be more sensitive to the memorandum of assistant commissioners than to the views of the select committee.

The hearings of Lord Ashley's committee met with the same fate: the committee failed to prove that the Factory Act was widely evaded. Testimony of the witnesses who had charged Stuart with laxness did not stand close scrutiny; it certainly did not offset the weighty testimony of Leonard Horner, who gave the committee a measured judgment of the Law's weakness and strength.[40]

On the whole, select committees afforded administrative officials

39. Hansard, 36 (1837), 987; 38, 1514. Finer, Chadwick, 129–31. PP, 17 (1837), Pt. I, 450–68 (15–33), 461–74 (1–13); 19 (1838), 172–73, 202–58; 18 (1838), Pt. II, 123–81, 460–75, 275–97, 125–89.

40. PP, 10 (1840), 64–81, 87–95; 19 (1839), 458–505 (25–72); 42 (1839), 423 (70).

a greater chance to influence the opinion of MP's than for the MP's to determine detailed administrative policy. The prison inspectors in 1850 lectured a select committee on the merits of their particular disciplines. The committee's twenty-one recommendations, re-flecting these lectures, were an amalgam of Jebb's passionate faith in hard labor and separate confinement, Perry's caution that such confinement be brief and modified by associated labor, and Hill's belief in the value of moral and religious instruction. The mining inspectors had a similar influence on the select committee of 1854, expounding the merits of furnace ventilation and the need for more inspectors armed with greater powers. Select committees, in fact, came to be useful governmental means to enlighten Parliament about administrative needs and social problems. Lord Palmerston in 1853 advised Lord John Russell to hold a select committee on settlement in order to prepare Parliament for legislative reform.[41]

With the exception of the Andover Committee, which led to the end of the Poor Law Commission, no select committee had great influence on administrative policy. What really counted was not the judicious reports of these committees but the temper of Parliament as shown in debates, resolutions, amendments to bills, and appropriations. Walters and his colleagues who opposed the New Poor Law influenced the policies of Lewis and Head by loud speeches and reiterated charges of cruelty. Lord Ashley and the ten-hour men triumphed in 1847 by prolonged debates, not by select committees. They also triumphed because they exploited the public's growing conviction that more than ten hours was harmful to women and young persons. Similarly the decision to grant £100,000 to the Committee on Education for aid to teachers and pupil teachers came only after prolonged debate. Parliament's greatest powers were those of cutting appropriations or abolishing agencies. Such powers were negative, not constructive, and were not to be lightly used. In this way, the day-to-day power of policy formation fell to ministers and civil servants.

41. PRO, 30/22/11, April 9, 1853, Palmerston to Russell. *PP, 17* (1850), iii–v, 98–101, 7–8, 117–33; *9* (1854), 252–71 (33–52), 271–80 (52–59), 320–25 (101–6).

Parliament also had the right to pass private and local acts, but only in the field of railways did it exploit the privilege, and then with disastrous results. The select committees of 1844, 1846, and 1849 all urged the government to take a greater role in planning railway legislation and supervising companies, but they also warned of the confusion involved when many small select committees passed on the merits of particular railway bills. Yet except for 1845, Parliament denied the Railway Department any say in railway legislation. Matters which in France and Belgium were planned by an executive department fell in England to the select committees, which the *Railway Times* called "nondescript tribunals [whose] decisions appear at variance with common sense, equity, and justice." [42] Hundreds of local acts, empowering companies to build, forced on England an inchoate system of railways. Some companies went bankrupt, some built shoddy lines, others became parts of powerful amalgamations able to defy governmental regulations and charge high rates. Parliamentary agents netted large fees from these local acts, as they did from the local improvement acts which large towns adopted, at considerable expense, in order to evade the meddling interference of the Board of Health. Vested interests knew well the art of securing local and private legislation, and they practiced it often. It was one of their chief weapons against the growing administrative state.

Parliament did not, in fact, exercise its imposing but largely negative powers with particular foresight or intelligence. Its attitude toward the Government's administrative departments was marked, at its worst, by irresponsibility, special pleading, and apathy. At its best Parliament imposed wise checks on impulsive administrative actions and showed an awareness of necessary reforms. But in the angry speeches of the anti-poor-law critics, it revealed its capacity for irresponsible charges. These outspoken men, encouraged throughout by the original promise that the Poor Law Commission would be only temporary, tried to kill it with slander and abuse. "The assistant poor law commissioners recommended and carried out a system of starvation," said William Busby Fer-

42. *PP**, *21* (1844), 3–33 (2–12, i–xix); *26* (1846), 165–71 (1–9); *29* (1849), 469–88 (i–xx). Hansard, 77 (1845), 246–98.

rand, "in order to drive the poor from the south to the north of England, into a servile state of existence horrible to contemplate." "The object of the poor law," said Thomas Wakeley in 1836, "undoubtedly was to turn the workhouses into prisons . . . and to subject [paupers] to every species of hardship and degradation." "In innumerable instances," said John Fielden, "persons had met death owing to rigorous imprisonments and spare diet enforced by regulations of the poor law commissioners." [43] They never wearied of tales of suffering and cruelty, and never relented from their unsupportable charges that the commissioners were unconstitutional, tyrannical, arbitrary, and despotic. From a passionate faith in parish self-government, a deep foreboding at the decline of a paternalistic squirearchy, and an antipathy for the workhouse, these courageous and sincere men felt impelled to use violent words and wild charges.

Their very violence hurt the cause they pleaded, alienating the sensitive MP's who thought the workhouse test too harsh. So violently did the critics of the poor law abuse the poor-law commissioners that Sir William James in 1843 confessed that "critical as he was of the poor laws, after hearing the language of its opponents, he was not inclined to support their resolutions against it." The resolutions in question, which Walters proposed and which demanded the end of the Poor Law Commission, were defeated—126 to 68. The critics never again won 68 votes. In 1847 a vote of 218 to 42 for the Poor Law Board destroyed any hope of ending the poor law with its centralization and its workhouse test. There was of course never any real hope of abolishing a law and a department that had reduced rates from a yearly average of £6,700,000 in the nine years before 1834 to an average of 4,500,000 in the succeeding nine years.[44] Measures promising low rates won immediate favor in a house filled with property-owners. Economic interests ruled the House far more than the cries of Old England against the economic calculations and hard administrative efficiency of the new age.

43. Hansard, *38* (1837), 455; *64* (1842), 137; *35* (1836), 722.
44. Hansard, *66* (1843), 1219–20, 1160–75, 1260; *97* (1847), 1235. *PP, 40* (1844), 13 (2).

Parliament Has Its Say

Economic interests also explained Parliament's treatment of the Railway Department and the General Board of Health. The great financiers of the railway world, the Hudsons and the Brunels, either sat in St. Stephen's or lobbied in its halls. They demanded and received power to run their lines through the estates of the squirearchy. They laid imperfect lines, formed monopolies, and were influential in the passage of new bills giving them power to build additional lines. So blatant was their lobbying that the *Liverpool Chronicle*, no radical journal, concluded: "It is painful to witness the interference which self-interest has on the legislation of this country."

Special interests also played havoc with legislation on sanitary questions. Chadwick, in commenting on Parliament's hostility to the Board of Health's burial measure, claimed that "the shareholding members and their supporters in the house—some of the most popular of the extreme radicals being amongst the most strongly influential—muster commonly as many as a hundred." Chadwick in his many memos and Lord Ashley in his diary list the many interests hostile to the Board: engineers, stockholders in water companies and cemeteries, Parliamentary agents, and owners of tenements. In explaining the fall of the Board of Health in July 1854, Chadwick wrote of water-company engineers and Parliamentary agents crowding the lobbies and canvassing against the Board. Vested interests that had thwarted the Burial Act and prevented the reform of London's water supply joined hands with metropolitan borough patriots to destroy the Board of Health by a vote of 74 to 65 in a thin House.[45] The vested interests were not as large as Chadwick and Shaftesbury imagined, but in collaboration with sincere advocates of laissez-faire principles, with ardent believers in local government, and with the indifferent they obstructed the Board's policies until 1854 and then ended its brief life.

Apathy in conjunction with vested interests might cause Parliament to veto the most desperately needed reforms, but apathy alone frequently gave a department remarkable freedom from harassing criticisms. Parliament said nothing about the policies of the Emi-

45. Chadwick Papers, April 10, 1851, unaddressed letter, and another unaddressed letter dated July 18, 1854. Hodder, *Shaftesbury*, 2, 42.

gration Commission and the Enclosure Commission and very little about the policy of the Merchant Marine Department. Lord Ashley and the commissioners of lunacy drew up their own rules and regulations, and quickly passed amending laws through a Parliament uninterested in nonrestraint or residential medical men. In these unexciting matters the central departments enjoyed considerable autonomy. Parliament was too busy with budgets, Ireland, foreign affairs, and party politics for such matters. Furthermore, it was rather ill-informed on these questions. Supreme over every agency, it bothered to exercise its power only when great issues were raised. Parliament's power was one of veto and criticism more than constructive guidance. The same was true of public opinion, which was sovereign in Victorian England.

PUBLIC OPINION

Sir James Graham presented to the Commons in 1843 a plan for local, rate-supported factory schools. Following the recommendations of factory inspector Robert Saunders and the Church, he advised a scheme that required all the teachers and a majority of the schools' committee of trustees to be members of the Church of England, into which the vast majority of MP's had been confirmed. There was only a handful of nonconformists in the Commons, yet the measure failed ignominiously—because of the protests of angry nonconformists out of Parliament. Their clamor was heard in pulpits and journals over the whole of England and led to thousands of petitions with millions of signatures. Congregationalists like London's Samuel Morley, Leicester's Edward Miall, and Leed's Edward Baines, Jr., organized every chapel and strained every resource. The bewildered Lord Wharncliffe, who headed the Committee on Education, asked Kay Shuttleworth, "Who and what are these Congregationalists?" Before such an upsurge of public opinion not even a Parliament overwhelmingly Anglican dared persist in the scheme. The Government withdrew the measure.[46]

John Russell and Lord Lansdowne in 1847 tried another edu-

46. E. Hodder, *Samuel Morley* (London, 1887), pp. 70–80. H. S. Skeats, and C. S. Mial, *History of the Free Church* (London, 1894), pp. 413, 494–95. Smith, *Kay Shuttleworth,* p. 158.

cational scheme. Following the recommendations of Kay Shuttleworth and the education inspectors they drew up a plan whereby the Government would supplement teachers' salaries and pay pupil teachers, both as apprentices in schools and as Queens' Scholars at normal schools. The measure sought to improve the abysmal state of instruction. The nonconformists once again entered the fray. They called protest meetings all over England and filled their newspapers with columns of abuse of this tyrannical and unconstitutional measure. Their national journals—*The Patriot, The Evangelical Magazine,* the *Non-Conformist,* and the *Eclectic Review*—warned that the state would aid schools promoting popery, Judaism, Socinianism, and infidelity. The press of the nonconformist towns, led by Baines' widely read *Leeds Mercury,* called on all dissenters to defend their liberties from the encroachments of the state and to complement free trade in goods with free trade in education. The *Mercury* on February 1847, under the banner headline AN ALARM TO THE NATION, gave a two-column warning of this unconstitutional system by which the state through bribery and corruption would enslave the pupil teachers and teachers. In Doncaster handbills called it "an unwarrantable interference in tax funds [that] endangered the retail trade of the United Kingdom." In Crosby Hall, London, Congregationalists met and applauded Baines, Edward Miall, and the other ministers who exposed the insidious aims of the government in establishing such "a vast engine of slavery," a "new star chamber," and "state nurseries"! They petitioned Parliament, though in fewer numbers than in 1843.[47] Parliament by 372 to 7 disregarded the intemperate and inaccurate protests and voted the Committee on Education £100,000.

The nonconformists, successful in 1843, failed in 1847. They

47. *Patriot,* April 5, 1847. *Leeds Mercury,* Jan. 2, March 6, 20, 27, 1847. *Economist,* 5 (April 3, 1847), 379–81. From the *Crosby Hall Lectures on Education,* London, 1847: R. Hamilton, *On the Parties Responsible for the Education of the People;* E. Miall, *On the Non-Interference of the Government with Popular Education;* R. B. Parsons, *The Unconstitutional Character of the Government Plan of Education.* Some of the provincial papers opposing the 1847 scheme were The *Sheffield Independent, Plymouth and Devonport Journal, Leicestershire Mercury, Macclesfield Chronicle, Manchester Times,* and in London the *Morning Chronicle,* a paper which, though nonconformist, was fearful of clerical dominance.

failed not from a lack of energy or inches of newspaper space, but because their cause in 1847 had less justification and less public appeal than in 1843. The 1843 scheme did treat the dissenters unfairly, excusing them from Anglican catechisms only if their parents so requested, and forcing on them Church of England teachers and trustees. The 1847 Minute treated them as equals. Nonconformist schools as well as Church schools could receive the new grants. Public opinion, so amorphous and changing, could on some occasions discriminate between just and unjust measures. On others, however, it could be intimidated by powerful minorities.

In 1848 a vicar of East Brent, Somersetshire, George Anthony Denison, addressed the National Society meeting at Willis' Rooms. Angered by governmental grants to Kneller Hall School for the training of workhouse and prison schoolmasters, he shouted: "We will not permit, so God help us, we will not permit that the land shall be filled throughout its length and breadth with the miserable offsprings of Kneller Hall." The assembled dignitaries of the Church, lay and clerical, broke into tremendous cheering. The Government gave way and ended grants to the Kneller Hall School. The Committee on Education also granted these High Anglican critics concessions in drawing up the management clauses that National Society schools needed in order to win a building grant. Henceforth all members of a school's committee would have to be members of the Church of England; the local clergy would be ex-officio members; and the local bishop could dismiss teachers and ban books if they dealt with the religious part of instruction.

Both of these stories illustrate how a minority of High Churchmen, through the National Society, had influenced the policy of the Committee on Education. But Kay Shuttleworth, supported by Lansdowne and Russell, would not give way to their insistence that every National Society school be able to choose which of four different management clauses it wished. Such a right would give the Society the right to choose in every instance clause D, and clause D, designed for underpopulated rural areas with a dearth of educated laymen, gave the dominant power to the clergy. Clause A, designed for towns, favored laymen. The High Church wanted all schools under the clergy and bishops and not laymen. This, in fact, lay behind their crusade against the Committee on Education. John Keble, after listening to Denison's portrayal of the Committee's insidious machinations, exclaimed with childlike sincerity, "I cannot believe any men could be so wicked." The journals and pamphlets of the High Church party expressed the same amazement, and villified the Committee as virulently as any of its critics.[48] But Kay Shuttleworth seldom misread public opinion. He knew the strength of the moderate Churchmen.

In the pamphlet war that ensued, and at the meetings at Willis' Rooms, the moderates seized the initiative and slowly gained a majority. Though a weak conservative government under Lord Derby in 1852 yielded temporarily on the management clause, in the final reckoning Kay Shuttleworth's policy, supported by moderate and more reasonable Churchmen, won out.[49]

Baines and Denison, with their nonconformist and High Church followers, represented the extremes of religious feelings. In 1847 the Wesleyans refused to support Baines, and in 1850 the moderate Anglicans defeated Denison. Both Wesleyans and moderate Anglicans favored state aid for voluntary schools. Yet even this solution to the education problem was only temporary. It may have had much support, but it proved unworkable in the long run. Kay Shuttleworth, reading public opinion accurately, knew that all policy must rest on compromise. But he was no prophet. The prophets of the day were the leaders of the National Public Schools Association. To Baines and Denison these men were vile secularists; to moderates they were impotent radicals; but they were irrefutably right when they reminded all church societies that the churches had failed to support their own schools, that good schools had to be based on local taxation, and that tax-supported schools had to rest on a comprehensive religious instruction. But public

48. Richard Dawes, *Crusade against the Education Plans of the Committee in Council on Education* (London, 1850), p. 28. *PP**, *13* (1849), 383–427. G. A. Denison, *Notes of My Life* (London, 1878), pp. 139–70. Metropolitan Christian Union, *History and Present State of Education*, London, 1850.

49. Some pamphlets by moderate Anglicans are E. Girdlestone, *The Committee of Council on Education*, London, 1850; E. Williams, *A Letter to the Hon. Mr. Talbot*, London, 1850; S. Robins, *A Letter to Lord John Russell on the Necessity and the Mode of State Assistance in the Education of the People*, London, 1850.

opinion, the supreme check on administrative policy, had not yet freed itself from religious jealousies.

The educational conflicts of 1839–54 made it clear that public opinion set fixed limits to the formulation of administrative policy by civil servants. They also reveal some of the traits that characterized the attitudes of Victorians to the reforms advocated by the civil servants. Like the Parliament it elected, the public exhibited various moods—quick to anger, irresponsible at times, given to exaggerations, apathetic on unexciting topics, intimidated by special pleading, and occasionally downright fickle.

The *Times,* the *Economist,* and the *Leeds Mercury* each demonstrated in the educational conflicts of these years how changeable a journal could be. In 1839 the *Times* opposed the creation of the Committee on Education; in 1847 it supported the work of that Committee. In 1842 it called the Pestalozzian principles of teaching "quackery," but in 1847 it favored the adoption of those principles. The *Economist* in 1847 wrote bitterly against any aid to education, but in 1850 it announced that "the advantages of the present system exceed our expectations." By 1852 the editors had again changed their minds. "The money of the voluntary societies is misapplied and wasted," they wrote, concluding that "our system is a reproach to us." [50] The *Economist,* which once wanted no tax money given to schools, now wanted rate-supported schools; their policies had come full circle. Edward Baines, Jr.'s *Leeds Mercury* had equal difficulty making up its mind. It originally supported the creation of the Committee on Education, but in 1847 it opposed the desire of that Committee to give grants to teachers. Not only on education policy but on other topics as well the press vacillated. In 1844 the *Times* argued for the Ten Hour Bill, and nine years later condemned it as socialism; in 1849 it urged that many prison schemes be tried as experiments; in 1853 it complained that "we are satiated with prison disciplines." On the health question it was again wayward, now supporting and now opposing Edwin Chadwick's efforts.[51]

50. *Times,* May 25, 30, June 3, 1839; Sept. 27, 1842; March 20, 1847; *Economist,* 5 (April 3, 1847), 379–81; 8 (March 2, 1850), 230; 11 (April 2, 1853), 364.

51. *Times,* March 11, 30, 1844; July 7, 1853; July 9, 1849; Oct. 13, 1853.

Public Opinion

Irresponsibility, not waywardness, was the unhappiest defect of the press' attitude toward England's new administrative apparatus. The *Times* in the 1830's is a case in point. In those years it gained its reputation as "the thunderer." Its editor, Thomas Barnes, wrote with righteous indignation of the sufferings of children in factories and the poor in the workhouses, but under his editorship the *Times* could misrepresent facts, exaggerate abuses and slander character. It was not alone; many papers were marred by these faults.

The attack on the poor law affords many examples of misrepresentations, exaggerations, and slander. Though the motives of those who made the attacks were humane, the means to which they resorted were dubious. In the writings and speeches of Oastler and Stephen, which appeared in Feargus O'Connor's *Northern Star,* vituperation and misrepresentation reached unfortunate heights. Oastler called the new law "a most horrible system of dastardly murder . . . damnable, infernal, detestable, despotic, unchristian, unconstitutional, and unnatural." Stephen called the assistant commissioner Alfred Power a traitor and told his readers that "it was not murder to kill a traitor." [52] The violence and hate of these radical Tories did not arise merely from changes in poor-law policies, changes they misunderstood; it arose principally from a passionate detestation of industrialism, urbanization, and centralization, and a deep affection for the village and the parish. They deeply resented the fact that mill-owners, poor-law guardians, and assistant commissioners had taken over the world once ruled by the squire, the magistrate, and the parson. A sense of reality was not to be expected from these passionate romantics.

The *Times* on the other hand represented power and intelligence. In their columns vituperation was softened and facts more respected. Their case against the poor law was more convincing because it was expressed in factual stories of individual suffering. They depicted in vivid detail the overcrowded squalor of the Sevenoaks workhouse, of the cruel relieving officer at Bridgewater, and of the pauper in Eye's workhouse who was so starved he ate potato peelings. Such tales aroused the readers' indignation at the

52. *The London Dispatch, People's Political and Social Reformer,* July 9, 1837. MH, 12/15224. *Northern Star,* Dec. 2, 1837.

cruelty of workhouses. The alarmed poor-law commissioners sent E. C. Tufnell to Sevenoaks, Robert Weale to Bridgewater, and Charles Mott to Eye. Their reports revealed that the *Times'* charges were a mixture of truth, misstatement, and exaggeration. Sevenoaks was overcrowded, but not as squalid as reported; the relieving officer at Bridgewater did not, as reported, stint on medical relief to sick paupers, and the man at Eye ate potato peelings not because he was underfed, which he wasn't, but because he was an idiot.[53] In its attack on the poor laws the *Times* often departed from the journalistic accuracy about which it boasted. The same can be said of other Tory journals, particularly in 1841, when for electioneering purposes they attacked the poor-law commissioners with great fierceness.

Still, the violence of Oastler and the inaccuracies of the *Times* apart, the press had its reasons for criticizing the New Poor Law. The commissioners were on occasion harsh and the local guardians often careless. The commissioners did separate husbands and wives in the workhouse, did order a diet of coarse bread, and did deny to the poor in some workhouses the right to leave on Sundays. To our age these acts seem cruel and their authors insensitive. The Webbs, for example, found the administration of the New Poor Law unjust, and they ascribed the injustice to the commissioners' enmeshment "in the subtlety of the workhouse test." A more convincing explanation is the fact that these commissioners were deeply involved in the problem of rural poverty. Paid only eight or nine shillings a week, the poor in the countryside lived in miserable cottages and seldom ate meat. William Day, the assistant commissioner for Wales, pointed out that even those who paid poor rates in Wales seldom ate meat and that some of the "Guardians are little removed from pauperism."[54] With the industrious rural laborer so near to poverty, what could be given to the pauper? Re-

53. *Times*, Dec. 1, 1841; June 16, 1838; Nov. 22, 1837. HO, 73/52. Charles Mott, *Report on the Workhouse at Eye*, London, 1838.

54. Webbs, *Poor Law*, 2, 157. MH, 32/16, Aug. 1839. Elie Halévy, *A History of the English People in the Nineteenth Century* (London, 1949–51), 3, 291: "It seemed as though it were the deliberate aim of the commissioners to make it impossible for the pauper to obtain relief. The paupers were deprived of sufficient bedding, warmth, and nourishment."

lief only attracted the poor to parish rolls. The commissioners favored the workhouse, where at least adequate food, clothing, and shelter kept the pauper in health. But anything more than this minimum only attracted the working poor to a life of leisure. The assistant commissioners thus saw a need for strictness which the Webbs overlooked. It was the deep poverty of the generality of the rural poor that led to a stern administration of the New Poor Law.

Still, its hard edges hurt, above all because it filled the poor with a morbid fear of incarceration and humiliation. Just as the prison inspectors advocated the hard doctrine of separate confinement, so the poor-law commissioners propounded a severe workhouse test. Perhaps the chief fault of both groups of men was their occasional insensitivity to human suffering. The critics of the poor law were more sensitive to the unpleasantness of the workhouse. Walters and Oastler, though irrational and irresponsible, were alive to the harder features of the law. Their outcry against the workhouse arose from sentiments of sympathy and humanity. And their intense opposition to it was shared by many, a fact which greatly thwarted the purists at the poor-law office. When Graham in 1844 boasted that 85 per cent of paupers received relief outside the workhouse, he reflected the broad current of public opinion and irritated the orthodox poor-law theorists—among whom Graham had once counted himself. When prosperity came in the 1850's, with Lancashire workers receiving 15 shillings and more a week, the outdoor labor test, with its low pay and enforced work, proved an adequate deterrent.[55] The workhouse test then lost much of its necessity. In 1854, 84 per cent of the paupers received outdoor relief, a testimony to the persistence of popular and local feelings against the doctrines of Somerset House. Public opinion, so liable to exaggerations, prejudices, and irrational fears, nevertheless occasionally placed judicious checks on the harsher views of close-reasoning civil servants.

Public opinion suffered also from a willingness to be led by vested interests. Its views on the General Board of Health, for example, were jaundiced by the influences of capital. Writers and

55. Hansard, 76 (1844), 348. McKay, *Poor Law*, 314. *PP, 46* (1855), 2-3.

publishers too often had connections with the propertied interests. Chadwick looked upon the London papers as a bought press. "On the water question," he said, "the corporation has all the papers but the *Times*." His friend Francis Mowatt repeated this view when he told the Commons: "The water companies have paralysed all the press but the *Times*."

And not only did the hired hacks of water and burial companies attack the Board of Health, but also the medical profession and those the *Eclectic Review* called "our Tory engineers." Both groups acted out of some real doubts of the Board's enthusiasms and some professional jealousy of its newer theories. In pamphlets and in the *Minutes of the Institute of Civil Engineers,* the engineers scoffed at the Board of Health's zeal for "self-cleaning" small-bore pipe sewers, all of which they condemned as "unscientific amateurism." The doctors on the other hand rightly ridiculed the Board's advice for cholera patients not to eat vegetables or fruits.[56] With important engineers and doctors against the Board, with representatives of water and burial companies attacking it, and with the opposition of borough and parish officials, the London press treated the Board severely. Even the *Times,* long a friend of sanitary doctrines, turned against Chadwick in July 1854. The provincial papers, so apt to take their copy from London journals, also opposed the Board. No administrative agency had such a bad press as the Board of Health in 1854.

Yet in this opposition there was a deep ambivalence. Most of the papers acknowledged the need of sanitary reform, the failure of parish government to carry it out, and the invaluable work Chadwick had accomplished. The *Examiner* on the eve of the Board's fall admitted that "A thousand useful things had been accomplished in England which would never have been attempted but for Mr. Chadwick." Yet they concluded, as did such important northern journals as the *Manchester Guardian* and *Leeds Mercury,* that the Board should be abolished because of Chadwick's unpop-

56. Finer, *Chadwick,* pp. 439–43. Chadwick Papers, Chadwick to R. A. Harvey, May 17, 1852; memo. on newspapers' attacks on the Board of Health, 1854; Chadwick to Mr. Branchman, undated; Hansard, *122* (1852), 848. *Eclectic Review* (Oct. 1853), 396.

Public Opinion

ularity.[57] The *Times* and *Economist* both praised Chadwick's works as highly, yet the *Times* boasted that Englishmen would rather be dirty than "bullied" into cleanliness, while the *Economist* agreed that Chadwick had "bullied" the local boards.

But was this accusation true? W. Hickson, writing to the *Economist*, asked them how many petitions local boards had sent in protesting against his bullying. During the summer of 1854 not one local board sent in a protesting petition.[58] Vast numbers of ordinary people had petitioned against the poor law and the minutes of the Committee on Education, while at the same time the main journals had supported the Government. In 1854 no large section of the people cried out against Chadwick and sanitary reform. Why then were the papers united against him in 1854? The answer is that no other Board had offended so many vested interests—local sewer commissioners, stockholders in water and burial companies, professional groups, and Parliamentary agents.

The outcry in the press against the Board of Health reflected only a segment of public opinion. In fact few of the extreme outbursts of press and pamphlets ever represented a majority opinion. Neither the anti-poor-law agitation nor the dissenters' crusade against the Minutes of 1847 were as widespread as the fury of their meetings and writings suggest. They were merely expressions of angered minorities, though their leaders naturally claimed that they spoke for the nation. Richard Oastler, the most ardent publicist in the campaign against the Poor Law Commission, claimed to speak for the people, as did Edward Baines, critic of the Committee on Education, and J. Toulmin Smith, leader of the movement against the Board of Health. Yet in December 1837 in Leeds, Oastler spoke to a hall only one-third full; and his triumphant welcome in London in February 1838, far from bringing out the expected 1,000, attracted only 200 to Exeter Hall. Hundreds at the time strolled indifferently on the Strand. Baines' attack on the minutes of 1847 attracted only 150 in Leeds, while his rival's meet-

57. *Examiner*, Aug. 5, 1854. *Leeds Mercury*, Aug. 5, 1854. *Manchester Guardian*, Aug. 2, 1854.
58. *Economist*, *12* (Aug. 5, 1854), 837; (Aug. 12, 1854), 871. *Times*, Aug. 1, 1854.

ing had the hall filled an hour early. And at Bristol J. Toulmin Smith found his hall only three-fourths filled, the meeting chaired by one of the town's shabbier personages, and the audience unresponsive to what the Bristol Mercury called his "one-sided exposition." [59] Unless the times and issues were critical, public opinion did not take to extreme solutions.

But if the public did not heed the declamations of Oastler, Baines, and Toulmin Smith neither did it accept the nobler sentiments of John Stuart Mill, Thomas Carlyle, and Charles Dickens, all three of whom had spoken well of the General Board of Health. Carlyle had praised "cholera doctors," Mill had argued for a London water system, and Dickens, most ardent of all, had given speeches to the Metropolitan Sanitary Association on the need of better sanitation. Dickens, never reticent in commenting on social questions, condemned the poor law (though not very accurately) in *Oliver Twist* (1841), separate confinement in *American Notes* (1842), the mill owners in *Hard Times* (1854), and the failings of vestries in several speeches on sanitation. In his *Household Words* he defended the factory inspectors' circular on fencing seven-foot shafts, earning from Harriet Martineau, who had written a pamphlet denouncing the order as worse than the ship money, a reprimand for "these late excrescences, the unwholesome growth of an unprincipled sensibility." [60]

Carlyle's praise, Mill's arguments, and Dickens' speeches probably had little influence with the public. The same may be said of the learned articles in the *Westminster* and *Edinburgh* reviews and in *Lancet*. Perhaps the lunacy commissioners winced when *Lancet* condemned them for being easy in granting licenses for insane hospitals, but the public didn't care.[61] Only a few of the greatest issues overcame their sluggishness—religious jealousies over education, the treatment of the poor, the hours of labor for 400,000

59. *Leeds Mercury*, Feb. 28, 1838, Dec. 30, 1837. *Bristol Mercury*, Aug. 17, 1850.

60. Carlyle, *Latter Day Pamphlets*, p. 64. Metropolitan Sanitary Association, *Memorials on Sanitary Reforms*, London, 1850. *Nonesuch Dickens*, 2, 384, 394. Martineau, *Factory Controversy*, p. 32. *Household Words*, *11*, No. 11, pp. 241–44.

61. *Lancet*, July 3, 1852.

operatives, cholera epidemics, and, as always, any reform involving the paying of higher rates. Beyond these matters they did not go— even when indifference to sanitation raised mortality rates, created crowded burial grounds, and caused foul water. They allowed the press to speak for water companies and local sewer commissioners, not for themselves. Where no such vigorous interests were present, the press tolerated or even supported those policies devised for the Government by civil servants.

The conclusion is that "successive changes in detail," ministerial compromises, Parliamentary jealousies, and occasional agitations by the public all played a role in the formulation of policy. Out of the play of these forces came those directives, circulars, amending laws, and personal advice by which the central departments hoped to inspire local agencies to deal adequately with the grave social problems besetting Victorian England. On the whole that process produced policies that were sound in detail, benevolent in aspiration, and moderate in scope. But however sound these policies might be, soundness availed little if they were not enforced. To see that they were enforced was the task of Her Majesty's inspectors.

9.

EXECUTION OF POLICY

THE POLICIES of the central government could be effective only if carried out by the local authorities. It was the inspectors' job to see that this was done, and the task was not easy. In 1854 the inspectors numbered about one hundred and the local authorities in the thousands. Some 600 boards of guardians and some 15,500 parishes administered to the needs of the poor; 4,600 schools educated the children of the working class; approximately 290 local committees of magistrates supervised an equal number of prisons; 182 local boards of health, 600 boards of guardians, and numerous town councils looked to the public's health. The owners of over 6,000 factories and 400 mines determined the condition of work for their employees and the owners of 205 railways and 8,000 ships the safety of their passengers. More than 2,000 magistrates were empowered to judge whether these private entrepreneurs maintained their positions of trust. These magistrates also supervised 37 county and 181 private asylums for the insane. Voluntary institutions added even more authorities to this crazy-quilt of local administration. Forty thousand private charities helped schools and hospitals, while 241 newly formed church districts, 851 newly formed benefices, and thousands of parishes administered to the spiritual needs of the British people. All told, the central departments relied on some 80,000 local authorities and an even greater number of local officials to improve the social conditions in which Englishmen lived. It was a highly dispersed system of public administration, one depending on the capacities of thousands of ordinary men.

The inspectors found among these local officials a great diversity of talent and temperament, ranging from the incompetent and truculent to the resourceful and cooperative. In general, especially after the first difficult years, the officials displayed moderate abilities and good intentions. But on certain occasions and certain issues they either fiercely resisted the inspectors' policies or by their ineptness frustrated the execution of policy. To overcome the resistance of such officials, particularly in the first years of a reform, posed for the inspectors their greatest problem.

THE RESISTANCE OF LOCAL GOVERNMENT

The battle against the New Poor Law in the 1830's together with the opposition that continued in the 1840's provides the classic instance of the resistance of local government to the new central administration. It also reveals the defects characteristic of local government: stubborn local pride, propensity to jobbing and party politics, fear of heavy expenditure and high rates, unwillingness to resist special interests, and a mentality too often a compound of prejudice, misinformation, complacency, and conservatism. To overcome these shortcomings as well as the general dissatisfaction with the New Poor Law presented a formidable challenge.

The commissioners chose the southern and rural areas to begin their revolution in the administration of poor relief. They sent down assistants to organize the parishes into unions and end the excesses of outdoor relief. They soon found that not all the poor shared their enthusiasm for the new law. Early in 1835 in Sittingbourne and Rodmersham, Kent, the poor rioted and drove the magistrates into the workhouse; a few weeks later riots broke out at Ampthill and Lidlington, Bedfordshire; in Hampshire there was incendiarism. Colonel Ash A'Court as early as November 1834 reported that the laboring classes were "decidedly hostile." By 1836 hostility was still uncomfortably active. "I was jostled rather roughly by the rabble," wrote Kay from Suffolk after his hat had been struck from his head and his coat torn.[1] The poor, about to be denied their few shillings of outdoor relief, responded with anger. But without leadership and without support from the respectable class their protests were—like the agrarian uprisings of past centuries—short-lived and futile.

It was in the towns, not the villages, that the poor law assistants met the most sustained and determined resistance. Here they came into conflict with a middle class wedded to local self-government and a proletariat seized by the first stirrings of revolt. Together they formed an imposing obstacle. In February 1837, for example, the commissioners learned that the people of Huddersfield wanted no part of the new law. The newly elected guardians refused to choose a clerk and adjourned till April, at which time they met and again left the clerkship unappointed. The commissioners had ordered them only to carry out the Registration of Births and Deaths Act, but the guardians and the agitators among the poor knew that the commissioners intended much more. The assistant commissioner, Alfred Power, reported in April that "so strong is the feeling against us that it is impossible to carry [the order] out." On July 10 the agitators sacked the workhouse, stoned the windows of the guardians' meeting place, and greeted Powers and Revans with "coarse ejaculations, groans, and insults." The hostility continued into 1838 with the enemies of the new law triumphant in the election of guardians. On May 9 they met and threw out the old clerk. With the Reverend Stephens and Feargus O'Connor attending, and with many of them drunk, they sat in the courthouse (according to Mott) "drinking wine in the presence of the gaping multitude." [2] The alliance of lower middle-class guardians and the operatives had thwarted the commissioners.

Similar outbursts of hostility occurred in the mill towns of Lancashire, Cheshire, and the West Riding of Yorkshire. In these milltowns mobs and riots greeted the assistant commissioners. Yet mob action, embarrassing and recurring as it was, did not present an obstacle as great as the tenacious and lasting opposition of par-

1. MH, 32/1, Nov. 21, 1834. *Examiner*, May 17, 24, 1835. HO, 73/51; MH, 32/44, July 3, 1836.
2. MH, 12/15,063, April 8, June 8, 14, 1837. *Leeds Mercury*, June 10, 1837. McKay, *Poor Laws*, 250. MH, 12/15,065, May 9, 1838.

ish officers and guardians, who either hated the new law or were simply incompetent to carry it out.

The assistant commissioners' reports on rural Wales and urban Lambeth and Bolton tell in detail of the contrariety and incapacity of such officers. In neither of these places was the law well administered. In Wales the prejudice and ignorance of the guardians made them quite intractable; they came mostly from the ranks of the poor farmers and many could not read. They clung tenaciously to the old parish habits: jobbing where they could, granting lax relief, neglecting the workhouse, falling into factional party squabbles. In Carmarthen the enemies of the law elected their men as guardians, and the result, according to George Clive, was "nothing but jobbing and dishonesty among the gentry, and ignorance among the farmers." Clive found the Cardiff board in a singular state: "they meet 50 strong, speechify, quarrel, and divide even from morning till night; it is a regular political club!" He found Welsh guardians generally inattentive, the overseers neglectful, the clerks idle, and the rate-payers penurious. William Day, after struggling with them for a year, finally expostulated: "the Welsh guardians are most provoking beasts. You harangue them at length, you discant upon principle, you expound the law, and when you think your oratory must have its due effect and look around for the plaudits of your audience, what do you think they are about? They are sitting with their hands in their trousers and their head between their knees, their mouth full of tobacco, and the floor at their feet an ocean of spittle. When you stop they look up in your face with a sardonic grin which if it could speak English would say Bravo! my eye and belly Martin." [3]

The guardians of Lambeth and Bolton were richer and better educated but no less obstinate. In Lambeth two furious radicals, Mr. O'Grady and Mr. Fall, led the opposition. Mr. Fall, twice a bankrupt and once a convicted slanderer, was a bellicose and hard-drinking champion of the poor. Mr. O'Grady, who professed to be a lawyer, had won fame as an open-air orator at Blackfriars Road. Once in power they immediately fired the union's clerk, rejected

3. MH 32/12, June 11, Aug. 24, Dec. 27, 1836, March 20, Oct. 20, Dec. 5, Nov. 24, 1837; MH, 32/14, Oct. 29, 1837.

the previous guardians' plans for a new workhouse, and held their meetings at night, when, with Mr. Fall half-intoxicated, they consumed their time in quarrels. They fired the schoolmaster and ridiculed the previous guardians' extravagant fancies on education. They refused to appoint a rector to the workhouse, though they decided to pay the porter—a friend of theirs—the inordinate sum of £35 a year and board and lodgings. They also offered handsome contracts to their friends in Lambeth, and persisted in giving outdoor relief to the able-bodied. In every possible way they thwarted the commissioners' policies.[4]

At Bolton the commissioners faced the same defiance. From 1837, when the union was formed, until 1842, when the chairman announced "they must knock down the commissioners and blow up the whole system," all was discord. In 1841 the guardians resolved to accept none of Mr. Mott's recommendations. The parish and townships refused to pay back rates, and the guardians insisted on cutting the salaries of the district overseers who had replaced the more numerous parish and township overseers. The guardians wished to return to the old system, and like their Lambeth compatriots they wanted no expensive workhouses.[5]

The conflicts that arose in Bolton, Lambeth, and Huddersfield and the incompetence of Welsh guardians provide the most dramatic episodes in the battle against the New Poor Law. Such conflicts did not occur in every union, and most particularly not in the rural areas. Real opposition came mostly in the mill towns of industrial England and in some of London's parishes, all urban and the home of new classes, a rising "shopocracy" and a proletariat. From the pride of the former and the anger of the latter came most resistance. Many historians of the poor law have judged the new law inapplicable to the towns because of the unemployment created there by industrial depressions. The crises of 1837 and 1842 support this judgment; in both instances widespread destitution made the workhouse test ineffective. But urban opposition to the law came also during periods of prosperity, at

4. MH, 12/12,456, Oct. 17, 1834; 12/12,457, April 10, 28, July 13, Sept. 28, 1838.

5. MH, 12/5593, April 8, 1836, Dec. 11, 1838, March 11, 1840; 12/5594, Jan. 25, March 30, April 19, 1841, Jan. 22, 1842. *Bolton Free Press*, Jan. 22, 1842.

which time the law was, as Chadwick insisted, even more applicable to urban than to rural areas. Urban areas were more prosperous than rural. The workers in the towns ate better, wore better clothes, and enjoyed better entertainment and schooling than did their confreres in the country. Only in matters of health did they suffer more acutely. It was not because they were poorer that they resisted, but because they were more literate, more articulate, even better paid and fed. They could buy and read Feargus O'Connor's *Northern Star*, the hammer of the poor law; and because they were concentrated in towns, they could organize associations, such as the South Lancashire Anti-Poor Law Association, which put into effect "an organized system of opposition to the New Poor Law." [6] Men such as Oastler, Fielden, and Stephens found in these restless and recently uprooted townspeople a source of anger against society which could be easily directed against the Whig aristocrats and mill-owners who, they felt, would deny them sufficient relief. Lesser leaders rose from their ranks. From Huddersfield came Mr. Nigby, a schoolteacher, and Joseph Hirst, a shopkeeper. They inflamed the operatives with false rumors and as guardians fervently defended the cause of the poor.[7] The poor in the South did not possess such leadership, did not enjoy such literacy and organization, had no consciousness of their ills, and found no shopocracy to exercise its franchise on their behalf. The anti-poor-law agitation of the North constitutes the first angry response of an industrial proletariat conscious of its grievances and its power. Only much later, after the frustrations of chartism and the diversion of its energies to the anti-corn-law leagues, would this proletariat find its true expression in trade unionism and a labor party.

More mundane motives and attitudes added strength to the guardians' obstinacy in the face of the commissioners' policies. Of these the seven most prominent were vested interests, party factionalism, fear of high rates, local pride, ignorance, prejudice, and a belief that the law was too harsh. The reports of the assistant commissioners differ as to which of these attitudes ran the deepest.

6. MH, 12/5593, March 23, 1839; 12/15,063, June 14, 1837. *Manchester and Salford Advertiser*, Nov. 11, 1837. Driver, *Oastler*, pp. 331-78.
7. MH, 12/15,065, Aug. 17, 1838; 12/5593, Dec. 11, 1838. *Bolton Chronicle*, Feb. 22, 1837. MH, 12/5593, March 10, 1837.

Execution of Policy

Edwin Chadwick, always quick to attribute resistance to selfish conspiracies, singled out vested interests as the villain of the piece, and his assistants' reports offer supporting evidence for his suspicions. They reported that most of those who obstructed the new law were shopkeepers and publicans who were anxious to keep the poor buying in their shops, small farmers and manufacturers who profited from an allowance system that kept wages low, and above all overseers whose peculations the commissioners would end. "One of the greatest obstacles to the formation of unions," wrote Day, "is the idea that the craft of the present participators in parish plunder will be interfered with." Jobbing was a widespread and tenacious feature of the old system. The majority of the Bolton guardians had once been paid officers of the townships and accordingly opposed the commissioners' plan for replacing the numerous township overseers with fewer and more efficient district overseers. The Lambeth guardians, said Mott, were the most skilled of jobbers; [8] part of the art of jobbing was that of dispensing favors for political reasons.

The conflicts of parish politics paralyzed the activities of the commissioners as much as did vested interests. "Our guardians," wrote Bolton's Ashworth to Chadwick, "make a complete party business of it." Party appeared in every part of the country. W. T. Hawley considered it "the main cause paralyzing the working of the law, and equal to all other causes combined." [9] Tories and ultra-radicals on the whole outdid their Whig friends in factious opposition. The Whigs were, after all, committed to the measure. The deep prejudices of Tories and the anger of extreme radicals, when excited by partisan aims, gave rise to a nearly immovable stubbornness. It was all the stronger when supported by ignorance. The assistant commissioners had an unflattering view of rural Tory guardians. Tufnell found them dull, slow, indecisive, and timid;

8. Chadwick Papers, Chadwick to Russell, Oct. 15, 1836; memo. on the multiplication of agencies, around 1840. *PP, 29* (1836), 328. MH, 32/26, Nov. 27, 1835; 32/28, Oct. 10, 1837; 32/14, July 24, 1835; 12/5594, Oct. 1, 1842; 12/12,457, April 28, 1838; 32/17, Nov. 24, 1837.

9. MH, 32/39, March 31, 1838; 32/35, Aug. 11, 1837; 32/76, March 13, 1836. Chadwick Papers, Ashworth to Chadwick, June 30, 1842.

Hall found them "usually very uncultivated and prejudiced persons, many of whom are unable to write their own name." [10] The ultra-radical shopkeepers and schoolmasters were more literate, but they more easily fell prey to misinformation. They had, for instance, an entirely erroneous impression of the law's harshness.

The exaggerated fears of the radicals, the special interests of publicans, the squabbles of party politicians—all these could eventually be removed by an energetic commissioner. Not so the pride of parishioners and townsmen in their town or parish and their fear of higher rates. These two feelings formed the continuing core of local resistance.

From the very beginning a firm attachment to parish government frustrated the commissioners and their assistants. Alfred Power wrote that "the reluctance of parishes to be united with their neighbours was the greatest impediment I have met with." Rural parishes hated to be joined with urban areas; each parish wished to give its own relief, to have its own workhouse, and to let out contracts to its own friends. They hated consolidation, though the parishes consolidated by local acts before 1834 were now profoundly attached to their new authority. The officers of these new authorities had a high estimate of their skill and policies, and where, as in St. Pancras and Marylebone, they represented large and wealthy areas, their disdain for the commissioners was as intense as their pride in themselves. Patriotic Englishmen took pride not only in the grandeur of the Empire but also in the local vestry or the town corporation, and they wished those august bodies left free and independent. John Bright told Parliament he had "a very excusable attachment to the old forms of local government." [11] It was a sentiment as hard to overcome as the fear of higher rates.

The main appeal of the Lambeth guardians to their electors was that the new workhouse was an unnecessary extravagance. Day and Parry found that rural guardians were commonly possessed by this fear. "With the farmer guardian," wrote Parry, "the whole

10. MH, 32/5, Jan. 6, 1836; 32/34, Jan. 28, 1836; 32/69, Nov. 14, 1835. *Bolton Chronicle*, Feb. 22, 1837.

11. BM, Add. MS 40,418, Peel Papers, Power to Peel, March 1835. *PP, 17* (1840), 256 (89). Hansard, 77 (1845), 719. MH, 32/26, Jan. 21, 31, 1836.

question is one of £, s, d." [12] In 1850 a fear of high rates still persisted, frustrating the Poor Law Board's hopes of district schools. One of the greatest failings in the administration of the law was represented by the dismal conditions of workhouses, and the reason for it, apart from apathy and indifference, was opposition to any undue expenditure.

According to the opponents of the law, their resistance stemmed from the highest Christian motive—a humane indignation at its severities. There is no doubt that Oastler, Stephen, and O'Connor fervently expressed such feelings, but there was a great distance between the humanitarian expressions of their speeches and the administrative negligence of the adherents who occasionally became guardians. The reports of the assistant commissioners and of local newspapers suggest that where the anti-poor-law forces controlled the board of guardians, the workhouses were the most distressing. In Lambeth, according to Mott, "the refractory paupers are placed in cold damp cells and treated worse than capital convicts." In Bolton in 1843 the guardians, most of whom opposed the commissioners, crowded sixteen persons of all sexes and ages into a single-room cottage, allowed the paupers' clothes to become infested with vermin, and hired a master whose conduct toward them was reported "utterly devoid of humane feeling." An inquiry into the death of a girl led to the exposure of these conditions. It was also found that the workhouse's nurse, being drunk, had sent the ill girl to the shed where the corpses of the recently dead were kept.

In 1848 the Huddersfield guardians, long hostile to the commissioners' interference, allowed their workhouse to become overcrowded and filthy. It had no proper baths, only two toilets, open cesspools near the house, and a foul stench. The Leeds guardians, jealous of their local act privileges and opposed to the commissioners' policies, allowed their workhouse to fall into a similar condition, while the Macclesfield guardians, to show the new law at its worst and so defy the commissioners' policies, allowed their work-

12. MH, 12/12,456, Feb. 15, April, 1837; 12/12,457, April 28, 1838; 32/60, Nov. 26, 1835; 32/14, Feb. 13, 1836.

house to become, in the words of the assistant commissioner, "a nursery of fanaticism and filth." [13]

On the whole, the worst workhouses existed where opponents to the new law managed them, for the guardians who believed in easier outdoor relief for the able-bodied gave the old, the sick, and the orphans who had to come to the workhouse dismal, dirty quarters. Their negligence, and that of apathetic guardians who feared large expenditures, formed the main problem with which the commissioners had to contend.

The prison, lunacy, education, and health inspectors found that the local officialdom with which they had to treat possessed the same defects: parsimony, pride, complacency, and self-interest. Those who feared heavy expenditures and those with special interests in local sewer commissions or water companies were sure to oppose sanitary reforms ordered from London. Chadwick saw the machinations of special interests everywhere, whether it was "the cupidity of butchers and fishmongers" or the selfishness of "the owners of cellar tenements." Rawlinson added to these, "publicans, beer sellers, spirit merchants, and owners of cottage property," while Edward Cresy believed that "the needy landlords are the stumbling blocks." [14] Men of property disliked higher rates and bothersome regulations. In alliance with them were vestry patriots and office-holders; together they all constituted an imposing phalanx.

At Durham this opposition was led by the local improvement commissioners, at Macclesfield by the police commissioners, at Cardiff by the street commissioners, and at Dover, Bristol, and Great Yarmouth by the paving commissioners. They defended with spirit their offices, their patronage, and the low rates desired by their friends. "Patronage," John Sutherland told Chadwick, "is a very powerful word and there is much of it." [15] Local commis-

13. *Macclesfield Chronicle*, June 17, 1848. *Manchester Guardian*, June 3, 1848. MH, 12/5595, Jan. 12, 17, Oct. 2, 1843; 12/12,457, Aug. 11, 1838; 12/15,226, Dec. 21, 1843.

14. Chadwick Papers, Chadwick to Morpeth, June 3, 1848; Cresy to Chadwick, May 17, 1849. Rawlinson to Chadwick, Nov. 2, 1854.

15. Ibid., Sutherland to Chadwick, Dec. 14, 1849. G. T. Clark, *Report of*

sioners hated to give up their remunerative and honorable offices. "Rate" was also a powerful word. As the clerk of the High Wycombe improvement commissioners said, "We have enough rates as it is, we don't want any more." In almost every instance the opponents of the Public Health Act, whatever their motives, claimed that the new improvements would be too costly. Actually, Chadwick's schemes were not extravagant, but allied with the fear of expenses was ignorance—"Not a single opponent," reported Rammel of Chipping Wycombe, "had read the measure." [16] A similar ignorance of the need and value of enforcing the Nuisance Removal and Disease Prevention Act in 1849 and 1854 hindered the Board's campaign to stop cholera. The guardians' inaction and incapacity was glaring, reaching a tragic height in Newcastle and Gateshead. Despite the cholera epidemic of 1849, the complacent corporation officers and the parsimonious tenement owners failed to make improvements. In 1854 cholera returned to the undrained courts and slums of Gateshead, and the guardians once again did not carry out the Board's plans for mitigating the spread of the dread disease. Only the arrival of an inspector stimulated them to action. The failures of the Newcastle propertied class moved Palmerston to write sharply of their faults:

> Our English tradesman has many good qualities. He does not grudge personal exertions, and he is ready enough with charitable subscriptions, but he has a great notion of his own sagacity, and cannot bear anything that may lead to an imposition of a rate, and they will often as at Newcastle see their neighbours perish around them and risk the lives of their wives and children and their own rather than ward off the dangers by arrangement which might involve a sixpenny rate

the *General Board of Health on Durham* (London, 1849), p. 6. *Macclesfield Chronicle,* Jan. 8, 1848. Rawlinson, *Report of the General Board of Health on Dover* (London, 1849), p. 3. *Bristol Mercury,* Dec. 7, 1850. *The Principality,* June 21, 1850. W. Lee, *Report of the General Board of Health on Great Yarmouth* (London, 1850), p. 58.

16. T. Rammel, *Report of the General Board of Health on High Wycombe* (London, 1850), pp. 38, 41. B. Babbage, *Report of the General Board of Health on Bromyard* (London, 1850), p. 5.

forgetting or not knowing that in the end such measures would be a real economy of money.[17]

The English tradesmen and rate-payers elected the boards of guardians and local boards of health whose negligence often led to miserable workhouses and unsanitary towns. Those who supervised the prisons were the magistrates, the celebrated unpaid magistrates—men of property and respectability. They represented the country's better families and the town's wealthier citizens, yet they proved little more helpful to Her Majesty's inspectors than the tradesmen. The reports of the prison inspectors tell of stubborn resistance to improvements. The prison inspectors, being the least powerful of Her Majesty's itinerant officials, could be the most easily ignored. Magistrates often refused to carry out their orders. In the East Riding of York they flogged children despite the inspector's condemnation; and in Great Yarmouth, notwithstanding the Home Secretary's orders, they did nothing to improve a defective prison. In Swansea in 1855 the debtors' jail was in every respect dismal; the *Newcastle Chronicle* in 1850 called its town prison "a school of corruption"; the Spalding Lockup, despite the inspector's protests, was a filthy black hole, with no ventilation, light, drainage, or conveniences; and the Spinning House at Cambridge, under the supervision of no less a person than the University's vice chancellor, was in 1842 in the same discreditable condition as in 1835.[18]

Such was the jealous pride of England's boroughs that by 1850 not one had chosen to consolidate with another borough or with the county in order to build a first class prison. But of all the prisons the ones that illustrated best the magistrates' defiance of the central government and enlightened reform were Newgate, Birmingham, and Leicester. Newgate in 1845 was defective and overcrowded.[19] In 1854 it was still, according to the *Times*, "the

17. Lewis, *Chadwick*, 355–56; Palmerston Papers, Palmerston to B. Hall, Aug. 20, 1854.
18. *PP, 21* (1842), 34. *Newcastle Chronicle*, June 7, 1850. *PP, 26* (1855), 37. *Lincoln, Rutland, and Stamford Mercury*, Aug. 22, 1851. *PP*, 34* (1844), 29.
19. *PP*, 37* (1845), 453; *PP, 17* (1850), 3.

worst prison in England." Its notoriety was rivaled only by the disclosure in 1853 of cruelty and whippings at Birmingham and Leicester. These two prisons made their inmates turn, while in solitary confinement, 14,000 turns of a crank, and if they didn't achieve this figure, their already meager diet was reduced, a punishment clearly against the law of the land and the policies of the inspectors.[20]

In the long run, however, it was more a passive than active resistance that hindered the inspectors—complacency and parsimony rather than truculence and anger. The agitators who drove the poor-law assistants out of town or the orators who excoriated the health inspectors in public meetings caught the headlines, but they were not so numerous as the negligent guardians, the complacent JP's, and the grudging rate-payers who unobtrusively frustrated the inspectors' most cherished reforms. The lunacy commissioners reported in 1850 seventy instances of negligence, uncleanliness, bad ventilation, want of attendants, scanty bedding, improper diet, lack of sheets, and use of mechanical restraint.[21] The busy and not too learned magistrates who supervised these asylums did not share the zeal of the commissioners for higher standards of care. Even when they did, the rate-payers objected to wasteful expenditures on resident doctors and new additions.

The state of the church societies' schools affords a good example of that financial poverty and local niggardliness which defeated the inspectors' hopes. Local committees were ardent for better teachers, books, and buildings but had no money to buy them. There was little active resistance to the education inspectors, either from teachers or from managing committees; the main problems were the indifference of working-class parents and the want of generosity on the part of subscribers. Inspectors Moseley and Watkins believed that the greatest hindrance was the want of money. In 1849 Moseley reported that prospects in the Midlands "are gloomy beyond description," because of "the parsimony of parishioners." One congregation that boasted a member worth one million pounds gave only £20 a year to its school; and a district of 10,000

20. HO, 12/7201, 8209, 4591. *Times*, July 29, 1854. *PP, 17* (1850), 66.
21. *PP*, 29* (1850), 37–38 (2–3); *PP, 49* (1853), 3–21 (1–18).

people, twenty-five of whom received over £50, 000 annually, gave only £50. Watkins in the North found that four-fifths of the schools were insolvent.[22] The English prided themselves on their attachment to local government, and the religious bodies spoke enthusiastically of voluntary efforts, but they did not support their ideals with adequate money or effort.

The owners and managers of factories, mines, railways, and ships do not formally constitute a part of local government, but their cooperation was no less necessary if the central government was to protect children from overwork, miners from explosions, the public from train wrecks, and seamen from abuse. That cooperation was not always forthcoming. Leonard Horner spoke in 1839 of "the continual violation of the law" and expostulated against those "of high station and property . . . who . . . shut their eye and silently acquiesced in the oppressive treatment of children . . ." In 1844 he reported "dishonest evasions in some mills of great magnitude" and by 1854 found the law still violated and his order on fencing openly resisted.[23]

The means of resisting the Factory Law varied over the years. In the 1830's mill-owners exploited children under age by using false age certificates. After 1848 they exploited the law's ambiguities on the use of relays of children in order to work some of them late into the night, and by such means to keep adult men engaged for longer hours. In North Wales they exploited the right of making up lost time to work extra hours; and in one factory they hurried the children into an attic as an inspector approached. Even if caught, they paid only light fines. Town magistrates were either mill-owners or friends of mill-owners. It was this weakness which most infuriated Horner and which helps explain why in 1846 Henry Moseley remarked candidly in his education report that "the factory law is openly and notoriously evaded," and why in 1853 the *Times* judged that "the Act is extensively evaded." [24] Only a mi-

22. *PP, 40* (1852), 378; *PP*, 14* (1847), 107 (93). *Education Times,* Sept. 1849. Scott F. Surtees, *Education for the People* (London, 1846), p. 5. *PP*, 9* (1846), 335.

23. *PP, 19* (1839), 449 (16). *Manchester Guardian,* June 12, 1839. *Wakefield Journal,* June 14, 1844.

24. *PP, 14* (1847), 108 (94). *Times,* July 7, 1853.

nority, of course, violated the Act; but it was the evasions of these few which posed for the inspectors their real problem, just as it was the directors of the Midland Railway Company and the Wigan mine-owners who caused the railway and mining inspectors great anxiety. Captain Huish of the Midland Company reflected a not uncommon view when he said, "his directors were not in any way affected by the remarks of the inspectors," while the Wigan owners, though in 1853 they lost fifty-nine men in an explosion, refused to carry out the inspectors' recommendations for better ventilation. In 1854 another explosion killed eighty-nine.[25] "When the simple truth is brought under the notice of the proprietor," Thomas Wynne wrote Palmerston in 1855, "the answer generally is 'the bully must know how to get the coal in the best and cheapest manner . . . accidents always did happen and always will.'" The embittered Wynne concluded that "a pit's company is without a head except so far as profits and loss is concerned." Mackworth reported that mine-owners seldom carried out his suggestions and that "reckless policy is the rule rather than the exception." [26] For many of the captains of industry the laws of Parliament and the orders of Whitehall were but vexations to be shunned and evaded. Many colliery owners fitted all too well Carlyle's image of capitalists who worshiped mammon more than humanity.

The colliery owners did not stand alone, however, for it was an age of exuberant capitalism. Everyone felt that property should be inviolate. Water companies and tenement-owners fought the Board of Health, and ship-owners balked at merchant marine regulations. The power of capital joined the staunch patriotism of old corporations, the complacency of rate-payers, and the tenacious adherence of local officials to patronage, as forces working against the efforts of the central government. Such forces were found everywhere in society. Even the august Ecclesiastical Commission with its array of cabinet ministers could not persuade a local bishop to carry out reform. "We can not check the Bishop of Exeter," Graham complained to Peel, "in his zeal to pull down his palace,

25. *Railway Times,* April 29, 1854. HO, 45/4678. *Mining Journal,* March 18, 1854.
26. *PP, 15* (1855), 575–76 (96–97), 693–95 (114–16).

to move it 100 yards, and to rebuild it out of Church funds." [27] Against bishops, JP's, railway magnates, sewer commissioners, poor-law guardians, mill-owners, and the mighty rate-payers, Her Majesty's civil servants, understaffed and insufficiently empowered, could win only by the vigorous and skillful employment of the art of persuasion.

THE ART OF PERSUASION

Lord John Russell in 1839 told the education inspectors simply to "inspect and report the facts," and let "opinion do the rest," since "authority never will." Kay Shuttleworth embodied that advice in official instructions that the inspectors should not, unless asked, offer advice. Sir George Grey repeated the same advice to the mining inspectors in 1850, urging them to "afford to any parties who may solicit it . . . advice and suggestions," but to "abstain from dictation." [28] Persuasion not coercion was the ideal of the Victorian administrators. Their belief in the power of intelligence and knowledge led them to overestimate the value of advice and suggestion. They feared compulsion. Even the sternest administrators shied away from the use of force unless compelled by necessity. Edwin Chadwick told Graham in 1841 that he wished the assistant poor-law commissioners "to carry all measures by persuasion," and later he told Russell: "however large the powers [of the Board] I have myself always preferred proceeding at the expense of great labour by persuasion and full exposition of the reason." [29] At the inauguration of each central agency there was a nearly unanimous faith in the power of persuasion. The Railway Board in 1842 said it would proceed by suggestion not compulsion, the commissioners of lunacy in 1847 claimed they sought to effect improvements not by threatening to revoke a license but by agreement. Horner disavowed, until 1852, the use of legal powers to order the fencing of machinery; and Stuart, in Scotland, was convinced that "the parties are far more likely to fulfill the humane intentions of the legislature by persuasion, than by having recourse . . . to penal-

27. Graham Papers, Graham to Peel, Dec. 27, 1842.
28. PRO, 30/22/3, Russell to Kay, 1839.
29. Chadwick Papers, Chadwick to Graham, undated, around 1841; Chadwick to Russell, undated, around 1854.

ties or coercive measures."[30] In a country jealous of a powerful central government and in an age convinced of the power of knowledge, a belief in administration by intelligence and not force was an agreeable axiom; but in practice it proved to be a less effective technique of administration than they hoped.

The plans of the Victorians for substituting intelligence for coercion depended above all on the inspectors' personal visits. Circulars and reports, no matter how brilliantly composed or eloquently written (and not many were brilliant or eloquent), could not induce reluctant and inefficient officials to make improvements. Urgent orders and long, detailed reports were indeed issued, and issued profusely, to poor-law guardians, health boards, asylums, prison and school committees, and factory- and mine-owners. In the later stages, when administration became more routine—when guardians and magistrates were won over to the new scheme of things—these written communications were of greater use, but in the early and tense stages and on controversial issues the local officials merely ignored them. At Dumfries, for example, the guardians, paying no heed to the circulars on cholera, did nothing to prevent the dread disease till John Sutherland arrived. In administration by persuasion everything depended on the personal contact of the inspector and the local official.

The first elements of the art of persuasion were tact and courtesy. "It is impossible to insist too strongly," said Robert Hall in an illuminating memo on how to persuade recalcitrant poor-law corporations to vote their own dissolution, "on the necessity of maintaining the most conciliatory deportment, the most perfect temper." Horner considered courtesy and kindness of manner an essential quality in all his assistants, and his colleague Rickards told his assistants: "your best chance of success will be courteous and conciliatory demeanour towards the mill-owners." Prison inspectors, said Captain Williams, should constantly exercise "great tact and delicacy."[31] The advice to the education inspectors was full of similar admonitions.

On the whole, the inspectors lived up to these ideals. Richard

30. *PP, 41* (1842), 34 (xxi); *PP*, 36* (1847), 22 (14); *PP, 31* (1837), 67; *32* (1847), 409 (38).

31. *PP, 21* (1852), 381 (4); *40* (1835), 698 (9). MH, 10/1, Nov. 1, 1834. *HO,* 45/451.

Dawes praised the education inspectors for "the gentlemanly and unobstrusive manners in which they inspected the schools." Numerous poor-law boards testified to the courtesy of assistant commissioners. The Manchester board found Mott "considerate, judicious, courteous." According to Edward Parry, Mott was "a mixture of good nature and firmness. Nothing gets him out of temper." Hall made a similar judgment about Gulson, praising his "surprizing tact . . . and invincible good humour." He also praised Richard Earle, whose deportment he found "perfectly ingenious, lively, and conciliatory." [32] Evidence of rudeness of brusqueness on the part of any of the inspectors is meager. Only Whitworth Russell seemed to have acted rudely and then, according to the affronted official, only after his courtesy and politeness were worn down by constant resistance to the idea of separate confinement.[33]

The second step in persuading local officials to adopt improved policies was to dispel their prejudices by presenting them with the fullest information and best reasoning available on any problem at hand. Though reason and knowledge did not influence everyone, they proved to be the strongest weapon in the inspectors' arsenal. Ignorance was always a great source of resistance—ignorance of what a workhouse meant, of the cost of sewers, of the means of ventilating mines, and of the harm of mechanical restraint on the insane. Such ignorance, when not bound too closely to prejudices and interests, could be dispelled by a clear exposition of the facts. "I explained the powers of the General Board of Health," said Rawlinson of his speech to Hexham's noisy ratepayers, "and of their intent to keep costs down and I traced disease to crowded tenements, undrained streets, lanes and courts; soon I had won the meeting." Ignorance of the crowded and diseased parts of town was widespread; few besides medical men, said William Lee, knew the true state of their towns. He added that nothing removed their opposition to the Public Health Act more quickly than a trip through the town's back alleys and tenements.[34]

The problem of pauperism and the purpose of the New Poor

32. Richard Dawes, *Observations*, p. 16. HO, 45/1463. MH, 32/60, April 25, 1835; 32/35, Dec. 12, 1837; 32/34, Jan. 6, 1837.

33. Chesterton, *Revelations*, p. 185. O'Donaghue, *Bridewell*, p. 229.

34. Chadwick Papers, Rawlinson to Chadwick, Sept. 30, 1852. W. Lee, *Report of the General Board of Health on Over Darwen* (London, 1853), p. 19.

Law were not as palpable as dirty sewers or uneducated school-masters. Boards of guardians and anti-poor-law agitators did not find the assistant poor-law commissioners' reasoning self-evident; and there were men of keen sensibility who found the new law repellent. Despite these difficulties, the assistants had modest success in dispelling the grosser prejudices by reason and fact. At Caistor, after Gulson explained the aims of the law and made it clear that the old and infirm would not be forced into workhouses, the chairman of the guardians confessed he had come to the meeting "unfortunately disposed" but "after the able exposition admitted his views had changed." Earl Fitzwilliam attended a violent Oastlerite meeting at York and reported that "the calm and candid explanations of Mr. Revans had a remarkable effect . . . persons who had come prepared to oppose the system, were induced to become its decided friend." [35]

Like Rawlings, Gulson, and Revans, most inspectors put their full acquaintance with the facts to good use. But in some circumstances they had to add the arts of the orator and the subtleties of the diplomat. Hall's memorandum on how to convince poor-law incorporations formed by local acts to dissolve themselves reads like a handbook on diplomacy; and it was not without Machiavellian overtones. After the first meeting, which should be devoted to a clear exposition of the facts, the assistant commissioner should meet the leading officers privately, attend their parish meetings, line up those who will support him, and prime them with arguments for the second meeting. At the second meeting the assistant commissioner should press his arguments more vigorously. The reports of the assistants show that they heeded Hall's advice on the need of forceful persuasion: "I was forced to lecture a good deal," wrote Clive in 1836, "and dragoon them all . . . with a good deal of driving they will I hope go." "I have been speechifying at the town hall for the last hour," wrote Ash A'Court, "and have succeeded in getting the two parishes to unite." "Yesterday," said Hall, "I held forth in the town hall for two hours." The job of the assistants was not for the gentle. Alfred Power in Huddersfield and Bolton had to bear the execrations of the mob and the resentment

35. *Lincoln Chronicle*, Aug. 19, 1836. *Leeds Mercury*, May 20, 1837.

of anti-poor-law guardians. He answered with firmness. Parker also, firmly if cynically, told the commissioners: "It is only constant opposition and not the weight of argument . . . which overcomes them."[36]

Diplomacy was everywhere needed to line up support. The assistants all agreed with Hall on the indispensability of private interviews. On personal contacts with the influential rested the success of an inspector. "My great object," wrote Ash A'Court, "has been to get willing agents to work with." Most of them succeeded in this art. "Earle possessed," wrote his colleague Hall, "a personal influence over his boards, to almost every member of which he is known, and with whom he has maintained an unbroken correspondence." Constant attention, artful pleading, firmness of character, a knowledge of when to yield and when to hold firm, tact, courtesy, sheer hard work—all these the inspectors employed to carry out the policies of the central government.[37]

Even when tact, reason, character, and ingenuity were happily combined (which did not always happen) the opposition did not invariably yield. The best suggestions and the most cogent arguments were wasted if a Squire Western ruled a poor-law board or a Bounderby and Gradgrind owned a factory. "My arguments are totally unintelligible" to the rural guardians, wrote Hall. The assistants, in such situations, often urged that Somerset House issue a directing order, clear and enforceable; but Somerset House eschewed such orders.

At times the preference for persuasion led to rather ambivalent courses of action. The poor-law commissioners, for example, told the Macclesfield guardians that they, the commissioners, had an undoubted power to order the guardians to alter their workhouse, "but that they were unwilling under any circumstances to exercise their powers." Then they added quite inconsistently, "though if the union refused they would compel the parishes to raise a sum

36. MH, 1/10, No. 7; 32/12, Aug. 12, 1836; 32/34, Jan. 28, 1836, May 8, 1835; 32/1, Nov. 15, 1834. Chadwick Papers, A'Court to Chadwick, Nov. 20, 1834, Jan. 1, 1837, Jan. 22, 1835. *Leeds Mercury*, Jan. 14, 1837. *Leeds Intelligencer*, Nov. 25, 1837.

37. MH, 32/35, Dec. 12, 1837. *Macclesfield Courier*, Feb. 22, 1851. Chadwick Papers, A'Court to Chadwick, Nov. 20, 1834. MH, 32/60, Oct. 12, 1838.

for such alteration." The poor-law commissioners' allegiance to the ideal of persuasion by intelligence and reason did not run so deep, however, as to preclude the wonderfully persuasive effect of a court order. "The commissioners are sensible," they said in a letter to Bolton's refractory guardians, "that they may be thought to have relied too much on the ultimate effects of reason and experience and to have been unwilling to have recourse to compulsory measures of other kinds." [38] The commissioners were fortunate in possessing the power to approve the appointments and dismissals of all union officers and to issue orders relating to workhouse rules and the kinds of relief to be dispensed. On critical occasions they used these coercive powers. Behind every order there lay the possibility of coercion. The law forced the local guardians to obey the commissioners' orders. For this reason Hall could force the dissolution of local-act corporations by threatening to swamp the local officers with detailed rules and regulations which they must obey. Rawlinson at Macclesfield, in urging on that town the Public Health Act, was similarly ready to use compulsion if words failed. Where the annual mortality was 23 per 1,000 or more the Board of Health could enforce the law on the inhabitants despite their fulminations; and where poor-law guardians and the officials of local health boards neglected to remove nuisances, the Board of Health, using common law, could prosecute them. Yet only in cases of gross negligence did they dare begin such a prosecution.

Greater coercive powers were available to the lunacy commissioners and the inspectors of schools, mills, mines, and railways. The education inspectors could refuse funds and the lunacy commissioners could revoke a license—though the drastic nature of such actions blunted their effectiveness in day-to-day administration. Both agencies were timid about shutting down badly needed institutions.

The railway and factory inspectors also shied away from coercion; their offices announced at the beginning that they were going to proceed by suggestion, a proposal as sanguine as the circular to the mining inspectors on giving advice only when it was solicited.

38. MH, 1/25, Oct. 12, 1840; 12/5595, Jan. 17, 1843.

The majority of factories, to be sure, did follow the advice of inspectors, but there were a few exceptions who had to be prosecuted. The mine-owners were less cooperative, and not all railways esteemed highly the proposals made by railway inspectors. The Brighton and Chichester refused to follow the inspectors' suggestion to improve its engines. The Railway Board countered by refusing to allow the company to open any new lines; and when the Great Western refused to complete the line from Oxford to Wolverhampton, the Railway Board, Isidore Brunel notwithstanding, issued a court order.[39]

The Victorian administrators, aristocratic minister and middle-class expert alike, soon realized that persuasion alone would not suffice. In 1854 the Home Secretary, Lord Palmerston, urged his inspectors to prosecute every violation of the factory and mining laws. Penalties on mill-owners, he told the inspectors, "should never be remitted, it is difficult enough to get them imposed," and he told the mining inspectors to prosecute even when the evidence was slim, for "it is right—to do everything in our power to protect these poor people."[40] Palmerston, a realist about administrative behavior, shared neither Lord John Russell's optimism about the power of persuasion nor Sir George Grey's conservative hesitation about irritating property-owners.

When the Home Secretary ordered a prosecution or the poor-law commissioners asked for a writ of mandamus, the Government's newest agencies found their policies under the review of the Government's oldest agencies, the courts of law. The courts alone could order a guardian to hold an election or require a factory-owner to cease working children after 6 P.M. The new bureaus, in asking the courts to enforce their policies, found themselves involved in the expanding province of administrative law.

By Order of the Court

Administrative law—that law which defines governmental rights and an individual's public duties—had obscure and controversial

39. *PP**, *32* (1850), 314–15 (12–13); *47* (1848), 201 (7).
40. HO, 45/5394, 45/5202.

origins in England.[41] The Tudors and the first two Stuarts enforced it through their council courts, which freely issued writs and heard cases on poor relief, wages of artificers, and the powers of the Justices of the Peace. England even then faced the possibility—though at the time it was still remote—of an administrative law developing from administrative courts. But the lawyers, parliamentarians, and puritans, resisting such encroachments, fought in Parliament to secure the abolition of council courts and won a triumphant victory in 1641 when Charles agreed to their demise. This dispute left as a legacy to succeeding centuries a deeply rooted hostility against all central administrative courts. Let the common, statute, and equity law—as expressed in the Queen's Bench, Common Pleas, Exchequer, and Chancery—rule supreme. Only such law would ensure the King's subject his rights.

Yet for all their animosity against the administrative law which came from conciliar courts, there grew up, in the regular courts, a large body of administrative law. It became extensive, even in the Tudor period, and it grew larger in the seventeenth and eighteenth centuries. A growing society needed to define the rights of its public officials. Most of this law was local and expressed itself in the countless powers of the local justices, such as the power to order overseers to give pauper relief or the highway surveyor to improve the roads. This law was also obscured by its proximity, and in some cases—as with malfeasance and misfeasance—by its identity with common law. It often rested on precedent and immemorial custom, though it was more often defined by statutes. The statutes, however copious, were frequently unenforced. A lax, unconscious laissez-faire attitude dominated English society in the eighteenth century.

The growth after 1833 of a larger and more active central government gave impetus to the expansion of administrative law and shifted its focus from the rights of JP's to the rights of central departments. Parliament, aware of new social problems, passed stat-

41. Some define administrative law as that promulgated by administrative agencies. In the following discussion the term is used in a broader sense, namely as any law which defines the powers and duties of administrative agencies. Such law may be passed by Parliaments or Congresses and heard before regular courts.

utes creating new agencies and defining the public duties and rights of old authorities. It defined the duties of the Excise and Customs Commissions, and the Queen's Bench sent writs to justices defining their public duties in managing prisons. By 1854 the courts found themselves preoccupied with a multiplicity of administrative matters.[42] They had to determine the rights of guardians, define the duties of mill-owners, and judge the competence of magistrates to supervise lunacy asylums. Bewigged barristers now argued the finer points of administrative law in the august chambers once dedicated to the finer points of land law.

Within this growing province of administrative law there arose the all-important question of defining a central agency's rights and powers to compel a local authority or individual to take certain actions. It fell largely to the Queen's Bench and the Exchequer to decide this question. The Queen's Bench ruled over such matters as the poor law and sanitation. The Exchequer dealt with the regulation of industry. The Queen's Bench often found itself harassed by cases arising from the ambiguous powers granted to the Poor Law Commission. Disputes concerning the commissioners' right to order guardians to take an action, along with an endless series of disputes on settlement and nonresident relief, dominate the law books of the Queen's Bench from 1833 to 1854.[43] The numerous clauses of the New Poor Law contained many ambiguities, which jealous authorities were quick to interpret according to their own interests. The courts were thus placed in the center of the controversy over centralization, and both central and local authorities looked to them for favor.

The Queen's Bench took no clear stand on this issue. Some of its decisions on the Poor Law Commission's powers were as ambiguous as the poor law itself. In two important cases the Queen's Bench decided once in favor of the Commission and once in favor of the local authorities. In 1837 it upheld the writ of certiorari of

42. Webbs, *Parish and County*, pp. 445–74. A. V. Dicey, *Introduction to the Study of the Law and the Constitution* (London, 1950), pp. xxvii–clvi. E. C. Wade's introduction provides an excellent discussion of administrative law in England.

43. W. G. Lumley, *An Abridgement of the Cases upon the Subject of the Poor Law*, London, 1843.

the St. Pancras local-act vestry that had questioned the validity of the Commission's orders for the election of twenty instead of forty guardians. The court decided that section 39 of the Law, which allowed the commissioners to issue rules and regulations to local-act corporations on matters of relief, did not include the power to define the number of elected guardians; and furthermore that to change the number of guardians was in fact to dissolve the union, which section 41 forbade unless two-thirds of the guardians agreed. One of the three judges dissented, however, maintaining with considerable logic that the power given to the commissioners to superintend the operation of the local-act unions so as to achieve efficiency and uniformity included the power to determine how many guardians should be elected. The other two judges decided for the St. Pancras guardians.[44]

A year later the same court upheld the commissioners. Though it had refused them the power of ordering a change in the number of guardians, it now allowed them to order local act or Gilbert incorporations to combine with regular parishes to form larger unions.[45] To argue that such an action did not imply dissolution (and so did not violate section 41) while insisting that the changing of the number of guardians to be elected did imply dissolution (and did violate section 41) was a refinement too subtle for the administrators to understand.

The court was equally ambiguous in judging the rights of the Poor Law Commission to order local guardians to employ certain paid officials. It ruled that the Commission could order unions to appoint chaplains (though the law did not mention them by name) but could not order the appointment of collectors of poor rates. The last decision, since it invalidated some 1,000 orders, caused Chadwick no little frustration. He complained to Sir Thomas Lewis about the so-called friendly attitude of the court toward the poor law.[46] Chadwick was the embodiment of administrative zeal, and it was natural that the court's restraint should have irritated him. But the fact remained that the local officials had more

44. *Law Journal Reports,* 6, m.c. 43–48.
45. Ibid., 7, m.c. 33.
46. Ibid., 9, m.c. 33, 10, m.c. 76. Chadwick Papers, Chadwick to T. Lewis, Feb. 3, 1841.

reason to believe that the courts were hostile to them than Chadwick had to believe the reverse. In their first anger at the law they contested many obviously valid orders. The Queen's Bench thus had to hand down far more decisions favoring the poor-law commissioners than the local authorities. The Queen's Bench, for example, upheld the commissioner's writ of mandamus ordering the overseer of the township of Todmorden to proceed with the election of guardians, a duty which the law clearly imposed on him but which took a court order and military force to carry out.[47] It was thus the court and the military that enabled the commissioners to force the last stubborn parish into the Todmorden union. The threat of such action led others to accede to the establishment of the New Poor Law in the North.

The factory inspectors also found themselves dependent upon the courts, which alone could fine the mill owners or interpret the law on accidents, relays, and time schedules. From the dignified Exchequer to the lowly petty sessions, the courts tended to favor the interests of property rather than the welfare of the workers. Many of the magistrates, themselves mill-owners, or relatives and friends of mill-owners,[48] naturally were disposed to favor the owners. The inspectors, for example, could not prevent the courts from legalizing the relay system used after 1847 to evade the ten-hour day which the law of 1847 required for young persons and women. The law of that year, however, merely reduced their hours from eleven to ten. It was the law of 1844 that defined the manner of time-keeping and required the owners to count the starting-time of all young people (13 to 18) from the time the mill began work in the morning, grant them uniform meal times, and inscribe their working times not individually but collectively to a fixed schedule.[49] Such rules meant after 1846 that all young people and women had to leave the mill by 6 P.M. To Horner, the Law Office, and the Attorney General, this also meant, as the authors of the 1844 act (Horner, Saunders, and Graham) had intended, that children below 13 must also work the very same hours throughout the

47. *Law Journal Report, 10,* m.c. 65. *PP, 20* (1839), 14–15.
48. HO, 45/1117.
49. 7 & 8 Vict. c. 15, ss. 26, 30, schedule C; 9 & 10 Vict. c. 29, s. 3, which applied the 7 & 8 Vict c. 15 clauses to young people and women.

day, all quitting six hours after the first of them started to work.[50]

But the mill-owners found a loop-hole. The act said nothing that literally precluded the mill-owner from excusing children below 13 for some hours during the day and using them in the evening. They could thus employ them in relays and beyond 6 P.M. With such children, needed to tend machines, the employers could keep the adult males busy a full twelve or thirteen hours—and possibly overwork some of the children since the relay system made it hard to detect violations. The relay scheme was of dubious legality and humanity, yet many owners exploited it fully.

Horner fought the mill-owners with prosecution upon prosecution, and with such vigor that the *Manchester Guardian* complained that he was putting the law in defiance.[51] After losing ten cases and winning only one in his district, a test case was sent to the Court of the Exchequer, which decided for the mill-owners. Two of the three judges insisted on the most literal reading of each separate clause and ruled that the relay was legal. The third judge dissented from their decision, insisting that the meaning of the act as a whole should be taken. In his opinion the meaning was clearly to prevent the working of children over six hours, measured from the time the mill started to work.[52] The decision was a severe defeat for Horner, convinced as he now was of the justice of the ten-hour day.

Ultimately his view triumphed. The ten-hour agitators in Parliament and Palmerston in the Home Office forced through a law, written by Horner in 1853, that prohibited the use of children after 6 P.M., and so in fact forced even the adult male on a ten and one-half hour day. The courts in this decision, as in all decisions on questions of public rights, were rigorous in judging particular cases, but they always had to base their judgment on the statutes of Parliament; common law had little to say. It was therefore Parliament who ultimately decided the extent and power of public authorities over local authorities and mill-owners.

50. HO, 45/ os 3094.
51. HO, 45/1117, undated clipping in file, around 1849.
52. *Times,* June 21, 1849. By this date Horner had lost ten cases and won one. Howells and Saunders were favored by magistrates who felt that the relay was illegal: *Law Journal Reports,* 19, m.c. 85–92.

In defining the limits of the government's power the courts usually took a narrow, technical and conservative view. Their common-law bias went against the ideal of a benevolent, active state, as did their respect for the rights of local government and private property. The Exchequer, a court increasingly active in administrative law, displayed in these years a record even more conservative than that of the Queen's Bench. They ruled in favor of the mill-owners on the question of relays, and in 1847 and 1848 they decided in favor of the private citizen against both the Railway and the Lunacy Commissions. The Lord Chief Baron of the Exchequer, in *Nottidge v. Ripley and another,* decided that "no person ought to be confined in a lunatic establishment unless 'dangerous to himself or others' "; and in *Chilton v. London and Croydon Railway Company* he determined that a person could not be seized for breaking the by-laws of a railway company unless he violated the particular statute that had established the railway.

Both decisions paralyzed administrative actions at crucial points. If literally carried out (which it wasn't) *Nottidge v. Ripley* would have freed thousands of mentally ill from needed care, while *Chilton v. London and Croydon* would have allowed an obnoxious railway traveler to endanger himself and discomfort others without the railway officers having the power to seize him.[53] The decision on the incarceration of the mentally ill was particularly unenlightened, if not preposterous: it was not only bad policy, it was bad law! Ashley's memorandum to the Lord Chancellor made it clear that other sections in other acts allowed the commissioners to order to an asylum insane persons who could not care for themselves yet who were not dangerous. Ashley told the Lord Chancellor that the court's decision would undermine the entire system of enlightened cure. To the Barons of the Exchequer, of course, all this was social philosophy, not law; in these years of expanding government they clung to a narrow interpretation of an agency's power and jealously checked the state's new powers.

The Law Office, the central government's supreme authority on the legal rights of each department, shared in part the conservatism of the courts. On health matters, said R. A. Lewis, it reflected

53. *PP**, *42* (1849), 64–65 (1–5); *47* (1848), 211 (17).

the lack of interest of the ruling class in sanitary reform. Typical of its conservatism was its answer to a question asked by the lunacy commissioners concerning the revoking of a license held by Mr. Wilkinson, manager of an asylum. The Law Office admitted that Wilkinson was guilty of a "very wanton and unnecessary outrage" but considered the revocation of his license too severe a punishment, "as it will deprive Mr. Wilkinson of a livelihood." [54] The Law Office always warned the aggressive Whitehall social reformers of the courts' narrow and literal interpretations of their powers.

Despite their conservatism and common-law bias, the Law Office, the Queen's Bench, and the Exchequer could not stay the avalanche of administrative law that descended on England. A check of an agency by a court invariably forced Parliament to give the agencies greater powers, and a myriad of new and amending acts multiplied the matters of administrative law. Despite this legislation, the courts continued to be chary of allowing the central departments the fullest interpretation of their powers. The courts, as well as the ministers, hoped that the new bureaucracy would carry out its policies by persuasion not compulsion, and so develop that working cooperation which finally characterized relations between the central inspectors and the local authorities.

A WORKING COOPERATION

The truculent local officials and self-willed industrialists who resisted and evaded the intrusions of the central government always constituted a minority; and those against whom a court order had to be issued were a minority among this minority. Most officials and industrialists cooperated with the central inspectors.

Those most receptive to the visits of the inspectors were the schoolmasters and school committees; the inspectors had only good words for their receptiveness and cooperation. "I have," said Henry Bellairs, "met with unusual kindness." He found the masters "anxious to listen to any suggestions offered." After inspecting schools for twenty months, William Brookfield did not remember "a single occasion in which any embarrassment or discomfort had risen between those interested and myself." The other school inspectors

54. Lewis, *Chadwick*, p. 303. HO, 45/5153, May 14, 1853.

reported the same happy receptions. The clergy, said the Bishop of London, esteemed the inspectors highly (a not unnatural circumstance, considering that most of the inspectors were clergymen). None of Whitehall's servants were more courteously received than these well-bred university men. An account by a teacher in Exeter of Frederick Cook's visit reveals the awe felt by local teachers for such distinguished and yet charming and kind personages: "His quiet tone, often very humorous . . . his excellent manners, his patience, the attention and respect which his great learning (never obtruded) commanded, had full play. He knew how to advise with effect, yet never seemed to dictate. I do not call to mind a single fracas, yet certainly there was never a more powerful inspector." [55] Similar reports were made of the other school inspectors. The cultivation and intelligence of the inspectors impressed the schoolmasters, and their Christian orthodoxy gained them the trust of the local clergy and school committees. The result was a fruitful partnership hindered only by a want of money. The Minutes of 1846, so radical to High Churchmen and dissenters, disturbed neither teachers nor committeemen, and they were adopted without anger or resistance. "It was," said Norris, looking back from 1862 to those dramatic events of 1847, "due to the cooperation of the clergy that the 1846 Minutes were successful." [56]

Cordiality also marked the relationship between other inspectors and their local officials, though it was not so universal as with the education inspectors. The strident shouts of Oastlerites against the bashaws of Somerset House and the protests of town councillors against the tyrants of Gwyder House quickly dispelled any hopes of a quick acceptance of the New Poor Law and the Public Health Act. Angry meetings and protests, not efficient cooperation, make good copy and won headlines. But if one looks beneath the headlines, one may find much evidence of a willingness, especially after initial fears and ignorance were removed, to accept the New Poor Law. "My suggestions," wrote Colonel Ash A'Court from Winchester, "met with a reception beyond my expectation." From

55. *PP**, 7 (1845), 304 (116); 37 (1850), 63. Hansard, 79 (1847), 878. Dawes, *Observations*, p. 4.

56. *Notes and Gleanings*, 2 (1889), 114–16. J. P. Norris, *The Education of the People*, p. 49.

Gloucester Robert Weale reported that "every suggestion of mine is received with the greatest possible respect and attention." [57] The reports of the assistant commissioners in 1837 on the public's reaction to the new law were encouraging. In Bedford, Buckingham, and Hertford "most are in favour," and in Dorset, Wiltshire, Gloucester, and Somerset "public opinion is almost unanimous in favour of the law."

The inspectors of the Board of Health had opportunities to write in like vein. "My visits and instructions," Lee told Chadwick, "have been received everywhere in the kindest manner." After inspecting sixty towns George Clark reported that not one public officer had declined to give him information.[58] There were no inspectors, whether of asylums, prisons, railways, or mines, who did not accompany their reports on the failings of some local officials with evidence of the ability and willingness of others. The picture they painted is a mixed one, telling of both resistance and cooperation.

The poor-law reports present the most checkered of these pictures. The quarterly reports of the early 1840's, with their terse three- and four-line summaries of each union, alternate between accounts of miserable workhouses and improved diets, or jobbing overseers and efficient guardians. Yet beneath this varied picture of the poor-law administration certain characteristics are discernible. In general the wealthier classes supported the new law, while the small farmers and shopkeepers (to the assistant commissioners, the "small-minded") opposed it. The assistants found their best allies among the aristocracy. Lord Northampton was chairman of Hardingstone Union, Lord Howe presided at Market Bosworth, Lord Portsmouth chaired the union at West Bromwich, Lord Radnor served on the Isle of Wight, and Lord Spencer presided at Brixworth. The Dukes of Rutland, Grafton, and Bedford were influential in helping the assistants in Northampton and Berkshire.[59] At Farringdon Richard Hall depended on Lord Ellen-

57. MH, 32/1, Nov. 15, 1834; 32/85, Oct. 24, 1835.

58. HO, 73/54. Chadwick Papers, William Lee to Chadwick, Feb. 9, 1854. *Bristol Mercury*, Feb. 16, 1850.

59. MH, 32/21, March 29, July 22, 1835; 32/34, Feb. 13, 1836; 32/4, Jan. 7, 1837; 32/21, July 11, 1835; 32/86, May 21, 1840.

borough, whose "practical knowledge of our measure is more extensive than almost anyone I have met with." "Nothing can exceed Peterboro's Board under Fitzwilliam," wrote Richard Earle; "he is quite the first chairman I have yet seen." Even royalty gave the law a benign blessing. His Majesty King William IV received Assistant Commissioner Walsham at Windsor with cordiality and pronounced the law "one of the greatest measures that has ever passed the legislature." [60]

Since most unions did not enjoy the presence of a peer of the realm, the assistants frequently turned to the MP's, the clergy, the magistracy, and all others of the "respectable" and intelligent class. In the countryside they found the gentry on their side. In the towns they depended on wealthy manufacturers like Ashworth of Bolton and Greg of Manchester. The law was by no means resisted in all the northern towns. In Manchester the shopocracy supported it. The board of guardians there, which included a jeweler, a solicitor, a woolen draper, a case-maker, two paper manufacturers, and some shopkeepers, worked very efficiently. Unhampered by party feuds or jealous townships, they imposed the workhouse test on the able-bodied and sent the pauper children to a newly built school for industrial and moral training. The guardians of Manchester, like the rural gentry, were men of property and respectability, and as Charles Mott said in 1836, "nearly all men of property and respectability . . . are generally decidedly in favour of it." [61] The law, as Oastler indignantly pointed out, favored the rights of property over the rights of the poor. It was class legislation, and as such its working depended upon men of property and education. Without their assistance the law would have failed.

In moments of bitterest resistance, when the agitators on the boards seemed to dissolve all into confusion, it was the magistrates, all of whom were ex-officio members, who held out firmly for the law. Richard Earle placed a high estimation on their work, praising "their moral worth, their judgement, and their capacity for business." [62] It was the active partnership of the assistant commis-

60. MH, 32/35, Jan. 3, 1837; 32/21, Feb. 7, 1837; 32/21, April 8, 1835; 32/26, July 25, 1835.
61. MH, 12/6040, Jan. 4, 1841; 12/6042, May 22, 1845. HO, 73/54.
62. MH, 32/21, June 25, 1836.

sioners with magistrates and peers, with educated gentry and respected manufacturers, that allowed the revolutionary poor law to triumph over the protests of the urban artisans and operatives and surmount the incompetence and prejudices of the rural farmers who so bitterly disliked it. Only with such a cooperation between local and central officials could the experiment in centralized supervision and local initiative have worked. Their agreement on basic principles and aims made success possible. In the same way a partnership between the clergy and the school inspectors brought better schools, and cooperation between medical doctors and health inspectors promoted sanitary improvement. In the case of the unsanitary towns, particularly, every bit of local cooperation was needed.

The Public Health Act demanded that one-tenth of the rate-payers sign a petition before the Board's officers could make an investigation. The rate-payers generally had a morbid fear of increased rates. Chadwick, aware of this fact, wished that a petition of one-fifteenth of the rate-payers be declared sufficient to warrant an investigation.

The upper classes were largely uninformed of the filth and disease of "the other part of town." Who but the clergy and doctors visited these wretched tenements? Their intimate acquaintanceship made them the inspectors' first and best allies. They accompanied the inspector on his tour, spoke for the act at public meetings, and, once the act was applied, served on the local boards. Rawlinson found that medical men invariably gave "the fullest evidence in favor of the Act," and he told Chadwick that "the country will ever owe them a debt of gratitude." Sutherland, after his arduous work fighting cholera in Scottish cities in 1849, found their parochial medical officers of the greatest help. At Derby it was Dr. Baker's indefatigable labors that led to a petition for the act, and at St. Oswyth it was the "zealous labours and exertions of the Reverend Mosse, the perpetual curate." [63] Once an investigation had forced a town to look at its disgraceful areas, the town dignitaries,

63. Rawlinson, *Report of the General Board of Health on Whitehaven,* London, 1849. *PP, 40* (1850), 263 (78). Cresy, *Report of the General Board of Health on Derby* (London, 1849), p. 10. Ranger, *Report of the General Board of Health on St. Oswyth* (London, 1854), p. 8.

the aldermen, councilors, and leading citizens came to the aid of the doctors and clergymen. The inspectors' reports acknowledge the general support of the educated and informed. They were the leaders on the boards of guardians, active on school committees, and became the visiting magistrates of prisons and asylums. They were men of ability and a sense of responsibility. Some were driven by a nonconformist conscience; others, like the peers on the poor-law boards of guardians, fell heir to the older traditions of squire-archical paternalism. They were never many, and some towns and parishes had none, but they constituted the indispensable few without whom the inspectors could not have carried out their policies.

The captains of industry were no heirs to paternalistic tradition; yet on their cooperation rested the efforts to mitigate the severities which unfettered capital visited on unprotected labor. Fortunately the majority accepted the limitations imposed on them. Most had fought the passage of such legislation; but once it passed, they dutifully obeyed the law. Instances of evasions never rivaled those of fulfillment. In general it was only the small, out-of-the-way mills that overworked children, and the small Midland mine that ignored safety regulations. The great mills of Manchester and the collieries of Durham and Northumberland cooperated, as did most of the railway companies. There were even paternalistic manufacturers and colliery-owners. Their attention to sanitation and their endeavors to provide excellent schools won the heartiest commendations from Leonard Horner and Seymour Tremenheere.[64] But they were not numerous. Those who went beyond the law by promoting benevolent schemes for schools and safeguards to health were fewer than those who determinedly evaded the law; but both were small minorities. The large middle group cooperated with the inspectors, some readily, some begrudgingly, but all enough to allow the inspectors to report that the law was "fairly well observed."

"The law is fairly well observed"—that is the monotonous refrain of the factory inspectors from 1837 to 1854. In 1839 it meant that the limitations on hours were generally observed, though by using false age certificates some small children worked more than

64. Leonard Horner, *Memoirs, 1,* 362. *PP, 31* (1837), 53 (1).

eight hours. In 1849 it meant 257 mills in Horner's district alone used 3,742 children in shifts to keep mills running longer than ten hours. To the inspectors this was a violation of the law; to the magistrates it was quite legal. By 1854 the phrase "fairly well observed" meant around 756 prosecutions and 500 convictions for evading the law and a general opposition to the order to fence shafts over seven feet high. Where the law was clear cut and allowed no evasions, the owners obeyed; where there were loopholes or ambiguities, the owners would attempt to balk the inspectors' orders.[65]

There are no statistics on the extent of cooperation among railway companies and mine-owners. The report of 1846 presents only an impressionistic view: "By far the greater number of railway companies evinced the utmost alacrity in complying with the provisions of the act." Matthias Dunn, the mining inspector for the Northumberland and Durham areas, gives an equally favorable though impressionistic view of the owners' cooperation, claiming that he enjoyed their "general good feelings and confidence . . ." Both he and the railway commissioners were apt to be overly optimistic. The rash of accidents which occurred in England in 1850 came from bad scheduling, running trains too close to each other, understaffing, bad discipline—all practices the inspectors had asked the companies to end. Galton's railway report of 1854 differs considerably from the 1846 judgment, and Wynne's and Mackworth's reports on mining differ from Dunn's. In mining, no doubt, those who violated the law were in a minority, but evidence suggests that the majority having obeyed the act (and what an ineffective act it was!) did little else to improve their fatally dangerous mines.[66]

To draw up a balance sheet between resistance and cooperation for the local authorities who carried out the New Poor Law, the prison act, and the health act is even more difficult than to assess the conduct of industrialists. By and large the resistance of these local agencies has been exaggerated and their cooperation min-

65. *PP, 21* (1852), 367 (14); *22* (1842), 340 (3); *19* (1839), 437 (4); *15* (1855), 278 (3); *19* (1854), 370 (113); *42* (1855), 363 (87); *45* (1851), 384 (6).
66. *PP*, 42* (1846), 11–29 (xi–xxix); *PP, 15* (1855), 584 (5), 675–76 (96–97), 693–95 (114–16).

imized, resistance being always more dramatic. Chadwick was right in pointing out that in the whole history of the Board of Health only six of the 182 local boards protested against the supervision of the General Board, and that the political outcry against the Board in Parliament and the press came largely from the metropolis, over which the Board had no control.

The poor-law commissioners were also not far from the truth when in 1847, the year of their disgrace and fall, they claimed, "at no other time has the administration been in a more satisfactory state." [67] The abuses at Andover, which the thundering *Times* attacked without stint, amounted to little compared to the conscientious work of thousands of guardians—no administrative geniuses and often negligent and lazy, but they met with the assistant commissioners, listened to them, argued with them, and tried their best to improve the care of the poor. To be sure, many objected to the harsh workhouse test, but they also adopted many useful suggestions emanating from Somerset House. In the same manner the prison authorities, according to Captain Williams, overcame their initial resistance and cooperated with the inspectors. In a memorandum to Sir George Grey, Williams recalled "the jealousy of interference with which this office was once regarded by local authorities, and the coldness of the reception experienced by the inspectors in the early execution of duties." He then went on to remark that after cautious and patient efforts, "that feeling is now in the happy but slow progress of extinction." [68] The inspectors, by a slow, hard, undramatic process, won the effective and working cooperation of local officials.

The reasons for the success of this fruitful partnership are three-fold: the existence of an élite of able and educated men in local government; the personal influence of energetic and intelligent inspectors; and the essentially sound, though cautious, policies of the central departments.

The period from 1833 to 1854 saw a great improvement in the first of these. Local government, under the tutelage of the inspectors, made great strides forward. Local authorities employed paid

67. *PP, 28* (1847), 7.
68. HO, 45/541.

officials, formed larger units of administration, kept better records, and adopted more humane ideas in the treatment of the poor and helpless. The reports of the inspectors are filled with evidence of these advances, of new attitudes toward the insane, of a more civilized approach to prison discipline, of more efficient techniques in auditing poor-law books.

But the improved local agencies could have done little without the inspectors. The arrival of the inspector, an official carrying the authority of Her Majesty's Government, a personage of status and education and with a wide knowledge of facts, often turned the tide in local affairs. Even when the poor-law guardian, prison magistrate, or town medical officer knew full well what was needed, he required the presence of the inspector to dispel the opposition. Without Rawlinson's persistence in lecturing to Macclesfield ratepayers, the town's own sanitary reformers would have lost; without Power's tenacity in Huddersfield, the New Poor Law would have remained a dead letter; the poor-law guardians of Edinburgh needed the presence of Sutherland before they took precautionary measures.

Yet the charm and vigor of the inspectors would not have secured the cooperation of local agencies if their policies had not been sound. It was in those very areas where the Government's policies were the most dubious—as in urging a strict workhouse test or demanding the rigorous separate confinement of prisoners—that local resistance was the most unbending. The opposition that reflected a just criticism of a harsh policy usually had a greater success than the opposition that arose out of special interests, prejudice or ignorance. By the end of the nineteenth century England was to enjoy, under the surveillance of central inspectors, consolidated water and sewer systems and safe mines, but it would never seek to have the workhouse test enforced *de rigueur* or ordinary felons placed in solitary confinement. The sounder the policy, the more efficient the relationship between local and central administrators.

The working relationship between inspectors and local officials was characterized by much friction. It was not an easy relationship. Conflict and hard-wrought compromises were the prices paid for the ideal of leaving to local authorities the burden of power and to the central inspectors only powers of persuasion and an occasional veto. Where the central inspectors possessed power, conflicts were more quickly resolved. Where they did not, they had to haggle and patiently endure defiance. In 1854 vested interests and frugal rate-payers were still thwarting the inspectors and hampering the Government in its attempt to remove the more glaring evils of an industrial and urbanized society. Offsetting these failures, however, were many more instances of local officials and men of industry working with the inspectors of the central government. By 1854 these inspectors had won the respect of local officialdom and capital, and so had created that early Victorian administrative state which, while abandoning few of the sacred liberties of local government and individual freedom, nevertheless promoted the well-being of the working classes, the imprisoned, the insane, and the poor.

10.

THE CENTRAL GOVERNMENT
AND SOCIAL PROGRESS IN 1854

IN 1833 THE TOWN of Macclesfield, in Cheshire, was the silk manufacturing capital of England. Like many another town in the North
it had lost its eighteenth-century rural aspect. Where pastures once
stretched down to the River Bollin, textile mills now stood; and
nearby Hurdsfield and Sutton, once quiet villages, now housed
thousands of factory operatives in crowded tenements. Macclesfield
from 1811 to 1831 doubled its population and between 1830 and
1850 grew in numbers from 30,000 to 40,000. It had become a
typical mill town, and in doing so had suffered all the attendant
growing pains. It had also, with the help of the central government, attempted to alleviate those pains, and to solve the problems
created by rapid industrial growth. How successfully it did this
and in what ways afford a vivid illustration of the impact England's expanded central administration had on the lives of ordinary people.

In the 1830's the Macclesfield laboring class had few opportunities to enjoy the good life. In fact it was all the people could do
to keep alive. Competition from new textile mills drove down the
earnings of the traditional hand-loom weavers, while child labor
depressed the wages of adult workers. Until 1844 one in every

three who tended the silk machines was 13 years of age or younger.[1] The Factory Law of 1833 had omitted silk mills; children of 8, 9, and 10 thus continued to work long hours in mills that remained unimproved. For the child operative, of course, there was little schooling. In 1833 only one in thirty of the inhabitants of Macclesfield attended a school. What few schools there were taught very little. Henry Moseley, after inspecting Christ Church Infant School, reported that half their students did no more than learn to read, that the schoolmaster had no training, and that fifty of the children worked half-time in the mill and all of them were "lamentably ignorant."

Hurdsfield's school was no better. It could accommodate 500, but in 1845 it had only one teacher and ninety-nine pupils; of these ninety-nine only fourteen could read with ease.[2] The children of the Macclesfield laborers had neither the time nor the opportunity to improve themselves and to gain that useful knowledge and sturdy morality which Victorian reformers believed would save the working class from crime, drink, and chartism. Consigned to congested and unhealthy slums as they were, the workers had little chance of enjoying even ordinary health. From 1841 to 1847 the mortality rate in Macclesfield was thirty-three per thousand every year, as compared to sixteen per thousand in the surrounding countryside. All the faults common to England's jerry-built towns were found in Macclesfield: unpaved and undrained streets, exposed dunghills, blind courts full of refuse, overcrowded tenements with few privies, overfull cemeteries, bad water, and filthy, vice-ridden common lodging houses. In sixteen blocks in Macclesfield the mortality rate exceeded fifty per thousand. In those areas one person out of every twenty would die within the year, almost all of preventable disease.[3]

Long hours of labor from childhood onward, no opportunity for education, and a mortality of thirty-three per thousand—these were the conditions of life for the laboring peoples of Macclesfield.

1. *PP*, 27 (1843), 352 (17).
2. *PP**, 7 (1845), 457; *PP*, *41* (1835), 82–83.
3. J. Smith, *Report of the General Board of Health on Macclesfield* (London, 1850), p. 15. Rawlinson, *Reply to Memorials against the Public Health Act for Macclesfield* (London, 1851), pp. 4–10.

In such circumstances it is not surprising that the less scrupulous turned to crime and the less industrious to pauperism, or that the weak fell prey to insanity. The propertied classes, to be sure, showed an occasional generosity toward some of the poor, but they displayed little wisdom or charity in the management of the workhouse. Of the £11,700 spent on the paupers, the greater share went to outdoor relief. The vestry gave 500 persons such relief, but seriously neglected the orphans, the aged, and the infirm who lived in a disreputable workhouse. They sent the children of the workhouse to the mills to work, a violation of the New Poor Law and a practice which, like all relief in aid of wages, depressed the wages of independent workers. The workhouse was in miserable condition. An assistant commissioner in 1841 called it "a nursery of fanaticism and filth." It had no system of personal classification, no probationary wards, no proper employment for its inmates, and no observed rules of cleanliness.[4]

For all that, it was a better fate for the poor than the town's two prisons. The debtors' jail, according to a prison inspector, was a "wretched place of confinement," dilapidated, unclean, and disorderly, with "windows out and wet coming through the roof." The lockup had no heat in the winter and inadequate ventilation in the summer. Those guilty of felonies, of course, went to the Knutsford House of Correction or Chester Castle, neither of which in 1833 made any attempt to reform the criminal.[5] The county also intended that the Chester Asylum should take care of the pauper insane, but according to the lunacy commissioners the "paupers are brought in such a bad state, in filth and rags, and from too long a delay, in a state where there is little or no chance of cure." The Chester Asylum could accommodate only ten patients, so for a pauper it was a back room of a workhouse "full of fanaticism and filth." [6] The Macclesfield governing class in 1833 had no real hope of reforming criminals, ending pauperism, or curing the insane. These evils, like child labor, ignorance, and a high mortality, were, they thought, an inevitable part of the life of the lower orders.

4. *PP, 28* (1834), 277. MH, 12/968, Feb. 27, 1841.
5. *PP, 25* (1843), 110; *40* (1851), 85.
6. *PP*, 26* (1844), 227 (223).

Macclesfield

By 1854 the Macclesfield laboring class was living in greatly improved conditions and the criminals, paupers, and insane were receiving a far more enlightened treatment. Children below nine no longer worked in silk mills, adults labored only ten hours a day, mills were well ventilated, machinery safely fenced, and walls whitewashed. Educational opportunities were much greater. The Exchequer granted £2,446 for the payment of teachers and pupil teachers in the schools of Macclesfield and Hurdsfield, and gave a further £302 for books. The teachers came from two nearby training colleges at Chester and Warrington, both of which were receiving Exchequer grants and were highly praised by Henry Moseley. Moseley admired Chester for its "remarkable industry" and for the "scientific attainments and skill" of its teachers, and Warrington "for employing the principles of de Fellenberg and Pestalozzi."[7] In 1853 Norris found Christ Church vastly improved: its master experienced, its three pupil teachers efficient, and its discipline and instruction good. The same held true (with a few exceptions) for Hurdsfield's new schools. Their enlarged curriculum now included industrial training. Macclesfield also had a school of design for training future artisans and craftsmen. Inspected and aided by the Board of Trade's Department of Art and Science it was, said the Reverend Edward Weigall, the "greatest step the town has taken towards school improvement."[8] Educational opportunities were much brighter in 1854 than in 1833.

By 1854 a local board of health was already alienating property owners by ordering improved drains. By 1858 mortality had dropped to twenty-two per thousand and was soon to drop even lower. A laborer's child could now expect an average life span of 34 years instead of 24.[9] Pauperism had also decreased; the authorities no longer doled out relief in aid of wages, and the new workhouse was praised for its cleanliness and good order. The workhouse children, whom the parish in 1833 had sent to the mills, were now given industrial education: fifty-four boys and girls were learning to garden, sew and knit, and do arithmetic.[10] The debtors'

---

7. *PP*, 42* (1855), 149–50, 313. *Macclesfield Courier,* July 5, 1851.
8. *PP*, 80* (1853), 519; *PP, 52* (1854), 201; *24* (1855), 130.
9. *Macclesfield Courier,* March 11, 1854. *PP, 23* (1858), 36.
10. *Macclesfield Courier,* April 22, 1854. *PP, 39* (1852), 269.

jail was no longer in use, and the lockup had heat in the winter and ventilation in the summer. The criminals sent to Chester Castle and Knutsford arrived at prisons that had been remodeled at the suggestion of the inspectors from Whitehall, while the pauper insane went to a much enlarged and improved county asylum.[11] A new humanity pervaded the public institutions.

That the silk operatives in Macclesfield worked fewer hours, that Christ Church offered better schooling, and that Hurdsfield tenement dwellers enjoyed better health was largely owing to the intervention of the central government. There is little evidence that local efforts alone would or could have carried these reforms. The mill-owners, the wealthiest and most respected citizens of Macclesfield, had petitioned Parliament in 1844 to allow those 4 to 12 years of age to work ten hours a day in the silk mills. The Macclesfield board of guardians had rivaled the guardians of Huddersfield and Bradford in opposing the New Poor Law. In order to show the new law at its worst they refused to improve the workhouse. The nonconformist *Macclesfield Chronicle,* which called the Factory Act a great abomination and oppression, described the Government's education plan in 1847 as "hostile to economic and civil freedom." [12] The same *Chronicle* and Macclesfield's 150 police commissioners, along with the town's two MP's and 4,000 ratepayers, protested vigorously in 1851 against the General Board of Health's plans for sanitary improvement, considering them too expensive.[13] Apathy and an antagonism to higher rates led them to tolerate the old lockup and to put pauper lunatics in the workhouse. All this would have continued but for the new acts of Parliament and the new civil servants from London.

The visits of Thomas Howells forced the mill-owners of Macclesfield to obey the provisions of the factory acts, and the visits of Henry Moseley, with assurances of aid, persuaded the Macclesfield schools to hire better masters, replace monitors with pupil teachers, and widen the curriculum. Only after Rawlinson's long and elo-

11. *PP*, 40* (1851), 84–85 (40–41). *Macclesfield Courier,* April 15, 1846.

12. Ibid., Feb. 24, 1844. MH, 12/968, Feb. 27, 1841. *Macclesfield Chronicle,* March 13, April 8, 1847.

13. Rawlinson, *Report on Macclesfield,* p. 3. *Macclesfield Courier,* June 31, 1850. J. Smith, *Further Report on Macclesfield* (London, 1851), p. 3.

quent plea in the packed town hall did the citizens support the Public Health Act, and only after Captain Williams' reprimands did they put heat in the lockup.[14] Charles Mott had to visit the guardians fifteen times a year in order to ensure that they did their duty. The authorities at Chester turned to the prison inspectors for plans for their new prison; and the visiting magistrates of the asylum followed the advice of Lord Ashley.[15] The local authorities were not unwilling to improve institutions and end social abuses, but they needed the stimulus, advice, and sustained energy of experts from Whitehall. The ordinary citizen of Macclesfield thus became, as did the mine worker in Durham or the wealthiest aristocrat who rode a railway, the beneficiary of a state that assumed a responsibility for the well-being of its citizens. However limited that responsibility, however meager compared to the responsibilities assumed by Whitehall today, it did mark the beginning of the welfare state.

Scarcely a single Englishman in 1833 either foresaw or desired that profound growth in the role of the central government which marked the beginning of a welfare state, and few of them, even among the Utilitarians, realized that their central government had become more paternalistic toward its subjects than any country in Europe. In 1833 the central bureaucracies of few governments in Europe did so little for its citizens as did England's. No country had so small a central bureaucracy, so strong a belief in local government and laissez faire, or so firm a resolve that its central government should grow even smaller. Yet in 1854 the central bureaucracies of few countries in Europe did more for the well-being of its subjects than did England's, and none of the governments of Europe intervened so decisively to regulate the hours of labor in factories, systematize poor relief, and promote the public's health. The English bureaucracy, to be sure, was still small compared to European bureaucracies; its powers were much more limited, its civil servants fewer, its organization much less rational, and its determination to reduce the central government much stronger. But

14. *Macclesfield Courier*, Feb. 22, 1851. *PP**, *40* (1851), 85.
15. *PP*, *29* (1840), 281. *Macclesfield Courier*, April 15, 1842. *Macclesfield Chronicle*, July 1, 1848.

despite all these disadvantages the central administration of England did more for its lower classes than the traditionally large and centralized administrations of the Continent. England, the historic home of Anglo-Saxon local government and the economic doctrines of Adam Smith, had begun to construct a welfare state.

Why this paradox? Why did England create an administrative state which she didn't want?

There is, to this question, an attractive and simple answer: the growth of an industrial and urban society brought serious social abuses which, since local government did nothing to remove them, forced the English to establish effective central departments. Child labor and unhealthy slums, in conjunction with negligent JP's and town councils, led inevitably to factory inspectors and a central Board of Health.

Much in the history of England's administrative growth after 1833 and in parallel developments on the Continent suggests that this conclusion, for all its simplicity, cannot be set aside. The creation of inspectors of mines, railways, factories, steamships, and noxious trades are certainly the responses to industrialization, while it is hard to imagine the establishment of a General Board of Health or burial inspectors without the growth of dirty towns and crowded urban cemeteries. And in the case of the Lunacy and Ecclesiastical commissions and of the inspectors of prisons and schools, it was from towns and cities that the loud demands arose for their establishment. Had England stayed agricultural, it might have been a long time before such departments would have been established.

A glance at developments elsewhere only confirms this conclusion. Industrialization in Prussia, France, New York, and Massachusetts brought with it the same abuses, the same failure of local government, the same growth of a central bureaucracy. In 1825, 66 per cent of the French lived in the country, by 1866 only 40 per cent. In 1841 France passed an education act, in 1841 and 1848 factory acts, in 1848 and 1850 public health acts, and in 1848 poor-law legislation.[16] Prussia passed its factory acts in 1839 and 1853,

16. Arthur Birnie, *An Economic History of Europe* (London, 1930), p. 205. E. G. Balch, *Public Assistance of the Poor in France* (Baltimore, 1893), p. 85. Gustav Amat, *Pouvoirs et rôle des maires au point de vue de la Protection de la santé publique* (Paris, 1905), p. 16.

poor-law reforms in 1840, and health reforms in 1852.[17] It is true, of course, that substantial industrialization in France and Prussia came later; but then, too, so did the really effective factory and health measures. As in New York and Massachusetts, effective factory and health reforms came after the 1860's.[18]

Prussia and France both had systems of poor relief and education before the first incursions of industrial growth. Not all reform by any means can be traced to the industrial revolution. But it would be dangerous to deny that wherever industrialism and urbanization occurred, there followed prison reforms, health boards, factory inspectors, and better poor relief and education.

The industrial revolution not only led to exploitation and abuses, it also brought increasing wealth, greater technological advances, and new classes. The poor got not poorer but better off and more articulate. The general increase in wealth made possible shorter hours, better schools, and more substantial asylums and prisons; technological advances in mining ventilation, railway engineering, drainage, and water supply made it possible to reduce accidents and disease; and the rise of the middle class and the formation of the proletariat produced the reformers and the agitators who insisted that the new possibilities be exploited, even if it meant intervention by the central government. The Government, to remove these initial abuses, appointed expert bureaucrats. And no sooner were such experts at work as inspectors than they exposed new abuses and urged new agencies. The administrative state itself became one of the causes of its further growth.

These conclusions are somewhat impersonal and Marxian: they attribute the growth of an administrative state to economic and social abuses, the rise of new classes, and greater wealth and technology. But how quickly would that growth occur, how efficient would it be, and how comprehensive? These questions depend

17. Gertrude Kroeger, *The Concept of Social Medicine* (Chicago, 1933), pp. 8, 13. A. Birnie, pp. 208, 232. George Stockhausen, *Das Deutsche Jahrhundert* (Berlin, 1902), pp. 320–27. Wilhelm Roscher, *System der Armenpflege und Armenpolitick* (Berlin, 1906), pp. 124–26.

18. S. N. D. North, *Factory Legislation in New England* (Boston, 1895), pp. 27–32. F. R. Fairchild, *The Factory Legislation of the State of New York* (New York, 1906) pp. 51–68, 96–113. Birnie, pp. 205–11. Albert Palmberg, *A Treatise on Public Health and Its Application in Different European Countries*, London, 1895.

on personalities and on the ideas and attitudes which the governing classes held concerning the role of government in a free society.

The most rational in their demands that an efficient central government promote administrative reforms were the Utilitarians, while the most passionate in calling on the Government to redress social evils were the Evangelicals. Together they constituted the creative minority that initiated and defined the basic reforms which led to the Victorian administrative state. But it would be a mistake to exaggerate their role. The ideas of Bentham and the convictions of the Evangelicals were never widely held. Far more common was the conventional attitude of supporting safe and necessary reforms. Most Whigs and Liberals—and to a lesser degree, many Tories—desired the removal of crying evils. Vaguely but ubiquitously, these men embodied what historians call the rise of humanitarianism and the spirit of reform. Their Christian consciences, however dull by Evangelical standards, were touched by the children's plight in mines, and their sense of order, however illogical to Benthamites, was disturbed by the rise of an ignorant and turbulent urban proletariat. They therefore voted for factory and prison inspectors and educational grants. The ideas of such men grew out of the Protestantism, the growing rationalism, and the traditions of English government which they imbibed from the Church, universities, and local government. From these intellectual currents came that humanity which, awakened and stimulated by industrial exploitation and urban abuse, led them to vote for reform and for the administrative state they didn't want.

Their anger against centralization could not prevent its growth, but it left an indelible mark on the resultant state. So great was Parliament's jealous regard for local government and private enterprise that it limited the powers and personnel of the new departments. And since it had established these departments, as it had won the Empire, piecemeal and in almost absence of mind, they did not constitute a model of administrative organization.

The Victorians did not want the central government to manage local affairs, or even to tell local officials what to do. All they really wanted, in most instances, was for the central government to prevent the worst abuses in local government and industry. They thus insisted on the ideal of an administrative system of checks and balances, with the central inspectors gaining the power to check abuses and local officials enjoying the sovereign power to form policy and manage their affairs. The idea of inspection was the crowning feature of the new state. It was the magical formula that was to preserve the autonomy of local government yet ensure that the worst evils of society would be alleviated.

The result was a series of agencies with little more than the power to investigate, report, advise, and—if the law was grossly violated—order prosecutions. Such powers were the usual ones granted to a central department and they could be, as in the case of the mining inspectors, grossly inadequate. But sometimes greater powers were given. Indicative of future developments was the power of the Poor Law Commission, the prison inspectors, and the Emigration Commission to make rules and regulations, or the power of the Committee on Education to grant money to local schools. Such powers of delegated legislation and grants in aid were destined to become the basis of a much larger and more powerful administrative state. In 1854 they were still handed out charily.

A budget-minded Parliament was just as chary in limiting the numbers of civil servants these new departments could employ. It kept nearly all the agencies undermanned. But in this deficiency England was not always alone. Prussia, the bureaucratic state par excellence, appointed only three inspectors to carry out the Factory Act of 1853, while the French appointed no central inspectors at all to carry out their 1841 Act. Most factories in Prussia and France went uninspected.[19] Industrial capitalism in mid-nineteenth century Europe could even withstand historic and established bureaucracies. England alone, in 1854, made them observe a ten-hour day.

Continental observers would have found the administrative organization of England's central administration most defective. No Napoleon or Frederick William I fashioned a rationalized bureaucracy with clear lines of responsibility. The English preferred instead to add casually another department to the Home Office or to create

19. Birnie, *Economic History*, pp. 205, 209. J. Kuczynski, *A Short History of the Labour Conditions in Germany* (London, 1944), p. 98.

a semi-independent Commission. Critics charged that such an expansion was done without planning, that the Home Secretary was much to busy to supervise his inspectors, and that semi-independent boards obscured responsibility and evaded Parliament's surveillance.

The Home Secretary's tolerance of divergent policies by prison and factory inspectors, and the troubles of the Poor Law Commission, General Board of Health, and Ecclesiastical Commission suggest that these critics had some grounds for their charges. But in truth these defects were not serious. European bureaucracies were not really as flawlessly organized as many imagined. Though the early Victorian administrative state might appear a patchwork of contrivances, some of its parts were brilliantly planned. The New Poor Law brought a national system of poor relief far more rational and uniform than the French system of overlapping church charities and state *bureaux de bienfaisances*. A flair for shrewd adaptations to *ad hoc* situations gave to England's administrative state a practical efficiency that allowed inspectors and commissioners to effect many reforms.

The large amount of discretion enjoyed by the inspectors and commissioners meant that such officials had to be men of responsibility, intelligence, tact, and firmness. This usually proved to be the case. The patricians who headed the ministries from 1833 to 1854 appointed, and increasingly by merit and not favor, able men, trained and expert in their fields. Coming from the middle class, privileged with a sound education, successful in their professions, these serious-minded Victorians hoped, through governmental actions, to alleviate the worst evils of society and, more importantly, to reform the lower classes—to make them independent, moral, educated, religious, temperate, and industrious. Despite their orthodox beliefs in laissez faire, these same inspectors looked to the government to effect these changes. To lay the basis for truly free society they had recourse to collective means. They thought a stern and reforming poor law, better prison disciplines, more schools, and reformatories, and healthier living conditions would create sturdier individuals less dependent on the government. But as bureaucrats their experiences made them more collectivist, and they vigorously urged governmental intervention to remove the physical, moral, and social evils that afflicted the lower classes.

The removal of such evils through governmental reforms constituted the central aim of the ablest inspectors. Not a Prussian sense of duty, not a French sense of bureaucratic logic, but an evangelical dedication to reform and ameliorate the condition of the distressed animated the Horners, Hills, Tufnells, and Allens who inspected the factories, prisons, workhouses, and schools.

The final test of the effectiveness of the new state and the men who served it was their success in removing the sufferings and injustices of an industrialized England. How effectively was this done?

To such a question there is no simple answer. Much depends on one's perspective and one's criterion. A close and exacting look at the England of 1854 encourages a rather negative judgement. There were so many ills left untouched, so many towns unhealthy and mines dangerous, so many children badly schooled or not schooled at all, and so many prisons, asylums, and workhouses in a deplorable condition. Railway wrecks were not declining and the merchant marine was still a miserable place for seamen. In 1854 because of bad sanitation 115,000 Englishmen would die of preventable diseases while dangerous mines would kill another 1,000.[20] Prison reports of the same year told of jails which were inadequate—some insufficient in their diets, others destitute of all discipline—while the reports of the lunacy commissioners noted that ten counties and fifty boroughs had yet to build an asylum and that the dismal conditions of many existing asylums discouraged any hope for curing the insane.[21]

Even more sobering to the Victorians than these facts were their failures in the field of education. It was, after all, by popular education that they hoped to end pauperism, reduce crime, improve morals, and extend democracy. But how could these improvements come about if, as was true, less than half the children of school age in Herefordshire went to school and less than half the working-class schools of England had good enough teachers or healthy

20. HO 45/5377. Chadwick Papers, Chadwick to Palmerston, Jan. 2, 1854.
21. *PP*, 29 (1854), 1–49; 26 (1855), 34, 56, 66, 85.

enough rooms to qualify for state aid? The Committee on Education would give no grants to schools with unheated rooms or untrained teachers. Yet with teachers' salaries averaging only 10 shillings (as they did in Herefordshire) trained teachers would look elsewhere for employment. A school system in which the pennies paid weekly by the children of the laboring classes exceeded the voluntary contributions of middle and upper classes could hardly remedy these failings.[22] There were, of course, good schools, just as there were efficient prisons and improved asylums. Improvements there were, too, but they did not occur everywhere. Textile operatives worked only ten hours and in whitewashed mills, while bleachers and dyers toiled fourteen or sixteen hours in sweat-shop conditions; Rugby had pure water, while Newcastle had dirty water; and nowhere were two workhouses exactly the same. In a system of public administration based on the ideal of a balance between local initiative and central checks the picture was bound to be spotty, salutary reforms being accompanied by persistent abuses.

The persistent abuses left unremedied by the new administrative state were so extensive and grievous as to suggest that something serious was amiss with the ideal of a limited central government merely inspecting and advising powerful local authorities and industries. Somewhere, in the process of day-to-day administration, failures occurred.

Such failures seldom originated in the investigations and reports of the inspectors. Allowing for a few unfair reports and the usual perfunctory reports, the inspectors by and large sought out the truth with vigor and told it with candor. Was the fault then in the confused and slipshod method of forming policy? In part, it was. In a process of policy formation that allowed inspectors great freedom to define the details of policy, there were bound to be variations and even negligence; and in a process that saw busy ministers confronted with inspectors demanding more reform, colleagues opposing those adopted, a Parliament angry at all expenditures, a press hostile to centralization, and aroused vested interests, a clear and vigorous policy of reform was bound to end in com-

22. *Economist, 11* (April 2, 1853), 364. *Times,* Jan. 28, 1854. *PP, 42 (1855),* 672.

promise, weakness, and even confusion. Dogmatic prison inspectors, on their own, could inflict the severities of separate confinement on criminals; Home Secretaries like Sir James Graham, confronted with Parliament's clamor for economy, could reduce the number of assistant poor-law commissioners and later disclaim responsibility; vested interests in Parliament could defeat the water schemes of the Board of Health; and a volatile public opinion, excited by religious fears and jealousies, could defeat the best proposals of the Committee on Education. Administrative policies that arose from the interactions of inspectors, commissioners, ministers, Parliament, and public opinion were bound to suffer. But such deficiencies lay less in the process of policy formation than in the widespread loyalties to local government, the earnest beliefs in laissez faire, and the activities of vested interests. Whether in the Cabinet, Parliament, or the press, these sentiments were bound to influence the formulation of policy.

It was the same localist and laissez-faire convictions, the same vested interests, that hampered the execution of the policies of Whitehall in the country at large. A close look at the angry protests of poor-law guardians against Somerset House and at the agitations of sewer commissioners against the Board of Health show how local interests, pride, and fear of change stood in the way of implementing sound policies. Twenty years of bureaucratic growth and administrative improvement had not dismayed the devotees of an untrammeled local government. Two of its staunchest protagonists, the Lord Mayor of London Sir Peter Laurie and Brighton's MP Sir Captain Pechell, had never faltered in their fight against centralization. Sir Peter, in 1834, had protested the establishment of prison inspectors and for twenty years as Lord Mayor had helped keep the City's Newgate Prison free of the inspectors' demands for reform. In 1848 he worked to prevent the General Board of Health from gaining authority over his sacred City and in 1854 to preserve the independence of the City's Bethlehem Hospital for the Insane he refused to testify before the lunacy commissioners.[23] Captain Pechell shared Sir Peter's hostility to Whitehall. In the thirties and early forties he attacked the cen-

23. *PP, 49* (1853), 14. HO, 45/5488. Palmerston Papers, Palmerston to Benjamin Hall, Aug. 4, 1854.

tralizing poor law and in the late forties and early fifties he worked industriously and successfully to keep Brighton free of the clutches of the health inspectors from Gwydor House.

The results of the Lord Mayor's and Captain Pechell's dedication to localism was not flattering. A Royal Commission of Inquiry into the Corporation of London showed it to be almost what Dickens and the *Times* said it was: "the worst government in Europe" and "the last of unreformable things." [24] Another commission, inquiring into Bethlehem in 1854, found its patients harshly treated, the bedding and clothing unfit, and the duties of the visiting physician very imperfectly performed. And as for Brighton, Lord Palmerston told Benjamin Hall in 1854 that it was "a triumph of prejudice and ignorance and private interest . . . its drainage is detestable, the water supply is about half of what it ought to be . . . yet the majority of the ratepayers and our friend Pechell at their head have obstinately refused to establish a local board." [25] In men like Sir Peter Laurie and Captain Pechell and in the corporations of England, local self-government still showed itself to be politically strong and administratively weak.

The failure to overcome local barriers to the execution of sound policies was due not to any lack of zeal or intelligence on the part of the inspectors but rather to the two principal defects of the Victorian administrative state: inadequate powers and inadequate personnel. Over and over again the halfway measures adopted in constructing the new bureaucracy meant that able civil servants could take only halfway measures to end social distress and to realize the hope of reforming the lower classes.

The above close look at the workings of England's central administration around 1854 has emphasized its failures. A broader and more tolerant look would modify that judgment. It was not an age which expected the government to guarantee an individual's security and well-being. France certainly fell far short of such a guarantee. She did even less for her lower classes than did England. Her mines and railways were, to be sure, safer, and her efforts at

24. *PP*, *26* (1854), 1 ff.; *49* (1853), 125.
25. Ibid., *49*, 127–57. Palmerston Papers, Lord Palmerston to Benjamin Hall, Aug. 20, 1854.

education roughly equal, but the children of her working class had less protection from factory labor, her slums were unhealthier, her mortality rate higher, and her central government much more indifferent to sanitary improvement and a general system of poor relief. Fifteen hundred of the local *bureaux de bienfaisance* had only 1 to 50 francs a year to spend on relief.[26] The prisons of France were also poor. According to a report in 1867 "our prison system is still so deplorable that, for the most part, it does but make the criminals worse." [27] France's central administration was not always efficient. Its factory acts remained unenforced and many of its unsanitary towns largely unimproved. In 1854 the working classes of Macclesfield received more benefits from a paternalistic Government than the workers of Lyon.

Prussia comes much closer than France to rivaling England's paternalistic care for the lower classes. It had long offered superior schooling. It, too, had an obligatory poor relief system. But its poor law was stricter, its factory law less effective, and its public health efforts much laxer. The Prussian factory acts of both 1839 and 1853 remained, in most districts, dead letters. The central government did little to push public health reform—choosing, like France, to leave the matter to local police.[28] If a worker did not wish his child in mill work, if he wanted a ten-hour day, greater longevity and health, and a more solicitous poor relief, it would have been best, around 1854, to have lived in England. London in 1854, for all the quarrels of the Metropolitan Sewer Commission with the General Board of Health, was still the healthiest metropolis in Europe, and the towns where the Public Health Act had been applied were even healthier.[29] The ideas and the work of Edwin Chadwick and his colleagues at the General Board of Health

26. Palmberg, *Treatise on Public Health,* p. 225. Balch, *Public Assistance of the Poor in France,* p. 101. Birnie, p. 205.

27. M. A. Corne, "Prisons and Prisoners in France," *Twenty-Fourth Annual Report to the Prison Association of New York* (Albany, 1868), p. 581.

28. Roscher, *System der Armenpflege,* pp. 124–25. In England in 1854 the annual mortality rate was 22.3 per 1,000 and in Germany, as late as 1875, it was still 26.4: Palmberg, pp. 514, 517; Stockhausen, *Das Deutsche Jahrhundert,* p. 327; Birnie, p. 208.

29. Palmberg, pp. 514–17. In 1855 Paris' mortality rate was 28.6 per 1,000, Berlin's 26.8, and London's 24.1.

gave England the same lead in sanitary reforms which she enjoyed in factory legislation. And her prisons and lunacy asylums were now among the most enlightened in Europe. Despite her aversion to centralization, despite her *ad hoc* bureaucracy, despite inadequate powers and personnel and the pervasive and deep hostility to governmental interference, her central government still did more for the welfare of the pauper, the child laborer, the tenement dweller, and the criminal, than did the bureaucracies of France and Prussia.

The early Victorians were not as calloused toward the poor as many have charged, nor were they, by the standards of that age in Europe or America, so indifferent to the welfare of the lowest classes. To admit this fact, however, is not to overlook the Victorians' calloused moments. Six out of every thousand English miners continued to die each year in accidents (in Prussia it was only one in every thousand), yet Parliament had refused to give the mining inspectors any power to order improvements in the mines. The same Parliament in 1854 abolished the one department whose work had most improved the lot of the lower classes—the General Board of Health.

A summary of the Victorian's first efforts at collectivism allows for no neat concluding judgment. The early Victorian administrative state and its work were marked by contradictions that reflected the deep ambiguities of their attitudes and interests. Their economic theories and their loyalties to local government were at war with their consciences, their paternalism, and their interest in public order. Individualism confronted collectivist necessities, localism the efficiency of centralization. From 1833 to 1854 reformers, MP's, bureaucrats, local officials, and captains of industry reflected these ambiguities in the halting and unsure construction of an administrative state. If that state seems crude by present standards, and if much distress in England remained unalleviated, it should at least be remembered that the early Victorians were the first in world history to experience the full consequences of the industrial revolution, and the administrative measures they took to meet them constituted the first beginnings of the welfare state which is today a distinguishing feature of the British Government.

APPENDIX

Her Majesty's Inspectors and Assistant Commissioners
(with sources of information about each)

Abbreviations

Boase	F. Boase, *Modern English Biography*
Burke, *LG*	Burke's *Landed Gentry*
Burke, *P*	Burke's *Peerage and Baronetcy*
Crockford	Crockford's *Clerical Directory*
DNB	*Dictionary of National Biography*
Foster	J. Foster, *Oxonienses Alumni*
GM	*Gentlemen's Magazine*
ILN	*Illustrated London News*
MG	*Manchester Guardian*
MT	*Medical Times*
Venn	J. A. Venn, *Alumni Cantabrigienses*

1. Factory Inspectors (does not include some 20 subinspectors)
    Leonard Horner: *DNB;* Boase; and K. Lyell, *Memoir,* London, 1890
    Thomas Howells: Boase
    Sir John Kincaid: *DNB;* Boase
    Alexander Redgrave: no information
    Richard Rickards: *MG,* Nov. 9, 1848

Robert Saunders: *Examiner,* Nov. 10, 1833

James Stuart: *DNB; GM,* Sept. 1848

2. HEALTH INSPECTORS (full list)

Henry Austin: *GM,* Nov. 1861; Boase

Benjamin Babbage: no information

Edward Cresy: *DNB;* G. L. Taylor, *The Auto-biography of an Octogenerian Architect,* London, 1870

George T. Clark: Chadwick Papers

Alfred Dickens: no information

Hector Gavin: Boase; *GM,* June 1855

P. H. Holland: Chadwick Papers

William Lee: Chadwick Papers

Gavin Milroy: *Lancet,* Feb. 27, 1886; Boase; *DNB*

Thomas W. Rammell: no information

William Ranger: Boase; *GM,* Dec. 1863

Sir Robert Rawlinson: Boase; *Times,* June 2, 1898; *Strand Magazine,* May 1889; *DNB*

James Smith: *Bristol Mercury,* Feb. 16, 1850; *Proceedings of the Institute of Civil Engineers* (1850), p. x

John Sutherland: Boase; *DNB; Lancet,* July 25, 1891; *Times,* July 24, 1891

3. POOR-LAW ASSISTANT COMMISSIONERS (full list)

Daniel Adey: Boase; *Harrow Register; Globe,* Nov. 11, 1834

Col. Ash A'Court: *Eton School List*

Alfred Austin: *Times,* May 22, 1884; Boase

Charles Clements: Boase

George Clive: *Harrow Register*

Lord Courtenay: no information

William Day: *Times,* Aug. 17, 1844; Hansard, *92* (1847), 1161; *85* (1846), 795

Andrew Doyle: Boase

Richard Earle: Venn

Harry Farnall: Foster

William James Gilbert: no information

John Thomas Graves: Boase; Foster

Appendix

Edward Gulson: City Archives, Coventry Library

Richard Hall: Venn

Henry W. T. Hawley: Foster; Burke, *LG; Globe,* Nov. 11, 1834

Sir Edmund Head: Bart., *DNB; GM,* 1868

Sir Francis Head: Bart., Anon., *Biography of Sir Francis Head,* London, 1879; *ILN,* July 31, 1875; S. Jackman, *Galloping Head,* London, 1958; *DNB*

Edward Hurst: no information

James Kay Shuttleworth: Frank Smith, *Life of James Kay Shuttleworth,* London, 1923

John Mainwaring: *Eton School List*

Charles Mott: Chadwick Papers, Boase; *Globe,* Nov. 11, 1834

Sir Richard Neave, Bart.: Burke, *P;* R. Brown, *The Baronetage,* 1844

Aneurin Owen: Boase

Walter Parker: Chadwick Papers

Sir William Edward Parry, K.C.B.: Burke, *P,* MH 1/2, Feb. 25, 1844

George Grenville Pigott: Burke, *LG*

Henry Pilkington: Burke, *LG;* Foster; *Globe,* Nov. 11, 1834

Alfred Power: Boase; *Law Journal,* June 16, 1888; *Biography and Review.*

John Revans: no information

Edward Senior: no information

Thomas Stevens: T. Mozley, *Reminiscences,* Boston, 1882; Boase; *Times,* May 21, 1888

Edward Boyd Twisleton: *Times,* Oct. 10, 1874; Mrs. Edward Twisleton, *Letters,* Hallowell, Me., 1925; *ILN,* Oct. 17, 1834; *DNB;* Foster

William James Voules: no information

Col. Thomas Wade: no information

Sir John James Walsham: *ILN,* Aug. 22, 1874; Chadwick Papers, Burke, *P*

Robert Weale: no information

Appendix

4. Prison Inspectors (full list)

William Crawford: *DNB;* W. L. Clay, *Memoir,* Cambridge, 1861

Frederick Bisset Hawkins: *Times,* Dec. 10, 1894; Boase; lancet, Dec. 15, 1894

Frederick Hill: *Autobiography,* London, 1893; Boase

Sir Joshua Jebb: *DNB;* Burke, *LG*

Capt. John Kincaid: *see* factory inspectors

Donatus O'Brien: Venn; Boase

John George Perry: *MT,* Jan. 22, 1870; Boase; *Monthly Notices, Royal Astronomical Society,* Feb. 10, 1871

Whitworth Russell: Venn; E. G. O'Donaghue, *Bridewell,* London, 1929; *DNB*

Herbert Poulton Voules: no information

Captain John Williams: no information

5. Education Inspectors (full list, but not including assistants)

John Allen: Crockford; Venn; R. M. Grier, *John Allen,* London, 1889; A. O. Allen, *John Allen,* London, n.d.

Matthew Arnold: numerous biographies

Henry Watford Bellairs: Boase; Foster

J. J. Blandford: no information

John Bowstead: Boase

Henry George Bowyer: Boase

William Henry Brookfield: Boase; Mrs. W. H. Brookfield, ed. *Sermons,* London, 1875

Thomas B. Browne: Foster

Frederick C. Cook: Venn; *Men of the Times,* 1887; Boase; *ILN,* June 29, 1889

James Cummings: Addison, *Roll of Graduates, U. of Glasgow*

Joseph Fletcher: J. Hutchinson, *Notable Middle Templars; Times,* Aug. 18, 1852; Boase; *DNB; Athenaeum,* 1852

John Gibson: no information

John Gordon: no information

Henry Longueville Jones: Boase; *Archaeologia Cambrensis,* Jan. 1871

Appendix

William James Kennedy: Boase; Venn; B. H. Kennedy, *Between Whiles*, London, 1887

Thomas Marshall: Venn; T. Marshall, *Clerical Friends*, London, 1873; *DNB*

Muirhead Mitchell: Boase, Crockford

Joseph D. Morell: Boase; T. Binney, *Memoir of Rev. Stephen Morell*, London, 1826; R. M. Theobald, *Memorials of J. D. Morell*, London, 1891; *ILN*, April 4, 1894

John Pilkington Norris: Boase; *The Biograph*, London, 1881; *Times*, Dec. 30, 1891

Joshua Ruddock: no information

David James Stewart: Venn

Scott Naysmith Stokes: Boase; *Times*, Aug. 5, 1891; *Merry England*, Dec. 1898

Jelinger Symons: Boase; *Law Magazine and Review*, May 1860; *GM*, 1851; *DNB*

Alexander Thurtell: Foster

Edward Douglas Tinling: Boase; Foster

Hugh Seymour Tremenheere: Boase; Foster; *Times*, Sept. 19, 1893; *Journal of Modern History*, 27, Dec. 1955

William Parsons Warburton: Boase; *Times*, May 7, 1900

Thomas Wilkinson: no information

Edward Woodford: Boase; *Register and Magazine of Biography*, Feb. 1869

6. LUNACY COMMISSIONERS (incomplete list)

John Bright: Foster

William George Campbell: no information

Edmund Starr Halswell: Venn

Bisset Hawkins: *see* prison inspectors

Cornwallis Hewlitt: no information

John Robert Hume: Boase

Samuel Gaskell: Boase; *Times*, March 27, 1886

James William Myline: Foster

James Cowles Pritchard: Venn; *DNB*; G. E. Weare, *J. C. Prichard*, London, 1898

Byron Walker Proctor: *DNB*
Capt. Self Sharp: no information
Edward Seymour: *DNB*
H. H. Southey: no information
William Henry Sykes: *DNB*
Cooke Taylor: no information
Thomas Turner: *DNB*

7. RAILWAY INSPECTORS (full list)
Captain Coddington: W. Porter, *Royal Engineers, 1,* (London, 1889) 326
Douglas Strutt Galton: C. M. Watson, *RE, 3* (London, 1911), 282; Boase
Sir Robert M. Laffan: Porter, *RE, 2,* 326; Boase
Sir Charles Paisley: Porter, *RE, 2,* 433
John L. A. Simmons: Watson, *RE, 3,* 259
Sir Frederick Smith: Porter, *RE, 2,* 433
Sir Henry Whately Taylor: no information
George Wynne: Porter, *RE, 2,* 327

8. MINING INSPECTORS (full list)
Joseph Dickenson: no information
Matthias Dunn: *Mining Almanac* (1849), p. 146; *Newcastle Chronicle,* March 23, 1849
William Lancaster: *Minutes of the Proceedings of the Institute of Civil Engineers, 18* (1858–59), 196
Robert Williams: no information
Thomas Wynne; Boase; *PP, 9* (1854), 261

9. TITHE ASSISTANT COMMISSIONERS (incomplete list)
Capt. Robert Dawson: *DNB*
Aneurin Owen: *see* poor law inspectors
Jelinger Symons: *see* education inspectors
Mr. Wooler: no information

10. LAND AND EMIGRATION COMMISSIONERS (incomplete list)
Frederick Eliot: no information
Mr. Alexander Wood: no information

Appendix

11. MERCHANT MARINE INSPECTORS (incomplete list)
    Capt. William Beechey: *DNB; Times,* Aug. 16, 1850
    Capt. W. H. Walker: *Times,* Aug. 16, 1850

12. INSPECTORS OF WELSH ROADS (incomplete list)
    Sir Henry D. Harness: *DNB;* Porter, *RE,* 2, 486
    Lieutenant Colonel Wortham: no information

13. CHARITY COMMISSION INSPECTORS (complete list)
    Thomas Hare: no information
    Walter Skirrow: no information

14. BURIAL GROUND INSPECTORS (full list)
    R. D. Grainger: *see* health inspectors
    John Sutherland: *see* health inspectors

15. INSPECTOR OF NOXIOUS TRADE
    Mr. Coulier: no information

16. INSPECTOR OF THE DEPARTMENT OF SCIENCE AND ART
    Ambrose Poynter: no information

BIBLIOGRAPHICAL ESSAY

BOTH PRIMARY AND SECONDARY sources dealing with the growth of the early Victorian administrative state are numerous. Every newspaper in England, for example, reported during the year on the increasing activities of the central government; every year the government published volumes of reports from administrative agencies; and a mere listing of published discussions of the New Poor Law or the Factory Act would take many pages. The following essay is therefore selective, its aim being to point out primary materials most rewarding to the scholar and secondary works most useful to the nonspecialist. Those who wish a more comprehensive list may consult the helpful bibliographies in Samuel Finer, *The Life and Times of Edwin Chadwick,* London, 1952; R. A. Lewis, *Edwin Chadwick and the Public Health Movement,* London, 1953; Frank Smith, *Life and Work of Sir Kay Shuttleworth,* London, 1923; Cecil Driver, *Richard Oastler, Tory Radical,* New York, 1946; and Roger Prouty, *The Transformation of the Board of Trade,* London, 1957.

1. GENERAL WORKS

The best of the general histories of early Victorian England are Volumes 2 and 3 of Elie Halévy's *History of the English People; The Triumph of Reform, 1833–1841,* London, 1927; and *Victorian Years 1841–1852,* London, 1947. They analyze the political developments in terms of social and economic changes and in relation to intellectual and religious attitudes. Halévy's study of the contradictions between the utilitarians' faith in laissez faire and their latent collectivism, in *Philosophical Radicalism* (London, 1928), is brilliant. And he is by far the best guide to Bentham's thought. J. H. Clapham has done the best work on the economic developments; his *An Economic History of Modern Britain* (London, 1926–38) is definitive for industrial growth, and his remarks on the institutional changes that followed are sensible and judicious. Barbara and John Hammond in their *Age of the Chartists* (London, 1930) show a flair for social psychology in their descriptions of the great social changes resulting from the urbanization of English life, but their work does not have the reliability of the many essays in G. M. Young, ed., *Victorian England* (London, 1934), nor does it have the profound grasp of Victorian conflicts and attitudes of mind shown in Young's unusually penetrating essay, *Portrait of an Age*.

Literature dealing with the intellectual attitudes of the Evangelicals is meager. G. W. E. Russell's *A Short History of the Evangelical Movement* (London, 1915) barely defines the social attitude implicit in that movement. Neither has much been done on the role of conservative thought in the growth of central government. Two general discussions of conservative ideas are Crane Brinton's *English Political Thought in the Nineteenth Century*, London, 1933; and R. J. White's *The Conservative Tradition*, London, 1950. The social ideas of the Evangelicals and the Conservatives await such monumental studies. as that of Sir Leslie Stephen on *The English Utilitarians*, London, 1900. A solid and safe study of the whole period is E. L. Woodward, *The Age of Reform*, Oxford, 1938; and a suggestive and imaginative account of its economic and governmental changes can be found in Karl Polanyi, *The Great Transformation*, New York, 1944.

2. SPECIAL STUDIES

No modern authorities except for R. H. Gretton, *The King's Government: A Study in the Growth of the Central Administration* (London, 1913) have dealt directly with the general growth of central administration in England from 1833 to 1854, almost all the work having been on particular agencies and particular social

questions; and Gretton's brief study is hardly more than an outline, comprehending as it does all of English history from the Con-
queror's household to the Local Government Act of 1870. K. B.
Smellie has written *A Hundred Years of English Government*
(London, 1937), but its scope is wide, dealing with problems of
Parliamentary and local government as well as central administration. J. Watson Grice, *National and Local Finance* (London, 1910)
touches upon the question of central and local relations, but only
in matters of finance and then for all countries of Europe. And
Emmeline Cohen, *Growth of the British Civil Service* (London,
1941), Robert Moses, *The Civil Service of Great Britain* (London,
1914), and J. D. Kingsley, *Representative Bureaucracy* (Yellow
Springs, Ohio, 1944) deal mostly with reform in the selection of
civil servants.

Interest in local government has always been keen in England.
Specialized studies, from Joseph Redlich's *Local Government in
England* (London, 1903) to the monumental work of Sydney and
Beatrice Webb, *English Local Government from the Revolution
to the Municipal Corporation Act* (London, 1906–24) and K. B.
Smellie's *A History of Local Government* (London, 1946), have
analyzed and traced the growth of parish, borough, and county
government. But no one has yet dealt solely with the problem of
the expanding central administration. Many, of course, have noted
its significance and B. L. Hutchins in her *Public Health Agitation*
(London, 1909) presents a brief but suggestive outline of the beginnings of the Factory, Poor Law, Education, and Health inspectorates.

Studies of particular social problems and particular agencies
provide considerable information on the growth of the central government. That the Factory Act of 1833 marked the beginning of
this administrative revolution has been noted in three studies of
the factory question: B. L. Hutchins and A. Harrison, *A History
of Factory Legislation,* London, 1903; Cecil Driver, *Richard Oastler, Tory Radical,* New York, 1946; and Maurice W. Thomas, *The
Early Factory Legislation,* London, 1950. Cecil Driver tells of the
dramatic events of the factory reform movement through a vivid
account of the life of its leading protagonist, Richard Oastler. This

work alone describes the struggles leading to factory reform in terms of the attitudes, conditions, and feelings of the workers. Maurice Thomas' survey is a dull, impersonal, and abstract analysis of the legislation and of its administration. He claims that factory inspection was the first "interference" in the economy by the central government, a notion which a glance at the work of the excise commissioners would have dispelled. The book is valuable for its lengthy citations from the inspector's reports and its appendix of Home Office papers.

Modern authorities have dealt with the poor-law question, though again more on the legislative and social side than on the administrative. None of the authors followed the assistant commissioners into the field and examined their work. The two main studies of the New Poor Law reflect two different periods of political and economic thought. George Nicholl, *History of the English Poor Law* (London, 1854)—completed and expanded by Thomas MacKay, *History of the English Poor Law* (London, 1896) —was written in the 1850's and 1890's and in the full flush of Victorian capitalism and individualism. MacKay defends the New Poor Law in every respect. Such a position was, among Fabian socialist circles, quite outdated by the twentieth century. In 1922, a decade after Sydney and Beatrice Webb wrote their minority report attacking the New Poor Law and its workhouses, they published the first of three volumes on the Poor Laws from Elizabeth to the present. *The English Poor Law History, Part II, The Last Hundred Years* (London, 1929) deals with the New Poor Law of 1834. The Webbs were critical of the Law's policy of a strict workhouse test and maintained that the authors of the Law did not seek to remove the causes of destitution. Filled with a socialistic desire to end poverty they overlooked the belief of Chadwick and the assistant commissioners that the end of easy relief, along with better education, improved health in towns, and workhouse schools for the young, would remove the cause of destitution. The Webbs' hostility to individualism prevented them from understanding the philosophy of the New Poor Law; and their failure to use the Chadwick Papers and to study the assistant commissioners has placed limitations on their work. But despite these limitations, their zeal, integrity, humanity, and thoughtfulness makes their study an accurate, full, and clear treatment of a difficult subject.

The Webbs also applied their prodigious energies to the problems of prisons, in their *English Prisons under Local Government*, London, 1902. Dealing mostly with prison legislation, they fail even to mention the important reforms of Frederick Hill. There are no other important works on prisons except Lionel W. Fox, *English Prison and Borstal System* (London, 1952), which is mostly of the modern period. Histories of individual prisons, such as Edward O'Donaghue, *Bridewell Hospital, Palace, Prison, School* (London, 1925), give valuable information.

Modern authorities have taken up the question of education in this period, but with little administrative analysis. John Adamson, *English Education, 1789–1902* (London, 1930), H. B. Binns, *A Centenary of Education, Being the Centenary History of the British and Foreign Society* (London, 1903), and Frank Smith, *A History of English Elementary Education, 1760–1902,* all describe the main story with its legislative and religious conflicts. Initial works about the public health movement (before Finer's and Lewis' biographies of Edwin Chadwick) were equally bare of administrative matters. Malcolm Morris, *The Story of English Public Health* (London, 1919), and W. W. Fraser, *English Public Health* (London, 1951), give brief expositions of the establishment of the General Board of Health and, in Fraser's study, a full account of the advances in medicine.

Two recent works have told of the expansion of the Board of Trade and of the work of the Commissioners of Lunacy: Roger Prouty, *Transformation of the Board of Trade,* London, 1957; and Kathleen Jones, *Lunacy, Law and Conscience,* London, 1956. Both works are based on official sources; both outline clearly the growth of these two departments and assess their significance. But neither deals with local conflicts—with the work of the merchant marine officer in Liverpool or that of a lunacy commissioner at Hanwell. True, the Parliamentary Papers are singularly deficient in Marine Department records, and the only way to reconstruct the field work of such officers is to use local newspapers. For the development of the Railway Department the best work is Edward Cleveland-

Stevens, *English Railways: Their Development and Their Relation to the State,* London, 1915. Like so many books on special departments, it too overlooks the inspectors and their work.

3. BIOGRAPHIES

Three biographies make up in part for the lacunae in the administrative history of the Committee on Education and the Board of Health: Frank Smith, *Life and Work of Sir Kay Shuttleworth,* London, 1923; Samuel Finer, *Life and Times of Edwin Chadwick,* London, 1952; and R. A. Lewis, *Edwin Chadwick and the Public Health Movement,* London, 1952. All three biographies were written from private papers and describe in detail the impact which these two earnest Victorians had on education, poor law, and public health reforms, and on the growth of the central administration. Frank Smith's biography is not as brilliant as Finer's or Lewis'; somewhat in the fashion of the editors of Victorian memoirs he helps himself copiously from Kay Shuttleworth's writings and letters. It is a helpful source nevertheless. Finer and Lewis show that two historians, working independently from the same sources, can, despite the warnings of relativists, come up with much the same conclusions. Finer is particularly strong on Chadwick's role at the Poor Law Office. He approaches the Poor Law with neither MacKay's nineteenth-century individualism nor the Webb's irritation with utilitarians for not being socialists. He analyzes the law instead in terms of the economic and social conditions of the 1830's, and of the then dominant ideas. His account of the workhouse scandal at Andover in 1846 is unusually exciting and dramatic. Lewis' analysis of the establishment, work, and fall of the General Board of Health is a masterful delineation of Chadwick's personality, and of the forces leading to the establishment and fall of the Board of Health.

Other biographies help fill in the personal element of the historical events that led to the growth of the central government. Cecil Driver, *Richard Oastler, Tory Radical* (New York, 1946), tells the story of the fight for factory reform and gives a lively account of the resistance in the north to the New Poor Law. Barbara and John Hammond, *Life of Lord Shaftesbury* (London, 1923),

praise the earnest and dedicated work of this Victorian humanitarian but unfortunately make significant errors in describing
the formation of the Board of Health and its work, and are in part
responsible for the harsh picture so widely held of Edwin Chadwick. Fabian historians, it seems, dislike Chadwick's stern view of
the poor and his rigorous bureaucratic manners.

W. Erickson, *Life of Sir James Graham* (New York, 1951), re-
counts uncritically Sir James Graham's work at the Home Office.
Charles Atkinson, *Jeremy Bentham* (London, 1905), and Marian
Bowley, *Nassau Senior and Classical Economics* (London, 1907),
add to one's understanding of the utilitarianism and political economy of the period. And standard biographies of government leaders—such as John Morley's *Life of Gladstone* (London, 1927),
Spencer Walpole's *Life of John Russell* (London, 1891), and
Herbert Bell, *Lord Palmerston*—reveal, though not thoroughly
enough, the basic social attitudes of those who headed the early
Victorian administrative state.

4. Manuscript Materials

Basic to any study of the expansion of England's central government after 1833 are the unpublished minute books, memoranda, letters, and reports of the central departments themselves. One frank confession of a frustrated administrator can
illuminate more administrative history than a long formal report. Such personal documents can be found in the Home Office
correspondence with factory, mining, and prison inspectors, and
in the voluminous correspondence of the Poor Law Commission
with assistant commissioners and the local poor-law guardians.
Both sets of correspondence are at the Public Record Office in
London. The Home Office correspondence, particularly the
papers listed under H.O. 45/–, though by no means complete,
reveal the inspectors' candid opinions and the attitudes of the
Home Secretaries. Quite a few of the letters and reports of the
inspectors tell intimately of the problems of truculent local
authorities. These letters and memos are not nearly so complete
as those of the Poor Law Commission with their assistants and
the guardians. The correspondence with assistants between 1833

and 1854 comes to nearly a hundred bulky volumes (M.H. 32/–) and those with the guardians (M.H. 12/–) many times that number. They reveal much more closely the workings of central and local government than any other source. Together with the Home Office papers on the Poor Law (H.O. 73/54–56) they make the evidence on the working of that law quite formidable and rewarding.

Far less so are the minute books and the chance correspondence of the Board of Trade (B.T. /–), the minute books of the Board of Health (M.H. 5 & 6 /–), and the occasional reports of the Commissioners of Lunacy (H.O., os/74/5488 & 5349)—all of which are at the Public Record Office.

Minute books are not too illuminating, since they record little but official decisions, and private papers are needed to fill in the gaps. None can compare in comprehensiveness and frankness with those of Edwin Chadwick at University College, London. The Chadwick Papers present an immediate, personal, and controversial view of the major conflicts involved in the passage of the Factory Act, Poor Law Amendment Act, and Public Health Act, and reveal the day-to-day administration of the Poor Law Commission and the General Board of Health. Chadwick also commented freely on general administrative and social questions. His papers include many letters from the assistant commissioners and the health inspectors as well as memos to and from the Home Secretaries, commissioners, and important public figures. Chadwick was not without strong biases: he was always arguing a cause or defending a policy; and despite his zeal for the facts and his undoubted integrity he does not tell a full story; but his papers nonetheless are the most revealing of any private papers dealing with the early Victorian administrative state.

Other private collections of value are those of Lord John Russell, at the Public Record Office; of Sir Robert Peel, at the British Museum; of Sir James Graham, at Netherby, Cumberland; of Lord Palmerston, at Broadlands; and of Bentham, at University College, London.

Manuscript sources on the growth of the central government reveal much which is not available elsewhere about decision-making and policy formation, but they do not form the largest source of information on the growth and working of the central government. The fullest account remains the official and published papers of the government, the *Debates,* the *Sessional Papers,* and the *Acts of Parliament,* which are the indispensable foundation to any administrative study.

5. PARLIAMENTARY PAPERS, DEBATES, AND ACTS

The Sessional Papers of Parliament are classified into four categories when bound: Public Bills, Reports from Committees, Reports from Commissions, and Accounts and Papers. They are in two series, one for the House of Lords and the other for the House of Commons, each having different volume numbers, a fact which must be kept clearly in mind if confusion is to be avoided. The various reports in the Sessional Papers can be located by reference to the indexes in the last volume of each year's Sessional Papers or in the *General Index to the Sessional Papers of the House of Commons, 1801–1852* (London, 1938) and the *General Index to the Sessional Papers of the House of Lords* (London, 1938). *The General Index for the House of Lords* is, of course, for those editions bound and numbered according to the House of Lords' series.

Among the Reports from Committees, those of the following select committees are the most valuable: child labor in factories, 1832, 1840, and 1841; the Poor Law, 1837, 1838, 1846, and 1847; prisons, 1835, 1836, and 1850; education, 1834, 1835, and 1838; and the health of towns, 1840 and 1842. The reports of the select committees on railways are too numerous to list. Dealing with less dramatic issues were the select committees on lunatic asylums in 1827, on lighthouses in 1834, on shipwrecks in 1836 and 1843, and on coal whippers in 1843. The hearings and reports of these select committees provide abundant information on social problems and administrative practices; their detail and thoroughness is sometimes quite surprising. The hearings of the select committee on the Poor Law in 1837 and 1838 come to five volumes and 2,813 pages, and they record the testimony of 102 witnesses answering, at 84 sessions, some 47,000 questions. Such hearings, in which both sides are heard, provide abundant evidence on the workings of administrative agencies.

Yet even more thorough are the inquiries of royal commissions. Such commissions investigated child labor in factories in 1833 and in mines and manufactures in 1842 and 1843, the old Poor Law in 1834, charities almost every year from 1833 to 1850, and the health of towns in 1843, 1844, and 1845. Edwin Chadwick always urged the inquiries of paid royal commissions instead of the hearings of select committees, because the committees always stayed in London while the commissioners and their assistants could travel throughout England ferreting out information. Furthermore, to Chadwick paid experts were preferable to unpaid MP's. The reports of the royal commissions are indeed fuller, more accurate, more interpretative, and more intelligent than the dialogues of select committees with their witnesses. They often, of course, show prejudice. Alfred Power, who worked on both the Factory and the Poor Law Commission of Inquiry could not hide his strong faith in political economy. The same was true of Chadwick, who wrote so many of the reports of the Factory and Poor Law Commissions of Inquiry.

The Sessional Papers of Parliament also include the annual reports of the central departments and of their inspectors. These reports are invaluable. Except in the case of the Poor Law Commission, the published reports of each department reveals much more of their general policies and practices than the manuscript materials at the Public Record Office. The accuracy, comprehensiveness, and bias of the reports are fully discussed in Chapter 7.

Supplementing these reports are the numerous returns made to Parliament by both central and local authorities, such as the annual returns on poor rates, prison commitments, expenditure of governmental departments, correspondence of the Committee on Education, and special returns, such as the number of sinecure offices (1837), power and duties of the Railway Department (1852), and number and names of health inspectors (1852). Very little escaped Parliament's watchful eye. The Committee on Education, for example, had to publish its entire correspondence with church societies, all of its minutes, and the returns from each local school. Parliament's jealousy has been a boon to the historians of this period, especially since some departments, like the Committee on Education, destroyed their unpublished papers.

Supplementing the Sessional Papers of Parliament are the Debates and Acts of Parliament. The third series of Hansard's *Parliamentary Debates of Great Britain* gives an almost complete account of the legislative battles which led to the establishment of the early Victorian administrative state. These debates are also informative of administrative practices, since very often an aroused MP or indignant peer declaimed on an administrative abuse of the Poor Law or Factory Act. The many complaints of MP's should be read especially critically.

The foundation of the administrative state was formed by Acts of Parliament. Only by meticulous analysis of these acts can one draw an accurate picture of the powers and organizations of the central departments. The acts of each year are published in *The Statutes of the United Kingdom of Great Britain and Ireland*. Recourse to law journals has often been necessary to determine their exact meaning, since the courts alone could interpret the statutes. The best accounts of their interpretations are the yearly *Law Journal Reports* and Adolph and Ellis, *Queen's Bench Reports*. For concise summaries of the cases involving the poor laws there is W. G. Lumley, *An Abridgement of the Cases upon the Subject of the Poor Law*, London, 1943.

6. Newspapers and Periodicals

The journalistic scene in England from 1833 to 1854 was crowded, varied, and growing. Over that scene loomed the majestic *Times*. It had the greatest circulation and enjoyed the reputation of speaking for the nation. In many respects it did speak the language and opinion of the sturdy, independent, practical, and moderately humane Englishman, proud of his liberties and local government but still concerned for those in distress. But it would be a mistake always to read the voice of the *Times* as the voice of the nation. On the controversial New Poor Law it spoke shrilly and irresponsibly. Two editors set the tone and color of the *Times* from 1833 to 1854: Thomas Barnes, "the thunderer," whose bombast, sarcasm, and sermonizing arose from an impulsive compassion unrestrained by a scrupulous objectivity, guided the paper from 1833 to 1841; after which John T. Delane, of soberer temperament, took over to advocate social reform. The owner of the *Times* was the independent, conservative John Walter, whose hatred of the New Poor Law brought the *Times* to oppose centralization but whose humanitarianism led his paper to support most social reforms.

The true conservative point of view on the growth of the central government found consistent expression in the *Morning Herald* and the *Standard,* while the Philosophical Radicals and Liberals read the *Examiner* and the *Morning Chronicle* until, in 1847, it went over to the interests of the City Corporation and opposed the General Board of Health. Its reporting of the public health question after 1847 is as stridently biased as was the *Times'* reporting of the poor law. The *Globe* was a Whig journal and the *Daily News* represented the liberalism of John Bright and Richard Cobden, as did, in the north, the *Manchester Guardian* and the *Leeds Mercury.* The extreme radicals had their *Northern Liberator* and O'Connor's *Northern Star.*

All these papers had their prejudices, yet they are the best sources for the dominant attitudes and interests that formed the environment in which the government's new departments had to work. They also reported on day to day administrative conflicts. The provincial papers are particularly valuable for such reporting. Often it is through their columns alone that one can read about those delicate conflicts that confronted the government's inspectors. Papers like the *Macclesfield Courier* and the *Bristol Mercury* tell in column after column of the health inspectors' battles to carry out the law in these hostile towns. These papers also printed, and quite fully, accounts of poor-law meetings or the reports of visiting magistrates on local jails.

The *Mining Journal* and the *Railway Times* provided some glimpses of the mining and railway inspectors in action, as well as the fullest picture of the problems these men faced. The *Railway Times* was strongly in favor of the railway companies and hostile to the government, but the *Mining Journal* was surprisingly favorable to greater government intervention to prevent accidents.

The weekly political journals represented even more clearly than the daily papers distinct political outlooks. The *Economist*, though abundant then as now in facts and hard reasoning, had a rigid and pure liberalism that made its reporting on factory, mining, and railway questions of dubious fairness. The *Patriot*, the *Non Conformist*, and the *Wesleyan* reported on education with the same antigovernment bias, only in their case largely because of their love of voluntary and free schools. They expressed the dissenters' jealousy of the central government. *John Bull* and the *Metropolitan Conservative Journal* spoke for the unbending Tories, the *Spectator* and *Observer* for the Whig-liberals. More specialized journals represented particular groups: the *Builders*, engineers with their dislike of the Board of Health; and the *Lancet*, doctors with their displeasure of the same board.

More sober and abstract were the quarterlies, containing useful information and a rational approach which the earnest Victorians valued. The *Westminster Review* argued for reform of social institutions in a true Benthamite spirit. The *Edinburgh Review*, though not as purely Benthamite, had a utilitarian outlook. More specialized and technical but again utilitarian in tone was the *Journal of the Statistical Society* with its extensive surveys of education, crime, prisons, and sanitation.

The *Quarterly Review* expressed an enlightened conservatism. It supported some definitely centralizing reforms, such as the New Poor Law and the Public Health Act, though in theory it believed in local government. In the *Eclectic Review* the nonconformists' pure liberalism and religious jealousies led to forthright attacks on centralization. The *British Quarterly* spoke for a more moderate liberalism. Other publications expressing definite attitudes were the Conservatives' *Frazer's Magazine* and the Dissenters' *North British Review*. The periodicals in this period were growing in number and quality, but those who could not write for them could always publish a pamphlet or a book, which they did in great numbers.

7. PAMPHLETS AND BOOKS

There are a large number of pamphlets on the many social and administrative questions of early Victorian England. On education alone they number in the hundreds, ranging from James Kay Shuttleworth's thoughtful *Recent Measures for the Promoting of Education* (London, 1840) and *The School in Its Relations to the State, the Church, and the Congregation* (London, 1846) to Edward Baine's fierce attack on the Government's plans of 1846, *Eight Letters Addressed to Lord John Russell,* London, 1846. Many congregational ministers and laymen echoed these anguished sentiments with like fulminations in *The Crosby Hall Lectures,* London, 1848. The liberal Anglicans, the moderate Nonconformists, and the secularists were also busy writing pamphlets. The liberal Vicar of Leeds, the Rev. Walter F. Hook, countered Baine's intemperate blasts with *On the Means of Rendering Efficient the Education of the People* (London, 1846), while Richard Dawes, the Anglican headmaster of Kings Somborne School, published *Remarks Occasioned by the Present Crusade against the Education Plans of the Committee on Education* (London, 1850) to dissuade the right wing of the Church from its opposition to government aid for schools. The Anglican forces in support of the government policy received further help from the publication of *Remarks on National Education* (Edinburgh, 1847) by George Combe, who along with Kay Shuttleworth did much to bring national education to England. Henry Dunn, secretary of the British and Foreign School Society, in his *National Education, the Question of Questions* (London, 1839) helped to reveal the dismal state of English education, and sharing in this task was Lord Brougham's outspoken and radical plea for public schools, *A Letter on National Education to the Duke of Bedford,* Edinburgh, 1839. These are only a few of the countless pamphlets published on the controversial question of government aid to church schools.

The New Poor Law called forth pamphlets of all kinds, semi-official and unofficial, for and against, declamatory and apologetic. The apologetic ones were usually calmer and more expository, and were occasionally officially inspired, such as the anonymous *Parish and Union* (London, 1837) and *The English Poor Law Commissioners*, London, 1847. Many also defended the New Poor Law unofficially, such as the Rev. J. Bosworth, *The Contrast: or the Operation of the Old Poor Law Contrasted with the Present Poor Law Amendment Act*, London, 1838. The pamphlets attacking the New Poor Law specialized in exposing hardships. An example of such an exposure is Pryce Jones, *The Poor Law, A Narrative of a Board of Guardians, Contingent upon and Arising out of the Death of a Pauper Child by Scalding*, London, 1841. G. R. W. Baxter's lengthy *Book of the Bastilles* (London, 1841) is one long series of abusive charges; its numerous citations from other pamphlets and periodicals makes it the most useful bibliographical guide to anti-poor-law writings.

Pamphlets on sanitary questions are also numerous. The most informative of those supporting reform, because of an extensive survey done by some 3,000 clergymen, doctors, and engineers, was the *Report of the Health of London Association on the Sanitary Condition of the Metropolis* (London, 1848), while the Metropolitan Sanitary Association's *Memorials on Sanitary Reform* (London, 1850) is valuable for its inclusion of a letter from John Stuart Mill arguing for the central government to control the water supply of the Metropolis. Many pamphleteers attacked the Board of Health but none so vigorously, and so singlemindedly on the issue of centralization, as Joshua Toumin Smith in *Centralization or Representation* (London, 1848), *Government by Commission, Illegal and Pernicious* (London, 1849), *Local Government and Centralization* (London, 1851), and *The Metropolis and Municipal Administration* (London, 1853). Some engineers, piqued by the Board of Health's small-bore drains wrote sharp criticisms of its ideas on drainage. Such a criticism was T. Hawksley's *A Letter to the Honorable Marquis of Chandos M.P.* (London, 1855) and George Burnell's *Letter to Lord Palmerston on the Administration of the Public Health Act* (London, 1854).

The factory controversy aroused many critics to write pamphlets, a list of which can be found in Driver's *Richard Oastler, Tory*

348

Radical. Very important to the conflict over the clause for fencing machinery is Harriet Martineau's *The Factory Controversy: A Warning against Meddling Legislation,* Manchester, 1855.

There are not many pamphlets on prisons, since these matters excited no great interest. The question of prison discipline did stimulate some to present their arguments to the public, as James Elmes, *Hints for the Improvement of Prisons* (London, 1817), and Rev. J. Field, *Prison Discipline* (London, 1846), both of which defend the virtues of separate confinement. Charles Pearson argued for hard labor in his *What Is to Be Done with Our Criminals?,* London, 1854.

Such pamphlets are few, as are discussions on lunacy and charities like *Observations on the Bill for the General Regulation of Lunatic Asylums* (anon., London, 1828) and J. P. Fearnon's valuable and orderly survey, *Legislation for Endowed Charities* (London, 1855). Thomas Clarkson, *The Grievances of Our Mercantile Seamen, a National Crying Evil* (London, 1847) provides a moving picture of the sufferings of the seamen, and J. J. Scott, *Railway Practice in Parliament* (London, 1846) gives a good picture of the confusions of railway legislation.

Contemporary books on the question of administrative centralization and social reform are few. Homersham Cox, *British Commonwealth* (London, 1854), offers the first account of the growth of the central executive after 1833, but it is a very brief sketch. The monumental work on administrative theory is of course Jeremy Bentham, *The Constitutional Code,* London, 1830, 1841. Carrying on the utilitarian tradition was John Stuart Mill, *Principles of Political Economy* (London, 1852), while not so specifically utilitarian are Nassau Senior, *Political Economy* (London, 1850), Lord Brougham, *Political Philosophy* (London, 1850), and J. R. McCulloch, *The Principles of Political Economy* (Edinburgh, 1825). Conservative political opinion had fewer theorists in this period. S. T. Coleridge, *On the Constitution of the Church and State* (London, 1830), dominated much of their thought on the education question and—along with Robert

349

Southey's, *Sir Thomas More: Colloquies on the Progress of Society* (London, 1829)—it gave slight encouragement to factory legislation and other mild reforms.

Books on social conditions were, in this period, revealing to the public the suffering of the lower classes. James Kay, *The Moral and Physical Condition of the Working Classes in the Cotton Manufacture in Manchester* (London, 1837) is a pioneer social inquiry. P. Gaskell, *The Manufacturing Population of England* (London, 1838) gives a graphic and somewhat statistical account of social conditions in the new towns but is not nearly so graphic and intimate a picture of the poor as that by Henry Mayhew, *London Labour and the London Poor,* London, 1851. George Porter in *The Progress of a Nation* (London, 1837), W. C. Taylor, in *Notes on a Tour of Lancashire* (London, 1842), and Edward Baines, Sr., *The History of the Cotton Manufactures* (London, 1836) all tell in optimistic terms of England's economic expansion. Sir Henry Bulwer Lytton, *England and the English* (London, 1833) is a useful and intelligent survey of both the social conditions and the dominant ideas of that age.

The novels of the period are also important. Benjamin Disraeli, *Sybil* (London, 1845) and *Coningsby* (London, 1844); Charles Dickens, *Oliver Twist* (London, 1838), *Hard Times* (London, 1854), and others; and Anthony Trollope, *The Warden* (London, 1855) and *Three Clerks* (London, 1858)—all recreate the political, social, and intellectual atmosphere of early Victorian England. But they should be read with caution: Disraeli's social feelings in *Sybil* never shone forth in his Parliamentary votes, and the factory conditions of 1855 and the Poor Law conditions of 1841 bear only a slight resemblance to the hardships described so imaginatively in *Hard Times* and *Oliver Twist*.

8. MEMOIRS

It was common for Victorians to collect the letters and speeches of their famous relatives or friends and to compose from them hagiographical memoirs. Such works can, in part, be used as primary sources, since their value lies more in the letters and speeches of their subject than in the pious praises and innocuous narratives which pin them together. Four such memoirs present an intimate picture of the attitudes and the day-to-day duties of the inspectors: Frederick Hill, *An Autobiography of Fifty Years in Times of Reform,* ed. Constance Hill, London, 1893; Katherine Lyell, *Memoirs of Leonard Horner,* London, 1890; R. M. Grier, *John Allen,* London, 1889; and Anna Allen, *John Allen and His Friends,* London, no date. The last two give the most complete picture available of an inspector's life and work. Similarly edited memoirs of Home Secretaries, commissioners, and prime ministers help in tracing down crucial conflicts and decisions. Most helpful are Rollo Russell, *The Early Correspondence of Lord John Russell,* London, 1913; G. P. Gooch, *The Later Correspondence of Lord John Russell,* London, 1925; Lloyd Sanders, *The Lord Melbourne Papers,* London, 1889; C. S. Parker, *Life and Letters of Sir James Graham,* London, 1907; Edwin Hodder, *The Life and Work of the Seventh Earl of Shaftesbury,* London, 1887; Gilbert Lewis, *Letters of the Right Hon. Sir George Cornewall Lewis,* London, 1878; and W. H. L. E. Dalling and Buller and Anthony Ashley, *The Life of Henry John Temple, Viscount Palmerston,* London, 1870, 1874, 1876. These memoirs are occasionally disappointing to administrative historians. High politics, not schools and drains, interested the editors of these memoirs. Often a memoir of minor figure is more valuable: Walter Clay, *Prison Chaplain: A Memoir of Rev. John Clay* (London, 1861) and G. L. Chesterton, *Revelations of Prison Life* (London, 1857). These two tell more than any other sources of the reaction of local officials to the dogmatic opinions of William Crawford and Whitworth Russell. In a similar manner G. A. Denison's *Notes of My Life* (London, 1878) offers an immediate and personal insight into the High Church's hostility to the government's education policy. Less valuable for pictures of opposition to bureaucratic reform but of interest for the utilitarian background of reform are Robert Leader, *The Life and Letters of John Arthur Roebuck,* London, 1897; Mrs. Grote, *The Personal Life of George Grote,* London, 1873; and Mrs. Lewes, *Thomas Southwood Smith, a Memoir,* London, 1895. The memoirs of G. L. Chesterton and G. A. Denison, mentioned above, were straightforward autobiographies. There are other such auto-biographies of value, pre-eminently John Stuart Mill's, London, 1873. The most revealing diary of the period is Lytton Strachey, ed., *The Greville Memoirs,* London, 1938. Kept day by day, it is a reliable first-hand source of the inner workings of the government.

9. WRITINGS OF THE INSPECTORS

Publications of the 140 inspectors who worked for the government between 1833 and 1854 come to more than 300 titles. Some wrote numerous works, others none at all. Many are of little value except as expressions of the inspectors' interests and talents. J. D. Morell, *History of Modern Philosophy* (London, 1845) or Henry Moseley, *Treatise on Mechanics* (London, 1847) tell little of their views on education. But some of the inspectors' works are more pertinent: Hector Gavin, *Sanitary Ramblings,* London, 1846; R. D. Grainger, *Unhealthiness of Towns,* London, 1845; Henry Moseley, *Faith in the Work of a Teacher,* London, 1854; J. P. Norris, *On Girl Industrial Training,* London, 1860; Leonard Horner, *On the Employment of Children in Factories in the United Kingdom and in Some Foreign Countries,* London, 1840; Thomas Stevens, *Poor Relief, No Charity,* London, 1845; Frederick Hill, *Crime, Its Amount, Causes and Remedies,* London, 1853; and James Prichard, *On The Different Forms of Insanity,* London, 1842. The many collected sermons of the education inspectors tell much of their religious convictions. John Allen, *Practical Sermons* (London, 1846), and Mrs. Brookfield, ed., *Sermons by the Late Rev. W. H. Brookfield* (London 1882), give eloquent expression to the deep convictions that inspired these men. Three works expressing the secular faith of utilitarian reformers are Jelinger Symons, *Popular Economy,* London, 1840; E. C. Tufnell, *Character, Object, and Effects of Trade Union,* London, 1834; and Seymour Tremenheere, *A Manual of the Principles of Government,* London, 1882.

From the above review of the literature on the early Victorian administrative state three characteristics emerge: there is a staggering amount of primary material dealing with the new departments, there are many secondary works touching on but not dealing directly with the establishment and work of these departments, and recent studies of particular departments and officials are remedying the gaps in administrative history. But even these particular studies deal mostly with the legislative battles leading to the new department and the high policy struggles which follow. They do not get out of London. They do not follow the inspectors into the field. And by their particular nature they do not present a wider and more integrated view of administrative developments as a whole. There is thus a double need in the study of nineteenth-century administrative history: for more detailed studies of departments and their field work—as, for example, of the Committee on Education—and for studies of the growth of the administrative state in its entirety.

INDEX

A'Court, Colonel Ash, 153, 154, 166, 176, 204, 221, 237, 273, 290, 291, 301, 302
Adderley, Charles, 91
Adey, Daniel G., 166, 171, 172, 221, 238, 239
Administrative law, 109, 113, 114, 293–300
Administrative organization, 118–36; inadequate, 319–20
Administrative powers, 105–18; to inspect and report, 105–7; to issue rules, 106, 108, 110, 319; to confirm appointments, 106, 109, 110, and dismissals, 111; to demand returns, 106; to arbitrate, 113, 115; to sanction rules, 113
Administrative techniques, 131; weekly diaries, 127, 129, 131, 233; circulars, 131, 288; personal visits, 233; 288
Admiralty, 15, 87, 143, 163
Agricultural laborers, 38, 101, 266
Alien Office, 15
Allen, John, 160, 165, 174; background and character, 185–93, 195, 197, 199; inquiry and reports of, 207, 210, 216; policies of, 229, 233–36
Allowance system, 3
Althorp, Lord, 33, 37, 41, 42, 133, 146
Ampthill, 273
Anatomy inspectors, 92, 94, 132
Andover Union, 68, 120, 121, 128, 140, 142, 241, 256, 307
Anti-Corn Law League, 72, 272

Anti-poor-law agitation, 43, 67; in Parliament, 256–57; in the press, 265–66, 269; riots, 273, 274; against guardians, 280, 301–3
Army, 13, 14, 17, 154; Pay Office, 15, 159
Arnold, Matthew, 107, 149, 161, 201, 206–8, 234; *Culture and Anarchy*, 202
Arnold, Thomas, 152, 161, 245
Arnott, Niel, 71
Ashworth, Henry, 278, 303
Asylums. *See* Insane asylums
Attorney and Solicitor General, 16, 297
Auckland, Lord, 19
Audit Office, 16, 18, 135
Auditor's Land Revenue Office, 15
Austin, Henry, 73, 153
Austin, John, 80–81

Babbage, Benjamin, 224–25
Baines, Edward, Sr., 44
Baines, Edward, Jr., 69, 79, 97, 220, 248, 260–61, 263, 269
Baker, Dr., 304
Bangor, 48
Bank of England, 18
Baptists, 68
Barnard Castle, 214
Barnes, Thomas, 229, 265
Beche, Sir Henry de la, 90
Bedford, Duke of, 302
Bedfordshire, 273, 302
Belgium, 257

355

Index

Bellairs, Henry, 192–93, 197, 212, 233, 300

Bentham, Jeremy, 19, 26; ideas of, 29–32, 39, 42, 55, 58, 71, 76, 80–81, 99, 105, 145, 148, 168, 175, 179; *Pauper Management*, 29; *Constitutional Code*, 29–30

Benthamites. *See* Utilitarians

Berkeley, Henry, 253

Berkshire, 302

Bernal, Ralph, 64

Berwick-upon-Tweed, 10

Bethlehem Hospital for the Insane, 323–24

Bethnal Green, 54

Birmingham, 11, 44, 49, 52, 91, 102, 175, 190, 283–84; prison scandal, 120, 122

Black, John, 42

Board of Control for India, 15, 127

Board of Health. *See* Health, General Board of

Board of Trade, 16, 19, 25, 43; growth of, 64–65, 88–89, 94, 135; personnel, 147–48, 156

Bolton, 52, 222; resists poor law, 275–78, 280, 290, 292

Borough Model School, 217

Boroughs: failures, 8, 10–11; oppose New Poor Law; 42; oppose Public Health Act, 74–75, 82; pride in self-government, 97, 102, 279, 283; hostile to General Board of Health, 268

Boswell, James, 163

Bowring, John, 222

Bowyer, H. G., 215–16

Bridgewater Union, 265–66

Bright, John, 64, 69, 96–97, 279

Brighton, 224, 252, 324

Brighton and Chichester Railway, 293

Bristol, 10, 270, 281

Bristol Mercury, 229, 270

British and Foreign School Society, 11, 24, 54, 165, 176, 207

British Association for the Advancement of Science, 185

British Quarterly Review, 69

Brixworth, 302

Bromyard, 224, 225

Brookfield, William, 160, 166, 190–94, 245, 300

Brougham, Lord, 12, 17, 25, 28, 33, 40, 42, 54–55, 86, 90, 145, 163, 198, 226, 243

Buck, Lewis, 82

Buckingham, James Silk, 89

Buckinghamshire, 302

Bull, George, 255

Bullar, George, 46

Buller, Charles, 55, 134

Bureaucrats. *See* Civil servants

Bureaux de bienfaisance, 320, 325

Burial grounds, 86, 91, 142–43; Act of *1850*, 87, 144, 249, 259; inspectors of, 92, 94, 132, 135, 149, 158; report on, 228; stockholders in burial companies, 259, 268–69

Burke, Edmund, 22–23

Butcher shops, 74, 281

Buxton, Thomas Fowell, 46

Byron, George Gordon, 189

Cabinet, 132, 135, 145, 151; in policy formation, 244–52

Calico Print Works Act, 63, 72

Cambridge House of Correction, 46, 283

Cambridge University, 31, 153, 155–56, 160–61, 186–91, 197; Senate of, 57, 168

Cambridge University Commission, 95

Campbell, Lord, 85

Canterbury, Archbishop of, 49, 51, 160, 165, 186

Cardiff, 275

Carlyle, Thomas, 66, 160–61, 175, 178, 189, 191, 219, 270; *Life of Sterling*, 189

Carmarthen, 275

Catholic Inspector of Schools, 191

Catholic Poor School Committee, 160

Cemeteries. *See* Burial grounds

Central Board of Health, 21, 23, 32

Central government (*1833*), 12–22; growth of, by *1854*, 93–95

Central Society for Education, 52

Centralization, 23–24, 31–32; growth of, 38–45, 51, 56, 64, 66; controversy over, 67–85; further development, 96, 98–100; Tocqueville on, 202

Chadwick, Edwin: administrative ideas, 31–33, 133, 245, 287; background and character, 29, 31–33, 99, 100, 148–51;

factory commissioner, 37; secretary of the Poor Law Commission, 110–11, 121, 127, 208, 221–22, 237–40, 246, 277–78; reformer, 71–72, 74, 85, 112, 218; commissioner on the Board of Health, 157–58, 165, 217, 224–25, 227, 233, 241–42, 249–50. Views on: Prison Act (*1835*), 48, Registrar General Act, 50, Metropolitan Building Act, 66, English government, 133, 245, 248–49, 253, 296, civil service reform, 163–64

Chancery, 15, 17

Charitable Donations Commission, 95

Charities, 24, 86, 112, 272

Charity commissioners, 12, 16, 22, 86, 91; reports of, 86; Permanent Commission of *1854*, 88, 92, 93, 119, 132, 151

Chartism, 52, 58, 178–79

Chelsea Hospital, 15

Cheshire, 274

Chester, 91, 191; Chester Castle prison, 312, 315; Chester Asylum, 312; Chester Normal School, 313

Chesterton, G. L., 177, 223

Child labor, 2, 4, 26, 36, 59, 60, 63, 88, 101, 180, 310, 311; Commission on (*1842*), 60–61

Chilton v. London and Croydon Railway Company, 299

Chimney sweeps, 26, 60, 125, 248

Cholera, 21, 23, 82–84, 103, 112, 117, 122, 135; *1850* report of the Board of Health, 227–28; policy toward, 242, 282

Chorley, 175

Christian Witness, 69

Church of England: abuses and reform, 24, 48–49; educational controversies, 51–58, 260–63; factory school controversy, 63–64; educational ideals, 187–94

Civil servants, 137–67; class background, 152–53; outlook, 168–202

Civil service reform, 110, 154, 162, 164–66

Clark, George, 302

Clarkson, Thomas, *The Grievances of Our Mercantile Seamen*, 6, 89

Clay, Walter, 223

Clay, Sir William, 83

Clement, Charles, 154, 237

Clergymen, 153, 301, 304

Clerks of: Estreat, 18; Hanaper, 18; Nichills, 18; the Pells, 16

Clive, George, 275, 290

Coal viewers, 154, 156, 209

Coal Whippers Commission, 93–94

Coast Guard, 15

Cobbett, William, 1, 3, 25, 26, 28, 43–44

Cobden, Richard, 79

Coldbath Prison, 177, 223

Coleridge, S. T., 28, 51, 57, 59, 162, 178, 188–90

Collectivism, 43, 76, 78–80, 83, 95, 202, 320; in the inspector's outlook, 179, 181–82, 184, 193, 195

Colonial Office, 15, 94, 127, 164

Colquhoun, John, 64

Colquhoun, Patrick, 28

Commander in Chief Offices, 15

Common law, 109, 294; commission, 16

Common Lodging Houses Act, 87; inspectors of, 94; report on, 214

Commons, House of, 26, 33, 42, 51, 58, 61, 63, 89, 90–91, 96, 128, 144, 223

Communism, 76

Comptroller of Army Accounts, 15

Congregationalists, 68, 69, 200, 210

Constable, 9; constabulary inspectors, 94–95

Cook, F. C., 160, 189–92, 194, 199, 200, 233, 301

Copyhold Commission. *See* Tithe Commission

Corn Office, 16

Cornwall Geological Society, 183

Corruption, 25, 75–76, 86, 275, 278

Cotton industry, 2, 181

Cottenham, Lord, 86

County Courts Commission, 95

Courier, 163

Courts of Justice, 13, 14, 15, 17, 108, 293–300

Coventry, 10, 174

Cox, Homersham, 102

Crawford, Sharman, 97–98

Crawford, William, 46, 124, 155, 172, 176–77, 185, 221, 223–24, 246

Cresy, Edward, 153, 159, 281

Index

Crime, 4, 46, 53, 58, 72, 182, 213–16, 229
Crimpage, 87
Crosby Hall Lectures, 69, 261
Cubitt, Sir William, 73
Cursutar baron, 18
Customs, 13, 14, 17–19, 87, 126, 128–29, 295

Daily News, 77, 81, 130
Dalhousie, Earl, 243, 250
Dame schools, 12, 54, 213
Dawes, Richard, 217, 228, 288–89
Day, William, 39, 53, 117, 128, 142, 162, 166, 170, 173, 176, 212, 237–38, 240–41, 266, 275, 279
Day schools, 12, 54
De la Beche. *See* Beche
Delane, John Thaddeus, 230
Denison, George A., 262–63
Depressions: (*1842*), 211, 230, 276; (*1847*), 211, 223, 276
Derby, 304
Derby, Earl of, 56, 57, 250, 263
Design Registry Office, 94
de Grey. *See* Grey, Lord
de Talby. *See* Talby
Dickens, Charles, 87, 96, 228, 270, 324; *American Notes*, 270; *Hard Times*, 270; *Oliver Twist*, 7, 270; *Our Mutual Friend*, 96
Discretionary powers, 109–11, 114, 252–53, 319
Disease, 72, 74, 87, 216, 311, 321
Disraeli, Benjamin, 56, 59, 61, 67, 73, 90, 96, 205; *Coningsby*, 65
Doncaster, 261
Dorset, 302
Douglas Jerrold's Weekly, 81
Dover, 11, 214, 281
Drainage. *See* Health, General Board of
Drunkenness, 53, 58, 89, 188, 212, 213–14, 216
Dunfries, 288
Duncombe, Thomas, 90, 97–98
Dunn, Henry, 54
Dunn, Matthias, 90, 169, 183, 306
Durham, 281, 305–6

Earle, Richard, 162, 289, 291, 303
Ebrington, Viscount, 72, 142
Ecclesiastical Commission, 49, 51, 78, 93, 56, 316; powers of, 114, 130–31, 140, 286
Eclectic Review, 69, 78, 261, 268
Economist, 61, 64–65, 70, 73, 75, 77–78, 164, 206, 220, 264, 269
Edinburgh, 175
Edinburgh University, 148, 155–56, 200
Education: want of, 5, 11–12, 53, 58, 188, 213–15, 311, 321–22; reform efforts, 27, 28, 37, 51–53, 72, 79–80
Education, Committee in Council on, 55–58, 68, 94, 145; *1839* Minute, 67, 79, 96, 98; *1846–47* Minutes, 68, 100, 114, 119, 220, 229, 245, 256, 261–62, 264; powers, 115, 252, 319; organization, 119, 131, 134, 140; policy of, 233–36, 242; management clause dispute, 245, 262–63
Education inspectors: background, 153, 155–61; outlook, 185–202; inquiries and reports, 205–8, 213—17, 226, 228, 242; policies, 235–36; execution of policies, 287, 289, 301; theories of education, 196–200, 233–34, 313
Educational Record, 230
Educational Times, 198, 230
Election disputes commissioners, 95
Eliot, George, 199
Ellenborough, Lord, 302–3
Emigration commissioners, 45, 94, 123, 206, 259–60, 319
Enclosures, 2; Enclosure Commission, *see* Tithe Commission
Engineers, 73–74, 103, 154, 156–57, 159, 183, 259, 268
Evangelical Magazine, 69, 261
Evangelicals, 5, 21, 26–27, 33, 37, 48, 89, 91, 99, 103, 168, 318
Evans, Colonel, 44
Examiner, 31, 42, 81, 268
Exchequer: Court of, 14–17, 295, 298–99; Chancellor of, 57, 130, 250; tellers, 16, 17
Excise Commission, 13–14, 17–19, 126, 128, 295; surveyors, 32, 109

Index

Exter, Bishop of, 49
Eye Workhouse, 265–66

Fabian socialism, 149, 179
Factory acts: (*1833*), 37, 40, 47, 51, 141; (*1844*), 61, 70, 108, 247, 297–98; (*1847*), 297; (*1853*), 248; (*1878*), 95
Factory Commission of *1833*, 22, 26, 33, 36–38
Factory inspectors: established, 53, 72, 78, 93, 109, 142, 144; powers, 108–10, 113; organization, 120, 123–25, 132, 163–64, 166; background, 153, 155, 157; outlook, 169, 177–78, 180–81; inquiries and reports, 204–6, 209–11, 215, 218, 226; policies, 234–35, 246–48, 253, 260, 262; efforts to enforce policies, 234, 285, 297, 305–6
Fall, Mr., 275–76
Farm schools, 195, 196
Fellenberg, 195, 197–98, 218, 313
Fencing of mine shafts, 143–44, 210, 247–48, 270, 287, 306
Ferrand, Colonel W. B., 97, 222, 257–58
Fielden, John, 205, 258, 277
Fine Arts Commission, 95
Fitzgerald, Edward, 186
Fitzroy, Henry, 152
Fitzwilliam, Earl, 290, 303
Fletcher, Joseph, 153, 155, 181, 185, 195, 198–99, 207–8, 213, 217; *Farm Schools*, 198
Floggings, 89, 122
Foreign Office, 15, 19, 89, **234**
France, 32, 202, 257, 316, 319, **324–25**
Frederick William I, 319
Fry, Elizabeth, 5, 46, 209

Galton, Douglas Strutt, 159, 209, 210, 220, 230, 243, 306
Gaskell, P., 4
Gaskell, Samuel, 158
Gateshead, 83, 282
Gavin, Hector, 158, 175, 182, 208; *Sanitary Ramblings*, 182
George III, 252
Gilbert, William, 62, 212

Gilbert incorporations, 296
Gladstone, William, 56–57, 59, 61, 63–65, 147, 251
Glasgow, 27
Globe, 31, 81
Gloucestershire, 302
Gordon, Robert, 21
Graham, Sir James, 124, 132, 163, 286; outlook, 19, 61, 142–44; on factories, 61, 63, 226; on the poor law, 121, 128, 133, 146, 204, 222, 267; on education, 207, 210, 246, 260, 323
Grainger, Richard, 156, 158, 166, 175, 178, 181, 183–84, 208; *Observations on the Cultivation of the Organic Sciences*, 183
Grants in aid, 106, 115, 116
Graves, Thomas, 162
Great Western Railway, 243, 293
Great Yarmouth, 281, 283
Greville, Charles, 4, 19, 21, 139, 141
Grey, Lord, 33, 35, 133
Grey, Sir George, 122, 125, 131, 142–44, 219, 247, 287, 293
Grey's Inn, 161
Grimsditch, Peter, 160–61
Grote, George, 43, 55
Gulson, Edward, 154, 174–75, 181, 212, 221, 237–38, 255, 289, 290

Hackney carriages, 91–92; Hackney Coach Office, 14
Haileybury, 151
Halifax, 237
Hall, Sir Benjamin, 224
Hall, Robert, 288–90
Hallam, Arthur, 160, 189
Hammond, John and Barbara, 7
Hampshire, 273
Hampshire and Southampton County Paper, 229
Handloom weavers, 7, 310; commission of inquiry into, 16, 22, 60
Hanwell Asylum, 62
Hardingstone Union, 302
Harroby, Earl of, 90
Hartley, David, 198

Index

Hartly, Jesse, 156

Hawes, Benjamin, 227

Hawkins, Bisset, 155, 158–59, 185

Hawley, W. T. H., 162, 171–72, 176–77, 213, 255, 278

Hayter, William, 250

Hazel School, Tottenham, 174–75

Head, Sir Edmund, 128, 143, 146, 163, 223, 240–41, 254, 256

Head, Sir Francis, 156, 162, 178; *Bubbles of Nassau*, 162

Health, General Board of: powers, 110–13, 117, 252, 254; organization, 122–23, 129, 132, 134, 135–36; inspectors, 135, 153, 175–76, 181–82, 185; personnel, 156–59, 165, 175; reports, 208, 214, 216–17, 221, 224–25, 227–29, 230–31; policies, 242, 249, 250–51; opposition to Board, 249–50, 259; cooperation with, 304, 305

Health of towns: bad conditions, 49, 65–66, 72–74, 80, 82–83, 86, 91, 102, 111–12, 214–15, 230; efforts at reform, 71–73, 75, 88, 140; Public Health Act of *1848*, 74–79, 82–86, 95–97, 143

Health of Towns Advocate, 158

Health of Towns Association, 72–73

Health of Towns Bill (*1847*), 68, 70, 73

Health of Towns Commission, 72–73, 74; *1842* report of, 72, 74

Herefordshire, 321, 322

Hertford, 302

Hickson, William, 269

High Wycombe, 282

Hill, Frederick, 53, 107, 116, 124, 155, 169; background and character, 173–75, 178–79, 181–82, 185; reports of, 209, 213, 218–19, 224; policies, 234, 256

Hill, Matthew, 90

Hill, Rowland, 20, 131, 148, 155–56, 169

Hill, Thomas, 152

Hirst, Joseph, 277

Hoare, Sir Samuel, 46

Holland, 32, 185

Holland, Lord, 19

Holyhead Road Commission, 16, 22

Home Office, 13, 16, 21–23, 46, 48, 50–51, 57, 93, 107, 110, 113, 123–26, 132–33, 135, 136–40, 142–45, 151, 162, 165, 219, 234–35, 292; permanent undersecretary, 125, 144; Parliamentary Secretary, 125–26

Horner, Leonard, 53, 60, 125; background, 155, 163; outlook, 169, 174–75, 178–81, 183, 185; reports, 210–11, 216, 218, 229, 230; influence on Parliament, 226, 227, 255, and Home Office, 234, 247–48; on duties of property, 285, 305; other views, 287–88, 297–98

Household Words, 270

Howard, John, 45

Howe, Lord, 302

Howells, Thomas, 153, 155, 169, 178, 314

Howick, Viscount, 47, 77

Huddersfield, 274, 277, 280, 290

Hudson, George, 82, 96

Huish, Captain, 286

Humanitarianism, 26–27, 62–63, 72, 88–89, 99, 103, 175–77, 227, 267, 318

Hume, James, 20, 38

Hume, Joseph, 18, 55, 73, 83, 88, 90, 100, 128

Hurdsfield, 310, 311; school, 313

Immorality, 53, 87, 181, 188, 192, 212–15

Individualism, 69, 70, 80, 151, 169, 171–73, 179, 180, 202, 320

Industrial schools, 91, 178, 188, 195, 201, 218, 303

Industrialization, 2–4, 52, 85, 99, 101–2, 178, 212, 316–17

Infidelity, 58, 215

Inglis, Sir Robert, 47, 49, 96

Inner Temple, 154, 187

Inns of Court, 31, 148, 153, 180

Insane asylums, 6, 24, 62, 158, 272, 312, 323–24

Inspectors. *See under* Education, Health, Factory, Poor Law, Prisons, Railways, Mining, *and other departments*

Inspector General of Quarantine, 16

Institute of Civil Engineers, 183, 224, 268

Interventionism, 26, 38, 64, 76, 321

Ireland, 32, 35, 248

Isle of Wight Union, 302

Index

James, Sir William, 258
Jebb, Sir Joshua, 107, 172, 234, 256
Jeffrey, Lord, 25
John Bull, 75, 77
Johnson, Dr. Samuel, 19
Jones, Henry Longueville, 160
Jones, Richard, 151
Journal of Public Health, 158
Journal of the Statistical Society, 81, 195
Justices of the peace, 8, 9–10, 17, 21, 38–41, 43, 47, 74, 102, 109, 112, 122, 132, 137, 144, 171, 176, 272, 283–84, 294, 297, 303
Juvenile crime, 86, 218
Juvenile Reformatories Act, 88, 90, 91, 103, 226

Kay Shuttleworth, James (before his marriage in *1841*, James Kay): background and outlook, 4, 148–51, 155, 165, 175–76, 181–82, 184; assistant poor-law commissioner, 53–55, 58, 71, 204, 218, 237–38, 255; Secretary to the Committee on Education, 99, 193, 197–98, 203, 235–36, 239, 245–46, 248, 260–63, 273–74, 287
Keble, John, 191, 263
Keighley Union, report on, 222
Kennedy, Benjamin, 190
Kennedy, Charles, 190
Kennedy, Rann, 152, 190
Kennedy, William, 160, 190, 197–98, 207–8, 228
Kent, 273
Kenyon, Lord, 44
Kincaid, Captain John, 156, 218, 234
King Edward's School, 152, 190
King's Bench, 15, 223
King's College, London, 153, 156, 159, 160, 183, 186, 190
King's Remembrance Office, 16
Kings Somborne school, 119, 217
Kingsley, Charles, 186
Kneller Hall School, 262
Knight Order of the Companion of the Bath, 159
Knutsford House of Correction, 312, 314

Labouchere, Henry, 89, 92, 98, 147–48, 156
Laffan, Captain, 157, 209, 243
Laissez faire, 30, 35, 64, 70, 76, 78–79, 85, 97, 116, 168, 169, 180, 201–2, 259, 320
Lambeth Union, 275–76, 278–80
Lancashire, 274
Lancaster Asylum, 158
Lancet, 158, 270
Landlords, 74–75, 83, 281
Lansdowne, Lord, 25, 55, 58, 98, 139, 141, 145, 147–48, 160–62, 165, 185–86, 199, 226, 233, 245–46, 260–61
Laurie, Sir Peter, 47, 323–24
Law Office, 135, 297, 299–300
Lawyers, 86, 153, 160–61, 180, 187
Lee, William, 230, 289, 302; *Experience in Disease and Comparative Rates of Mortality*, 230
Leeds, 44, 52, 102, 150, 248, 260, 269, 270, 280
Leeds Mercury, 38, 44, 60, 69, 70, 75, 77–79, 134, 220, 261, 264, 268
Lefevre, John Shaw, 128, 146, 237, 238–39, 240
Leicester, 7, 10; prison, 46, 120, 122, 260, 283–84
Lewis, Sir George, 121, 128, 140, 142–43, 146, 163, 223, 240–42, 253–54, 256
Lewis, Sir Thomas Frankland, 127–28, 146, 237, 239–40
Liang, Samuel, 239, 243
Liberalism, 69, 168, 175
Liberals, 37, 61, 78–79, 97, 168, 170, 187, 201, 318
Lighthouses Act, 88
Lighting commissioners, 10–11
Lincoln, 48; asylum at, 62
Lincoln, Lord, 141
Lincoln's Inn, 155
Lingen, Ralph, 236
Liverpool, 4, 5, 10, 49, 52
Liverpool Chronicle, 89, 259
Local act authorities: for health, 74, 83, 253, 281; for the poor law, 279, 288; and railways, 257
Local government: defects of, 6, 7–12,

Index

Local government (*continued*)
32–33, 38–39, 41, 45, 48, 74, 76, 80, 82, 93, 102–3; loyal attachment to, 75, 77, 79, 85, 95–96, 117–18, 258–59, 279, 323; resistance to centralization, 21, 23, 43–44, 102, 117, 205, 221, 268, 300; causes of resistance, by poor-law guardians, 272–81, by prison authorities, 283–84, by boards of health, 284–85, by school committees, 284–85; and by others, 285–87; cooperation of local authorities, 300–9

Local Government Act (*1871*), 95

Locke, John, 192, 198–99

London: bad sanitation, 4, 5, 10, 11, 86–87, 91; strong parish hostility to centralization, 23, 42, 269; juvenile delinquency, 91; want of education, 52; in *1854* healthiest capital in Europe, 325

London, Bishop of, 49, 71, 84, 87, 186–87, 301

London, Corporation of, 23, 75, 87; commission into (*1854*), 95, 324

London Workingman's Association, 52

London University, 80, 159, 163

Londonderry, Lord, 61, 90

Longsight, 31

Lonsdale, Bishop of Lichfield, 187

Lonsdale, Lord, 82–83, 90, 96, 134

Lord Chancellor, 16, 17

Lord Lieutenant, 137

Lords, House of, 42, 55, 57–58, 90, 91, 226

Lunacy Act of *1842*, 60, 62–63, 97

Lunacy commissioners: background, 156–58; powers, 116; organization, 120, 122, 130, 132; outlook, 185; inquiries and reports, 206, 217, 219; policy, 239, 242–43, 260; administration, 270, 287, 292, 299; asylums, *see* Insane asylums

Lunacy conditions, 59, 62, 102, 284, 321; reforms in care of, 5, 6, 21, 27, 103, 173

Lunacy inspectors, Ireland, 32

Lutwidge, R. W. S., 239

Lyttleton, Lord, 160

Lytton, Bulwer, 3, 29, 31, 34–35, 72, 93, 96, 172; *England and the English,* 35

Macaulay, T. B., 4, 34, 211

Macclesfield, 150, 280–81, 291–92, 310–15

Macclesfield Chronicle, 314

Macclesfield Courier, 79, 230

M'Culloch, John R., 28, 168–69

Mackworth, Herbert, 124, 157, 169, 183, 210, 235, 306

Malthus, Thomas, 25, 170

Manchester, 4, 5, 9, 11, 49, 52, 53, 305

Manchester Committee for Education, 52

Manchester Guardian, 268, 298, 303

Manchester Statistical Society, 5, 27, 53, 150, 184

Manners, Lord John, 249–51

Manning, Henry, 176, 187

Market Bosworth, 302

Marshall, Thomas, 191

Martineau, Harriet, 25, 270

Marine boards, local, 113

Marylebone, London, 44, 102, 279

Massachusetts, social reforms, 316–17

Maule, Foxe, 152

Maurice, Frederick, 189

Mechanic institutes, 25

Medical officers, 111, 115, 208, 304

Medico Chururgical Review, 158

Melbourne, Lord, 33, 35, 40, 42, 58, 123, 124, 139, 140, 147, 163–64

Mercantile Law Commission, 95

Merchant Marine: conditions, 6, 85, 147; reforms, 87, 89, 101; *1850* Act, 89–90, 147; *1854* Act, 147; Department, 88, 94, 98; power, 106, 109, 113; organization, 130, 135

Methodists, 55–56, 263

Metropolitan Building acts, 66, 254; Commission, 94

Metropolitan Commissioners in Lunacy, 16, 22, 24, 32, 62, 103

Metropolitan Police, 16, 21–23, 88, 94, 132, 140

Metropolitan Sanitary Association, 270

Metropolitan Sewer Commission, 91, 94, 130, 134

Metropolitan turnpike commissioners, 16, 22

Miall, Edward, 260–61

Index

Midland Railway Co., 286

Migration, 2

Mill, John Stuart, 31, 35, 76–77, 80–81, 97, 100, 202, 219, 270

Millbank prison, 176

Mill-owners, 24, 37–38, 74, 97, 109, 112, 178–80, 209, 216, 226–27, 252, 272, 277, 285, 298, 305, 314

Milne, Monkton, 91, 189

Milroy, Gavin, 158, 175

Mine-owners, 112, 218, 272, 286, 293, 305–6

Mining conditions, 7, 59–61, 79, 85, 216, 230, 321; ventilation, 103, 183, 218, 256; moral conditions, 213–14, 216

Mining inspectors: powers, 92, 107–9, 113, 116–17, 144, 319; organization, 119, 123–24, 132, 140; background, 153, 156–57; appointments, 165; pay, 166; outlook, 169, 183; reports of, 209–10, 217, 230; policy, 234–35, 256; reluctant to use coercion, 292

Mining Journal, 90, 107, 119, 230

Mining reforms: *1842* Act, 61, 65, 67, 70, 97, 147; *1850* Act, 87, 90–91, 98, 144; *1877* Act, 95

Ministry of Interior, France, 12

Monitorial system, 54, 197, 207, 236

Monmouthshire, 5; mining conditions, 205, 213, 216

Monthly Law Review, 223

Moral reform: by education, 175–77, 183–85, 187–88; 195–96, 201, 218–19; by the New Poor Law, 173, 184, 192

Morant, Robert, 161

Morell, Joseph, 160–61, 179, 199, 200, 217, 224, 234; *History of Modern Philosophy*, 161, 199

Morley, Samuel, 260

Morning Advertiser, 75

Morning Chronicle, 31, 38, 41–42, 75–76, 98, 111

Morning Herald, 23, 41, 57

Morning Post, 23

Morpeth, Lord, 70, 72–74, 82, 136, 145–46, 241

Mortality, 86, 11, 311, 313

Moseley, Henry, 119, 160, 183, 189–92, 194–95, 197–200, 214, 217, 220, 233, 236, 284–85, 311, 314; *Astro Theology*, 194

Mosse, Reverend, 304

Mott, Charles, 154, 171, 181, 222–23, 266, 274, 276, 278, 280, 289, 303, 315

Mowatt, Francis, 268

Municipal Corporations Commission, 16, 22–23; Act of *1835*, 48

Murray, James, 89

National Debt Office, 16

National Public Schools Association, 263

National School Society, 11, 24, 54, 100, 207, 262; schools, 185–86

Navy, 13–15, 17, 154

Navy Pay Office, 15

Navy surveyor, 15

New Poor Law. *See* Poor Law Amendment Act

New York, 316–17

Newcastle, 82, 282–83, 322; Cholera Commission, 95

Newcastle Chronicle, 230, 283

Newgate Prison, 10, 46–47, 209, 223, 283, 323–24

Nicholls, Sir George, 39, 151, 237, 238–41

Nigby, Mr., 277

Non Conformist, 68, 261

Nonconformists, 49, 50, 58, 68–70, 75, 77–78, 97, 148, 174–75, 221, 247, 260–62, 301, 314

Norfolk, 53, 205, 212, 237

Norris, J. P., 161, 173, 191–93, 195, 197, 199, 214, 301

North British Review, 209

Northampton, 302

Northampton, Lord, 302

Northern Star, 265, 277

Northumberland, collieries, 218, 305, 306

Norwich, 23

Norwich, Bishop of, 90

Nottidge v. Ripley, 299

Noxious trades, Inspector of, 94

Nuisance Removal and Disease Prevention Act, 84, 112, 252, 282

Index

Oastler, Richard, 4, 25–26, 36, 67, 265, 267, 269, 270, 277, 280, 303
O'Brien, Donatus, 213, 243
O'Connor, Feargus, 67, 265, 274, 277, 280
O'Grady, Mr., 275–76
Ordnance Department, 14
Oriel College, 176
Overseers, 8, 109, 208, 275–76, 302
Owen, Robert, 28
Oxford University, 31, 92, 153–56, 160–62, 168, 180, 187; Convocation, 57; Commission of Inquiry (*1854*), 92, 94, 132

Paisley, General, 209, 243
Paley, William, 197
Pall Mall Gazette, 95
Palmerston, Lord: Whig views, 25, 35; for juvenile reformatories, 91; for chimney sweeps, 125; praises permanent undersecretaries, 127; as Home Secretary, 144–45, supports factory inspectors, 247–48, 251–52, 298; and mining inspectors, 210, 235, 293; and Board of Health, 134, 227–28; castigates local government, 282, 324
Panopticon, 29
Parish government, 8, 9, 17, 21, 38–40, 44, 50, 74, 87, 92, 102, 268, 279
Parker, Henry, 121–22, 128, 142, 241, 291
Parkhurst Prison Act, 246
Parkinson, James, 153
Parliament: factory questions, 38, 40; poor-law matters, 41–45, 240–41, 257–58; emigration, 45; prisons, 46–47, 223–24; ecclesiastical commissioners, 49; education, 56–57, 261–62; health, 82–85, 249, 259–60; economy-mindedness, 118, 120–23; relation to inspectors' reports, 223–27; participation in forming policy, 252–60; jealous regard for local government, 318
Parliamentary agents, 74, 253, 257, 259, 269
Parry, Edward, 279
Patent and invention commissioners, 94
Paternalism, 78, 139, 145, 169, 177–79, 193
Patriot, 68, 261

Patronage, 43, 50, 64, 75–76, 80, 82, 126, 162–64, 281
Paving commissioners, 8–11, 75, 281
Pechell, Captain George, 224, 227, 252, 323, 324
Peel, Sir Robert, 21, 23, 33, 39, 49, 57, 59, 61, 63–65, 68, 120, 122, 128, 139, 141, 143, 241, 251
Pensions, 25
Penzance, 10
Perry, John, 122, 124, 159, 209, 256
Persuasion, administrative art of, 106–7, 287–93
Pestalozzi, Johann, 150, 195, 197–98, 200, 236, 266, 313
Peterboro Union, 303
Philosophical Radicals, 1, 43, 78
Physicians, 73, 103, 153, 158–59, 183, 191, 268, 289, 304
Pigott, Grenville, 212–13
Pilkington, Henry, 153, 161, 177
Pilot authorities, 88
Pitt, William, 39
Playfair, Lyon, 90, 148, 151
Police, 27, 79, 96; opposition to police bill (*1854*), 102, 144, 251
Police commissioners, local, 10, 11, 281, 314
Police inspectors, Ireland, 32
Political economy, 24, 28, 43, 59, 65, 75, 80, 141, 168, 170, 179, 188, 193, 196
Poor Law Amendment Act of *1834* (New Poor Law): passage of, 43–45, 47, 51, 59; pauperism under, 71, 173, 181, 212, 214–15, 221, 313; opposition to, 102, 273–76; support of, 141, 143; good effects of, 222, 255; harshness, 266–67
Poor-law auditors, 109, 115
Poor-law board of *1847*, 96, 115, 120, 130, 132, 134, 208, 241, 248, 258
Poor Law Commission of Inquiry (*1834*), 22, 33, 40, 162; report of, 40–41, 53
Poor Law Commission of *1834–46*: powers, 108–13, 117, 295, 319; organization, 120–23, 126–28, 132–33, 135, 140, 164, 320; inquiries and reports, 203–4, 208, 212, 217, 219, 221, 225, 227–28, 239, 242; policies, formation of, 236–37, 239,

253; medical relief, 237–38, 241, 253; outdoor relief, 246, 255; attacked by Parliament, 254, 258, on lunacy, 109, poor-law schools, 109, 110, 115, 219, 241, 280, settlement, 248, the workhouse test, 170–1, 177, 222, 237–38, 240, 267, 276, 280, 303, 308; justices of, 266–67; enforcement of policies, 273, 291–92, 297.

Assistants: inquiries and reports, 53, 71, 203–4, 206, 208, 211, 213, 215, 221–23, 229, 236, 275; alienated from commissioners, 128, 240; background, 153–55, 157, 161–62; appointment, 164; pay, 166; outlook, 170–72, 176–77, 180–82, 192; policies, 237, 240; influence of, 246, 255, 257; carrying out policy, 273, 290–91, 293; cooperation with local guardians, 303–4

Poor-law guardians, 40, 84, 109, 117, 208, 272–75, 277–78, 290, 302–3, 307, 314

Poor-law rates, 2, 38, 42–43, 71

Population, 2

Porter, George, 148, 239, 243

Portman, Lord, 226

Portsmouth, Lord, 302

Post Office, 14, 17

Powers, Alfred, 162, 170, 180, 181, 211, 238, 255, 265, 274, 290–91, 308

Press, the, 63, 75, 77–78, 81–82, 122, 226–29, 231

Preston Gaol, 223

Prichard, James Cowles, 158–59, 173–75, 183; *Observations on the Medical Treatment of Insanity*, 158

Prime ministers, 132, 138–39, 141–42

Prison acts: (*1824*), 46; (*1835*), 45, 47, 48, 67, 77; (*1838*), 246; (*1877*), 95

Prison Discipline Society, 27, 45–46, 176

Prison inspectors: established, 47–48; inquiries and reports, 53, 70, 204, 213, 217, 218, 223–24, 226, 229–30, 321; powers, 88, 113, 115, 117, 283, 319; organizations, 120, 122–24, 132, 143–44; background, 155–57; pay, 166; outlook, 172–73, 176, 185; policies, formation of, 234–35, 246, 267, expressed to Parliament, 250, resisted, 283; on diet, 122,

235, 284; separate confinement, 124, 144, 172–73, 177, 223–25, 246; discipline of silence, 124, 224, 234, 256, 267, 284, 308; useful labor, 124, 144, 224; the treadmill and crank, 144, 172, 234–35, 284; cells, 235

Prisons: conditions, 5, 6, 21, 102; reforms, 27, 46–47, 72; Magistrate Committees, 272, 283, 307

Private bills, 65, 252, 257

Privy Council, 14, 21, 57, 84, 94, 112, 134–35, 141; presidents, 57, 138, 162, 163

Privy Seal Office, 16; Lord of the Privy Seal, 57

Progress, belief in, 103, 179, 182, 193–94, 196

Propertied interests, 74, 82, 96–97, 99, 103, 117, 258–59, 267, 281, 309

Prosecutions, power to order, 106, 108, 109, 292

Prostitutes, 46

Protectionists, 84

Prussia, 32, 316–17, 319, 325

Public opinion, 225, 227–28, 232, 247, 260–72

Puritanism, 69, 215

Quakers, 6, 27, 172

Quarantine, 134; Surveyor of, 21

Quarterly Review, 28, 41, 50, 60, 80

Quartermaster General's Office, 15

Queen's Bench, 109, 114, 295–97

Radford debtor's gaol, 209

Radicals, 23, 25–26, 35, 37, 43–44, 57–58, 69, 77, 90, 97–99, 244, 278–79

Radnor, Earl of, 162, 302

Railway Acts: (*1840* and *1842*), 64; (*1844*), 65, 67, 70, 147

Railway Commission of *1846–51*, 251, 257

Railway Department (from *1846* to *1851* the Railway Commission), 64–65, 94; powers, 108, 113–15; organization, 129, 130, 135; inspectors, 157, 159, 164, 243; reports, 209, 220–21, 227, 230, 306;

Index

Railway Department (*continued*)
policies, 239, 242, 251; administration
of, 287, 292–93

Railway owners, 65, 108, 112, 210, 221,
259, 272, 293, 305–6

Railway Times, 220, 257

Railways: condition of, 6, 64, 101, 140;
accidents, 209, 306; panic, 209, 251

Ranger, William, 159, 166, 182, 214–15

Rate-payers, 74, 83, 111; fear of rates,
273, 275, 277, 279, 280–82, 309, 314

Rawlinson, Sir Robert, 153, 156–57, 159,
175, 182, 185, 214–15, 281, 289, 304, 308,
314

Record, 69

Reform, spirit of, 85, 88–89, 91, 92, 183,
203

Reformatories, 86, 93, 116, 178

Registrar of Joint Stock Companies,
Office of, 94

Registrar General of Births, Deaths, and
Marriages, 49–51, 78, 93, 163, 274

Registration and Conveyance Commission, 95

Reports of inspectors, 206–31

Revans, John, 274, 290

Ricardo, David, 25, 151, 168, 171

Richmond, Duke of, 46, 90, 98

Rickards, Richard, 169, 180, 210, 288

Rochdale Union, 128, 223

Rodmersham, Kent, 273

Roe, John, 242

Roebuck, Arthur, 55, 100

Rousseau, 198

Royal College of Physicians, 183, 224

Royal Engineers, 156–57

Royal Engineers School, Chatham, 153,
156, 158

Royal Marine Hospital, 15

Royal Military Academy, 153, 156

Royal Society, 158–59, 162–63, 183

Rugby, 152, 161, 191

Russell, Lord John: pushes social reforms, 25, 49, 50, 55–59, 89, 98, 130; on
education, 58–59, 246, 248, 260–61; as
Home Secretary and Prime Minister,
141–42, 205; uses patronage, 163; on
the poor law, 204, 238, 245, 255; on
health, 227; on powers of persuasion,
287

Russell, Whitworth, 172, 176–77, 185,
209, 217, 221, 223–24, 234, 246, 289

Rutland, Duke of, 302

Sadler, Michael, 24, 26, 36–37

St. Andrews, Madras College, 160

St. Bartholomew's Hospital, 156

St. George's Hall, Liverpool, 159

St. George's Hospital, 158

St. John's, Cambridge, 190

St. John's College, Battersea, 150, 176,
197–98, 236

St. Luke's Hospital for the Insane, 24

St. Oswyth, 304

St. Pancras, 11, 279, 296

St. Paul's School, Birmingham, 190

St. Thomas School of Medicine, 153, 158

Salford, 5

Salisbury, Bishop of, 252

Satire, 81

Saunders, Robert, 60, 125, 178, 180, 247,
260

Savings banks and friendly societies,
commissioner of, 45, 169

Say and Sele, Lord, 154

Science, impact on administrative
growth, 63, 90, 92, 102, 182–83; and
religion, 193–94

Science and Art, Department of, 92, 94,
151, 220, 313

Scotsman, 31

Secularism, 51, 56, 57

Select committees on: Andover Union
(*1845*), 241; Children in Factories
(*1832*), 36; Education (*1838*), 54; Factory Law (*1840*), 247; Keighley Union,
222; Mining Accidents (*1849*), 90,
(*1854*), 256; Poor Law (*1837* and *1838*),
39, 254–55; Prisons (*1835*), 46, (*1850*),
256; Railways (*1844*, *1846*, and *1849*),
257; Registration of Births and Deaths,
50; Shipwrecks (*1836*), 85, 89

Senior, Nassau, 28, 33, 39–41, 133, 162,
164–65, 170–71, 181

Sevenoaks Union, 265–66

Sewer commissioners, 74, 87, 92, 269

Index

Seymour, Edward, 158

Seymour, Lord, 136, 142, 145, 224, 227, 249–50

Shaftesbury, Earl of: on labor in factories and mines, 26, 36, 59, 60, 63, 163, 255–56, 266; on education, 56; on lunacy reform, 60, 260, 299, 315; on Evangelical, 60, 99; attached as socialist, 70, 250; and sanitary reform, 72; on juvenile crime and chimney sweeps, 91, 125; at the Board of Health, 134, 136, 142, 241, 249, 259

Sheffield, 52, 190

Sheffield Independent, 79

Ship owners, 89, 272, 286

Shopocracy, 276–77, 282, 303

Sibthorp, Colonel, 77, 97–98

Simmons, J. L. H., 159, 243

Sinecures, 18, 25, 35

Sittingbourne, Kent, 273

Six Acts, 25

Smiles, Samuel, 149

Smith, Adam, 23, 70, 168–69

Smith, Sir Frederick, 209

Smith, J. Toulmin, 76–77, 79–80, 100, 269–70; *Centralization or Representation*, 76

Smith, James, 157, 159, 169–70

Smith, Southwood, 33, 37, 60, 71–72, 74, 151

Smoke Regulation Act, 87–88, 144

Somerset, 302

South Easter Railway Company, 164, 243

South Lancashire Anti-Poor Law Association, 277

South Shields Committee, 90

Southey, Robert, 24, 27, 47, 51, 57, 59, 178, 201

Spalding Lockup, 283

Spectator, 42, 78–79

Speenhamland, 3, 4, 9

Spencer, Lord, 302

Spitalfield, 7

Stafford, 82

Stamps, Commissioners of, 14, 17–18, 126

Standard, 23, 41, 75–76

Stanley, Lord. *See* Derby, Earl of

Star Chamber, 76

State Paper Office, 16

Stationary Office, 16, 219–20

Statistical Department, Board of Trade, 16, 21

Statute Law Commission, 95

Statutory authorities, 8, 10–11

Stephen, James, 127, 164

Stephen, Raynor, 67, 265, 274, 277, 280

Stephenson, Robert, 74, 153, 156

Sterling, John, 189

Stevens, Thomas, 161, 171–72, 176–77, 221–23, 237; *Poor Relief, Not Charity*, 171

Stewart, Dugald, 25, 27, 145, 168, 198

Stockport, 180, 211, 223

Stokes, Scott Nasmyth, 160

Strickland, Sir George, 252

Strutt, Edward, 107, 141

Stuart, James, 155, 163, 205, 209–10, 221, 255–56, 287

Suffolk, 237, 273

Sunderland, 4

Sutherland, Dr. John, 158, 182–84, 281, 288, 304, 308

Sutton, John Manners, 152

Swansea, 283

Sykes, Colonel, 185

Symons, Jelinger, 195–96, 198–99, 201, 207, 233

Talby, Lord, 90

Tamworth Manifesto, 59, 140

Taxes, Commission on, 14, 17–18

Taylor, Sir Henry, 19

Taylor, Jeremy, 189

Technology, influence on administrative growth, 93, 103–4, 317

Ten-hour day, 24, 36, 61, 65, 143, 147, 169, 170, 247; Ten Hour Act of *1847*, 180, 256, 226, 227, 264

Tenements, 72, 83, 86–87, 111, 181, 216, 311

Tennyson, Alfred Lord, 160, 189, 190

Thackeray, William M., 160, 186, 190; *Curates Walk*, 190; *Vanity Fair*, 190

Thompson, Poulett, 43

Thurtell, Alexander, 160

Index

Times (London), 41, 50, 55, 57, 67–68, 77, 80–81, 86–88, 100, 103, 120–21, 133, 220–21, 228–30, 240–41, 248, 251, 264–65, 268–69, 283, 285, 307, 324

Tinling, Douglas, 119

Tithe Commission, 95; Commissioners, 51, 56, 130, 134; assistants, 51, 113–14; powers, 113–14; organization, 132; reports, 208, 216, 220, 229, 260

Tithes, 7, 49–50; *1836* Act, 51

Tocqueville, Alexis de, 76, 202

Todmorden Poor Law Union, 297

Tooke, Thomas, 60, 73

Tories, 22–23, 26, 35, 37, 42–44, 49, 55–59, 61, 65, 67, 75, 77, 82, 90, 96–97, 116, 244, 278, 318

Trade unions, 169

Traditionalism, 74, 77, 96–97

Treasury, 13–14, 17–18, 20, 123, 126, 129–30, 135, 151; and fight with Board of Health, 142–43, 166, 249–50

Tremenheere, Seymour, 91, 119, 178–79, 181, 183, 185, 186–87, 193, 195–96, 198–99, 204; reports, 207–8, 212–13, 216, 225, 228–30

Trevelyan, Sir Charles, 130, 162

Trinity College, Cambridge, 189, 191

Trinity College, Dublin, 153

Trinity House, 88

Trollope, Anthony, 64, 86; *Three Clerks*, 64

Tufnell, E. C., 71, 91, 170, 172–73, 176, 178, 180–81, 184, 195, 197–99, 201, 213, 215, 218, 234, 238, 241, 266, 278

Tufnell, Henry, 162

Turnpike trusts, 8, 23

Twisleton, Edward Boyd, 154, 161–62, 180–81, 211

University College, London, 31, 162

Urbanization, 2, 3, 4, 9, 27–28, 48, 52, 78, 91, 101–2, 155, 178, 180, 182, 277, 316–17

Urquhart, David, 82, 96

Utilitarians, 5, 26–27, 30–33, 37–38, 40, 55, 73, 78–79, 89, 99–100, 103, 139, 145, 232, 315, 318

Vagrancy, 212, 213

Victoria, Queen, 138

Victualling Office, 15

Voluntaryism, 24, 51, 54, 58, 86, 102, 179, 236, 263

Voules, Herbert, 222

Waddington, Henry, 151

Wade, John, 25

Wakeley, Thomas, 258

Wales, 22, 240, 275

Walsham, Sir James, 213, 222, 239, 303

Walters, John, 44, 229, 254–56, 258, 267

War, Secretary for, 14

War Office, 14

Warrington teachers college, 313

Watchman, 57

Water companies, 74–75, 83, 91–92; stockholders of, against Board of Health, 259, 268–69, 286

Water inspectors, 92, 94

Water supply, 12, 72–73, 80, 86, 91, 135, 149; *1851* Bill, 250; *1852* Act, 250; Board of Health proposals, 254, 259

Watkins, Frederick, 197, 214–15, 284–85

Weale, Robert, 266, 302

Webb, Sydney and Beatrice, 7, 8, 211, 222, 266–67

Webb School of Medicine, 153, 156

Wellington, Duke of, 17, 49

Wells, Reverend A., 69

Wesley, John, 26, 103

West Bromwich Union, 302

Westminster, Marquis of, 90–91

Westminster Review, 5, 25, 28, 31, 50, 60, 78–79, 81, 93, 99, 121–22, 125, 128, 163, 208, 229, 270

Westminster School, 186

Wharncliffe, Lord, 61, 141, 145, 246, 260

Whigs, 22–23, 25–27, 33, 35, 37, 44, 50, 55–56, 58–59, 65–66, 68, 75, 98–99, 103, 116, 142, 163, 244, 251, 277–78, 318

Wigan Mine Company, 286

Wilberforce, Robert, 176

Wilberforce, William, 26

William III, 252

William IV, 138, **303**

Index

Williams, Captain John, 124, 156, 182, 185, 209, 218, 224, 234, 288, 307, 315

Wilson, James, 37

Wiltshire, 302

Winchester, 187, 301

Wood, Sir Charles, 129, 136, 250

Woodford, Edward, 160

Woods, Forests, Land Revenues, Public Works, and Buildings—Commissioner of, 14–15, 18, 84, 128, 134–36, 142, 159, 248–50

Wordsworth, Christopher, 189

Wordsworth, William, 201

Working classes, 51, 53, 58, 101, 179, 181, 188, 205, 211–14, 274, 276–77, 318

Wynne, George, 209, 210, 243

Wynne, Thomas, 286, 306

York, 5, 290; East Riding, 283; West Riding, 274

York Retreat Hospital, 6

Young England, 65, 73